MR. BRYAN'S RESIDENCE, FAIRVIEW, LINCOLN, NEBRASKA.

The Commoner
Condensed

BY

WILLIAM JENNINGS BRYAN

VOLUME III.

Published by
THE WOODRUFF-COLLINS PRINTING CO.,
Lincoln, Nebraska
1904

CONTENTS

EDITORIALS.

	PAGE
A Big Navy League	41
A Black Spot	325
A Conscience Campaign	322
A Correction	10
Administration's Position	138
Address to the Czar	221
A Fallacious Defense	178
Afraid of 16 to 1	312
A Good Suggestion	445
Aldrich Bill	78- 290
Alexander Hamilton's Plan	21
Altgeld's Plain Talk	412
American Commons	219
A Momentous Problem	453
An Income Tax Decision	52
An Inquiry Answered	223
An Interesting Dispute	228
"An Item For Reflection"	92
Another Anti-Pass Congressman	303
Another Argument Gone	309
Another Gold Bug Fallacy	280
Another Negro Burned	193
Another Wall Street Demand	241
A Party in Court	30
A Perpetual Debt	42
A Real Trust Fighter	11
A Reformer in Office	20
A Republican's Views	39
Arguments Against Second Term	190
A Rise in Silver	324
A Permanent Truth	54
A Somersault	410
"Asset Currency"	451
Ballot Box, Serving God at	451
Beginning of Evil	297
Bennett's Bequest to Colleges	326
Bennett, Philo Sherman	254

Contents

	PAGE
Bennett Will, The	314
Bimetallism	342
Bimetallism Not a Panacea	35
Bribing Congressmen	259
Call to Arms	31
Cannot Keep It Down	240
Cleveland and Francis	195
Cleveland and the Income Tax	279
Concerning Advertising	93
Congratulations to Cuba	147
Conscience Campaign	322
Consumers Are Nervous	405
Courage, Value of	55
Corruption in Politics	171
Criminal Clause	404
Criminals, Treatment of	439
Decision in Bennett Case	327
Defeat Explained	269
Demanding Army Increase	262
Democracy Defined	156
Democracy, Mr. Bryan's	230
Democratic Opportunity	422
Democratic Party	362
Democratic Substitute	14
Dishonest Argument	51
Drawing the Line	62
Defend Democratic Principles	89
Dodging the Issue	288
Does It Dare Answer?	120
Dropping the Mask	311
Election of Senators by the People	442
Elkins Law, Saved by	179
Enforcing Instructions	105
Emergency Currency	164
Expansion vs. Imperialism	184
Experiences of a Juryman	68
Ex-Secretary Long on Roosevelt	321
Eyes Are Opening	278
Farming as an Occupation	399
Financiers Against Tariff Reform	25
Foreigners in China	239
Fourth at Fairview	222
Fowler Currency Bill	27
Fraud of Ultra-Protectionists	5
From P. O. Department	227
Getting Rich Quick	61

Contents ix

	PAGE
Gifts From Monopolists	166
General Miles Retires	247
Get Rich Quick Schemes	162
Good Roads	122
Good Suggestion	445
Gorman's Leadership	416
Governor Black's Strong Words	199
Government by Injunction	62-84
"Graft"	303
Harmony and Harmony	74
Harmony, Recipe for	84
History Distorted	191
How Rich Should One Be?	175
How the Skies Were Cleared	37
Idle Rich	304
Ignorant of the West	19
Initiative and Referendum	59
Jewish Petition	238
Jones, Dr. Hiram K.	202
Judge Lochren's Decision	446
Law Made Value	278
Laziness	183
Leadership	149
Legislation, Not Petition	260
Light Out of Darkness	174
Local Self Government	34
Lottery, Newspaper	249
Making the Issue Plain	246
Malignant Partisanship	450
Manana	294
Masked Batteries	155
Marplots	411
Marplots, Speaking of	107
Melting Pot Test	240
Memorial Day	146
Miles, But He Forgot	314
Miles on the Philippines	148
Missouri Hits the Trusts	72
Misinterpreting Providence	242
Momentous Problem	453
Money Their God	65
Money Question	248
Monroe Doctrine	33
More Money is Needed	94
Mr. Bryan's Democracy	230
Mr. Shaw as a Legislature	295

Contents

	PAGE
Municipal Ownership	419
Natural Rights	26
Negro, Another Burned	193
Newspaper Lottery	249
Nominees, What About	66
"Non-Partisan" Republicans	310
Northern Securities Case	440
Not Yet Enough Money	191
Oklahoma and Statehood	7
On Mammon's Side	235
Orator's Preparation	157
Organized Wealth	185
Organized Against Labor	196
Passes Unlawful	27
Persecutions in Russia	147
Philanthrophy,	408-444
Philippine Question	286
Philo Sherman Bennett	254
Picayune Wrong Again	188
Playing For Trust Support	261
Platform Building	414
Political Weekly as an Advertising Medium	341
Post Office Department, to the	226
President's Message	337
Post Office Scandal	169
Protect Life and Limb	56
Pure Municipal Government	340
Price of Silver	132-224
Race Problem	249
Race Problem Discussed	281
Race Question Again	264
Real Difference Between Parties	18
Recipe For Harmony	84
Reform the Senate Now	12
Religious Freedom	98
Republican Tariff Reform	137
Riot Cartridges	88
Roosevelt and the Coal Trust	430
Roosevelt Defends the Trusts	84
Roosevelt's St. Louis Speech	116
Rockefeller's Prayer	187
Roosevelt's Masterly Retreat	200
Saved by the Elkins Law	179
Selecting Candidates	198
Selfishness Admitted	277
Serving God at the Ballot Box	451

Contents

	PAGE
Shaw as a Legislature	295
Slavery in the Philippines	230
Slump in Stocks	334
Silver Dollar, The	301
Silver, Price of	132-224
Silver, Why Coined	121
Speaking of Marplots	107
Speculation in Stocks	263
Squeezed by the Trusts	182
Strikers Win	80
Strong and Weak	269
Sunday Reading	160-224
Tariff Logicians	229
Tell the Senate	320
To the P. O. Department	226
To Secretary Shaw	270
The Administration's Position	138
The Aldrich Bill	78
The American Commons	219
The Bennett Will	314
The Criminal Clause	404
The Fifty-Seventh Congress	57
The Hard-Up Disease	264
The Idle Rich	304
The Jewish Petition	238
The Lesson of 1894	140
The Munroe Doctrine	33
The National City's Schemes	197
The Orator's Preparation	157
The People in Art, Government and Religion	204
The Political Weekly as an Ad. Medium	341
The Price of Silver	132-224
The President's Message	337
The Silver Dollar	301
The Strikers Win	80
The Test of Democracy	43
The Value of Courage	55
The Voting Machine	114
The Postoffice Scandal	169
The World Mourns	237
Three Questions Answered	122
Treatment of Criminals	439
Truth Omnipotent	115
Value of an Education	406
Very Poor Advice	405
Victory for Workingmen	82

Contents

	PAGE
Voting Machine	114
Wages of Sin	258
"Wall Street Knows"	437
What About Nominees?	66
Why Not Freight Ships?	92
Why Silver is Coined	121
Worth Remembering	288

THE COMMONER CONDENSED

FAIRVIEW.

In this volume will be found a picture of the family residence at Fairview. The house was not completed as soon as expected, and is not entirely finished yet, but sufficiently so to present an accurate exterior view. The ground upon which the house stands was purchased in the summer of 1893 and the house has been in contemplation ever since that time. The original five-acre piece has been added to from time to time until the tract now comprises thirty-five acres.

Ground was broken for the house on the 1st day of October, 1901, the seventeenth anniversary of our marriage and the fourteenth anniversary of our location in Nebraska. We moved into the barn March 19, 1902, and into the unfinished house October 1, 1902. The architect was asked to prepare plans for a house that would cost about $10,000, but owing to the numerous alterations in the plans, to the expense of delivering materials so far from town and to the recent increased expense of building, the house cost considerably more than I anticipated it would. This is not an unusual experience, I believe, with those who start out to build a permanent home.

Fairview is nearly four miles southeast of the business center of the city of Lincoln and overlooks as beautiful a piece of farm land as can be found anywhere. It is reached by the College View street car line, which runs within about a third of a mile of the house. My editorial work is done in a basement room, fitted up with a working library, and here I am always glad to see any of the readers of THE COMMONER who may chance to pass through Nebraska's capital.

It is not often that one finds it necessary to dispute exaggerated reports of his wealth and income, but the erroneous accounts have been so persistently circulated as to have deceived friends.

From the tone of some reports it is evident that they were intended for a political purpose, namely, to create the impression that my views on public questions are determined by the amount of money to be made out of them. It ought to be apparent to any one that I would take the corporations' side rather than the people's side if my object was to make money. As it is, but a small portion of my time is devoted to remunerative work. Since 1896 more days have been devoted to my correspondence than to lecturing, and more days also have been devoted to speaking without remuneration (and often at my own expense) than to lecturing where compensation has been received. There is no reason why the readers of THE COMMONER should not know the facts and thus be prepared to meet the criticism of unfair opponents.

In the beginning the republicans made me appear poorer than I really was, and now they go to the other extreme and multiply my possessions from ten to a hundred times. One paper reports me as receiving $750,000 from subscriptions to THE COMMONER, and says that none of this money has been used for expenses, alleging that the receipts from the advertising exceed by $125,000 the cost of running the paper. Even democratic papers have been misled by these reports into assuming an accumulation entirely beyond what it would have been possible for me to make had I devoted all my time to money-making.

On another page will be found an editorial from the New Orleans *Times-Democrat* which defends the means employed for the accumulation of such wealth as I possess although it has accepted the republican estimate. The truth is, that in addition to my house, the tract of land on which it stands and my household goods, I have property, real and personal, that might at a fair market price be considered worth from $15,000 to $20,000. Of this, a sum amounting to between two and three thousand dollars (some of the land has not yet been disposed of) came to me by inheritance, and between three and four thousand was saved between the time I began the practice of the law and my first nomination for the presidency. The acquaintance and notoriety given me by the presidential campaigns largely augmented my earning power as well as largely increased my expenses and the demands upon my purse. In 1897 I received $17,000 as royalty from my book, "The First Battle," an equal amount, the remaining half of the royalty, being distributed among the various committees that were carrying on the campaign for the restoration of bimetallism. Since that time, except when in the army, I have derived my income from lectures and from articles written for newspapers and periodicals. Since 1896 I have contributed to the advancement of political reforms more than twenty thousand dollars, and that the reader may know that all my thoughts have not been centered on politics it may be added that donations for educational, religious and charitable purposes have in that time amounted to nearly half as much as my political contributions.

As I write editorials when on the road my lecturing has not interfered with my editorial work, but I expect to do less lecturing in the future than I have in the past, because I desire to spend more time with my family and to do more book-reading than I have had opportunity for in recent years. I shall only lecture enough to cover my personal and household expenses and to lay aside a little for old age.

The Commoner, while a success in a business way and in the increasing circle of its influence, has not reached a position where I feel justified in drawing any considerable amount from it. The paper was not started as a money-making scheme, but as a means of contributing toward the advancement of those principles for which the democratic party stands. It was necessary that the paper should be self-supporting and it has been self-supporting from the beginning. It will be published as long as the patronage is sufficient to pay running expenses, and in view of increasing encouragement received it seems likely to live as long as its editor does.

As the subscriptions are payable in advance and when paid

must cover the expense of the paper for the full subscription term; THE COMMONER fund has been kept by itself and held in trust for the benefit of the subscribers. The only reductions made from it have been made to pay running expenses, and there is now enough in this fund to guarantee that each subscriber will receive the paper for the time during which he has paid it. I draw no salary from the paper myself, and have taken out for my personal use on an average of less than five thousand per year during the two years of the paper's existence.

If the reader is surprised that the paper has not made the fabulous sums reported, he must remember that the subscription price was fixed at $1.00 per year in the beginning and has not been increased even though the paper has been doubled in size. He must also remember that agents' commissions must be paid out of the dollar, and that when the paper is furnished at clubbing rates the amount realized is considerably less than a dollar for each annual subscription.

In the effort to get the paper before as large a number of readers as possible, combination rates have been made which still further reduce the amount realized from each subscription. While, on the one hand, the paper has been furnished at a low price, the advertisements, on the other hand, have been restricted far below the amount that most papers of similar circulation carry. There are three reasons for this: First, no trust advertisements are accepted—this excludes an increasing number of advertisements; second, a great many advertisements which appear in some less discriminating papers have been rejected because not suitable for a paper that goes into the household and is read by all the members of the family. Third, the paper had to encounter the prejudice of many large concerns, managed by republicans, who carry their politics into their business and object to a paper that persistently exposes and opposes the plans of organized wealth.

The care, however, taken in the selection of advertising matter, while it has lessened the receipts of the paper for the time being, has given it standing with those advertisers who are admitted to its columns.

FRAUD OF ULTRA-PROTECTIONISTS.

The revolt among the rank and file of the republican party against ultra-protection found expression in the speech delivered in the senate by Mr. Dolliver of Iowa on January 13.

The spirited retort made by Mr. Aldrich, who is recognized more as the representative of the tariff barons than as a senator from Rhode Island, indicates that, however weary the republicans may have become of bearing the burden of special interests, the men whom Mr. Aldrich represents do not intend to yield any of the privileges that they now enjoy.

Mr. Dolliver indorsed the statement that had been previously made and fairly established by democratic senators to the effect that the tariff schedules in the Dingley law were purposely placed high so as to provide a margin in order that they might be reduced as a basis for reciprocity treaties. Mr. Dolliver said that he stood for the policies of James G. Blaine and for the policies advocated by William McKinley in his last speech. He said: "I do not intend to sit quiet in this chamber while it is said to be infamy that anybody should have the notion that tariff schedules once framed could not be honorably modified by sensible trade negotiations with the world." And he added: "I for one have made up my mind that the time has come when somebody whose convictions do not lie along the path of silence and quietude and ease in our political science should declare here that the whole future of the protective system in the United States depends upon the wisdom with which the congress of the United States fulfills the aspirations which found an expression so lofty in the last public utterance of William McKinley."

Some idea of the disposition of the ultra-protectionists may be obtained by those who are yet strangely ignorant as to that disposition from a statement made by Mr. Aldrich in reply to Mr. Carmack, Mr. Aldrich said: "I imagine that the senator from Tennessee and myself would never agree as to whether the protective duties in any bill were placed too high." In other words, perhaps, if the tariff rates were even higher than they are in the present exorbitant tariff schedules, Mr. Aldrich would not be willing to agree with Mr. Carmack that the rates were excessive.

Newspapers generally are complimenting Mr. Dolliver upon his speech and are referring to the "fine courage" displayed by the senator from Iowa. Does it not seem strange that when a senator from the big state of Iowa rises in his place to cross words with the senator from the little state of Rhode Island, giving expression to views which he believes are entertained by the people of Iowa, this should necessarily be referrd to as a display of "fine courage?"

Senator Dolliver is an orator and a man of more than ordinary ability. If he possesses any traits of cowardice his intimate friends have so far failed to discover it; and yet there is justification for the statement that Mr. Dolliver displayed "fine courage." The justification is found in the fact that the thing he pleaded for was justice for the people at the hands of the powerful interests that control our federal government, and that are represented in the senate by Mr. Aldrich and his associates.

It was not a display of fine courage for Dolliver to cross swords with Aldrich the man, because Dolliver in debate is Aldrich's superior. But the interests which Aldrich represents dominate the party to which Dolliver belongs, control the senate of which Dolliver is a member, and have a firm grasp upon all the machinery of the federal government. These interests, so we have been told and if we mistake not Mr. Dolliver has on several occasions been our informant, are the "business interests" of the country; they represent the "intelligence and patriotism" of the land; their wisdom should control the judgment of the people and their choice for public officials should be the people's choice. Even though Dolliver merely pleaded for the fulfillment of an explicit pledge made by the republican party, although he did not ask the representatives of his party to go so far as a real tariff reformer would desire, he knew that he was placing himself in the attitude of defying the decree of men who having provided the republican party with its campaign funds expect at the hands of that party and its leaders prompt and complete submission in return for those favors.

Mr. Dolliver's speech is simply an index to the growing sentiment among the rank and file of republicans in opposition to ultra-protection. Mr. Dolliver's argument shows that the high protectionists practice fraud upon republicans as well as upon the people generally; they secure a higher tariff than they even claim to need by promising a reduction through reciprocity treaties; and after securing these exorbitant rates they refuse to lower the duties even for the purpose of obtaining reciprocity. This, too, in face of the fact that Mr. Roosevelt referred to reciprocity as "the handmaiden of protection" and the republican national convention of 1896 said: "Protection and reciprocity are twin measures of republican policy and go hand in hand."

OKLAHOMA AND STATEHOOD.

My recent visit to Oklahoma convinced me, first, that the interests of Oklahoma imperatively demand immediate statehood, and, second, that the people of the territory fear that admittance to statehood may be prevented by the differences of opinion which exist as to the propriety of incorporating the Indian territory. The situation may be summed up as follows: The arguments in favor of single statehood for the two territories are, first, that either territory alone would be small in area, compared with other western states, and small in population, compared with most of the states of the union; second, that the two territories supplement each other in products and resources; third, that there is no natural boundary line between the two territories, while the two together are compact and shapely. Arguments in favor of separate statehood are, first, that Oklahoma, having organized counties, a large area of well improved land, and an admirable school system in operation, is better prepared for statehood than the Indian territory. Second, that the school fund of Oklahoma would have to be divided with the Indian territory, and, third, that the expense of enforcing the criminal law in the Indian territory would be a burden to the people of Oklahoma.

Besides these arguments there are arguments of a political nature and others of a local character. For instance, some republicans favor single statehood because they prefer to have two democratic senators from one large state rather than four democratic senators from two small states—admitting that both territories are democratic; while other republicans favor double statehood with the hope of saving Oklahoma to the republicans. Some democrats, too, favor double statehood with the belief that it would give the party four senators, while others think that it is necessary to include the Indian territory in order to make Oklahoma surely democratic. The location of the capital also affects opinions to some extent, some towns hoping for the capital under single statehood while others expect it under double statehood.

So numerous are the conflicting interests and opinions that it is difficult, if not impossible, to ascertain the wish of the majority of the people. In the late election the republican candidate for congressional delegate ran on a platform declaring for the immediate admission of Oklahoma, leaving for future decision the question of adding the Indian Territory, while the democratic candidate was committed to single statehood for both territories, but the result was not decisive because many on both sides placed their political preferences above their opinions on statehood and, besides, there is a contest over the seat. The republican received the certificate, but the democrat demands the counting of several thousand ballots which were thrown out because marked twice.

In view of the impossibility of deciding certainly as to the desire of the majority, and in view of the further fact that each side claims a majority in support of its position it would seem wise to leave the question to a vote. Let Oklahoma be admitted to statehood and before the time set for admission let the people of both territories declare their preference. If a union of the two territories is desired by the people of both territories no objection ought to be made by those who live outside. If, on the other hand, the people of either territory object to the union there ought to be no disposition on the part of the outside public to force a consolidation.

If Oklahoma is admitted by itself the name, of course, would remain unchanged, but the name, Jefferson, has been suggested as an appropriate one in case the two territories are united. The main argument advanced in favor of this name is that as this is the last state remaining in the territory known as the Louisiana purchase, it would certainly be a fitting honor to the author of the Declaration of Independence This question, too, ought to be left to the people and it can be decided at the election called to pass upon the question of single statehood. If a majority of the people of the two territories favor the name it can be substituted for Oklahoma. If, however, the people of the Indian territory favor the name, Jefferson, but it does not command a majority of the total vote, the name can be given to the Indian territory, in case the two territories are not united.

These suggestions are made because I am convinced that great injustice is being done the people of Oklahoma by the continuation of territorial rule. The population there is intelligent and energetic, and it represents every section of the country.

At Lawton I attended a democratic dinner at which some 125 or 150 guests were present. I was so impressed with the cosmopolitan character of the population of the territory that at this dinner I called the roll and found that all the states and territories of the union, except six, were represented either as the former home or birthplace of some person present.

In Lawton, Hobart, Anadarko and the other towns which sprang up a year ago last summer schools were at once established, churches built and literary societies organized, and now the inhabitants enjoy all the advantages of advanced civilization except self-government. The older communities of Oklahoma and the Indian territory are not surpassed by communities of equal population anywhere. It is a grievous wrong that the rights of the enterprising and progressive people of Oklahoma who have converted a wild prairie into a vast garden dotted over with busy marts of trade—it is a grievous wrong, I repeat, that the rights of these people should be sacrificed to the whims of republican politicians. There is no doubt about Oklahoma's fitness for statehood and it surely ought to be possible for the senators and members to agree upon a plan which leaves all disputed questions to be settled by the people of the territories. If Oklahoma and the Indian territory are admitted as one state it is only fair that the question be decided at once so that the people of the Indian territory may have a voice in the framing of the constitution and in the location of the capital and state institutions. It is only just, too, that in the opening of Indian lands hereafter some provision should be made for a school fund whether the Indian territory comes in by itself or in conjunction with Oklahoma.

If by the vote of the people it is determined that the two territories shall be admitted separately then the Indian territory should be given immediate representation in congress with a view to early statehood.

It is believed by many that the eastern republicans, notwithstanding platform promises, are really anxious to prevent the admission of any of the territories, but this is only the greater reason why the democrats in congress should redouble their efforts. If the omnibus bill is so amended as to leave the disputed questions to a vote of the people it will be hard for the most partisan republican to stand out against its passage.

The union of Arizona and New Mexico has been suggested by those who oppose their separate admission. While this would be unjust to those who have redeemed the desert places and would hardly be accepted by the people of those territories, yet it might be well to leave the question of united or separate statehood to be decided by a vote of the people if such a provision would secure the passage of a statehood bill.

A CORRECTION.

The editor of THE COMMONER is always glad to make a correction when his attention is called to a mistake. In a recent issue he said that, so far as he knew, no representative of the administration had ever explained why the criminal provisions of the Sherman anti-trust law had not been enforced. An Ohio reader takes the editor to task for this statement and says that Senator Foraker, in his speech opening the Ohio campaign last fall—the speech in which the "stand pat" phrase was used—said "these trust magnates are some of our best citizens and we will not put them in jail to please Mr. Bryan." This would seem like a sufficient explanation, and yet the reader above referred to suggests that even if the trust magnates were not put in jail to please Mr. Bryan it might still be wise to put them in jail because the law says that they should be put there.

A REAL TRUST FIGHTER.

The *Globe-Democrat* in a recent issue tells how President Diaz of the Mexican Republic thwarted the Standard Oil company. According to the *Globe-Democrat* the oil trust got control of a Mexican railroad and attempted to freeze out a rival by putting a prohibitive rate on oil from the competing well. The matter was brought to the attention of the president and he at once put the legal machinery into motion and the railroad soon had to choose between the restoration of the old rate and a forfeiture of its charter. The result was that the railroad reduced its rate for carrying oil and the Standard Oil company had to meet the competitive price of oil.

Our president could do the same thing in effect if he desired to do so. If he was really anxious to exterminate the trusts he could do so in short order. He could prepare a bill making it unlawful for any corporation to use the mails, railroads or telegraph lines for interstate commerce until that corporation showed that its stock was not watered and that it was not trying to monopolize any branch of business or the production of any article of merchandise. His power to appeal to the people and his ability to focus public attention upon a question would enable him to secure the passage of a really meritorious law—but such action would antagonize the money power and bring a fight in the next national convention.

REFORM THE SENATE NOW.

The constitution of the United States provides that a constitutional amendment shall be submitted to the several states for ratification whenever two-thirds of both houses shall deem it necessary. The same article also provides that congress shall call a convention for proposing amendments "on the application of the legislatures of two-thirds of the several states."

The people have been trying for years to reform the method of electing United States senators. A resolution proposing the necessary amendment to the constitution has passed the house four times and, as proof that the sentiment was not confined to one party, it may be added that this resolution passed two democratic houses and two republican houses. The last national democratic platform contained a plank demanding the election of senators by direct vote of the people, and similar action has been taken by several states.

In Illinois, last November, the question was voted upon, and although the state went republican by about 90,000, there was a large majority in favor of the election of senators by the people.

Having waited a reasonable length of time for the senate to acquiesce in this public demand, it is now time for the people to reform the senate whether it wishes to be reformed or not, and this power is in their hands. If the legislatures of two-thirds of the states will adopt resolutions asking congress to call a convention for the purpose of submitting this amendment, it then becomes an imperative duty which even the senate cannot refuse to perform.

THE COMMONER proposes the following resolution and urges its adoption by legislatures now in session:

JOINT RESOLUTION.

"Whereas, Article V. of the constitution of the United States provides that 'the congress, whenever two-thirds of both houses shall deem it necessary, shall propose amendments to this constitution, or on the application of the legislatures of two-thirds of the several states shall call a convention for proposing amendments, which in either case shall be valid to all intents and purposes as part of this constitution, when ratified by the legislatures of three-fourths of the several states, or by convention in three-fourths thereof,' etc., and,

"Whereas, The house of representatives of the congress of the United States has on four separate occasions passed by a two-thirds vote a resolution proposing an amendment to the constitution providing for the election of United States senators by direct vote of the people, and,

"Whereas, The United States senate has each time refused to consider or vote upon said resolution, thereby denying to the people of the several states a chance to secure this much desired change in the method of electing senators, therefore, be it

"Resolved, By the senate and house of representatives of the state of ——————, that, under the authority of article V. of the constitution of the United States, application is hereby made to congress to forthwith call a constitutional convention for the purpose of submitting to the states for ratification, an amendment to the federal constitution providing for the election of United States senators by direct vote of the people; and,

"Resolved, That the secretary of the state be, and is, hereby directed to forward a properly authenticated copy of these resolutions to the president of the United States, to the president of the senate of the United States, and to the speaker of the house of representatives of the United States."

The various legislatures are urged to take up and pass immediately the above resolution or some resolution of the same import to the end that this question may be brought before the present congress and action secured before adjournment.

Of course, it is much more cumbersome to call a convention for this purpose than to secure an amendment through a resolution passed by congress, but where congress refuses to act this alternative is necessary. It is probable, however, that if two-thirds of the states make application for a convention the senate will act on the resolution now before it and thus make the convention unnecessary. Surely, no senator would be likely to stand out against the proposition after his state had passed a resolution asking for a constitutional convention. In this way the power that remains with the legislatures can be used to compel action by the senate.

It is to be hoped that the democrats who favor this proposition, as nearly all democrats do, will not attempt to make party capital out of it. In legislatures that are republican the democrats should allow some republican to introduce the resolution in order to give it greater probability of immediate consideration. In democratic legislatures the democrats can take the initiative. Let no time be lost. Act at once.

DEMOCRATIC SUBSTITUTE.

The democrats of the house and senate will not do their full duty if they merely support a republican anti-trust measure and then complain that it does not go far enough. A republican measure satisfactory to the trusts (as any republican measure is likely to be before it passes) may have enough of the appearance of good to justify democrats in voting for it. In fact, the democrats are so anxious to legislate on the trust question that they will in all probability vote for any measure, no matter how feeble or ineffective, if it at all recognizes the power of the government, and the desire of the people, to extinguish the trusts.

But it is incumbent upon the democrats to do something more than point out the short-comings of the republican measure; they ought to present a democratic measure as a substitute, in order that the country may see the difference between a real attempt at anti-trust legislation—such an attempt as the Kansas City platform promised—and the puerile and faltering efforts that are being made by the republican leaders.

Congressman Shallenberger of Nebraska has introduced a bill which more nearly than any other measure that has been brought to the editor's attention carries out the Kansas City platform plan. It provides for the appointment of the commission to be known as the foreign and internal commerce commission. The bill provides that the commission shall consist of five persons, not more than three of whom shall be members of one political party. This is intended to make it bi-partisan, but a bi-partisan board appointed by a partisan official is likely to divide responsibility without accomplishing the purpose sought. The president has already appointed several bi-partisan commissions, but the men appointed to represent the democrats have almost in every case been pretended democrats who earned their places by supporting the republican ticket—men whose only political service, since appointment, has been to give a quasi democratic indorsement to republican policies. It might be well to have one of the commsisioners a member of the opposing party as a guaranty that any partisanship attempted by the majority would be exposed. But to make sure that this minority member shall be really and positively with the minority the appointment ought to be made from a list of names suggested by the democratic national committee or by the democrats of the senate and house acting in caucus. A minority member who owes his appointment to his party rather than to the opposition is much more likely to represent the minority than one whose salary places him under obligations to political opponents.

The Shallenberger bill provides that it shall be the duty of this commission to investigate and report on all matters effecting foreign commerce and the trade between the states, together with methods and means of transportation and the customs that prevail among the corporations in regard to management and issue of stock, bonds, etc. It is also the duty of the commission to inquire into the consolidation of corporations and associations and to ascertain whether any attempt has been made to restrain trade or monopolize business.

The bill provides that corporations proposing to engage in interstate commerce shall file a statement showing stock, liabilities, indebtedness, etc., and applying for authority to engage in interstate commerce, and the commission is not allowed to grant such authority if the statement shows any watered stock or if the corporation is attempting to monopolize or control the manufacture, product, sale or transportation of any article of trade or merchandise.

The president is authorized, upon the recommendation of this commission, to suspend wholly or partially for such time as he may direct, the collection of import dues on such articles as compete with articles produced by any corporation which is attempting to monopolize an industry. If any official of a corporation or member of an association of individuals is guilty of perjury in making the statements provided for in the bill he shall be subject to the penalties provided for perjury. All corporations attempting to engage in interstate commerce without first complying with the conditions of the act and obtaining a license from the commission shall pay a tax of 10 per cent on the capital stock issued and outstanding, and the same annual tax is levied upon all stock issued in excess of the actual money invested in the enterprise.

Such, in brief, is the Shallenberger bill. The bill is in line with the Kansas City platform and is a much more effective measure than anything proposed by the republicans or likely to be proposed by them. It places the entire matter of interstate commerce under the control of the commission to be created. Corporations organized for the purpose of engaging in a purely state industry are not at all interfered with or embarassed, but a corporation organized to engage in interstate commerce must secure a license before going outside of the state of its origin. The attempt to engage in interstate commerce might be more accurately defined as the use, or attempted use, of railroads, telegraph lines or the mails for any business outside of the state in which the corporation is created.

This bill does not interfere with the right of the state to create any corporation it needs for its own use, but it makes it impossible for a state to convert itself into a den of thieves and organize great industrial combinations to prey upon the rest of the country. The bill ought to provide that the license issued by the commission is not to interfere with the right of every state to regulate foreign corporations doing business in the state. The license contemplated is simply a license that permits the state corporation to engage in interstate commerce—it cannot leave the state of its origin without obtaining this license—but when the license is obtained it does not protect the corporation, or should not, from the laws deemed necessary by any state for the protection of its own people. In other words, the federal remedy should be added to the state remedy, not substituted for it.

The bill ought to go a little further in the way of penalties. The tax to be collected is all right, but there should be a criminal penalty imposed upon any corporation official who attempts to engage in interstate commerce before the license is obtained, or who in any way takes part in the issue of watered stock. The bill should also provide for the revocation of the license by the commission whenever the corporation violates the conditions upon which the license was granted, and when the license is revoked the interstate business of the corporation must be suspended until a new license is issued.

The Shallenberger bill is sound in principle and would be effective in practice. Instead of compelling the government to search the country for violations of the law it would compel the corporations to seek the government and obtain a license before engaging in business. The system proposed by the bill is similar to the license system now in operation, but much more easily enforced. If the government attempted to collect a tax from each liquor dealer after he had sold liquor, or attempted to enforce provisions against persons who sold without first requiring a license, it would find its task a very difficult one. But when it requires the payment of the license fee in advance the work becomes much easier. In the case of a corporation it could not do much interstate business without being detected. Under such a law it would be impossible for a corporation to do any real harm without the fact coming to the knowledge of the government.

The democrats in the senate and house ought to agree upon a substitute which follows the lines of the Shallenberger bill and offer it in lieu of the republican measure. Such a substitute would draw the line between honest and effective legislation desired by the democrats and the weak and partial measures thus far proposed by the republicans.

If it is thought an unnecessary requirement to compel all corporations engaged in interstate commerce to take out the license a beginning might be made by requiring it of all corporations having a capital of more than a certain amount, fixing the same low enough so that no monopoly can be secured.

It is imperative that the democrats shall take a positive and aggressive position. Criticism is well enough in its way, but affirmative action is necessary for a party that proposes to do something in the interest of the masses of the people.

REAL DIFFERENCE BETWEEN PARTIES.

The editor of THE COMMONER is in receipt of a letter from a man born in Russia, but recently naturalized. He says that he appreciates the responsibility of citizenship and desires to discharge his duty intelligently and patriotically. He has some difficulty in deciding with which party to act, because he says that the party names represent the same ideas of government, and that if the parties are true to their names they are much alike. Yet, thinking there must be a wide distinction to justify active party contests, he asks for information as to the real distinction between them.

The party names themselves do not indicate any essential difference between the parties. In fact, the democratic party, when organized by Jefferson, was known as the republican party. As the democratic title brings out the idea that the people rule, while the republican name emphasizes the fact that the rule is through representatives, it might be argued that the democratic party would bring the government a little nearer to the people, while the republican party would have more faith in representatives of the people than in the people themselves, and yet this distinction is not necessarily indicated by the names, although there is this general distinction between the beliefs of many of the members of the two parties. It is not unusual, however, for party names to be twisted from their original meaning and applied to different ideas at different times. The democratic party stands for the doctrine of "equal rights to all and special privileges to none." It protests against the use of the government for the benefit of a few at the expense of the many, whether this favoritism be shown in a protective tariff that burdens the consumers for the benefit of manufacturers, or in a financial system that sacrifices wealth-producers to the money-changers, or in imperialism which barters away fundamental principles of government to enable syndicates to exploit distant lands. It is not strange either that the democratic party, jealous of any infringement upon the rights of the masses, should oppose private monopolies which, under the pretense of developing industry, simply gather in the profits of industry and reduce to a minimum the number of those who are to be the recipients of the benefits of industrial progress.

The republican party, on the other hand, has turned from the defense of human rights to the emphasizing of property rights. It has helped manufacturers to levy tribute upon the rest of the people; in return for campaign contributions it has permitted the financiers to make laws for their own enrichment, and in order to open new fields for corporations it has adopted the English colonial system. Without daring to defend the trusts as beneficial it has failed either to enforce existing laws against them or to devise new laws for their extermination.

This difference between the parties is not due to party name nor entirely to the fundamental principles advocated by the party leaders. It is partly due to environment. The republican party was in power during the war; the foundation for a great many fortunes was laid in government contracts and in legislation that was primarily enacted under the spur of what was called a war necessity. It was natural that the recipients of benefits should not only turn with gratitude to the party that granted them, but should seek to keep that party in power in order that the benefits might continue. The republican party has thus become obligated to, and identified with, predatory wealth, and it is not in position to punish those who are so influential in its counsels. Since 1896, however, the democratic party has not only stood for the rights of the plain people, but has been free from the embarrassing support of the great money magnates.

IGNORANT OF THE WEST.

Those eastern statesmen who seem so ignorant of the west and so indifferent to the welfare of the territories would do well to compare the opinion expressed by Daniel Webster a little more than fifty years ago with the development which has taken place since that time. Webster was one of the greatest statesmen of his time. His long connection with public life gave him as good an opportunity to know the country and its possibilities as any one then living and yet he opposed an appropriation that was intended to establish mail connection between the Pacific coast and the Atlantic seaboard.

Those who allow their sectional prejudices or their partisanship to stand in the way of the admission of Arizona and New Mexico (the same objection cannot be made to Oklahoma) ought to read the following extract from Webster's speech in 1844:

"What do we want of the vast, worthless area, this region of savages and wild beasts, of deserts of shifting sands and whirlwinds of dust, cactus and prairie dogs? To what use could we ever hope to put these deserts or these endless mountain ranges, impenetrable and covered to their bases with eternal snow? What can we ever hope to do with the western coast of three thousand miles, rock-bound, cheerless and uninviting and not a harbor in it? What use have we for such a country? Mr. President, I will never vote one cent from the public treasury to place the Pacific coast one inch nearer Boston than it is today."

A REFORMER IN OFFICE.

The readers of THE COMMONER had occasion to rejoice when a Kansas City platform democrat, Hon. Lucius F. G. Garvin, was elected governor of Rhode Island, for they knew that he was interested in doing something more than drawing his salary and enjoying the honors of the position. They will be glad, though not surprised, to know that Governor Garvin is justifying their hopes and expectations. He begins his message to the legislature by using language which the republicans may regard as sacrilegious. He points to the great productive capacity of the United States during the year 1902, but instead of attributing this prosperity to the republican administration he attributes it to our "vast natural resources and to the industry and enterprise of our people." He calls attention to the abuses of governmental functions of the state—first, the passage of laws by one general assembly which cannot be amended or repealed by subsequent assemblies; second, the establishment of a board of police commissioners which spent money raised by taxation, although not responsible to the people who pay the taxes; third, the post-election sessions of the general assembly which passed laws that they would not dare to pass before an election; fourth, the domination of a third house, causing legislation to be sold to the highest bidder. He also points out that the theory of representative government is constantly violated in Rhode Island, and that under the constitution of Rhode Island one-twelfth of the inhabitants living in small towns possess as much influence as eleven-twelfths of the people living in large cities. He calls for a constitutional convention, and points out other needed reforms.

The eastern democrats are looking around for a presidential candidate. Why is it that they ignore such timber as that furnished by Rhode Island? Why is it that they pick up men who have never expressed themselves on public questions and have never given any evidence of sympathy with the people? Why? Because the reorganizing element of the party does not want a president who would be democratic in office and who would use the great prestige of the presidency to protect the people from the encroachment of organized wealth.

Governor Garvin lives in an eastern state, but he would be as obnoxious to the reorganizers as any western or southern believer in the Kansas City platform. If he were to announce his candidacy for the presidency he would be assailed as a small, insignificant, narrow-minded man, "an accident in politics," and as a person lacking the breadth and depth which the metropolitan papers are in the habit of conferring upon those who are under secret obligation and pledge to the corporations.

The democrats, however, who are interested in good government—and such democrats are quite numerous on election day—will rejoice that little Rhode Island is going to have a taste of democracy. Governor Garvin will have their best wishes as he tries to secure remedial legislation for his constituents.

ALEXANDER HAMILTON'S PLAN.

A Chicago reader of THE COMMONER takes the editor to task for saying that Hamilton's proposed plan of government provided for a president and senators for life. The reader referred to says that that statement "has no foundation in fact," and suggests that Hamilton's plan was to have them serve during "good behavior." What is the distinction? If a man holds office during good behavior and cannot be put out except by impeachment, wherein does his term differ from the term of one who holds office for life, but can also be put out of offiec by impeachment?

Hamilton's plan will be found in the appendix to the Madison papers, page 584. In a note it is stated that Colonel Hamilton placed in the hands of Mr. Madison for preservation a document outlining his idea of "the constitution which he would have wished to be proposed by the convention." A copy of this document was kept by Mr. Madison and published by him, the original having been returned to Mr. Hamilton and found among Hamilton's papers at his death. In future years Hamilton, forgetting the text of the paper, was under the impression that in his plan the president's term had been limited to three years. Section 9, article 4, of Mr. Hamilton's proposed constitution says of the president that "he shall hold his place during good behavior, removable only by conviction, on impeachment, for some crime or misdemeanor." Section 6, article 3, says of the senators that they "shall hold their places during good behavior, removable only by conviction, on impeachment, for some crime or misdemeanor."

According to Hamilton's plan the senate was to consist of persons chosen by electors "elected for that purpose by the citizens and inhabitants of the several states," and then he proceeds to fix a property qualification for the electors who are to choose the senators. They must have "in their own right or in the right of their wives, an estate in land for not less than life or a term of years whereof, at the time of giving their votes, there shall be at least fourteen years unexpired."

Not only did he want the president to hold office for life (unless impeached), not only did he want senators to hold office for life (unless impeached), and elected by electors having a prescribed property qualification, but article 8, section 1, of his plan provided "that the governor or president of each state shall be appointed under the authority of the United States and shall have a right to negative all laws about to be passed in the state of which he shall be governor or president, subject to such qualifications and regulations as the legislature of the United States shall prescribe."

Section 2, of the same article, provides that "each governor or president of a state shall hold office until a successor be actually appointed, unless he die or resign, or be removed from office by conviction on impeachment." It will be seen that Mr. Hamilton wanted life terms in the federal government and also wanted the federal government to appoint the governors of the states who were to have a veto over state legislation, and these governors, unless they resigned or were impeached, should hold office during life unless the federal authorities saw fit to supersede them. The people of the state had no authority in the matter whatever.

But why this dispute as to the views of Alexander Hamilton? The record is clear, and there is no excuse for misunderstanding it. The trouble is simply this: Hamilton did not believe in a republican form of government. It is so stated on page 244 of the Madison papers. Here is the language used: "He acknowledged himself not to think favorably of republican government; but addressed his remarks to those who did think favorably of it, in order to prevail on them to tone their government as high as possible."

Hamilton's distrust of the people manifested itself at every turn. On page 203 of the Madison papers will be found a report of his speech in the convention in which he praised the English house of lords, as "a most noble institution," and added, "Having nothing to hope for by a change, and a sufficient interest, by means of their property, in being faithful to the national interest, they form a permanent barrier against every pernicious innovation, whether attempted on the part of the crown or of the commons. No temporary senate will have firmness enough to answer the purpose."

He argued that a seven-year term for the senators would not be sufficient to give the senate an "adequate firmness," and said that those favoring a seven-year term did not duly consider the "amazing violence and turbulence of the democratic spirit." On the same page he argued that a government could not be good unless it had a good executive, saying: "The English model was the only good one on this subject. The hereditary interest of the king was so interwoven with that of the nation, and his personal emolument so great, that he was placed above the danger of being corrupted from abroad; and at the same time was both sufficiently independent and sufficiently controlled, to answer the purpose of the institution at home."

His preference for life tenure was also alluded to on the same page as follows: "Let one branch of the legislature hold their places for life, or at least during good behavior. Let the executive, also, be for life."

Senator Henry Cabot Lodge, in his Life of Hamilton (published by Houghton, Miffin & Co., Boston), calls attention to the fact that Hamilton did not believe our constitution "equal to the burden imposed upon it," that he "considered the government too weak." Again Lodge says, on page 282: "He did not believe in democracy as a system of government. He strove with all his energy to make the experiment of the constitution succeed, but he doubted its merit at the outset, and finally came to the conclusion that, in its existing form, it was doomed to failure. He believed in class influence and representation, in strong government, and in what, for want of a better phrase, may be called an aristocratic republic."

Hamilton's very death was due to his lack of faith in our form of government; he was looking for an uprising and thought that a strong man would be needed, and he was to be that strong man. He fought the duel in which he died because he feared to refuse lest it should be attributed to cowardice and make him useless in the crisis for which he was looking. Here is the paper which Hamilton left giving his reason for accepting the challenge. It is quoted by Lodge on page 251:

"The ability to be in future useful, whether in resisting mischief or affecting good, in those crises of our public affairs which seem likely to happen, would probably be inseparable from a conformity with public prejudice in this particular."

The republicans are today making Hamilton their saint, and the fact that they do so shows that they are turning from the democratic republic of Jefferson to the "aristocratic republic" of Hamilton. In 1856 the republican national platform appealed to all who wanted "to carry the government back to the principles of Washington and Jefferson." In 1859 the republicans of Boston celebrated the birthday of Thomas Jefferson, and Lincoln wrote his famous letter expressing regret that he could not atend the meeting, and eulogizing Jefferson. But that was in the earlier days of imperialism. Now republicans denounce Jefferson as a demagogue, ridicule his idea of government by the consent of the governed, and pay their homage at the shrine of the man who would have made this government little less than a limited monarchy.

No wonder the republicans wince when Hamilton's real views are brought out. But they might as well get used to it; if they are going to favor imperialism in the Philippines they must not be squeamish about applying the principles of imperialism at home. They are admitting today charges that they indignantly denied a few years ago, and it will not be long before they will be praising the most undemocratic utterances of Hamilton as the highest evidence of statesmanship.

FINANCIERS AGAINST TARIFF REFORM.

Hon. Flavius J. Van Vorhis of Indianapolis, Ind., in an argument recently made, points out that the republicans have made the great financiers pecuniarily interested in the defeat of any tariff reform legislation. He says that the banks are now using without interest a large sum of government money, approximating $150,000,000, and that they would have to give up this money and lose the interest upon it if the surplus was reduced by the lowering of revenue duties. Six per cent interest on $150,000,000 would yield nine millions; 5 per cent, seven millions and a half. This is a tremendous sum, and operates, first, as a bribe to the banks to oppose any reduction of the surplus, and, second, it forms a fund from which the republicans can draw in their campaigns. Surely, banks that receive as a gratuity so large a sum in the shape of interest each year could afford to give a very considerable sum to the campaign fund every four years. If, for instance, they gave the equivalent of one year's interest for the opportunity to collect four years' interest, they would give to the republican campaign fund more than twenty times as much as the democratic national committee has had in either of the campaigns of 1896 and 1900. The fact that the elections can be carried by the interest collected on the people's money shows the perversion of the national government, and ought to make honest republicans recognize the abuse of power of which the republican party has been guilty.

Mr. Van Vorhis has done the public a service in pointing out the vital connection between the republican method of running the treasury department and the opposition which the great financiers show to tariff reform. It will be remembered that in 1888 the republican national platform denounced Mr. Cleveland's administration for doing the very same thing, although on a less scale, that the republican administration is doing now. The fact is that both the republican administration and Mr. Cleveland's administration purchased the active support of the financiers with the loan of public funds.

NATURAL RIGHTS.

A reader of THE COMMONER asks: "What are natural rights?" and says that some of his acquaintances declare that the whole theory of "natural rights" died soon after the French revolution. The Declaration of Independence has reference to natural rights when it declares that there are certain inalienable rights given by the Creator to every human being, and among these inalienable rights are enumerated "life, liberty and the pursuit of happiness." The right to life is not a right given by the government or by society. It is an inalienable right, and the taking of it cannot be defended except in self-defense or where it is taken by society because of some crime done against society. Those who oppose the death penalty insist that even society has no right to take it, no matter what the crime.

Every individual has the right to liberty and the pursuit of happiness, the only condition being that he shall not trespass upon the equal rights of others.

The doctrine of natural rights is not yet absolute, and it is this doctrine that will ultimately destroy imperialism and overthrow the imperialists.

PASSES UNLAWFUL.

Attorney General Cunneen of the state of New York has, at the request of one of the legislators, prepared an opinion on the pass question. He holds that according to the new constitution it is a misdemeanor for a corporation to offer a pass to a member of the legislature, and that the official would forfeit his office if he accepted a pass. The New York constitutional convention deserves great credit for inserting the anti-pass section in the constitution. It is a pity that every state has not such a constitutional provision. The political pass ought to be abolished and it is to be regretted that congress voted down an anti-pass amendment offered when the house was considering the bill to raise the salaries of federal judges. Surely the officials who draw salaries ought to be as able to pay railroad fare as the ordinary citizen, and if he is not willing to pay his fare he ought to be compelled to do so. The pass is not always a bribe, but it is issued by corporations that understand its value and it would not be issued without a purpose.

THE FOWLER CURRENCY BILL.

During the recent campaign republican organs and orators persistently denied that there was any serious intention of passing the Fowler bill. In spite of the fact that the Fowler bill was reported in the first session of the present congress by the republican majority of the house committee, republican newspapers and in some instances republican congressmen who were candidates for re-election, assured the people that the Fowler bill was dead beyond all hope of resurrection, and that democrats who referred to that measure were merely employing it as a scarecrow.

Today the Fowler bill is before congress and it is being pushed with such vigor that it is impossible for republican leaders to longer deceive the people. It is true that there is a difference between the Fowler bill as reported at the last session and the Fowler bill that is now being pushed in the present session. The change in the details of the measure does not imply any surrender on the part of the money trust. The change has been made in response to the protest on the part of republican members that they dare not enact a law containing all the ill-advised provisions contained in the old Fowler bill. The money trust, while not making any surrender as to any of the so-called "reforms" which they hope to bring about, have yielded to the protests of the republican congressmen to the extent that they are willing to demand at this time the adoption of one of the iniquitous features of the Fowler bill, holding other features in abeyance.

The old Fowler bill authorized the establishment of branch banks and provided also for the retirement of the greenbacks, together with other provisions contemplated by the policy adopted by the so-called Indianapolis monetary conference. Republican congressmen pointed out to the backers of this measure that the time was not yet ripe for the retirement of the greenbacks; the people were somewhat partial to the greenbacks and it would not be "good politics" to insist upon their retirement at this time. With respect to the branch bank feature, the smaller bankers throughout the country made such a vigorous protest against this plan that Mr. Fowler and his associates thought it inadvisable to undertake at this moment to push through a measure providing for the branch banks. But one of the most important, if not the most important, features of the old Fowler bill relates to asset currency, and the so-called new Fowler bill as it was reported to the house by the republican majority of the committee on banking and currency on January 13, 1903, provides for the asset currency. This bill is known as House Roll No. 16228. Its title is, "A bill providing for the issue and circulation of national bank notes." The bill is printed in full in another column of this issue.

In the report accompanying the recommendation of the Fowler bill, the republican committee says: "The time has come when every one realizes that United States government bonds will no longer furnish a sufficient basis for an adqeuate supply of currency, even though that form of currency were profitable, which it is not. Indeed, were it not for the policy of force applied by the secretary of the treasury, the banks would now be retiring their circulation, because unprofitable, at the rate of

$3,000,000 per month, the maximum allowed by law, and this, too, in the face of a constantly increasing demand for more bank notes." Although a national bank having invested in United States bonds may deposit those bonds with the government and may, by reason of that deposit, issue bank notes to the full amount of the face value of those bonds, that bank will be permitted to draw from the government interest on the bonds thus deposited and at the same time will have the use of the money in the shape of national bank notes to an amount equal to the face value of those bonds which it may loan to the people and obtain interest or in other ways derive profits. And yet this form of currency, according to Mr. Fowler and his associates, is not profitable. These people are not satisfied with the already generous advantages given them under the national banking law. They want privileges and advantages that cannot, in reason, be defended and that are without precedent even in the record of the greedy demands made by their predecessors in the financial world during the history of this government.

In conclusion this republican committee recommending the adoption by the United States of the asset currency plan, says: "First, that there is an exigent demand for some provision to relieve the present situation if our unparallelled prosperity is not itself to prove the source of a commercial crisis. Second, that neither silver nor gold nor United States bonds, much less any other kind of bonds, can be a proper source of a safe, economical, and elastic currency. Third, that in the six billions of liquidated assets of our national banks there is an incomparable security many times over for the credit notes that our trade demands; and that no currency can be truly elastic that does not spring into being at the bidding of business, and as certainly disappears when that business is finished."

It is interesting to be told that there is some danger under a republican administration that "unparalleled prosperity" may in itself prove the source of commercial crisis. It is interesting to be told, by the representatives of a party that claims to represent "sound money" and that insisted that the single gold standard would provide the solution of all our financial problems, "that neither silver nor gold nor United States bonds, much less any other kind of bonds, can be a proper source of a safe, economical, and elastic currency."

In the opinion of this committee "no currency can be truly elastic that does not spring into being at the bidding of business, and as certainly disappears when that business is finished." In other words, although this republican committee was not frank enough to admit it, in the opinion of these financiers, no currency will be satisfactory, no financial system will be complete, unless they are so arranged that the money trust can, by the mere pushing of a button, make money scarce, and therefore dear, or when the so-called elasticity shall better suit their purpose, are enabled to make money plentiful during a period to be designated according to their selfish inetrests.

It would be well if the American people could have made a note of the statements made by republican orators and republican newspapers during the presidential campaign of 1896. Then these republicans inveighed against anything in the form of "wild-cat money." Then they wanted a financial system based upon a "solid and substantial foundation." They then would be content with nothing but gold as a proper source of a safe currency; and yet today they tell us "that neither silver nor gold nor United States bonds, much less any other kind of bonds, can be a proper source of a safe, economical, and elastic currency." This, then, is "sound money." This is the "preservation of national honor and international credit!" This is the "reasonable, intelligent financial system based upon the experience of years;" a system that "makes for the permanent prosperity of the people;" a system that gives "high promise to business interests;" and for this system the republican party assumes the role of prophet!

A "PARTY" IN COURT.

An Ohio reader of THE COMMONER sends in a circular letter issued by Caleb Powers, ex-secretary of state for Kentucky, appealing for funds to assist him in his defense. It seems to be a letter directed to the postmasters throughout the country, as it is typewritten, addressed "To the Postmaster," and then the name of the town to which this letter was sent is added in ink on a dotted line. We have no means of knowing how many postmasters have been appealed to, but as this is sent to a postmaster in Ohio it is probable that the appeal has been quite general.

In the letter Mr. Powers speaks as a representative of the republican party. He says that the party "should not ask him to make the fight alone," and insists that he is making it in "the party's defense" as well as in his own. He wants the money to help him in "maintaining the integrity of our party."

In order to make the appeal more effective he says "the effect on the republican party in the state if I should be driven to surrender this fight would be disastrous." It is a pathetic appeal and all who are anxious to secure the acquittal of the republican party through the acquittal of the accused should hasten to contribute.

How complacently many of the republican papers have taken the assassination of Governor Goebel. How little interest many of these papers have felt in the prosecution of the guilty party. If a republican official had been killed by democratic politicians the country would have rung with denunciations of the assassins and every democrat would have been accused of belonging to a party of law-breakers. But it is different when a democratic governor dies at the hands of republican partisans. No democrat thinks of accusing republicans generally because a few republican politicians resorted to murder, but the republicans ought to resent the attempt of one of the accused to make it appear that the republican party is on trial.

A CALL TO ARMS.

Democrats who are democrats from principle should assert themselves. Not only is it their duty to do so, but they need to do so if they would save the party from disaster and demoralization. Reports from every section of the country make it certain that those who left the party in 1896 under the pretense of opposition to bimetallism are making a systematic effort to regain control of the party with a view to placing it in the position it occupied under Grover Cleveland's administration. In this they are being aided by the less extreme representatives of the corporation element that voted the ticket for regularity's sake without endorsing the platform. These elements do not work openly and honestly, but covertly and through agents who beg for "harmony."

It is time that loyal democrats were aroused to the danger confronting their party and its principles. It is time they were organizing to combat the insidious influences at work within the party to republicanize it and make it acceptable to the corporation interests, for a democratic party that espouses principles acceptable to the trusts and the money power is democratic in name only. Only thorough organization will be effective against these undemocratic influences. This work of organization should begin now and be prosecuted with vigor. The best way to go about this work is the organization of clubs within the party in every voting precinct in the country. These clubs can arouse enthusiasm, perfect organization and see to it that delegates elected to nominating conventions are men whose opinions are known and who may be relied upon to carry out the wishes of the majority; and they should be instructed by the people at the primaries. These clubs will enable Kansas City platform democrats to know each other and to act together. They will also furnish a means of supporting democratic principles. By circulating democratic literature and debating public questions they may bring pending propositions and existing policies before the people. The work of organizing these clubs should begin without further loss of time. With a view to forwarding the work of organization THE COMMONER will furnish upon application a form of constitution and membership blanks to all who request them, and every reader of THE COMMONER should appoint himself a committee of one to perfect the organization of a club in his precinct without delay. A course of study will be outlined in THE COMMONER, and from week to week the editor will discuss the subjects suggested.

Secretaries are asked to report organizations, notice of which will be made in THE COMMONER for the information of other communities. DO NOT DELAY! ORGANIZE NOW.

THE MONROE DOCTRINE.

The Monroe doctrine was not intended, nor has it been used, to shield the republics of Central and South America from the performance of international duties and obligations. It is more in the nature of a homestead or exemption law. It is considered good policy to protect the family homestead from seizure and sale under execution and the law is defended on the theory that the state, if it must choose between the two, is more interested in the preservation of the home than in the collection of a debt. In like manner the United States declares that the maintenance of the integrity of the southern republics is paramount and while the collection of just debts will not be prevented, if collectible in ordinary ways, no execution shall issue against the national homesteads of South and Central America. How important this doctrine is can be judged from two incidents within the memory of all. During Mr. Cleveland's last administration England claimed a part of Venezuela in a boundary line dispute. Venezuela wanted to arbitrate and England refused to submit the question to arbitration; then our nation told England she ought to arbitrate and she replied in a diplomatic way that it was none of our business. Then the Monroe doctrine was called into use and England was informed that in case of her refusal to arbitrate our nation would independently conduct an investigation, ascertain the boundary line and then insist upon the recognition of that line. Thus we protected Venezuela from an unjust demand that she could not, if left to her own strength, have resisted.

Just now several European nations are united in making a pecuniary demand upon Venezuela. One of the allies has, without excuse or pretense of justification, sunk the Venezuelan navy and shelled a fort—thus wantonly destroying property. But for the guardianship of the United States Venezuela would be in danger of being divided up among greedy European land-grabbers; but for the Monroe doctrine all the South American republics would be in danger of being forcibly annexed to the monarchies of the old world, and we have some Americans so destitute of American spirit as to think that such a change would be desirable, but these unworthy citizens—call them monarchists, plutocrats, aristocrats, or what you will—are fortunately comparatively few in number. The great mass of the people, irrespective of party, believe in the Monroe doctrine—the national homestead law—and will not permit any surrender of it.

Neither is it necessary for the southern republic or our country to bear the burden of enormous navies to enforce this doctrine. Our nation has reached a position where its strength is recognized and if we did not have a single battleship the Monroe doctrine would not be molested. A few ships are necessary for the training of officers and seamen, but there is no more reason for our loading ourselves down with an enormous navy than there is for an individual to break himself down carrying arms for his own protection. The Monroe doctrine was asserted and defended without a big navy when our nation was feeble as compared with European nations and we do not need a large navy to defend the doctrine now. The administration has properly insisted upon arbitration in the present dispute, and there is no doubt that arbitration will be resorted to, and in the finding Venezuela should be awarded damages for the malicious destruction of her fleet and the unnecessary shelling of her forts.

LOCAL SELF-GOVERNMENT.

A reader of THE COMMONER asks why the president should not be allowed to interfere in a state for the preservation of order, even when the state authorities do not request it. The answer is plain and very conclusive. The people of a state know best what they need, and they are in position to punish any state official who abuses his power. A president far removed from the state is not likely to be so well informed. In fact, as he must secure his information from some source he is much more apt to be misinformed than those near the scene of the disturbance, and if he abuses his power the people of the state are unable to administer punishment. Local self-government is essential to free government, and it is necessary that we shall preserve the equilibrium between the state and the nation, the state administering its domestic affairs, the nation supreme in all that concerns the country as a whole.

BIMETALLISM NOT A PANACEA.

A Massachusetts reader of THE COMMONER calls attention to the fact that the cost of living has, during recent years, increased more rapidly than the rate of wages, and complains, justly, too, that the masses are not receiving their share of the boasted prosperity. He asks whether any legislation on the money question would furnish a complete remedy.

Those who advocate bimetallism do not insist that the restoration of free coinage would cure all the ills which afflict the body politic; it is not put forward as a panacea. As a matter of fact, the forces that are at work in society are so numerous that no one cause is entirely responsible for conditions complained of. It is for this reason that the discussion of public questions is so difficult and the confusion of the public mind so easy. The most that can be said in favor of any system is that, other things being equal, it would improve conditions, but as other things are not equal, the good done by one policy may be off-set by the injury done by another. There is, however, a general principle running through the policies of a party, and those who apply the principle to one question are apt to apply it to others.

Democrats believe that a high tariff is responsible for the fact that a large amount of money has been transferred from the pockets of the consumers to the pockets of the protected industries. The farmers sell in the open market and buy at prices artificially fixed. Democrats also believe that a large amount of money has been transferred from the masses to the speculative classes by the watering of railroad stocks, the people being compelled to pay rates sufficient to realize dividends on money never invested, but represented by stocks and bonds that have been issued.

Democrats also believe that the gold standard has transferred a large amount of money from the producers to the money changers. This condition has been relieved for the time being by an unexpected discovery in the supply of gold, but the financiers are still at work attempting to overcome by legislation the benefit which the masses have received from an increasing quantity of money.

Democrats believe that the national banking system has enabled the financiers to make a large amount of money from the people by means of the law that permits national banks to draw interest on the bonds (the interest being paid by the people through taxation) and at the same time receive back in bank notes the money represented by the bonds. If the money were issued by the government instead of by the banks the people would save the interest paid on the bonds.

The democrats believe that the trusts, through their power to monopolize the market, are collecting tribute from all the people, and building up enormous fortunes in the hands of a few. The trusts use the tariff wall as a bulwark, and also use the railroads to obtain an unfair advantage over competitors.

The democrats further believe that an imperial policy, aside from the un-American principle involved, taxes the masses to support a colonial policy, while a few syndicates and office-holders make all the profit.

There are other matters that need attention, among which are extravagance and government by injunction. Extravagance is due to the fact that the tax-eaters have more influence with the republican leaders than the tax-payers; government by injunction is used by the corporations to secure an advantage over their employes.

These are some of the causes that are at work, and the

elimination of one cause would not work an entire cure; but there is a remedy for each evil, and these remedies are but the application to each question of the maxim of "equal rights to all and special privileges, to none."

Those who favor the applying of this maxim to one question as a rule favor its application to other questions, while those who resist reform on one line are apt to resist it on other lines. While circumstances may make one issue paramount at one time or another issue paramount at another time, the democratic party must stand ready to apply democratic principles to all questions, and to protect the people's rights wherever those rights are attacked.

HOW THE SKIES WERE CLEARED.

The Littlefield anti-trust bill passed the house by an unanimous vote on February 6. The democrats were not permitted to amend the measure. They voted for it, not that it exactly suited them, but because they regarded it as a step in the right direction.

Mr. DeArmond, the well-known democrat from Missouri, speaking upon the bill pointed out that the bill under consideration was quite a different measure from that originally introduced by Mr. Littlefield. Referring to Mr. Littlefield's original measure, Mr. DeArmond said: "When the gentleman from Maine started out he had blood in his eye and a tomahawk in his hand, but by the time he and his colleagues caught up with the trusts they were smoking the pipe of peace, the sky was clear and the pickings continue food for the trusts."

It will be interesting to follow the process of "sky clearing," referred to by Mr. DeArmond; and, fortunately, there is an unbroken chain of incidents, testimony in support of which is provided by republican authorities.

The St. Louis *Globe-Democrat*, a republican paper, in its issue of January 16, printed a dispatch under date of Washington, January 15, as follows:

"The plans of Congressman Littlefield and his associates on the judiciary committee to report his trust bill to the house tomorrow from the full committee have been abandoned. This was a direct result of a conference which was held this afternoon at the home of Mr. Knox. The publicity provision is entirely too drastic. He took the bill to Pittsburg with him tonight and will submit a substitute for the publicity provision which he believes can be passed by congress."

The newspapers receiving the Associated press dispatches printed in their issues of January 17 a dispatch under date of Pittsburg, Pa., January 16, as follows:

"An informal dinner was tendered tonight by H. C. Frick to Attorney General P. C. Knox at his palatial home 'Clayton.' None but representative business men of the city were present. No speeches were made and the function was purely a social affair. Tomorrow Mrs. Knox will be given a reception by Mrs. Frick."

The newspapers receiving the Associated press dispatches printed in their issues of January 19 a dispatch under date of Washington, D. C., January 18, as follows:

"There were several officials prominent in legislative and executive circles at the White house in conference with the president tonight. Among them was Attorney General Knox who remained with Mr. Roosevelt some time. It is supposed the trust question was considered."

Let the thoughtful citizen read and re-read these telegrams. The republican attorney general for the United States concluded that the Littlefield bill as originally introduced was "entirely too drastic."

Under date of January 15 it was announced that "he took the bill to Pittsburg with him tonight and will submit a substitute for the publicity provision which he believes can be passed by congress."

Under date of January 16 it was announced that Mr. Knox was tendered an informal dinner by H. C. Frick, the great steel trust magnate, at Mr. Frick's palatial home "Clayton."

Under date of January 18 it was announced that Mr. Knox and other officials were in conference with the president and that "it is supposed the trust question was considered."

In the light of these dispatches, it is not difficult to understand how the "sky" happened to "clear."

In a dispatch to the Chicago *Record-Herald*, under date of Washington, February 11, William E. Curtis said that Mr. Littlefield was surprised to learn that he could not expect any encouragement from Mr. Roosevelt in the effort to push the Littlefield anti-trust bill through the senate. Doubtless Mr. Littlefield remembered that Attorney General Knox had taken the bill to Pittsburg and that as a result of that visit the provisions of the bill which Mr. Knox regarded as "entirely too drastic" were trimmed down to suit the wishes of the trust magnates; and it is not suprising that he should be a bit disturbed on learning that in spite of these radical changes in his bill he could not depend upon the administration's support for his measure.

Is it possible that in the light of such exposes as this, republicans who are really opposed to the trust system and who hope that the people may find practical relief from impositions will continue to affiliate with a party that depends upon the trusts for its campaign funds and that trims its measures to suit the wishes of the trust magnates?

A REPUBLICAN'S VIEWS.

The New York *Independent* of December 4 prints the "Biography of a Bootblack" as told to its representative by Roco Corresca. The following extract will be of interest to readers of THE COMMONER:

"These people are without a king such as ours in Italy. It is what they call a republic as Garibaldi wanted, and every year in the fall the people vote. They wanted us to vote last fall, but we did not. A man came and said that he would get us made Americans for 50 cents and then we could get two dollars for our votes. I talked to some of our people and they told me that we should have to put a paper in a box telling who we wanted to govern us.

"I went with five men to the court, and when they asked me how long I had been in the country I told them two years.

Afterward my countrymen said I was a fool and never would learn politics. 'You should have said you were five years here and then we would swear to it,' was what they told me.

"There are two kinds of people that vote here, republicans and democrats. I went to a republican meeting and the man said that the republicans want a republic and the democrats are against it. He said that democrats are for a king whose name is Bryan and who is an Irishman. There are some good Irishmen, but many of them insult Italians. They call us Dagoes. So I will be a republican.

"I like this country now and I don't see why we should have a king. Garibaldi didn't want a king, and he was the greatest man that ever lived."

From the above it will appear that Roco was a republican. The only reason he gave was that he was informed at a republican meeting that the republicans wanted a republic while the democrats were for a king. It is evident that while he had some prejudice against the Irish he was most influenced by the fact that he thought the republicans most friendly to the liberty which Garibaldi had taught his people to love. It will also be noticed that this republican did not have a very high idea of the right of suffrage, valuing it at $2.00 a year.

It can be said to his credit, however, that he told the truth about the time he had been here and thus lost a chance to make $2.00 that year.

The editor of THE COMMONER has often heard it said that many foreigners vote the republican ticket because the name sounded so much like "republic" that, without comparing the policies of the parties, they came to the conclusion that the republican party is more nearly an exponent of the ideas of a republic, but this Italian's testimony would indicate that the delusion is not a natural one arising from the similarity of the words, but one studiously cultivated by unscrupulous republican leaders. The absurdity of this republican claim is the greater at this time when the administration is carrying out the strenuous policy of imperialism while the democrats are defending those principles of human liberty which have raised up patriots in every land.

A BIG NAVY LEAGUE.

The most un-American movement recently started under the guise of patriotism is the "Navy League of the United States," organized with ex-Secretary of the Navy Tracy at its head. An official statement of the purposes and plans of the league will be found on another page. It will be noticed that similar leagues have been formed in England, Germany, France, Italy and Belgium, and the activity of the other leagues is given as a reason for the formation of this league. The object of this league is "to aid in strengthening our sea power," and the members are "to learn what the navy means, what is, and what should be its actual efficiency and what is its relative standing with other navies." These leagues are mutually helpful; as soon as the leagues in England, Germany, France, Italy and Belgium secure an increase in the navies of those countries the increase thus secured will be used as an argument in favor of an increase here and the increase here, when secured, can be used by the leagues abroad as an excuse for further increases, and so on ad infinitum. There is no limit to such increases except the burden-carrying power of the taxpayer and the object of these leagues is to convince him (or those who act for him) that it is his patriotic duty to carry a big navy on his back because the deluded citizens of other countries are carrying big navies. This is another outgrowth of imperialism and the league's growth will be in proportion to the imperialistic sentiment developed. The league's work may be illustrated by a parable:

A, B, C, and D have farms surrounding a lake. Mr. Navy League calls on A and explains to him that he is in constant danger of being attacked by his neighbors and that as a matter of precaution he should keep an armed boat anchored in front of his house (Mr. Navy League probably knows of some competent boat builders who are willing to build the boat and he can also furnish men to take charge of it). Having convinced A that he needs a boat, Mr. Navy League finds it easy to convince B that he needs two boats, C that he needs three boats and D that he needs four boats. By this time A is in a position to be convinced of his need of several more boats to put him upon an equal footing with his neighbors, and Mr. Navy League is thus kept busy stimulating patriotism, recommending ship builders and furnishing men to be given life commissions in the navy. Question: How long before A, B, C, and D would find out that boat building was absorbing too large a share of the income from their farms? How long before they would find out that it was better to have fewer boats rotting in the water, waiting for war, and more wealth producing assets convertible into war vessels on demand? There is, in the nature of the case, no limit to the compilation in navy building for each nation tries to overstep the others and each stimulates the others to new enlargements. We need fewer "navy leagues" and more associations for the cultivation of sentiment in favor of justice and fair dealing which make for peace.

A PERPETUAL DEBT.

Secretary Shaw is the first secretary of the treasury to suggest the advisability of a permanent national debt. To be sure, he puts it in the alternative and uses it to scare congress into an asset currency, but the fact that he considers it at all shows the length to which he has gone in surrendering to the dictation of Wall street. He says:

"The frequent purchase and retirement of bonds renders the amount available for circulation gradually less, while a rapidly growing population, additional banking facilities, and expanding trade suggest the need of an ever increasing circulation. I therefore believe the time has arrived when it will be necessary to adopt one of two policies; either the government debt must be perpetuated as a basis for national bank circulation, and additional bonds issued as occasion may require, or some other system must be provided."

What is that other system? The asset currency that does not require a bond basis.

During the war national banks were established to give a market for bonds, now bonds must be issued to give a basis for banking. And if the people do not like a perpetual debt, let them accept an asset currency as the least of the two evils. That is the same logic that was applied to the treasury notes and greenbacks. The administration first announced that they would be redeemed in gold on demand and then the people were told they must choose between an endless chain and the retirement of government paper. The financiers refused to consider the wisdom of exercising the government's right to choose the coin of payment—a plan which would have stopped the endless chain without retiring the paper—a plan the mere mention of which by Secretary Manning stopped a run on the treasury gold. And so now it never occurs to Secretary Shaw and his tutors in finance that the substitution of greenbacks for bank notes would render a perpetual debt unnecessary and at the same time remove the excuse for an asset currency. The greenback is better than a bank note, for it is as secure as a bank note with a government bond behind it and has the advantage of being a legal tender.

But no. The greenback is not a part of Mr. Shaw's plan, for the bankers get no profit out of its issue and can not control the volume in their own interests.

Here is the money question again—an important phase of it—and yet the reorganizers are as silent about it as the republican leaders are. The republicans seem to think they can do anything now, but the test of a system comes in the storm rather than in the calm, and when the storm comes neither a perpetual debt nor an asset currency will prove acceptable.

But Secretary Shaw is certainly earning a position at the head of some big New York bank—the reward that usually comes to the treasury official who turns the treasury department over to the New York financiers.

THE TEST OF DEMOCRACY.

The following is the substance of the speech delivered by Mr. Bryan at Columbus, O., February 12, at the dinner given on Lincoln's birthday by the Jefferson-Jackson-Lincoln league. Hon. John J. Lentz was toastmaster and ex-Governor Budd of California and Mayor Tom L. Johnson of Cleveland also made speches. Mr. Bryan said:

It is entirely appropriate that we celebrate this day. In April, 1859, the republicans of Boston celebrated the birthday of Thomas Jefferson, and Abraham Lincoln in a letter expressing his regret that he could not be present eulogized the author of the Declaration of Independence in eloquent terms. Lincoln said at another time that he had no political principles that he had not drawn from that Declaration. If the early republicans could honor the natal day of Jefferson in 1859, we democrats can at this time observe with fitting ceremony the birthday of Lincoln.

I am glad to be present on this occasion, and I appreciate the generous words of compliment spoken by the toastmaster, Mr. Lentz. We are fortunate in having with us in our fight against foes within the party and against foes without, so able and courageous a democrat as Mr. Lentz has shown himself to be. I was glad to listen to the distinguished ex-governor of California. You are to be congratulated upon his presence, not only because of the pleasure his speech has given you, but because he is a living proof that we have active and vigorous democrats on the Pacific coast. Pardon me if I call him a Budd of promise—and we have them all over the country. I was gratified to hear him refer to the work that Mr. Hearst has done personally and through his papers. Mr. Hearst has been of immense service to the party. He has shown that wealth need not lead a man away from the people; he has shown that he is willing to trust his fortune to the care of laws made by the masses. The democratic party has never condemned the accumulation of money by honest means. A man can have any amount of money—if he makes it legitimately—and still be a democrat. It is only when his money has him that he finds it necessary to become a republican in order to find congenial company. Jefferson, the greatest democrat of all time, was rich in this world's goods—richer for his day than Hearst or Johnson are now—but Jefferson asked for no class legislation and lived up to the maxim, "Equal rights to all and special privileges to none." It has delighted me also to hear again the voice of Cleveland's mayor. I rejoice that Senator Hanna finds in his own home city a foe like Tom Johnson, who has the brains and the bravery to meet him and overthrow the commercial standard which the republican leader has set up. Mr. Johnson says that he has no higher ambition than to be mayor again. Well, God speed him in the realization of that ambition, but as long as I believe—as I believe now—that he only desires office because the office will enable him to protect the rights and interests of the people, I shall be glad to aid him. I care not to what he may aspire.

I have taken as my subject tonight, "The Test of Democracy," but I do not come to preach a new gospel or to formulate new rules. The principles to which we hold are not new principles; they are truths—self-evident truths—and truths are eternal. Jefferson did not invent the principles set forth in the Declaration of Independence; he merely stated them in language so apt that the words will always linger in the memory of man. Jackson did not create new principles; he simply applied with matchless courage the political doctrines handed down from a preceeding generation. Neither did Lincoln originate new principles. He built upon the foundation laid by Jefferson. And we today are not seeking to secure the adoption of a new theory of government; we are only trying to make the government what the fathers intended it should be—a government of the people, by the people, and for the people.

So with the rules for measuring men and parties, they are not new rules, they are rather the every day rules which we apply in the ordinary affairs of life. Nations and parties and men are judged by their performances rather than by their promises; by their works rather than by their words. In every calling, profession and occupation men are measured not by what they say of themselves, but by what they do, and it is even so in politics.

Christ laid down a rule that applies to the world as well as to the church. He knew that false prophets would arise to deceive and to mislead, and He gave to his disciples this sound, but simple test for distinguishing the false from the true: "By their fruits ye shall know them." He stated it even more strongly and said: "Many will say to me in that day, Lord, Lord, have we not prophesied in thy name? and in thy name have cast out devils? and in thy name done many wonderful works? And then will I profess unto them, I never knew you; depart from me, ye that work iniquity."

There have been false prophets in politics also. There were false prophets in the days of Jefferson—men who professed great love for the people and yet would not trust the people. There were false prophets in the days of Jackson, and he was warning his countrymen against them when he said. "The path of freedom is continually beset by enemies who assume the guise of friends." The nation has its false prophets today who are declaring that duty to the Filipinos compels us to make subjects of them, and yet these false prophets are not willing to do their duty to citizens of the United States. Democracy has its false prophets now. They stand in the market places and talk about harmony—the very thing that they themselves destroyed. They demand the leadership and say to the party: "Did we not hold office in thy name, and in thy name draw large salaries?" If the party has learned wisdom by experience it will say: "Depart, I never knew you, ye that work iniquity."

Those who are old enough to aspire to leadership have made a record during the last seven years and by that record they must be judged. The great fight between manhood and mammon began in 1896, and is not yet decided. Those who did not realize the nature of the contest then ought not to ask to be put in command over those who did, and those who knew the nature of the contest and yet directly or indirectly aided plutocracy must repent and bring forth works meet for repentance before they can be trusted with control.

We want harmony, but there can be no harmony between the party and men who call themselves democrats and yet oppose loyal democrats more bitterly than they do republicans. It is much easier to convert the republicans who really desire just government and equal laws than it is to draw back to the party those who, understanding the issues, supported the republican ticket in 1896 or voted for Palmer and Buckner, for many republicans, though not approving of republican policies, were held to the party by the strength of party ties, while the democrats who left their party gave positive proof that they preferred republican principles to democratic principles. Many republicans were held within their organization by the recollection of early republican arguments, but the democrats who went over in 1896 were attracted by the vices and hypocrisy of modern republicanism, and we do not want them to come back until they are disgusted enough to come back for good. They told us how it pained them to leave the party in 1896 and I do not want them to be compelled to go through the same anguish again, as they will have to do if they return to us with the hope of transforming the democratic party into a republican party.

The struggle between democracy and plutocracy is still on and must continue until one side or the other is completely triumphant. It is a real contest with the welfare of the race at stake, and we are not willing to have it converted into a sham battle. The platform of 1896 was democratic and the questions raised by it have not been settled. The platform adopted at Kansas City was also democratic, and the issues raised by it have not been settled—and the republicans have no plans for settling them. The reorganizers tell us that the money question has been disposed of, but no statement could be farther from the truth. True, we have some five hundred millions more money in circulation now than we had in 1896, but it only proves that we were right in asserting that more money would make better times. And yet with all this unexpected increase in the circulation we still have too little money in the country. Reserves are loaned and reloaned and Secretary Shaw had to rush to the aid of Wall street and tide the financiers over a panic by giving them the free use of more than $130,000,000 of government money. Not satisfied with this scarcity of money they are now seeking to make the silver dollar redeemable in gold and abroad the financiers are endeavoring to make gold dearer by driving silver-using nations to the gold standard.

Talk about the money question being settled! Secretary Shaw in his latest report declares that we have just reached one phase of the money qustion. Your own splendid exponent of democracy, the president, has already called attention to it. Mr. Shaw says: "The frequent purchase and retirement of bonds renders the amount available for circulation gradually less, while a rapidly growing population, additional banking facilities, and expanding trade suggest the need of an ever-increasing circulation. I therefore believe the time has arrived when it will be necessary to adopt one of two policies; either the government debt must be perpetuated as a basis for national bank circulation, and additional bonds issued as occasion may require, or some other system must be provided."

Here is a financial proposition that must be met and it involves the same question raised by other phases of the money problem, namely, whether the government shall be run for the benefit of a few financiers or in the interest of the whole people. The democratic party is pledged to oppose a bank currency whether based on bonds or on the assets of the banks. It is pledged to the greenback issued and controlled by the government and every democrat nominated for a federal office must take his stand upon this question. If he opposes the bank currency he will disturb "harmony" and "disrupt the party" again; if he favors a bank currency he will not be satisfactory to any opposed to the money trust. The democrat who attempts to ignore the money question is either deceived himself or is trying to deceive others.

Neither can the reorganizers be trusted to deal with the evils of private monopoly. Mr. Cleveland is the head and front of the reorganizers and we can judge by his record what the party would do on this subject if again under his leadership. He was elected in 1892 by money collected from the corporations, and his administration was dominated by the corporations. One trust contributed $175,000 to his campaign fund—more than half as much as we were able to collect from the more than six million who supported our ticket in 1900. His administration was mortgaged to the trusts and his record has hung like a mill-stone about the neck of the party in two campaigns. He is nearer to organized wealth than any living republican and as a presidential candidate, if his nomination were possible, he would be more acceptable to the monopolies than any republican that could be named. What mockery to talk about harmonizing with him or those who worship at his shrine.

No matter what question is considered, whether tariff, money, trusts, imperialism or the labor question, the same principles must be applied and the democratic party must meet them all and on all of them deal fairly and honestly with the people.

Even on the low plane of expediency success can not be won by aping republican policies and methods. With a party as with an individual character is all important, and what the democratic party needs today more than recruits is to get rid of those so-called democrats who use the democratic name as a cloak while they carry out undemocratic designs. They repel honest seekers after good government because their record is such that their very presence in the party casts suspicion upon the purity of the party's motives. The democratic party must stand for democratic ideals and it must apply democratic principles to all questions regardless of the prospect of temporary victory or the danger of temporary defeat. If a young man asks my advice I tell him to be honest and industrious, performing well every duty as it comes. If he asks me if that will guarantee immediate success, I tell him that immediate success can not be guaranteed by any one, but that merit is the only basis upon which permanent success can be predicated. If a man seeks the truth constantly he will become better and better able to discern it. If he is willing to ignore it for a reward he ultimately loses the power to distinguish the true from the false. And I may add that it is not probable that a man of ability can live an upright life in any community for twenty-five years without so winning the confidence of his neighbors as to be called upon to serve them.

And so with a party. If it seeks the truth and stands by it, it not only improves in its perception of truth, but it is sure to be needed in the administration of public affairs. The democratic party must stand erect, neither indorsing the wrong nor surrendering the right. It must invite the confidence of those who want good government and are willing to have the government administered for the benefit of the whole people. Instead of trying to make the democratic party so much like the republican party that we shall get a few republicans by mistake, let us make it so different from the republican party that we shall get many repubcans by design—republicans who turn from the mammon-serving leaders of that party and seek a party that puts the man before the dollar. When we gain such recruits the party will be strengthened both in numbers and in purpose. The republican party can not long conceal its degeneracy. The commercialism that now dominates will so degrade it that there will be a revolt. The protectionists in the party will not allow any revision of the tariff, the financiers are becoming more and more exacting, the trust magnates insolent by refusing to permit any effective legislation, and Philippine syndicates continue to demand that their pecuniary ventures shall be made profitable at the expense of the American people. This can not last always. Republican conscience and republican judgment must finally protest and to what party can republicans turn for relief? Let us make the democratic party their hope and their reliance. Let us prove its right to their support by giving assurance that it has the courage to fight and the strength to resist temptation. Let us make the word democracy stand for positive and aggressive principles. Let it apply to citizens who are unterrified and incorruptible. Let it be so holy a name that none will assume it who lack sympathy with the struggling masses or who are unwilling to trust the people with the management of their own affairs. The democratic banner may be an inspiration and an aid to those who are not in full harmony with all the party's purposes, but that banner can not be placed in the hands of men about whose democracy there is any question. As in a church so in a party, the organization must be in the control of those who are strongest in the faith and whose lives are a living creed.

If our party will but maintain its integrity and convince the country of its steadfastness of purpose the flag of the party will yet be placed beside the flag of the union and the words "democracy" and "republic" will be recognized throughout the world as representing liberty, self-government and justice.

KILL THE TRUSTS NOW.

The larger the number of stockholders of the trusts, the harder it will be to destroy them. It is exceedingly difficult to persuade the average man to sacrifice a specific and definite sum, however small, to secure a large but undefined public good. His selfishness and his conservatism are both arrayed against the reform. He says: I know I will lose a certain number of dollars, and while I might gain more, the gain is uncertain, while the loss is certain.

The editor of THE COMMONER once met upon the train a prominent minister of the gospel and his wife, and in the course of conversation learned that the wife held stock in a well-known trust. It is scarcely necessary to say that a careful perusal of the minister's sermons failed to disclose any attack upon the trust evil. It is difficult to convince a person that the public suffers from a system so long as he is sure that he himself profits by the system, and it is not easy to convince the average man that he ought not to take advantage of the profits on trust stock so long as the trusts are allowed to exist. In the beginning he is opposed to the trusts, but he says—how often we have heard the argument—that as long as the trusts are allowed to exist there is no harm in his making the profit; somebody will make the profit, why not he? Of course, in the beginning he is in favor of legislation that will destroy the trusts and only intends to make the profit until this legislation is enacted. After a while he begins to enjoy the profit and the thought of losing that profit makes him conservative about remedies. He gets to feel as the president expresses himself, that we must act "with great caution" and "deliberation," or, as Mr. Knox says, that it is more necessary to act "wisely" than to act "speedily," and one is not apt to think a measure wise that lessens his income.

The New York *Journal* is right in saying that it will be easier to destroy the trusts now than five years from now. Some of the republicans say that in ten years from now the trusts will have died a natural death. The trouble about that argument is that it gives the trusts the benefit of ten years of unmolested activity without guaranteeing to the people either that the trusts will be dead then or that it will be as easy to kill them then as now.

By the watering of stock a large sum is made by the organization of a trust, but this profit can be realized at once by selling the stock, and the trust magnates are now unloading. If a trust violates both a statute and a moral law, how can a person in good conscience hold trust stock any more than he can share in the profits of any other criminal act? But observation shows that a large number of people do not apply conscience to such a subject and, therefore, it is more necessary that the government act speedily, before too large a number acquire a pecuniary interest in the protection of the trusts.

DISHONEST ARGUMENT.

"When you handle a plunk you handle one of Bryan's 37-cent dollars."—An Iowa republican paper.

"Oh, no, Bro. ——; it is what would have been a 37-cent, or less, dollar had Mr. Bryan and his party had their way. You now handle a good, 100-cent plunk, thanks to republican success and wisdom."—Another Iowa republican paper.

The above items from republican papers illustrate the style of republican arguments on the money question. One hardly knows whether to attribute the language to ignorance or to a desire to mislead. The silver dollar answers all useful purposes, and is more used by the masses than gold ever was. And why is it good? Because the government makes it a legal tender for all public debts and for all private ones, too, (except where the contract specifically excludes silver). Money is a medium of exchange and no one objects to receiving a dollar in payment of a debt or in exhcange for a purchase if he is able to dispose of it in the same way, and the legal tender enables him to dispose of it. But for the fact that gold bullion is convertible into coin no one would be willing to receive it at a fixed amount per ounce, and when money is scarce and the coin actually needed for immediate use no one will receive gold bullion at the same price that he will legal tender money. The unfairness of the republican argument consists in the ignoring of the effect of law upon money. The law that makes money of a particular kind of metal increases the demand for that metal; the law that makes it possible for a man to convert a given weight of metal into a given sum of money fixes the market price of that quantity of bullion. After legislating against silver and in favor of gold the republican editors chuckle to themselves and even boast with their pencils that silver is not able to keep up with gold. It is difficult to believe that such editorials as the ones above quoted are due to lack of knowledge of the subject, and yet it is more charitable to attribute them to lack of knowledge than to evil intent.

AN INCOME TAX DECISION.

An important decision was rendered February 9 by United States Circuit Judge Gilbert at the circuit court of appeals, San Francisco. This decision related to the income tax and while it immediately applied to the constitutionality of the income tax law adopted by the territory of Hawaii, because of some of the statements made by the court, it will be of general interest.

Referring to this decision the San Francisco *Chronicle* says:

A bill was passed by the legislature of Hawaii in 1901, fixing a tax of 2 per cent on incomes above $1,000. W. C. Peacock and fifty-nine other merchants of Honolulu instituted an action against J. W. Pratt, assessor and collector of the division of Honolulu, Hawaiian territory, to enjoin that official from the collection of the tax. The government planned to collect $8,056.68 on a net income of $402,834 of the complainants.

The complaint was filed in the circuit court of Hawaii, and set forth that the act was invalid by reason of being in conflict with the organic act of the territory, and also with the federal constitution. Complainants maintained that the exception of incomes below the amount of $1,000 was illegal, and that the salary of judges should have been excepted.

A demurrer was filed by the government, and sustained by the judge, and the bill dismissed outright. The appeal was then made. Judge Gilbert decides that a territory has a right to legislate in the matter of taxation, and, in affirming the opinion of the lower court, says:

"The appellants by their bill seek to enjoin the enforcement of the income tax on the ground that it violates both the organic act of the territory and the constitution of the United States in that it contains illegal discriminations, fails to exempt the salaries of judges and compels taxpayers to furnish evidence against themselves that may result in their criminal prosecution. It is contended that the exemption of incomes to the extent of $1,000 is an illegal discrimination. The power of state legislatures to grant reasonable exemptions is undisputed. It has been upheld on grounds of public policy, a public policy which seeks to exclude from taxation the living expenses of the average family and thus enable the poor man to escape from being a public burden. It rests upon the theory that the exemption results in ultimate benefit to the taxpayer. It does not apply to corporations, for they have not the same expenses as the individual. We are unable to discover any ground for holding that an exemption of income to the extent of $1,000 from an income tax law is unreasonable, or that its allowance is an abuse of legislative discretion.

"Upon a careful consideration of the act and of the averments of the bill, we discover no ground for enjoining the collection of the tax, and find therefore no equity in the bill. The act was undoubtedly intended to remedy the depletion of the revenue of the territory. It contains no evidence of an intention to unjustly or unfairly discriminate. It places the burden of taxation upon the points of strongest resistance, where it is easiest borne."

The fact of general interest is that this federal court having the Hawaii income tax under consideration said: "It contains no evidence of an intention to unjustly or unfairly discriminate. It places the burden of taxation upon the points of strongest resistance, where it is easiest borne."

The objections that were raised against the Hawaii income tax are similar to those that are raised against a proposed income tax within our own country. And yet in spite of all these specious pleas the intelligent man must understand that the income tax is the most rational of all taxes and that in the language of the federal court at San Francisco "it contains no evidence of an intention to unjustly or unfairly discriminate. It places the burden of taxation upon the points of strongest resistance where it is easiest borne."

And now the question suggests itself, if the income tax in Hawaii "contains no evidence of an intention to unjustly or unfairly discriminate" and if the Hawaii income tax "places the burden of taxation upon the points of strongest resistance where it is easiest borne," why not an income tax within the United States of America?

A PERMANENT TRUTH.

The republicans who try to justify a colonial policy patterned after Great Britain's rule in India are in the habit of saying that the Declaration of Independence was only intended to accomplish an immediate purpose, namely, the arousing of the people to the necessity of securing independence. It has been denied that the Declaration was really intended to set forth any permanent governmental principles.

Those republicans who have been deluded into accepting this statement would do well to read the speech made by Abraham Lincoln at Springfield, Ill., June 26, 1857. In that speech Mr. Lincoln not only pointed out that the doctrine that "all men are created equal" was not necessary for the securing of independence, but that it was presented as an eternal truth and was intended for future use.

In these days of boasted prosperity the republicans may find it valuable to remember that Lincoln spoke of the proneness of prosperity to breed tyrants and pointed out that it was at just such times that the Declaration of Independence and its doctrines were needed. He said:

"The assertion that all men are created equal was of no practical use in affecting our separation from Great Britain; and it was placed in the Declaration not for that, but for future use. Its authors meant it to be—as, thank God, it is now proving itself—a stumbling block to all those who in after times might seek to turn a free people back into the hateful paths of despotism. They knew the proneness of prosperity to breed tyrants, and they meant when such should reappear in this fair land and commence their vocation, they should find left for them at least one hard nut to crack."

THE VALUE OF COURAGE.

If there is demoralization apparent among some of the democratic leaders it is due to a lack of moral courage. Instead of standing up and fighting republican policies all along the line, many of them are afraid to be democratic for fear they will offend the men who left the party in 1896 and who now refuse to return unless the party avoids disputed questions. Aside from the moral depravity involved in the offer to sell the party's convictions for the votes of plutocrats or for campaign contributions, it is disastrous from even the low standpoint of expediency. Jefferson once said of a man that he had not yet learned the important truth that firm adherence to principle was the best handmaid even unto ambition. There is a crying need for a real, pure and fearless democracy. The republican party is delivered over into the hands of organized wealth, and a bold attack upon that party's policies—not one, but all of them—would win more votes than the party would lose among those who call themselves democrats merely because they were born that way or joined the party before they became pecuniarily identified with great corporate interests. A few brave exponents of democracy who can not be terrorized by the financiers are worth a whole yard full of weak-kneed drawers of salary who divide their time between running from their shadows and flirting with purse-proud ex-democrats. The attitude of these timid democrats is illustrated by the remark of a colonel who was retreating with his regiment and who reproved some of his men for firing an occasional shot. He shouted: "Quit shooting! You just make them madder!" It is time that those who aspire to leadership should face toward the enemy and make an attack. In a political fight an ounce of moral courage is worth a pound of office-itch. Unless a man thinks more of principle than of office he is not deserving of official reward—and furthermore is not likely to hold office when the people awake to their duty.

PROTECT LIFE AND LIMB.

Mr. H. R. Fuller, the legislative representative of the Brotherhood of Locomotive Engineers, the Brotherhood of Locomotive Firemen, the Brotherhood of Conductors, the Brotherhood of Railroad Trainmen and the Order of Railroad Telegraphers—an imposing array of labor organizations—is in Washington seeking to secure legislation for the protection of the lives and limbs of trainmen. The various organizations of railroad employes have been endeavoring for ten years to secure safety appliances that will lessen the risk of those who operate the trains. During the period beginning July 1 and ending October 1, according to the interstate commerce commission's bulletin, 130 persons were either killed or injured while operating trains which used air-brakes upon but a portion of the cars. This would make nearly five hundred accidents a year, a number sufficient, it would seem, to arouse interest in the subject. The corporations have been fighting the measure from the beginning. First, they offered to consent to a bill requiring 75 per cent of the cars to be operated by air-brakes. Then they objected to more than 65 per cent; now they are opposing a law that compels them to use air-brakes on at least 50 per cent. The fact that they are now opposing a law requiring the use of air-brakes on only 50 per cent when a few years ago they agreed to a bill requiring the use of such brakes on 75 per cent shows the aggressiveness of the corporate interests and the increasing control which they exert over legislation. Both parties have declared in favor of such legislation and President Roosevelt recommended it in his recent message, and yet there is still a determined opposition to it. It is strange that representatives of the people can so far ignore public interests at the command of corporate greed.

THE FIFTY-SEVENTH CONGRESS.

The adjournment of the Fifty-seventh congress completes the work of the federal legislators chosen in 1900. They have succeeded in increasing the expenditures of the government about 50 per cent over the expenditures of the Fifty-first congress, which startled the country with its "billion-dollar" extravagance.

The increase in the per capita cost of government is largely due to the fact that the great manufacturing industries are using the taxing power for their own enrichment and they, therefore, encourage extravagance to make an excuse for a high tariff: Then, too, the imperial policy upon which the government has embarked is adding a considerable amount to the appropriation bills. The army expenditure is more than double what it was before we began to experiment with colonialism and the navy is feeling the stimulus of the war spirit.

While heavier burdens are constantly being laid upon the people by the government, those in authority are more and more negligent of the rights and interests of the people. The failure of the president to secure, or even seriously attempt to secure, effective anti-trust legislation is the most promnient feature of the second session of congress. It will be remembered that the president made some anti-trust speeches last summer—or at least speeches which his political friends construed as antagonistic to the trusts. It was even said that Mr. Littlefield had been selected to lead the fight against monopolies. "Just wait until congress meets in December," said the president's supporters, "and then you will see a strenuous attack on the trusts." Many democrats were deceived by the noise of preparation and a minister went so far as to say that Mr. Roosevelt had been raised to the office providentially to meet the aggressions of organized wealth.

Well, congress convened and the papers told us how the bills were pouring in, how the committee was combining the good features of the various bills, and finally how a draft of the committee bill has been submitted to the attorney general. But he regarded it as "too drastic." At last the bill was drawn so as to effect only corporations hereafter organized, leaving existing trusts to continue their depredations. The democrats of the house were denied an opportunity to present amendments and the bill was rushed through and sent to the senate. The senate committee kept it until the democratic members, together with a minority of the republican members, reported it over the protest of the majority of the republicans. By the same vote the committee added an amendment making the bill apply to existing corporations as well as to future ones, but when Senator Blackburn, acting under instructions from a democratic caucus, moved to take the bill up for consideration in the senate only two republicans voted with the democrats to consider the measure.

Can anti-trust republicans be deceived any longer? It is not fair to lay all the blame on the republicans of the senate because Attorney General Knox, speaking for the administration, said that the two little clauses inserted in the Nelson amendment and the Elkins bill in regard to rebates and publicity were entirely satisfactory. It was in the power of the president to focus attention upon this subject, to point out the necessity for strong and vigorous legislation and to insist upon immediate action, but instead of this he abandoned the fight before any decisive victory was won. Whether the president lacks purpose or only lacks moral courage is a question about which people may differ, but there is no doubt whatever that his anti-trust campaign, begun with great flourish of trumpets, has ended in an inglorious rout.

Just before adjournment Senator Elkins pointed out that for the third time the republican party had failed to keep its promise to admit the territories of Oklahoma, New Mexico and Arizona. Having spent the session doing little of importance it is now necessary to have an extra session of the senate in order to secure the ratification of the Panama and Cuban treaties.

Surely it must be a partisan republican who will point with pride to the record of the Fifty-seventh congress.

INITIATIVE AND REFERENDUM.

In a recent issue of THE COMMONER the editor called attention to the principle involved in the initiative and referendum, and criticised the Chicago *Chronicle* because of its attempt to defeat the will of the people on this question. On another page will be found an argument recently made against the initiative and referendum by one of the citizens of Chicago. It is published because it shows the standpoint from which the opponents begin to reason. The writer of this article asks the question: "Is it reasonable to assume that the placing upon the masses this great responsibility of making or selecting laws, is logical or safe?" Here is the secret of all the opposition. The opponents of the initiative and referendum distrust the masses; they assume that the people as a whole are incapable of passing judgment upon their own affairs; they must select officers to think for them and to act for them. The democratic idea is that the people think for themselves and select representatives to carry out their thoughts. The democratic idea is that the people think for themselves and select representatives to carry out their thoughts. The democratic idea is that the representative is a necessary evil—necessary because the people are too numerous to act directly upon all questions, but an evil still because the representative is often led by his own interests to sacrifice the interests of the people.

In the article referred to, we are told that the making of laws is a science calling for the highest talent. Here, again, the opponent of the initiative and referendum is trying to get the government out of the reach of the people. Jefferson said that the art of government was simply the art of being honest, and that the principles of right and wrong were so easily discerned that they required not the aid of many counselors. Is it because they are skilled in the science of government that the members of city councils vote away valuable franchises to corporations, or is it because the members of such councils sell for a price that which they themselves do not own? There is a great deal more danger that representatives will not do as well as they know than there is that the people themselves will not know enough to protect their own interests.

The writer of the article referred to lectures the people for not selecting "broad-minded, honest and courageous representatives." The admonition is often needed, but the trouble is that men are often selected who have not been dishonest before election, but who bcome dishonest when subjected to the temptations that surround their position. It is not always easy to detect corruption in legislators. Very few confess, and conclusive proof is often hard to secure. If the people have a right under reasonable restrictions to pass upon a law, temptation will be removed, because it will be of no advantage to a corporation to bribe a legislature if the people have a right to sit in judgment upon the law afterward. And so a corporation can not bribe a legislature to avoid a subject upon which the people, through the initiative, have demanded action.

The initiative and referendum do not supplant representative government; they simply purify it and perfect it. If the reader of THE COMMONER will pursue and consider the argument made against the initiative and referendum he will have his faith strengthened in this popular reform.

It is neither necessary nor desirable that the people should attempt to decide all questions by the referendum, but when any considerable proportion of them desire a question submitted it is only fair that it should be submitted. Likewise, when a proportion of the people desire to vote upon a law passed by the legislature they should have a right to do so. Experience has shown that they do not have to avail themselves of the right very often, because the mere fact that they have the right makes the legislature more obedient to their wishes, thus giving the protection of the initiative and referendum without the expense of it.

GETTING RICH QUICK.

The recent exposure of several "get-rich-quick" concerns shows both how many people can be fooled and also how certain those are to be fooled who take up with short-cut schemes for making money rapidly. It is hard to sympathize with people who lose money in this way, and yet it is due to an ignorance of the fundamental principles of morality, and this ignorance can only be secured by education. Modern commercialism has led too many of our people to measure life by the amount of money accumulated rather than by the amount of service rendered. The man whose highest aim is to "get rich" is apt to violate the moral law, if not the statutes of the state, in his effort to secure the object of his search. It is useless to preach honesty or equity to such a man. As long as the purpose remains it is likely to break all the restraints placed upon it. When money becomes the master the man who possesses it is really possessed by it and is in bondage unto it. It is not even necessary to possess money to become a servant; a poor man who regards money as the measure of success can be as subservient to Mammon as the most opulent.

The frauds that have been perpetrated by the turf investment companies and similar swindling gangs can be turned to a useful purpose if they lead parents to impress upon the minds of their children the viciousness of all schemes that promise profits out of proportion to the investment, or profits to be secured by chance or luck.

There is only one honest and honorable way of accumulating money, and that is to give to society a service equal to the compensation received. If young men are taught that it is better to be underpaid than overpaid, better that they give overflowing than scant measure, they will be proof against all kinds of deception and fraud. If a swindler, when he offers something for nothing, is met with the reply that the person addressed is not willing to accept something for nothing, he will go away in search of greener pastures. It is possible to render a child immune to the gambling disease that seems to be epidemic at present, but it must be done by inculcating a proper view of life. Manhood and womanhood, not money, must be made the standard, and the child must be taught that no amount of ill-gotten wealth can make a person worthy of respect—much less of envy.

DRAWING THE LINE.

The old democratic party of Tilden and Cleveland is extinct outside the east and south. In its place is a populistic and socialistic aggregation which is animated by a blind hatred of property and corporate wealth and by an unreasoning discontent with social conditions and social order. This aggregation is a menace to the financial and industrial stability of the land, and so long as it exists every man of sound ideas and every man who owns property in any form will ally himself with the republican party if for no other reason than the instinct of self-preservation.—New York *Commercial Advertiser*.

The above, from the New York *Commercial Advertiser*, shows how the republican papers are drawing the line between the protection of human rights and the worship of Mammon. The democratic party has never attacked property. It is, on the contrary, the best friend of honestly acquired wealth, for it distinguishes between honest wealth and predatory wealth. Republican organs like the *Commercial Advertiser* are endangering legitimate accumulations by confusing them with the enormous fortunes which are being secured by force, or cunning, or favoritism. The democratic party as now organized puts manhood before money, but it also protects all wealth accumulated without a surrender of manhood.

GOVERNMENT BY INJUNCTION.

The democratic platform of 1896 declared: "We specially object to government by injunction as a new and highly dangerous form of oppression by which federal judges in contempt of the laws of states and rights of citizens, become at once legislators, judges and executioners."

This plank was bitterly denounced by republican newspapers and was frequently referred to as an assault upon the courts.

Interest in this protest against government by injunction has recently been awakened because of the writ issued by Judge Adams in the United States circuit court at St. Louis. Upon application by the officers of the Wabash Railroad company, Judge Adams granted an injunction restraining representatives of the labor unions from "ordering, coercing, persuading, inducing or otherwise causing" the employes of the railroad to strike or quit the service of the company. Representatives of the labor union were also enjoined from "ordering, advising, or influencing employes on connecting lines to refuse to interchange traffic."

It is somewhat interesting to observe that even republican papers are finding it necessary to protest against this "highly dangerous form of oppression by which federal judges in contempt of the laws of states and the rights of citizens become at once legislators, judges and executioners."

The Chicago *Record-Herald*, a republican paper, in referring to Judge Adams' injunction, says that it "is such an extraordinary exercise of the power of injunction that it may well invite public apprehension regarding the extent to which this arbitrary instrument of the court may be used in the future."

The *Record-Herald* further says that "if this injunction stands and is finally written into the laws of our country, it is difficult to conceive of the possibility of fixing any limit to government by injunction."

The Des Moines *Register and Leader*, also a republican paper, says that heretofore it has been assumed that the right of labor involved the corresponding right to refuse to labor and that the exercise of this latter right means men acting as individuals or collectively. The *Register and Leader* points out that if Judge Adams' injunction is sustained, "it will revolutionize the relations of organized labor to its employers and will practically eliminate the strike as a weapon of defense."

Judge Tuley, an Illinois state judge at Chicago, makes interesting comment upon the Adams injunction. Judge Tuley says that he is not surprised at any injunction of any kind being issued, and he adds:

"I regret it very much because I believe that the issuing

of such writs of injunction brings the administration of justice into contempt. It breeds discontent and will reap a whirlwind some day from the seeds so sown.

"The day may come in the not distant future when the working classes will have political control and will appoint judges who will also issue writs of injunction—in their favor. I see no reason why a writ of injunction should not as well issue against a railroad enjoining it from discharging any employes or from failing to pay such employes a certain fixed rate of wages. It would be no greater departure from the true principles that ought to govern when issuing such writs.

"We judges are getting to be the whole thing in government. We are approaching a condition that will be without precedent in the history of the world, in which the governing power will be exercised by the judges, with the executives and legislators as mere figureheads in carrying on the government. It is time to call a halt."

Will any intelligent man undertake to say that Judge Tuley is desirous of bringing the courts into disrepute? Is it not true, on the contrary, that men who protest against this "highly dangerous form of oppression" as Judge Tuley does show a much deeper anxiety for the maintenance of the dignity of the courts than do those who, either directly or indirectly, are responsible for the effort to establish government by injunction?

Judge Tuley well says, "It is time to call a halt." That is what the democrats said in 1896; and it is significant that while the government by injunction plank of the Chicago platform was bitterly denounced and many claimed that that plank had considerable to do with the defeat of the democratic ticket, since then injunction writs issued by federal judges have become, by reason of their radical terms, more and more oppressive, and this form of oppression has come to be so "highly dangerous" that even republican newspapers are moved to enter vigorous protest.

MONEY THEIR GOD.

The Chicago *Record-Herald* of last week contains a report of a sermon delivered by Dr. H. E. Kittridge of the Madison Avenue Presbyterian church, New York, at the Third Presbyterian church of Chicago. Dr. Kittridge had formerly been pastor of the Chicago church and the paper reports the audience as "dumfounded" and adds that the congregation "left the church in silence."

Bravo, Dr. Kittridge! The country needs more sermons like that if it is to be saved from the corroding influence of greed and avarice. The following extracts show the nature of the reproof administered to those who profess the name of the meek and lowly Nazarene and yet allow a love of money to lead them into all kinds of conspiracies against their fellows:

"Thousands of our prominent business men who call themselves Christians and go regularly to church are being driven —driven rapidly against the rock of destruction by their tremendous absorption in money making, which is one of the greatest perils of the land today. We see it in the business of daily life. They are diligent in business, fervent in spirit, and think they are serving the Lord, all the time they are being carried away by this lust of money.

"Take it in social life: Do you not know of multitudes of men and women who have good enough intentions, but because of the luxury in which they live and the society in which they move day after day, their lives are lives of absolute idleness, bent wholly upon self-gratification? They are animated solely by the low, mean motive of self-gratification. To me there is no spectacle more pitiful than that of men or women trusting their souls to God and hoping for salvation while they spend their efforts and time day after day in quest of self-enjoyment. When their lives have been closed they are empty to all real joy.

"So I have come here tonight simply judging of you in the time in which I left and went to another city to speak a few plain words of warning. Let me tell you, young men and women, if ever there was a time for men and women to act as the children of God and to realize the full possibilities of such life, that moment is now. Here, I may say, as in New York, the cry raised is that the great peril of civilization is the constant friction between labor and capital. But there is a question far more thrilling. It is this tremendous current of passion and of love for money and show which is sweeping God's people away from the passion of the Lord and the teachings of Jesus Christ."

WHAT ABOUT NOMINEES.

The Commoner has called attention to the demerits of some of the candidates suggested by the reorganizers, and it proposes to call attention to the merits of a number of men who are worthy of the democratic nomination. As has already been stated, there is no lack of presidential material among those democrats who are really wedded to democratic principles. It would be possible to find in every state in the union men sufficiently honest, sufficiently able and sufficiently experienced to discharge the duties of the office of president. There are many men who have never been heard of before outside of their own states who can poll two or three million more votes than any candidate named by the reorganizers. A man who has had no chance to make a conspicuous record, but whose record has been good as far as made, would be a much better candidate than a man who has made a conspicuous record on the wrong side of public questions. It may be suggested as a guiding principle that no man ought to be considered for the presidential nomination on the democratic ticket about whose democracy there is a shadow of a doubt. When a campaign is on our party has business enough on hand assailing republican policies and defending democratic principles. It cannot afford to spend any time trying to prove the democracy of its candidate. And how shall we know whether a candidate's democracy is beyond question? Not merely by his perfunctory support of a democratic ticket, but by his own convictions upon the issues involved. In every campaign many men vote their party ticket without being in sympathy with all or even the most important parts of their platform. With some men the party name is more than a party platform; but such men could not expect to represent their party in positions of leadership. The struggle between the gold democrats and the Chicago platform democrats was not a struggle over gold and silver. It involved a far more important question—namely, whether the financiers should control the financial system in their own interests or whether it should be controlled by the people in the interests of the people. That question is still an issue, and must ever remain an issue, and no man whose sympathies are with the financiers and against the people can or should expect to be the nominee of a party that stands for the people. The effort to put at the head of the democratic party a man who bolted in 1896 would be ludicrous if it were not serious. Would the republican party think of nominating for president a man who supported the democratic ticket in 1896? Some of the silver republicans who were with us six years ago have gone back to the republican party, but they have not attempted to change the party's policy; they have simply adopted their party's position on the money question. The gold democrats, on the other hand, are impudent enough to assume not only that they are entitled to leadership, but that they are entitled to it without in the least modifying their views on the questions that separated them from their party.

THE COMMONER will from time to time present the names of real democrats whose position on public questions cannot be questioned and whose fidelity to the party cannot be made an issue in a campaign. These names will be presented without any effort on the part of THE COMMONER to urge the candidacy of any particular Kansas City platform democrat as against any other Kansas City platform democrat. THE COMMONER has no choice between those who stand for democratic principles; it simply draws the line between those who look to the rank and file of the party for their promotion and those who rely upon the corporations, first, to aid their candidacy; second, to secure their election, and, third, who will allow the corporations to dominate their administration.

THE EXPERIENCES OF A JURYMAN.

The readers of THE COMMONER may be interested in some comments upon the jury system from a juror fresh from the service of his country. For five days of last week I served as a juror on the regular panel of the district court of Lancaster county, and I may add, incidentally, will draw from the county $10.00 for my services and 30 cents mileage (being five cents for each full mile to and from the farm.) I was called on three juries, and having neither formed nor expressed an opinion upon the merits of the cases, was each time accepted.

A word as to the method of selection. The law in Nebraska provides that each side shall be allowed three peremptory challenges. In some places the attorneys are required to make their peremptory challenges from among the twelve men who are not subject to challenge for cause, and then new men are called to take their places in the box. In the district court of Lancaster county, however, the judges have adopted a plan of calling eighteen jurors instead of twelve. If one is challenged for cause his place is filled and when at last eighteen have been passed for cause each side strikes off three, alternating in the striking, leaving twelve jurors to try the case. This has an advantage over the method sometimes employed in that the peremptory challenges are made after all have been passed for cause, and thus each side can strike off the three least acceptable. If all the peremptory challenges are exercised and then the places filled, it may be that the new jurors, though not subject to challenge for cause, may be less acceptable than men already challenged. In other words, the method now in vogue in Lancaster county seems most likely to secure a fair and impartial jury.

The first case tried before our jury was a suit against an insurance company, but as the case turned upon the construction of the policy it was taken out of the hands of the jury and a verdict given for the defendant in pursuance of specific instructions from the court.

The second case considered by the jury upon which I served was an action brought against the county by a person who had suffered injury due, as he alleged, to the negligence of the county in the care of a public highway. The evidence showed that the injury sustained was small. The doctor's bill was $5.00, the horse was lame for a few days and the buggy damaged, but not rendered useless. There were three questions involved. First, was the road properly cared for and sufficiently safe for travelers exercising reasonable care; second, was the plaintiff guilty of any act of negligence that "approximately," as the court instructed, contributed to the accident; and, third, what was the amount of the damage. As soon as the jury reached the consultation room and a foreman was selected (it happened in this case, as in the others, that I was selected as foreman), a vote was taken first upon the proposition, "Shall the verdict be for the plaintiff or defendant." Upon this ballot it was found that a majority favored a verdict for the defendant. Then followed a discussion of the merits of the case, each juror giving his reason for voting as he did, and this discussion was exceedingly interesting because it showed the various points of view from which twelve unbiased men could look at the testimony. It soon developed that some of those who voted for the defendant believed that the road was not properly cared for, but that the injury was so small that the plaintiff should have no considerable award, and as no one felt that the injury was sufficient to justify more than nominal damages, the jury finally agreed to a verdict of $5. This was a compromise verdict and was accepted by all as doing substantial justice both to the county and the plaintiff. While the decision of a case in the district court is not considered as establishing a legal precedent binding upon other courts it may be worth while to say that the negligence complained of consisted in the county's maintaining a road only thirty-two feet in width, (the usual width is sixty-six feet), around the bank of a creek (a deviation from the section line) with nothing to protect travelers from falling over the bank and into the creek bottom some eight feet below. The plaintiff having occasion to pass there on a dark night went over the bank and suffered the injuries complained of.

The third case was a replevin suit, appealed from the justice court, and involved the title and right to possession of about four tons of wild hay. In this case the evidence showed that the plaintiff obtained a lease to eighty acres of land which included about seven acres of hay land, the land belonging to a young woman whose mother was in the habit of attending to the business for her. The mother made a verbal agreement in regard to the renting of the land with the expectation that a lease would afterwards be drawn up and signed. After the plaintiff had gone into possession under this verbal agreement the lease was presented by the defendant in the case, the brother of the young lady who owned the land. When the tenant read over the lease he noticed that the hay land was not specifically mentioned and wanted to insert a clause in the lease, but the defendant objected, and upon this point there was a difference in the testimony, the plaintiff testifying that the defendant said that the hay land was included and that there would be no trouble about it, and the defendant denying the statement. The evidence showed, however, that the plaintiff obtained a mower from the defendant and mowed a part of the hay, but that owing to the wet season the hay was spoiled. The defendant afterwards went in and cut the remainder of the hay claiming that he did so to protect his sister's rights and that he did so with her acquiescence, although he testified that she had not expressly authorized him to cut it. He also admitted that his mother, in the presence of his sister, told him he had better not cut it. As soon as the jury entered the consultation room a vote was taken and a majority of the jurors expressed themselves in favor of the plaintiff. In the discussion that followed it became apparent that all the jury desired substantially the same thing, namely, that the plaintiff should be declared entitled to the hay, but that as the defendant was acting, as he believed, in the interest of his sister, the judgment should carry as little cost as possible. The jury returned a verdict for plaintiff and fixed the damages at $12, but as the parties and nearly all the witnesses were related either by blood or marriage, the foreman, at the request of the jury, submitted two recommendations, and asked that, if possible, they be made a part of the judgment of the court. The recommendations were, first, that as the plaintiff, if entitled to recover, would owe one-half the value of the hay to the owner of the land, the sister of the defendant, the defendant be permitted to satisfy one-half of the judgment with a receipt from his sister for her share of the hay; and, second, that each party pay the fees of the witnesses called by him. While the judgment was not made contingent upon the acceptance of these conditions, the plaintiff's attorney signified his willingness to have them made a part of the judgment. And thus my services as a juror came to an end.

Having had some experience in trying to convince others, it was a refreshing change to sit in the jury box and listen to the arguments of the attorneys. Having heard the evidence and having measured it, as one must as the case proceeds, it was instructive to note the manner in which each attorney made clear and emphatic the points that strengthened his client's case. I have so often taxed the patience of hearers that I could not well ask that a limit be placed upon those who talked to us. In the jury room the merits of the lawyers was at times discussed. In one case two prominent young lawyers were opposed to each other, and each had made a gallant fight for his client. One juror, speaking of the lawyer for the plaintiff, said that he was especially eloquent and convincing. "But," replied another juror, "who couldn't make a good speech on that side? The facts were on his side and that made his speech necessarily convincing; but look at the defendant's attorney—see how skilfully he presented a bad side." It reminded me of the conversation between two men as to which was entitled to the more credit, the sun or the moon. The advocate of the sun thought he had his case won when the moon's defender overwhelmed his antagonist with the assertion that the sun only gave his light by day when it was not necessary, while the moon gave her light by night when the light was badly needed.

A fact clearly brought out by jury service was that the opinion of the judge had great weight with the juror even aside from the instructions given. The manner in which he admitted or excluded testimony and any suggestion which he made that bore even remotely upon the merits of the case had its influence. This was complimentary to the judge before whom the case was tried because it showed the confidence the jurors had in his integrity.

Five days of jury service before the court and in the jury room deepened, if possible, my confidence in the jury system. It is not only good for what it does, but also for what it prevents. Our judges are better because either party can summon a jury in a case at law. If all cases were necessarily tried before a jury the great corporate interests which have grown up in the country would be even more tempted than now to use their influence in the selection of judges friendly to them before nomination, or who could be obligated to them during the campaign. There is much more latitude in the decision of a question of fact than in a decision which rests upon a question of law, and the judges themselves may feel grateful that the jury not only relieves them of much labor, but also shields them from a pressure that might be difficult to bear.

The judge before whom the hay case was tried, in dismissing the jury for the term, took occasion, not only to commend the jurors for the manner in which they had discharged their duty, but to testify to his increasing love for the jury system as a part of the court of justice.

MISSOURI HITS THE TRUSTS.

The Missouri supreme court has found five great beef packing companies guilty of maintaining an unlawful combination to control the price of beef in that state, and has levied a fine of five thousand dollars on each of the companies. The opinion of the court was unanimous, and the companies affected are the Armour, Cudahy, Hammond, Swift, and Schwarzchild and Sulzburger companies.

A fine of five thousand dollars in such a case is, of course, insignificant when compared with the profits made by the companies, and this calls attention to the fact that in large violations of the law the punishments are not in proportion to the magnitude of the offense. It may be said that from a moral standpoint the crime is as great when one steals a small amount as when he steals a large amount, and yet it is well known that public opinion does not condemn large violations as it does small violations, and therefore the pecuniary penalty ought to be great enough to protect the public from repeated infractions of the law. In the cases mentioned, the fines imposed, while they may be the maximum fines allowed under the law, will hardly restrain the companies from another conspiracy against the public. The court could, upon the evidence, have prohibited them from doing business in the state, and yet such a judgment might have hurt the people of the state as much as the corporations.

These cases bring plainly to view the inability of one state alone to furnish a complete or satisfactory remedy and prove the wisdom of the Kansas City platform, which suggested a federal remedy.

The present anti-trust law, the Sherman law, is sufficiently broad to cover such a conspiracy against trade as that formed by the packers, and, if enforced by imprisonment, would strike terror into the hearts of the trust magnates. But the present law only relates to conspiracies between separate individuals or corporations. Another remedy is necessary when a number of corporations are merged in one and the one corporation controls the market. In the case recently tried in Missouri it was shown that five distinct and separate corporations conspired together to fix the price of meat, but suppose the five corporations should consolidate, and form one corporation? The injury to the public would be even greater because, instead of having to agree among themselves, the corporation would act as a unit, and yet if such a consolidation was formed neither the Sherman anti-trust law nor the anti-trust laws of the various states would reach the evil. The Kansas City platform remedy does, however, reach this very evil, and that remedy added to the present remedy, and the two remedies enforced by an administration really in sympathy with the public, would kill the trusts.

Let the criminal clause of the anti-trust law be enforced against the officials of the various corporations if they combine against the public, and then let congress declare that large corporations, before engaging in interstate commerce, must secure a permit from the federal government which permit can be granted only upon conditions that will make a private monopoly impossible.

The state of Missouri is to be congratulated upon the enforcing of its state law against these powerful companies, and the federal government is to be censured for not having used the criminal law against these same corporations. But congress and the administration cannot escape blame for failure to enact the legislation needed to protect the public from trust extortion. The failure of the president and congress to do something really effective shows how absurd it is to expect the trusts to be killed so long as the government is in the hands of officials who secure election through the aid of contributions collected from the corporations.

HARMONY AND HARMONY.

The editor of THE COMMONER has received an unsigned letter—such letters are usually unsigned—asking why Mr. Bryan is not willing to work for "democratic harmony;" why he does not "make an effort to unite all men believing in democratic principles;" why he "keeps up a war in the democratic camp?" This unknown correspondent insists that "peace and harmony are essential to success," and suggests that Mr. Bryan ought to "try to rehabilitate the democratic party and bring it into public favor." As a clincher he asks who is to be "the proper judge or judges of genuine, sound and sterling democracy?"

There are other things in the letter which indicate that the writer's sympathies are really with those who bolted the ticket rather than with those who supported the party in recent campaigns, but an answer is given for the benefit of those readers who have to meet these inquiries.

Mr. Bryan is interested in securing democratic harmony, and certainly has more personal reason to regret a lack of harmony in the party than the men who, after voting for the republican ticket, now clamor so loudly about "letting by-gones be by-gones." Mr. Cleveland was elected by the democratic party in 1892, and no one will seriously dispute the fact that he proceeded at once, knowingly and wilfully, to misrepresent the people who elected him upon an issue which his own conduct made paramount for the time being. Waiving for the present the right of a party nominee to betray those who nominated him and to barter away the suffrages that he had received, it is sufficient to say that Mr. Cleveland was the greatest disturber of party harmony of the present generation. Never before in the history of the party did a democratic president undertake to change the party's attitude upon a great public question, or to force upon the party as a party measure a bill identical in purpose and almost identical in language, with a bill drawn by the leaders of the opposing party. This Mr. Cleveland did. The bill introduced by Congressman Wilson in August, 1893, was almost an exact copy of a bill introduced for the same purpose by Senator John Sherman a year before.

The president's action was made the issue in the fight for delegates to the national convention of 1896, and in spite of the influence of patronage, the influence of money and the influence of all the great corporations, the rank and file of the party by a large majority repudiated the president's policy and adopted a platform that in effect condemned his course and pointed out a course directly opposite.

This was the most democratic convention held in fifty years and probably the most democratic ever held in the United States. Seldom, if ever, before had a battle been waged between the voters at the primaries on a definite principle, and never before did a convention more perfectly reflect the sentiments of the voters of the party. What was the result? The administration and all who could be influenced by the administration, the great financiers, the great corporation lawyers and all who held their service to corporation above their party allegiance, joined in an effort to defeat the democratic ticket and elect the republican ticket. Some of these bolting democrats went directly into the republican party and have been there ever since; some stopped half way, and tried to organize a new democratic party. Having failed in this, some of these went over to the republican party and some returned to the democratic fold. Of the prominent ones who returned nearly all boasted of what they had done, and few have ever announced a change of heart or a change of opinion upon public questions. They now demand harmony. And at what price? The complete and abject surrender of those who made the fight in 1896 and in 1900. And this surrender is not confined to the party's position on the money question. It means that the party must stop its opposition to the demands of organized wealth on all questions, must nominate a ticket composed of men who are in the confidence of the money magnates and the trust magnates, and then allow the party to be so organized that it can collect an enormous campaign fund from the men who are enjoying special privileges and immunities at the hands of the government. Reorganizers do not stand for any real or positive reform.

This is the harmony program, and there is no reason why any true believer in democratic principles should be deceived by it. If the men who talk about harmony so much really want harmony, why do they not content themselves with contributing their mite toward democratic success? Certainly those who helped to defeat the party, if they realize the gravity of their offence, will be ashamed to ask for leadership, and those who are not restrained by a sense of propriety can hardly be trusted with the reins.

The voters who in 1896 and 1900 risked social and business ostracism are perfectly willing to welcome back and forgive those who went astray, provided those who return come back changed in sentiment and purpose. But why welcome men whose only object in coming back is to make the democratic party an adjunct and an aid to the republican party? Why have a fight in the convention if it is going to result in renewed alienation unless the party sounds a retreat? Instead of inviting harmony these so-called "harmonizers" are only planning for more contention.

Mr. Bryan's views and conduct affect only himself and those who choose to be influenced by what he says or does, but he can no more shirk his responsibility, be it great or little, than other democrats can. Every democrat owes a duty to himself, to his party and to his country, to contend for those things which he believes to be best. If Mr. Bryan could relieve himself from this responsibility merely because those who have opposed him would be gratified by his silence, then democrats might, with the same logic, be urged to cease contending for democratic principles because their silence would gratify the republicans. If Mr. Bryan, with his knowledge of the plans and purposes of the reorganizers, refrained from pointing out their menace to the party's welfare, he could justly be accused of apostacy or cowardice. Who is under greater obligation than he to the democrats who were loyal in both campaigns? The fact that he is not a candidate for any office makes it more imperative rather than less that he should do a citizen's part in the discussion of public questions and in the plans proposed for making democratic principles effective. What would be thought of a neighbor who failed to give notice of an attempted burglary merely for fear of disturbing the quietude of a neighborhood? The leaders among the reorganizers are making a burglarious attempt to enter the democratic party for the purpose of carrying away whatever it has of value to those who occupy the house, and it is time to sound the alarm.

If any real democrat is deceived he has himself to blame, for the admissions of the reorganizers are sufficient to put all on their guard.

Let us have harmony; not the harmony that would enable the wolf to enter the lamb fold unnoticed, but a real harmony between those who believe in a government of the people, by the people and for the people, administered according to the doctrine of "equal rights to all and special privileges to none"— a government which would protect the people from every arm uplifted for their injury. No other harmony is either desirable or possible, and harmony banquets that are designed to obliterate the distinctions between democracy and plutocracy can only bring evil, however well intended.

THE ALDRICH BILL.

In order that the readers of THE COMMONER may know what to expect from the republican party when congress meets in December, the Aldrich bill is printed in full on another page. It was called up near the close of the last session of congress, but there was not time enough to force it through. It will be noticed that the secretary of the treasury designates whatever national banking associations he likes as depositories of public money, and that they are to be employed "as fiscal agents of the government, performing whatever reasonable duties may be required of them." In these designated depositories the secretary may deposit public moneys received from all sources, and may accept as security any of the interest-bearing obligations of the United States or of any state, also municipal bonds of any city of 5,000 inhabitants, provided the city has been in existence twenty-five years, has not for ten years defaulted in the payment of interest and whose indebtedness does not exceed 20 per cent of the value of the taxable property. It is also provided that first mortgage railroad bonds may be used as security for such deposits, provided the road has paid not less than 4 per cent per annum on its entire capital stock for a period of not less than ten years. The banks are to pay a rate of interest to be fixed by the secretary, amounting to not less than 1 1-2 per cent and the United States is to have a general lien on all the assets of the bank, in addition to the special security above named.

The objections urged against this bill range themselves under four heads. The first objection was very forcibly stated by Senator Blackburn in reply to Senator Bailey. The senator from Texas made a speech in favor of the Aldrich bill. He said that while he was opposed to the collection of unnecessary revenue, he thought it better to deposit the money in the banks, and thus return it to circulation, than to lock it up in the vaults. He estimated the amount thus to be deposited at $300,-000,000; he not only favored depositing the money with the banks, but he objected to the charging of interest. He said: "Another provision in this bill that I would prefer to have stricken out, is the provision for interest. I believe that it would be better to avoid the question about the government loaning money as contradistinguished from depositing it." He also objected to the provision giving the government a general lien on deposits, saying: "There is an amendment reported by the committee to which I object. It is the provision that gives the government a first lien upon the assets of the bank as against all other depositors. The government takes a special security for its deposit, and the power of the secretary of the treasury to demand more security is ample if what he has becomes imperiled." He was at first inclined to object to the deposit of railroad bonds as security, but says that the objection was more sentimental than substantial.

These quotations are made to show Mr. Bailey's attitude upon the subject, and to give a better understanding of Mr. Blackburn's answer. The reader of the Congressional Record will be impressed with the feeling that Mr. Bailey's argument lacked the force and logic that usually characterizes his speeches. Mr. Blackburn in making his reply was frequently interrupted by Mr. Aldrich and Mr. Stewart, and other republicans, but he held his ground against them, and showed how well one is armed who has the right side of a question. He pointed out that it was to the interest of the people to have the government indebtedness paid off rather than the money loaned to the banks at a low rate of interest, while the government itself was paying a higher rate of interest. Instead of allowing republicans to collect large sums and then insist upon loaning the money out to get it back into circulation, he demanded that they either reduce the taxes and leave the money in the pockets of the people, or if they collected too much, apply the surplus on the reduction of the public debt. He very forcibly pointed out the interest the national banks have in preventing the reduction of the debt, because the bonds are the basis of the bank-note issue.

The second objection to the Aldrich bill is that the loaning of the money gives to the bankers a pecuniary interest in keeping the taxes high and surplus large. As long as they can collect money from the people and then get the money at a low rate of interest, their influence will be thrown upon the side of high taxes and large surplus.

The third objection is to be found in the fact that the administration, if allowed to loan out government money at a low rate, will be able to lay the foundation for an enormous campaign fund, and there is no doubt that this method has been employed in the past. It will be remembered that Secretary Gage was required to make public some correspondence which he had with some New York bankers, and it appeared that one of the bankers had pleaded his campaign contribution as a reason for favors.

The fourth objection to the bill is to be found in the fact that the government would become a partner in the stock jobbing transactions of Wall street. As the secretary of the treasury would have the right to select bonds that came within the provision of the statute, he could raise or lower the price of bonds to the enormous advantage of the speculators, and as Senator Blackburn pointed out, it would be possible for a railroad magnate engaged in the banking business, to secure loans from the treasury at a low rate of interest, while the ordinary citizen would have to borrow from the banks at prevailing rates.

A careful inspection of the Aldrich bill and a consideration of the arguments made for and against it, ought to convince any unprejudiced mind that the republican party is in the clutch of Wall street and is making the federal treasury merely a business asset of the New York financiers.

It is absurd to say that the money question is settled while the financiers are persistently hanging about congress and demanding further and further concessions in the interest of organized wealth. It is fortunate for our party that it has in the senate champions like Senator Blackburn, who are always on the watch and ready to point out the iniquities of republican measures.

THE STRIKERS WIN.

The findings of the board of arbitration were given to the public just as THE COMMONER went to press last week, and an abstract of those findings was published in the news columns.

The award was unanimous and was a substantial victory for the strikers. The commission recommended a general increase of wages, amounting to about 10 per cent, and also recommended a decrease in the hours of labor. These are important advantages gained. The commission also recommended a minimum wage with a sliding scale that enables the miner to profit by an increase in the price of coal. A discontinuance of the system of employing what are known as a "coal and iron police" was also recommended, and a stricter enforcement of the laws in relation to the employment of children was urged.

The recommendation of the commission in regard to a permanent board of arbitration deserves especial consideration. It insists that the state and federal governments should provide machinery for the making of a compulsory investigation of labor difficulties by a commission similar to the commission in the case just closed.

Republicans have been inclined to give the president great credit for the appointment of a commission and the settlement of this strike after tremendous loss had been suffered by all the parties interested, and yet these same republicans refuse to give the democratic party credit for having insisted in 1896 and also in 1900 upon a permanent system of arbitration which would have made this strike unnecessary because it would have enabled the miners to secure a settlement of their grievances without a strike.

According to the commission, the strike cost the mine owners $46,000,000, and employes $25,000,000, and the transportation companies $28,000,000. Here was a loss of about $100,000,000 that might have been avoided if the democratic plan had been adopted, that is, this much might have been saved in this one strike, not to speak of the saving in other strikes. And yet there are republicans so partisan that they toss their hats in air in praise of the administration because, after waiting until enormous loss had been suffered, it secured the settlement of one strike without guaranteeing the country against a constant recurrence of strikes.

The laboring men have been pleading for arbitration for years, and the democratic party has been insisting upon it, but the republican leaders are too busy looking after the interests of the corporations to give time or consideration to legislation imperatively needed, not only in the interests of the wage-earners, but in the interest of the public generally.

Is it not time for the rank and file of the republican party to demand a plan for the settlement of all labor disputes rather than the tardy settlement of one only?

VICTORY FOR WORKING MEN.

Organized labor won a decided victory in the United States circuit court at St. Louis when Judge Adams refused to make permanent the temporary restraining order which he had issued in which order the railroad men were forbidden to quit work.

Judge Adams holds that laboring men have the right to organize, that they have a right to demand higher wages and to quit work if their demands be not complied with. He holds that the effect of a strike in delaying the movement of freight or passenger trains would be too remote and incidental to make the authors of it even constructively guilty of conspiracy to interfere with interestate commerce or defy the authority of the United States by obstructing the transit of the mails, which were some of the allegations set up in the petition on which Judge Adams issued his temporary restraining order.

While the decision is a victory for the workingmen, Judge Adams undertakes to justify the temporary restraining order. That order should not have been issued even if the facts alleged were true; and we need go no further than the statement of the conclusions reached by Judge Adams himself to justify this claim. If workingmen have an unquestioned right to organize, if they have a right to demand higher wages and to quit work if their demand be not complied with—and Judge Adams says they have these privileges—then the court was not justified in issuing the restraining order forbidding these men to quit work, even accepting the statements made in the railroad company's petition as being entirely correct.

This is true because it may be said, with respect to the temporary restraining order as Judge Adams says in his refusal to grant the injunction, that while the results of a strike might be delay in the movement of trains, interference with interstate commerce, and obstruction of the transit of the mails, these are too remote and incidental to make the authors of it even constructively guilty of a conspiracy; and it is also true because it was never intended to confer upon a court the privilege of interfering, by the issue of a writ, with the unquestioned rights of men.

The objection to government by injunction is not merely against the evidence on which the writ is based; it is against the writ itself, as it is applied in enabling powerful men to interfere with the plain rights of other men and as it represents that extraordinary power assumed by a judge which power has, properly, no place in our system of government.

The very men who have been quick to resort to the writ of injunction against workingmen would become very indignant if the workingmen could summon sufficient influence to persuade a judge to issue an injunction in their behalf denying to the employer the exercise of his unquestioned rights.

One of the most striking utterances with respect to the temporary restraining order issued by Judge Adams was made by Edward M. Shepard recently in a speech delivered in Chicago. Mr. Shepard asked: "Is it anything less than calamitous that in the armory of law weapons should be found to restrain that kind of freedom, when thus far the armory of law has been ransacked in vain for weapons equal to the prevention of combinations expressly forbidden by statute?"

Men who have been ready to resort to the injunction in order to deprive laboring men of their plain rights would not only be indignant if they were made the victims of similar injunctions, but they have never been slow to give expression to their indignation when it has been suggested that the armory of law be ransacked for weapons in order to protect the people and in the effort to require powerful and influential men to abandon their impositions upon the weak and the helpless.

GOVERNMENT BY INJUNCTION.

A reader of THE COMMONER desires to know the meaning of "government by injunction." It is the name given to that process of the court by which judges, mostly federal judges, have at the request of corporations restrained the employes of the corporations from doing certain specified acts. If such acts are already prohibited by law, then the violation of the law should be punished in the ordinary way and the accused be given a trial by jury. If the acts prohibited by the court are not prohibited by statute, then the court is making criminal law, and this is not its province. A bill was introduced some years ago and passed through the senate making it unlawful for a court to punish for contempt unless the contempt was committed in the presence of the court. This bill passed the senate practically without opposition, but as soon as the corporations discovered the purpose of this bill they succeeded in defeating it in the house, and since that time it has never been able to pass either house, or, in fact, to obtain consideration.

RECIPE FOR HARMONY.

The recipe for harmony usually given by the reorganizers is as follows: Mix sixteen parts of loyal democrats with one part of unrepentant bolters and stir until all the bolters are on top. Then skim off the top with an official ladle and throw the balance away.

ROOSEVELT DEFENDS TRUSTS.

On another page will be found the speech of President Roosevelt, delivered at Milwaukee a few days ago and reported in the *Chicago Tribune*. The full text is given because it is the president's defence of his administration's record on the trust question and after a careful study of it the reader can better understand the criticisms herewith submitted.

In the first place, it is evident that Mr. Roosevelt neither desires nor intends to kill the trusts. He starts out by saying that he does not "approach the subject from the standpoint of those who speak of themselves as anti-trust or anti-corporation people," etc. He thus admits that he is not opposed to the trust as such.

Then he proceeds to defend the trusts by declaring that they are "in many cases efficient economic instruments, the result of an inevitable process of economic evolution." This is the phraseology of the trust magnate and, strange to say, it is also the language used by the extreme socialist. Both the trust magnate and the extreme socialist regard the trust as natural and necessary, the former accepting it as a blessing to be distributed through the benevolence of private individuals, the latter considering it a blessing to be administered by the state acting for all the people.

The all-important point at issue is whether the trust is really "an economic evolution." If it is, we may as well prepare to meet the question proposed by socialism. The word, trust, is usually understood to mean monopoly, and if the monopoly is a natural growth, if it is an "economic evolution," the only question that remains is, whether the benefits of monopoly shall be enjoyed by a few who hold stock in the private corporation or by all the people as shareholders in the government.

Is Mr. Roosevelt prepared to discuss the question which his argument inevitably raises?

Again, a careful reading of his speech will convince any candid student of public affairs that the president is at heart in full sympathy with the trust magnates. This is evident, first, from the language he uses. He is bitter when he speaks of the anti-trust people and apologetic when he speaks of the trust themselves. He praises the feeble efforts put forth by the administration and says that they were "removed as far as possible from rancor, hysteria and unworthy demagogic appeal." He says that "nothing of value is to be expected from ceaseless agitation for radical and extreme legislation." He also fears "legislation of a general and indiscriminate character." He thinks that "many of the alleged remedies are of the unpleasantly drastic type." "We are against all radical and unwise change"—this is the keynote of his speech and it is apparent that he is more alarmed lest good trusts may be embarrassed than he is lest bad trusts may hurt the people. He spends more time warning against radical anti-trust legislation than he does in pointing out a remedy. In the second place, to relieve the trusts of further apprehension he eulogizes Knox and declares that the legislation already secured is all that is now needed. He does not hold out hope of anything more effective than the anti-rebate bill which Mr. Archibald, the attorney of the Standard Oil company, expressly indorsed in a telegram to Senator Quay, and the publicity amendment which was so weak and ineffective that Littlefield, the blue-ribbon, far-famed republican "trust-buster," refused to vote for it.

When he attempts to quote from his Minneapolis speech which it will be remembered led many to believe that he was against the trusts, he quoted the part wherein he defended the large fortunes and left out the "violent and radical" part wherein he suggested that it might become necessary to "shackle cunning" as we have "shackled force." This, too, shows that he wants the trust magnates to understand that "there is but the scantiest justification for most of the outcry against the men of wealth, as such," but he is willing to allow the public to forget the harsh things that (in a fit of "hysteria?") he inadvertantly said about the shackling of cunning.

He says nothing of the bill framed by a republican committee of the house of representatives, passed by the house almost without opposition, and then strangled by the trust representatives in the senate. It was not an adequate remedy and yet strong enough to make Attorney General Knox call it drastic and certainly worthy of passing notice if the president intends to do anything further on the trust question.

The suits brought by the government are mentioned as conclusive proof that the present laws are being enforced. The merger suit is referred to and yet it is well known that there have been more consolidations among railroads the last few years than ever before; he speaks of enjoining the packers' combine, but he neglects to say that the packers have now formed a trust that avoids the farce of the injunction; he speaks of the Federal Salt company, but neglects to say that the big salt trust is still in undisputed control of the salt supply of the nation and is not vexed by suits. He has mentioned a few instances where civil process has been used, but does not explain why he refuses to use the criminal clause. If a mail carrier steals a dollar out of a letter he does not have the attorney general enjoin him from doing so again. If a man sells a gallon of liquor without license he does not use the injunction against him. Why are small violations of the law punished in the criminal court and the large criminal only enjoined? Then, too, why does he overlook the oil trust, the sugar trust, the cracker trust, the starch trust, the harvester trust, the steel trust, the tobacco trust and the hundreds of other trusts? The conclusion is irresistable that he has no objection to a trust, but thinks the government ought to interfere only when the trust does some outrageous act. For instance, the Federal Salt company raised prices several hundred per cent and that was considered ground for prosecution, but what about the plate glass trust that takes advantage of a protection of over one hundred per cent?

One of two conclusions must be drawn from the president's speech; either he has no idea of attacking the principle of private monopoly, or, if he has any such purpose, it does not manifest itself. What motive could he have for concealing his purpose if he really intended an active crusade against private monopolies? Does he doubt that the people are prepared for energetic action? He cannot so mistake the sentiment of the people. Is he afraid of the influence of the trust magnates in the next convention? If he must conciliate them to secure a nomination, will he not serve them after the election?

Here is an opportunity for the display of moral courage, but where is the courage? O, strenuosity! what frauds are committed in thy name! The overawing of the Filipinos—even the ride up San Juan Hill, how insignificant both would seem in comparison with a real, sure-enough attack on the citadel of the trusts. All his boasting about "iron in the blood," all his scoffing at "cowards and weaklings" only give emphasis to the timidity he shows in the presence of insolent and arrogant monopolists.

The Milwaukee speech would seem to be the death-knell of the anti-trust movement so far as the president is concerned.

RIOT CARTRIDGES.

It is a little singular that the national administration should announce its readiness to furnish riot cartridges to the various state administrations just at the time when republican leaders are boasting of universal prosperity, universal contentment and universal approbation of republican policies. The very discussion of a riot cartridge is suggestive of conditions that need remedying. Victor Hugo has described the mob as "the human race in misery," and it is as important that mobs should be prevented as that they should be dispersed. It is not an indication of the application of the imperialistic idea to domestic conditions, that the administration should spend more time devising means to put down a mob than it does in devising remedies for the evils that lead to the formation of mobs?

Imperialism rests on force rather than justice; imperialism coerces rather than persuades; imperialism, instead of curing evils, compels silent submission to those evils. The republican party today is loading the masses with taxation while it permits great aggregations of wealth to plunder with impunity. When reminded that there may be clashes between labor and capital, instead of providing boards of arbitration for the settlement of conditions, it prepares riot cartridges for distribution; instead of destroying government by injunction it prepares to back up the judge with the army, while he uses the courts to enforce the demands of the employer as against the claims of the employe.

And yet a sleeping people must be awakaned and it may be that the riot cartridge will do what reason and logic have failed to accomplish. If the rank and file of the republican party are not ready to administer a rebuke to the leaders of the party their decision may be hastened when they are brought face to face with the horrid realities for which the administration seems to be preparing.

The democratic party is sometimes accused of being radical. As a matter of fact, it is the conservative element in the country today. It seeks to apply well settled principles to gross evils; it seeks to preserve law and order by the most effective means, namely the establishment of justice. The republican party, on the other hand, boasts of its love of law and order, and yet it fosters and promotes injustice and favoritism.

The democratic party has been accused of being hostile to the well-to-do. This indictment is as absurd as it is false. The democratic party is the best friend of honestly acquired wealth, and by attempting to protect each person in the enjoyment of that which he earns it offers the greatest stimulus both to industry and to thrift. The republican party, on the other hand, by confusing wealth acquired by spoliation with wealth acquired by brain and muscle, is liable to bring upon honest accumulations an odium that ought to be reserved for predatory wealth.

It is to be hoped that the riot cartridges will never be needed, but the mere issuing of them ought to educate the people to the gloomy and melancholy end of republican theories and republican policies.

DEFEND DEMOCRATIC PRINCIPLES.

Reports received by THE COMMONER show that the work of organization among democrats for the protection of the party and the preservation of democratic principles is progressing at a gratifying rate.

While the organs of the reorganizers are preaching "harmony," they are insisting that men who subscribe to the democratic national platform must have no voice in the democratic convention of 1904. These gentlemen have worked themselves up to the point where they are bold enough to declare that devotion to the principles set forth in the democratic platform is thoroughly "undemocratic." Indeed, the New York *World*, in a recent issue, went so far as to say that a certain man who did not subscribe to the platform, but who in 1900 is said to have voted the ticket, would not be a strong candidate for the reorganizers to present, because the fact that he had supported the ticket in 1900 would be to his disadvantage.

In the view of these gentlemen, then, the real democrat is the man who has not only repudiated the party platform, but who has voted against the party candidates. In the view of these gentlemen, the real democrat has so conducted himself as to win the approval of J. Pierpont Morgan and other trust magnates. To be sure, the organs of the reorganizers do not frankly admit this much, although their arguments in favor of reorganization and relating to the work to be performed by the democratic convention of 1904 is clearly susceptible to this interpretation.

Henry Watterson, who advocates practically the same things favored by Grover Cleveland, seems to be very much alarmed lest Mr. Cleveland become the nominee. It cannot be doubted that the leaders of the reorganizers would prefer Mr. Cleveland as the nominee and it must be admitted that he is the logical candidate; and yet even though time shall demonstrate that it is not good policy to urge Mr. Cleveland's candidacy, it may be depended upon that the candidate agreed upon by the reorganizers will represent the same influences and the same policies that dominated Mr. Cleveland's second administration.

In a recent newspaper interview, Senator Morgan of Alabama said that he was willing to welcome to the democratic party the prodigal sons and he insisted that there was no reason for closing the democratic doors in the faces of penitent men. But there is nothing to indicate that these men have repented. On the contrary, they boast of their repudiation of the democratic platform and the democratic ticket. In the *Courier-Journal* of Wednesday, April 8, Mr. Watterson has an editorial in which he says:

"The editor of the *Courier-Journal* has nothing to regret except a series of disasters, for which he was nowise responsible. Looking back over that record, he asserts that, from first to last, he, and those democrats with whom he acted, were right, and that events have amply vindicated them."

This, then, is the spirit of the reorganization now undertaken by the men who deserted the democratic party. They do not come as penitents. They resent the imputation that they are in the attitude of the prodigal son. They assert, in the language of Mr. Watterson, that from first to last they were right and that events have amply vindicated them. As a mater of fact, none of the policies for which they stood have been vindicated.

While at this very moment they are engaged in declaiming loudly against the party which they helped to place in power, they charge that that party is "rotten to the core" and that the administration is controlled by selfish interests and is not actuated by patriotic purposes. These gold standard reorganizers insisted more vehemenlty even than the republican gold standard champions did that an increased volume of money would not bring better times; and yet today they are confronted with the fact that the American people are enjoying better times; and if there are any who yet doubt that the enormous increase in the volume of money had much to do with this improvement they need but to observe the fact that republican leaders are insisting upon an even larger increase in the volume of money in order to maintain "existing prosperity."

The democratic party cannot change its principles to suit the purposes of these reorganizers unless it becomes so similar to the republican party that, so far as the patriotic voter is concerned, there will be small choice between the two organizations. There is but one position for the democratic party to take. It is the plainly defined democratic position. It is the position on the side of the people as clearly defined in the conscience of every thoughtful man.

The republican party represents the plutocracy of this country. The democratic party cannot successfully compete for favors in that direction. Even upon the low plane of so-called practical politics, it will be wisdom for the democratic party to stand faithfully by the people and to resent, without apology and without equivocation, the encroachments which the strong would make upon the weak.

In order that the democratic party shall remain steadfast, it will be the duty of every one who believes in the principles set forth in the democratic national convention to manifest an active interest in the work of organization. In every precinct throughout the United States democrats should organize. They should carefully scrutinize the record of every man who aspires to be a delegate to democratic conventions; and they should see to it that no man is sent to a democratic convention, county, state, or national, who cannot be depended upon to faithfully represent and defend the opinions of the rank and file. THE

COMMONER will be glad to furnish a form of constitution and membership blanks to all who contemplate the organization of democratic clubs. When clubs are organized THE COMMONER will make notice of the fact for the information of others.

The only hope which the reorganizers may entertain is that the rank and file of the party may become indifferent and will remain away from the primaries. If the rank and file of the party will but take part in the primary elections, there is not the slightest doubt that the democratic party will remain faithful to its principles and that the trust magnates will be required to bestow their smiles upon the republican party and to look to that party for special favors at the expense of the people.

WHY NOT FREIGHT SHIPS?

The president is urging a larger navy under pretense that we need it to enforce the Monroe doctrine. No nation is likely to assail that doctrine, but if we need more ships, why not build transport ships? When the war with Spain broke out we had to buy a lot of vessels of doubtful value and pay for them at a high price. Why not build a few vessels that can be used for transport service in time of war and for merchandise in time of peace? With such vessels our government could establish lines between our seaports and the seaports of South and Central America. They would give experience to our officers and seamen, establish communication with the countries whose rights we guard, improve mail and freight facilities and at the same time give us vessels that can, in time of need, be added to our fleet? Why not? This would be a far more useful expenditure of public money than that which the president contemplates.

"AN ITEM FOR REFLECTION."

Forman, Ford & Co., of Minneapolis, have sent out to their customers a postal card containing the following suggestions under the head, "An Item for Reflection:"

"If there was no duty to be paid on imported plate glass, based on today's market, an ordinary store front would cost $100 f. o. b. Minneapolis. The same store front, with the present tariff added costs $275, the consumer being obliged to pay $175 extra for duty, which is the 'protection' given the 'trust.' As plate glass is manufactured entirely by machines, no skilled labor entering therein, (and machines are operated about as cheap in America as in Europe), it must be clear to any one that the 'trust' is not entitled to such enormous and unreasonable 'protection' as it has at present at the expense of the consumers of plate glass."

It certainly is worthy of reflection, and yet there are republicans who will assure without further argument that the tariff is necessary and that the country would go to ruin were it not for the power of the trusts to extort from the people.

CONCERNING ADVERTISING.

One of the readers of THE COMMONER has discontinued his subscription because THE COMMONER declined to publish an advertisement of the stock of a corporation in which the subscriber was interested. While one always dislikes to lose a subscriber, it is impossible to so conduct a paper as to please every one, and THE COMMONER prefers to lose a few subscribers rather than risk the injury of the readers by the advertisement of stock in corporations. As a rule, the corporations that advertise stock for sale are purely speculative, such as mining, oil and developing companies, and while many of these companies are entirely legitimate, the value of stock depends partly on chance and partly on the management of the companies, and as the management may change any day THE COMMONER has thought it best not to take such advertisements. Of course, in refusing such patronage THE COMMONER virtually loses the money that might be obtained from these advertisements, but the proprietor prefers to suffer this loss rather than make himself responsible for a far greater loss that might come to his readers if through such advertisements they were led into unsafe investments.

MORE MONEY IS NEEDED.

The New York *Sun* of March 9 contains an article on the financial situation written by Daniel F. Kellogg, admitting all that THE COMMONER has said in regard to the scarcity of money. He points out that the financial situation is anything but satisfacory. The following quotations present the salient points:

"But it would be idle to deny that in a broader sense the money situation is causing some serious reflection. Apart from routine business matters it is the chief topic of discussion in all the great banking and commission houses down-town, the querry taking this general form: 'Have we, as a matter of fact, enough money with which to conduct the financial operations of the country at their present rate and volume?' Those raising the question admit and lay great stress upon the sound and substantial nature of all legitimate business conditions—the vast development of the iron and steel business, the tremendous railway traffic, the huge purchase of commodities of all sorts by the once poverty-stricken dwellers on the western prairies, and the fact, attested in every way, that, despite all its great strides, production in our country has still not kept pace with consumption. But what is troubling these observers is what they declare to be the continual indications that the mere mechanical operation of financing all this prosperity is becoming difficult, that the money supply of the country is, in plain words, inadequate to the demands made upon it. They say that no sooner is one period of financial stress, owing to tight money, at an end, and money rates once more approximate their customary ease, than one corporation after another so swoops down upon the money market with requirements for cash for extensive improvements, new construction and acquirements of various properties at high prices that the supply of lendable funds in bankers' hands becomes exhausted.

"It has been said in answer to all this that there would be money enough in the country for all legitimate business if speculation could be kept quiet. But this objection is without force. Speculation cannot be kept quiet. It is the natural complement of business prosperity, and so-called legitimate business itself is largely speculative in its nature. A circulating medium which did not allow and provide for the needs of speculators would be worthless; by which is meant, of course, that reasonable and not unreasonable provision of the kind is necessary; undoubtedly, present circumstances will strengthen the demand that has recently arisen for an 'asset' currency system; but if it is said that the flood of money or of the paper promises of banks to pay money that the establishment of such a system will bring, is necessary to afford proper elasticity to the conduct of business affairs in our country, one must recall the increase in the circulating medium that has already occurred under existing laws and wonder at the voracity of the demands, which, it appears, this increase has stimulated and is no longer able to satisfy. The circulation has increased in the last six years almost as much per capita as in the famous war time period between 1862 and 1868; and the volume of the circulation now is twice as great as it was then. A change in the currency system cannot, however, be effected for a twelve-month at least, and there are those who hold that recent developments, instead of emphasizing the wisdom of placing the currency on a bank asset basis, militate against it."

It will be noticed that the *Sun's* financial authority raises the question whether we have money enough, and his argument is clearly in support of the negative side of the question. It will also be noticed that he regards the circumstances as strengthening the demand for an asset currency, and yet it is apparent that he is not so sure that it will meet the requirements of trade. In fact, he closes his article with a suggestion that the circumstances which he has described may militate against an asset currency rather than emphasize the wisdom of it.

Now what does all this mean? It simply means that the business world is fast coming to realize that our supply of money is so inadequate that even the loaning of bank reserves over and over again will not suffice to furnish the money required to meet the needs of the country. The bank reserves ought not to be loaned at all. The law requiring banks to keep a reserve against their deposits ought to be so amended as to require the reserve to be kept in the bank vaults. To allow this reserve to be loaned when all is sunshine only to be suddenly contracted at the approach of a storm is utterly without defense. It means that when money is easy it is too easy, and that it cannot get a little tight without necessarily becoming very tight.

The scarcity of money can be understood when one inquires what the result would be if the government required banking to be done on a safe basis and the reserve to be kept in the vaults. Such a result would produce a stringency that might bring on a panic, and yet instead of providing more money with which to do business, the financiers insist upon the gold standard with all the danger that it involves.

The asset currency is urged for four reasons: First, because the banks fear that in the course of time the national debt will be paid off, and they know that with the payment of the bonds the present basis of bank-note circulation will disappear. Second, the banks also know that as the national debt is reduced the struggle to get bonds will raise the premium and lessen the profits of national banking. Third, the bankers know that there is more profit in the issue of bank notes on their assets than in the issue of notes on government bonds, both because it is necessary to invest money in the bonds and also because the money invested in the premium cannot be off-set by bank notes. The fourth reason why the bankers favor the asset currency is that it enables them to issue a larger amount of money and they everywhere feel the need of more money.

Why not satisfy this need by the coinage of silver rather than by the issue of paper promises to pay, resting upon the shifting banking assets of a banking institution? Every well-informed student of finance knows that the coinage of silver under the Bland-Allison act and under the Sherman law conferred a great benefit upon the world by increasing the amount of real money. The government will soon finish the work of coining the silver in the treasury, and there is then no law for the further coinage of silver. Not satisfied with this, the financiers are attempting to make the silver dollar redeemable in gold, thus lessening the volume of real money and increasing the volume of credit money. While it is possible to issue a certain amount of credit money upon a given amount of real money, it has never been possible to establish with mathematical certainty just what that safe relation is, and it varies with financial conditions. When everything is running along smoothly a given amount of real money will carry a larger amount of credit money than it will in time of panic or industrial depression. Then, too, the government can carry a larger amount of credit money on a given amount of real money than an individual or private corporation can, because the government, with its taxing power, stands back of its paper (This is assuming that the government paper like the banking paper, is redeemable in standard money.)

It is merely a statement of a self-evident truth to say that a financial system becomes weaker and less secure in proportion as the ratio of credit money to standard money is increased. It is easy to understand why the great financiers insist upon a gold standard, bank paper and an asset currency. But why should anybody else advocate these things? The farmer, the laborer, the business man (the business man who thinks for himself and is not under the thumb of some financial magnate) are all interested in having a volume of money that is not only safe, but sufficient in quantity. If the government should open the mints to the coinage of silver today, and coin all that was presented, it could not furnish money more rapidly than it is now needed. With a sufficient volume of real money we could require the banks to keep their reserves on hand and thus save the country from spasmodic inflation and contraction of the loanable money of the country; we could replace the bank currency with silver or silver certificates, and then, if there was need for more money than the gold and silver furnished, we could issue United States notes, like our present greenbacks, that are a legal tender and about whose value there can be no question. These advantages would come to us at once, not to speak of the advantage that wuold come from an increase in the price of silver. That would increase the export value of the silver we send out and improve our trade with the silver-using nations of the world, and raise the value of those exports which have suffered because of their competition with the exports of silver-using countries.

Because, during the last six years, the country has been benefited by the increased production of gold and by the enlargement of the volume of our currency many people have thoughtlessly declared the money question settled, but no one who reads the news from other countries and knows of the struggle that is going on everywhere to get money enough to carry on the world's business can believe that the money question is settled or can be settled by any system that curtails the volume of real money or substitutes the unsubstantial fabric of an asset currency for a legal tender standard money.

The fall in the price of European consols is only an indication, but taken in connection with the *Sun's* article, it shows how unsupported is the confidence of those who expect the financiers to take care of the people and solve their financial difficulties for them.

RELIGIOUS FREEDOM.

Address delivered by Mr. Bryan at a Dinner given at Washington, D. C., April 13, 1903, by the Thomas Jefferson Memorial association.

Mr. Toastmaster, and Fellow-Citizens: I hardly feel that I ought to detain the banqueters or take their thoughts away from the magnificent speech to which we have just listened from the governor of the state which gave Thomas Jefferson to the Union. It was so complete, so felicitous in expression and so true, that nothing can be added in the way of eulogy; and if it were not that I have been assigned a particular subject I would not attempt a speech.

This evening has been one of great delight to me. I am a believer in Thomas Jefferson, and in his principles, and I am glad to come from Nebraska to Washington to join this association in the inauguration of this movement to raise a monument to his memory. I deem it an honor to attend this dinner, given under the auspices of an association at whose head stands Admiral Dewey, the highest man in the navy of the nation, and to sit at the board with General Miles, the highest soldier in the army of the nation; to follow Senator Hoar, the nestor of the United States senate, and to speak with ex-Secretary Smith, who represents a profession—which I must admit to be an influential profession—namely, journalism; and with so distinguished an educator as President Needham.

I can not say anything about the purpose of this organization that has not been better said by Mr. Lipscomb, who shares with Mr. McKean the honor of originating it; but I can join with them in the enjoyment of this occasion, and, my friends, if any of you wonder why one who advocates as earnestly as I do the political principles of Thomas Jefferson, should on this occasion take Religion rather than Politics as his theme, I might explain to you that to hear republicans praise Jefferson as they have tonight makes a democrat feel religious.

I can give a general indorsement to the general eulogy pronounced by Senator Hoar, and a particular commendation to the particular indorsement given by the gentlemen from Philadelphia. I have heard Zacheus mentioned in connection with Philadelphia, but I confess that the version of the story as I heard it tonight was new to me. The only reason I have ever heard given why Zacheus and Philadelphia should be named in the same breath was that there was a request preferred to Zaccheus which is often preferred in Philadelphia— "Come down."

I am not disposed to be controversial tonight, but it requires all the Christian forbearance that I have been able to cultivate since I joined the church at the age of 14, not to say something in reply to the remarks made about expansion.

I agree with Jefferson rather than with my friend from Pennsylvania in estimating the relative importance of what Jefferson did. It gave me, I think, a better insight into the character of Jefferson than I had ever had before when I read the inscription which he himself suggested for his monument—the inscription to which our toastmaster has eloquently referred. Jefferson was a political philosopher, and as has been said, he thought far in advance of his time. And yet he differed in one essential particular from the philosophers who do not live to see the triumph of their ideas. He proclaimed great living truths, and then applied those truths to the questions with which he had to deal. Some have contented themselves with laying down abstract principles, and have not sought to give them vitality in the present day; but Jefferson not only saw the future, but he saw the present, and we have this great advantage in the study of the principles of Jefferson, that he gave us those principles embodied in legislation. I have been more and more surprised as I have studied the questions with which we have to deal, to find that there is no subject with which our people grapple today that he did not consider in principle. Take the questions that are subjects of controversy and you will find that he stated principles and applied principles at that time that apply to the questions at this time; and today we do not have to go beyond his writings to find principles that will solve aright the problems of today. He saw great fundamental truths, self-evident truths, if you please, and I am coming to believe that there are not only self-evident truths, but that all truth is self-evident, and that the best service that a man can render to a truth is to state it so that it can be understood. Jefferson had the power of statement, and he stated the truths so that they could be understood. I do not mean to speak lightly of the work of Jefferson in purchasing the Louisiana territory, but, my friends, if that territory had not been bought then it would have been bought afterward, for it was there and it was necessary that it should became American territory; I can not believe, therefore, that the purchase of that land—dull, inanimate matter—can be compared with the proclamaion of immortal truth. I place far above any purchase of acres or square miles, the utterance of those truths upon which human liberty must rest. Philosophy is above geography. Jefferson rightly measured his own work when he looked back over a long and eventful life, and, ignoring the foot-hills of honor saw only the mountain peaks of service. He gave to us proof that the Bible is right when it fixes service as the measure of greatness. You will remember that when there was a controversy as to which should be greatest in the Kingdom of Heaven, and the question was brought to the Master, He said: "Let him who would be chiefest among you be the servant of all."

So Jefferson, when he looked back over his life saw, not the things that he had received, but the things that he had given to the world; not the things men had done for him, but the things he had done for mankind.

I have been asked to speak of the statute for establishing Religious Freedom, written by Thomas Jefferson, and enacted by the state of Virginia in 1786, about eight years after it was drafted. Let me read you the statute:

"That the general assembly do enact that no man shall be compelled to frequent, or support, any religious worship, place or ministry whatsoever, nor shall be enforced, restrained, molested, or burdened in his body or goods, nor shall otherwise suffer, on account of his religious opinions or belief; but that all men shall be free to profess, and by argument to maintain, their opinions in matters of religion and that the same shall in no wise diminish, enlarge, or affect their civil capacities."

The conciseness to which Governor Montague has referred is well illustrated in this statute. Read it over. There is not a superfluous word, and yet there is enough to guard religious liberty. It is not strange that this doctrine so well set forth by Jefferson more than a century ago, is now a part of the constitution or bill of rights of every state of this Union. Not only is that today the law of this land, but it is spreading throughout the world. It was only a few weeks ago that the czar of Russia issued a decree in which he acknowledged the right of all the subjects of his empire to worship God according to the dictates of their own consciences. And, my friends, I believe that when we come to measure the relative importance of things, the importance of an act like that, the very foundation upon which we build religious liberty, the importance of an act like that which, gradually spreading, has become the creed of eighty millions of people, and is ultimately to become the creed of all the world—when we come to consider the vast importance of a thing like that, how can we compare lands or earthly possessions with it?

In the preamble to this statute Jefferson set forth the main reasons urged by those who believed in religious freedom. Let me call attention to some of the more important ones. He said, in the first place, that to attempt to compel people to accept a religious doctrine, by act of law, was to make, not Christians, but hypocrites. That was one of the reasons, and it was a strong one. He said, too, that there was no earthly judge who was competent to sit in a case and try a man for his religious opinions, for the judgement of the court, he said, would not be a judgment of law, but would be the personal opinion of the judge. What could be more true? No man who has religious convictions himself bears them so lightly that he can lay them aside and act as a judge when another man's religious convictions are involved. Then he suggested—and I think that I am justified in elaborating upon this suggestion a moment—that religion does not need the support of government to enable it to overcome error. Let me read the exact words, for I can not change them without doing injury to them:

And finally, that truth is great and will prevail if left to herself; that she is the proper and sufficient antagonist of error, and has nothing to fear from the conflict unless by human interposition disarmed of her natural weapons—free argument and debate; errors ceasing to be dangerous when it is permitted freely to contradict them.

Tell me that Jefferson lacked reverence for religion! He rather lacks reverence who believes religion is unable to defend herself in a contest with error. He places a low estimate upon the strength of religion, who thinks that the wisdom of God must be supplemented by the force of man's puny arm.

Jefferson paid a tribute to the power of truth when he said that truth was able to overcome error in the open field; and it was this sublime confidence in the triumph of truth that distinguished him from many of the other great men of his time. In fact, of all the men who have lived upon this earth I know of no man who has surpassed Jefferson in his confidence in the ultimate triumph of truth; and, my friends, upon what can people build if not upon faith in truth? Take from man his belief in the triumph of that which is right and he builds upon the sand. Give a man an abiding faith in the triumph of that which is true, and you give him the foundation of a moral character that can withstand all temptation.

It was this belief in the triumph of truth that made Jefferson favor free discussion, not only in religion, but in everything; and one of the virtues of Jefferson was that he was consistent in applying his principles to all questions. I am not one of those who beleive that Jefferson was inconsistent when he advocated the Louisiana purchase. He was in doubt whether the language of the constitution, unamended, was such as to authorize the purchase of this territory; but never for a moment did he think that there was anything in the constitution, in its letter or its spirit, to confine the United States to the original states. When he bought the territory his first thought was to ask for an amendment to the constitution that would expressly ratify the act. But when the question was discussed it was found that his act was so universally approved that it was not considered necessary even to ask for an amendment. I do not believe that the purchase was inconsistent with any principle he had ever advocated or with any utterance that he had ever made. I repeat that one of the virtues of Jefferson was that he was consistent in applying his principles no matter where those principles led him.

The same doctrine that he applied to religion he applied to the press—and I suppose no American, certainly not one who lived before the time of Andrew Jackson—ever had more reason than Jefferson to find fault with the untrue utterances of the press. Yet, so great was his faith in the triumph of the truth, and so willing was he to have error presented if truth could only be left free to combat it, that he was opposed to censorship of the press, and I believe that he gave expression to the strongest eulogy of the press that any statesman has ever uttered, when he said that if he must choose between a government without newspapers, and newspapers without a government, he would prefer to risk the newspapers without a government. He said that public opinion would measurably correct things if public opinion was left free; but that a government without the free expression of public opinion would soon become a despotism.

In the preamble to the statute for religious freedom Jefferson put first that which I want to speak of last. It was that the regulation of the opinions of men on religious questions by law was contrary to the laws of God and the plans of God. He pointed out that God had it in His power to control man's mind and body, but that He did not see fit to coerce the mind or the body into obedience to even the Divine will; and that if God Himself was not willing to use coercion to force man to accept certain religious views, man uninspired and liable to error ought not to use the means that Jehovah would not employ. Jefferson realized that our religion is a religion of love and not a religion of force.

There has recently been published a little book called The Jeffersonian Bible, and in the forepart of that book there is a letter, written by Jefferson in reply to an inquiry, in which he states his estimate of the teachings of Christ as compared with the philosophies of other religious teachers, and he shows the superiority of the philosophy of the Nazarene in that, while other philosophies have dealt with man's conduct, Christ's philosophy purifies the fountain at its source—cleanses the heart.

He recognized that our religion is a religion of the heart, that it is propagated from heart to heart; and he recognized, too that the heart controls human life. Jefferson was great in his intellect. I know of no mind that our nation has produced that could express itself with more clearness, or with more logic; but I believe that there was in Jefferson that which was greater than his head. It was his heart. Greater than his intellect was his love for all mankind.

It has been said that it marks an epoch in history when God lets loose a thinker in the world. God let lose a thinker when Jefferson was born. But Carlyle, who says that thought is stronger than artillery-parks; that thought moulds the world like soft clay; that it writes and unwrites laws, makes and unmakes parliaments—Carlyle adds that back of every great thought is love; that love is the ruling force in the world. I believe it is true. I believe that Jefferson's greatness rests more upon his love of humankind than upon his intellect—great as was his intellect—and that he was great because his heart was big enough to embrace the world. And the people loved him "because he first loved them." He wanted our religion to rest on the basis of love and not on the basis of force; and, my friends, when we get down to the root of our government, and the root of our religion, we find that they alike rest on the doctrine of human brotherhood—"that all men are created equal," "that they are endowed by their Creator with certain inalienable rights," rights that government did not give, rights that government cannot take away; that the object of government is to secure to the individual the enjoyment of his inalienable rights and that governments derive "their just powers from the consent of the governed." But all of these things rest upon that conception of human brotherhood which one cannot have unless he has the love that is back of every great thought. I believe that, when Jefferson assisted in establishing religious freedom, he assisted in giving to our government its strongest support. Chain the conscience, bind the heart, and you can not have for the support of our form of government the strength and the enthusiasm it deserves. But let conscience be free to commune with its God, let the heart be free to send forth its love, and the conscience and the heart will be the best defenders of a government resting upon the consent of the governed.

I believe that Jefferson gave a complete theory of government when he gave us the doctrine of the Declaration of Independence, and he gave us the two great supports of free government when he gave us universal education and an unfettered conscience. I am glad that this association is going to erect a monument to his memory. I say going to erect it, because I can not believe that the American people need more than an opportunity to contribute to insure their contribution. I want this monument to be in keeping with the services of the man. I want it to stand as high as the monuments erected to warriors, I want it to testify to the world that the heroes of peace are as great as the heroes of war; that those who save human life are as great as those who take it, even though they take it in defense of a righteous cause. I want this monument to testify that a man can live for his country as well as die for his country.

But, my friends, anxious as I am that this association shall erect a monument worthy of Jefferson, I thank God that Jefferson's memory needs no marble or bronze to perpetuate it. Erect your monument as high as you can, make it of material as enduring as you may, time will destroy it; the years will come and go, and at last that monument will disappear; but there is in the hearts of the people a monument that time can not touch, and this monument, growing as the world grows, increasing as civilization increases, is a greater monument than the hand of man can rear. And as people measure the influence of Jefferson upon the destinies of the human race, they will be convinced that the Bible is true when it says that it is "more blessed to give than to receive," for he gave the largest measure of service that man ever gave to man.

ENFORCING INSTRUCTIONS.

The following bill has been introduced in the Pennsylvania legislature by E. M. Herbst, a democratic senator from Burks county:

Section 1. Be it enacted, etc., That in all cases where a person is elected or chosen or shall act as a delegate to any convention to make nominations for offices and who shall have been previously instructed by his constituency at any primary or special election, nominating convention or other organic branch of any party organization where such instructions are not inconsistent one with the other, to vote for a certain candidate, said delegate shall vote for said candidate, so long as the said candidate shall be a candidate before the said convention, and failure to so do shall be a misdemeanor punishable as hereinafter provided.

Sec. 2. That in all cases where a person is elected or chosen or shall act as a delegate to any convention to make nominations for offices and who shall have been previously instructed by his constituency at any primary or special election, nominating convention or other organic branch of any party organization, and where such instructions conflict and are inconsistent one with the other, then the instructions by the primary or special election polling the largest vote shall be deemed the binding one, and said delegate shall vote for said candidate so long as he shall be a candidate before said convention.

Sec. 3. Any person who shall violate any of the provisions of this act shall be guilty of a misdemeanor and shall upon conviction thereof be sentenced to pay a fine of five hundred dollars and undergo an imprisonment not exceeding two years and shall be disfranchised for the period of five years.

Sec. 4. All the acts or parts of acts inconsistent with the provisions of this act are hereby repealed.

This bill is the outgrowth of a very palpable case of misrepresentation. In the republican convention of last year a number of delegates who had been instructed to vote for John P. Elkin for governor were in some way brought to the support of Judge Pennypacker, who at the last moment became the Quay candidate. While the Pennypacker nomination brought this question prominently before the people of that state, there have been other instances of it and these cases have not all been confined to the republican party.

The principle involved in the bill is a correct one. According to the democratic theory of government a delegate represents not himself, but his constitutents, and a misrepresentation of his constituents is a blow at representative government. It is not sufficient to say that the people have it in their power to vote against one nominated by unfair means, but it ought not to be necessary to elect one of an opposite party in order to correct such mistakes. Even the fact that the people have it in their power to retaliate by defeating the candidate nominated is no excuse for the man who violates his instructions. We do not excuse a crime because it may be possible for the loser to recover the stolen goods.

The country needs to be awakened to a more active appreciation of the duties and responsibilities of citizenship and the punishment of a few who betray their trust and who would embezzle or convert to their own use the power intrusted to them, will have a salutary influence.

SPEAKING OF MARPLOTS.

The Boston *Herald* in a recent issue complains that Mr. Bryan is acting the part of "a marplot." This is so serious a charge that the editor will be pardoned if he devotes a little time to it. The Standard Dictionary defines a marplot as "one who, by meddlesome interference, mars or frustrates a design or plan." It is evident to all that one must understand something of the plan or design to be frustrated before he can pass judgment upon the merits of the attempt to frustrate it. If, for instance, a group of persons should plan to do injury to an innocent person, to a city or to a country, it would hardly be fair to denounce as a marplot one who frustrated such a design or plan. The term "marplot" can be properly applied only to one who not only meddles with affairs which do not concern him, but interferes in the carrying out of some good plan or thwarts some laudable effort. What is Mr. Bryan doing to earn the name of marplot?

The *Herald* attempts a sketch of Mr. Bryan's career. The following is an extract:

"Now, how did this come to be? It is one of the most curious manifestations of modern politics. About a dozen years ago William J. Bryan was a clever young democratic representative in congress from a newer western state, a state that no one expected to see furnish a candidate to the presidency from any party in this generation. He did not stay long in that body, being defeated by a republican competitor.

Then he transferred his allegiance—or, at least, a good part of it—to another, the populist party. The populist party, having in effect taken possession of the democratic party in his locality, sent him to the democratic national convention, in which he made a speech so electrifying in its eloquence that it drew the presidential lightning upon him and made him the party candidate for the presidency."

It will be noticed that Mr. Bryan's first crime was to come from one of the newer western states—"a state that no one expected to see furnish a candidate to the presidency from any party in this generation." It was perfectly proper that Maine, with less population than Nebraska, should furnish a candidate for the presidency, although Maine was in one corner of the country, but Nebraska, almost in the geographical center of the country and much nearer to the center of population than Maine, was not expected to take a prominent part for a generation yet.

The editor of the *Herald* next informs the public that Mr. Bryan did not stay in congress because he was "defeated by a republican competitor." Mr. Bryan served in congress for two terms, and was not a candidate for re-election, but instead became a candidate for the United States senate, being the unanimous choice of the democratic state convention. The editor of the *Herald* then asserts that the populist party sent Mr. Bryan to a democratic national convention. He either knows better, or convicts himself of an ignorance that would be surprising if manifested by the editor of any other paper than the *Herald*. Mr. Bryan was never a member of the populist party, was never a delegate to a populist convention, and was never nominted for office by the populist party until he was nominated by the populist party two weeks after he had received the democratic presidential nomination. In Nebraska the democrats and populists have co-operated in the selection of state officers, congressmen and senators, but before they had ever united on a state ticket they united in the election of William V. Allen to the United States senate, and this action was recommended by the democratic steering committee of the United States senate. It may be added that Mr. Cleveland's secretary of agriculture advocated co-operation between democrats and populists in 1890, two years before Senator Allen was elected. Most of the democrats of Nebraska, by the direct and specific instructions of Mr. Cleveland's national committee, voted for the populist electors of 1892 for the purpose of taking the state out of the hands of the republicans. It was confessedly impossible to elect the democratic electors, and as the house of representatives was democratic, the national committee very wisely planned to throw the election into the house in case it was impossible to secure a majority in the electoral college. So much for the *Herald's* attempt at history.

The *Herald* proceeds to commend Mr. Bryan for the manner in which he conducted himself in the two campaigns, and then laments the change which it thinks it discerns in his conduct. It says:

"We hardly recognize the amiable, and aside from his capital error in participating in the free silver delusion, this discreet Mr. Bryan in the man that he has since become, and who is now addressing the public. His modesty has departed, and his discretion has vanished with it. His amiability has given place to resentment and something resembling rancor toward those who he thinks have thwarted his purposes. We can not believe he fully realizes it himself, but in his present attitude he is like a man who, having failed to continue to rule the party that he lately represented, has now set himself to ruin it. His later position toward the democrats is that of a marplot—a marplot who is determined that as far as he has influence it shall be exerted to prevent union upon any policy that does not render party defeat inevitable."

Mr. Bryan was nominated for the presidency by a convention more truly democratic than any other convention in recent years. The platform eminated from the voters. While the phraseology of the platform, so far as the money question was concerned, was practically the same as the phraseology of the Nebraska platform two years before, the fact that this phraseology was indorsed by a large majority of the voters of the party made it their platform rather than the platform of any state or individual. Certainly no one will charge that the delegates to the national convention were influenced in making the nomination by anything other than their own judgment. They may have erred in judgment, but they were under no coercion whatever either in writing the platform or in the nomination of the ticket.

During the campaign Mr. Bryan spoke in defense of the principles enunciated in the platform, and whatever strength he acquired was not a personal strength, but a strength due entirely to the priciples for which he stood. As soon as the election was over he announced his purpose to continue the fight for those principles, and between that day and the date of the next national convention he visited all parts of the country, everywhere discussing and defending the Chicago platform.

When the action of the republican party brought the question of imperialism before the country, he immediately took a position upon it, making a speech against a colonial policy on June 14, 1898, before any party or association had spoken on the subject. This question he treated as an additional one rather than as a substitute for any of the other questions before the country. When the time came for the holding of the state conventions it was found that with two exceptions every sate and territory instructed for his renomination. As this nomination came to him in spite of the misrepresentations, criticisms and protests of the papers which, like the Boston *Herald*, opposed the ticket in 1896, he was constrained to believe that the people still adhered to the principles that he advocated, and still repudiated the sordid and mercenary arguments of commercialism advanced by the plutocratic press which, although claiming to be independent or democratic, defended the republican position on most questions.

It is often asserted by the metropolitan papers that Mr. Bryan prevented a repudiation of the Chicago platform at Kansas City. The fact is, that the delegates at Kansas City were nearly all of them selected by conventions that reaffrmed the Chicago platform, and the only question that excited debate at Kansas City was whether the silver plank should be reiterated or simply reaffirmed. As an honest reaffirmation meant the same as reiteration, no one could strenuously oppose the latter if he sincerely favored the former, and all that Mr.

Bryan did at Kansas City was to say that a reaffirmation intended not to reaffirm but to abandon the question was not a fair treatment of the subject, and that if the convention desired to ignore the money question it should select candidates who were willing to carry out such a program. He did not attempt to control the convention, but he did insist upon his right to control his own conduct and upon his right to refuse a nomination if he could not conscientiously indorse the platform.

The convention made imperialism the paramount issue, and while the party's position on the money question was not abandoned Mr. Bryan and all the other speakers spent the greater part of the time in discussing imperialism. It is a common practice for the plutocratic press to charge the defeat of the party to the money plank. This is neither true nor is it honest. In 1900 the republican party had the advantage of having carried on a successful war, and it had the further advantage of being in power during a period of good crops and increasing currency. The result of the election showed that the democratic leaders gave too little rather than too much time to the discussion of the money question, for the improved industrial conditions which followed the increase in the currency vindicated the party's position on the money question and showed how much greater the advantage would have been could silver have been added to the gold supply.

We are now preparing for the campaign of 1904, and the reorganizers, not satisfied with Mr. Bryan's announcement that he will not be a candidate, insist that he must either indorse the views of those who are responsible for the party's defeat in recent campaigns or, at least, keep silent while they plan the emasculation of the platform and the demoralization of the party. Is it meddlesome for Mr. Bryan to take part in politics? Does the fact that he has been a candidate for the presidency impose silence upon him? He is only forty-three; if he lives forty years longer he will witness ten more presidential campaigns. Must he be a mute observer of what transpires from now on, merely because he can not agree with the men who in a great crisis voted the republican ticket, and the neswpapers which for business reasons supported the republican ticket? This would be a high price to pay for a nomination to any office.

The responsibilities of citizenship rest upon Mr. Bryan as much as upon the bolting democrats in general or upon the bolting editors in particular. It would not be presumptuous to say that Mr. Bryan's responsibility is even greater than the responsibility of those who question his right to discuss present issues. Responsibility is measured by opportunity, and if Mr. Bryan has had an opportunity to know the purposes as well as the plans of those who, failing to destroy the democratic party from without are now trying to destroy it from within, could he excuse himself if he hid himself under the cover of two nominations rather than subject himself to the venom and detraction of those editors who bend the suppliant knee to organized wealth? Who is under greater obligation to the rank and file of the democratic party than Mr. Bryan? And who has more reason than he to co-operate with them in the gigantic task of defending the wealth-producers against the attacks of exploiters and monopolists?

The *Herald* belongs to that class of papers which pretends great solicitude for the welfare of party. Has not Mr. Bryan shown as much solicitude for the welfare of the party as those who have aided and contributed to the enemy?

The reorganizers assume that the men who supported the Chicago and Kansas City platorms are ready to go back and apologize for their party's position. This is a groundless assumption, and is known to be so by those who make the assumption. There has been no change among the voters; those who were opposed to a financial system made by the financiers for the financiers, are still opposed to such a system; those who were opposed to a high tariff, even when the reorganizers were supporting a high-protectionist for the presidency, are still against a high tariff. Those who were opposed to the trusts, even when the leading reorganizers were helping to elect an administration pledged to the trusts, are still against the trusts; those who opposed government by injunction, even when the leading reorganizers were helping the corporations that rely upon government by injunction, are still opposed to this tyrannical process of the court; those who opposed imperialism, even when the leading reorganizers were willing to surrender the Declaration of Independence at the demand of Wall street, are still opposing the separation of our people into citizens and subjects.

If Mr. Bryan were to remain silent in order to escape hostile criticism, his silence would not change the convictions of those who voted for him; if he were openly to join the reorganizers and proclaim a conversion to the opinions of those who seek to republicanize the democratic party, he could not carry a dozen men into the opposition camp. He would simply forfeit the confidence and excite the contempt of those who have supported him. The contest between democracy, on the one side and plutocracy on the other, is still on, and the result of that contest means much for weal or woe to the American people. The democratic party ought to be kept democratic in order that it may be an efficient instrument in the hands of the people for the protection of the people's rights. Those who believe in the Kansas City platform are not ashamed of the part that they have played, and they do not intend to surrender the control of the party into the hands of those who have openly antagonized those principles and who boast of their intention, if successful, to take the party back to the position which it occupied under Mr. Cleveland's administration. All that the friends of the Kansas City platform ask is that all questions be submitted to the voters in order that the policy may be determined by the voters, and to this end they propose to organize and marshall their forces at the primaries. They know by bitter experience that they have powerful and cunning enemies to meet—enemies who are not only in close and constant communication with the monopolists in trade and finance, but who will employ republican methods of coercion, deception and corruption wherever those methods can be employed. No amount of abuse or villification will deter the friends of the Kansas City platform, for they have an interest in the preservation of their party's virtue and in the protection of their country from the assaults of predatory wealth.

THE VOTING MACHINE.

Some time ago the Chicago *Record-Herald* contained an article by a special correspondent who gave a description of a voting machine which has been successfully tried at Rochester, N. Y. The article is given in full on another page, THE COMMONER being an advocate of this method of voting.

Election-day frauds are, generally speaking, due to the corruption of the judges or to repeating. Of these the corruption of the judges is the most difficult to detect and punish. The voting machine, when perfected, as the one described in the article seems to have been, is a sure preventive of corruption. The ballot is secret and the voter is free from intimidation, and then, too, and it is a very important advantage, the result of the vote is announced at once so that there can be no changing afterwards as is often the case where remote precincts are held back until it is known how many votes are needed to decide the contest. The people generally, in their calmer moments, are anxious for honest elections, and men who might in a moment of temptation yield to the desire to gain a party advantage will, when they can consider the question dispasionately, support any reform that guarantees a correct expression of the public will. Although the voting machine is somewhat of a reflection upon the honesty of judges it is likely to grow because of the justifiable desire of the people to avoid temptation for fear of not being able to withstand it.

Registration has been adopted in nearly all the cities as a precaution against repeating, but it has not proven entirely successful. It may become necessary to provide that voters shall assemble at a certain time in all the precincts and remain in the voting places until they have voted. By fixing two hours, one in the forenoon and one in the afternoon, it will be possible to accommodate every one, and yet make it impossible for a crowd of repeaters to be sent from precinct to precinct. This may occupy a little time, but surely self-government is valuable enough to justify a citizen in giving half a day to the service of his country and to the protection of his own rights.

The *Record-Herald* article is commended to the careful consideration of all who desire to purify politics, and the editor of THE COMMONER assumes that all of his readers belong to this class.

TRUTH OMNIPOTENT.

The time-serving politicians and the "anything-to-win" democrats who call it wisdom to fall in with the crowd and to accept as final the insolent boastings of commercialism and plutocracy, will find food for thought in the last volume of the French Revolution. In Chapter VII, entitled "The Whiff of Grape-Shot" Carlyle testifies to the omnipotence of truth. "Hast thou considered how Thought is stronger than Artillery-parks, and (were it fifty years after death and martyrdom, or were it two thousand years) writes and unwrites Acts of Parliament, removes mountains; models the world like soft clay? Also how the beginning of all Thought worth the name is Love; and the wise head never yet was, without first the generous heart? The Heavens cease not their bounty; they send us generous hearts into every generation. And now what generous heart can pretend to itself, or be hoodwinked into believing, that Loyalty to the Moneyy-bag is a noble Loyalty? Mammon, cries the generous heart out of all ages and countries, is the basest of known gods, even of known devils. In him what glory is there, that he should worship him? No glory discernible; not even terror; at best, detestability, ill-matched with despicability!" If the democratic party is to build upon a permanent foundation it must recognize the fact that truth alone can give to the pary hope of perpetuity, and that back of all thought must be love. Deep love for the common people and belief in human brotherhood will make the democratic party an invincible force. Unless the party is an exponent of thought and truth; unless it is built upon love—not self love, but brotherly love—it can not hope for more than temporary and trifling success. Democracy when rightly understood is a religion, for it is founded upon the doctrine of equal and inalienable rights. Let no sacrilegious hand drag the party down to the sordid plain of Mammon worship.

ROOSEVELT'S ST. LOUIS SPEECH.

The president's speech at the dedication of the St. Louis exposition is mainly important, first, because of his failure to emphasize Jefferson's connection with the purchase. He only referred to Jefferson once in the entire speech, and then only incidentally. In mentioning the trans-Mississippi country he speaks of "this great region acquired for our people under the presidency of Jefferson." One would suppose that so important an addition to our territory would have justified the president in giving some slight praise to the man whose foresight and statesmanship led him to see at an early date the importance of making the trans-Mississippi country a part of the American republic.

The second thing noticeable in the speech was his attempt to turn the occasion to partisan advantage. The whole burden of his speech was expansion, expansion, expansion. The entire speech was an effort to justify the Philippine policy of the United States without expressly mentioning it. He started in by declaring that the Louisiana purchase determined that we should be a "great expanding nation, instead of relatively a small and stationary one." He said: "This work of expansion was by far the greatest work of our people during the years that intervened between the adoption of the constitution and the outbreak of the civil war;" that "our triumph in this process of expansion was indissolubly bound up with the success of our peculiar kind of federal government;" that "only the adventurous and far-seeing can be expected to welcome the process of expansion, for the nation that expands is a nation which is entering upon a great career, and with greatness there must of necessity come perils which daunt all save the most stout-hearted," etc.

He took occasion to discuss the different forms of colonization, condemning both the Greek and the Roman forms.

Greece, he explained, formed colonies, but each colony as created became entirely independent of the mother state, and in after years often an enemy. "Local self-government, local independence," he said, "was secured, but only by the absolute sacrifice of everything representing national unity." "National power and greatness were completely sacrificed to local liberty." Rome, he asserted, did exactly the opposite. "The imperial city rose to absolute dominion over all the peoples of Italy, and then expanded her rule over the entire civilized world by a process which kept the nation strong and united, but gave no room whatever for local liberty and self-government. All other cities and countries were subject to Rome. In consequence this great masterful race of warriors, rulers, road-builders and administrators stamped their indelible impress upon the after-life of our race, and yet let an overcentralization eat out the vitals of their empire until it became an empty shell, so that when the barbarians came they destroyed only what had become worthless to the world."

He then explained the American plan of making each acquisition a component part of the whole. "We," he said, "expanded by carving the wilderness into territories, and out of these territories building new states when once they had received as permanent settlers a sufficient number of our own people. Being a practical nation we have never tried to force on any section of our new territory an unsuitable form of government merely because it was suitable to another section under different conditions. Of the territory covered by the Louisiana purchase a portion was given statehood within a few years. Another portion has not been admitted to statehood, although a century has elapsed—although doubtless it soon will be. In each case we showed the practical governmental genius of our race by devising methods suitable to meet the actual existing needs; not by insisting upon the application of some abstract shibboleth to all our new possessions alike, no matter how incongruous this application might sometimes be."

It will be noticed that in commending the system of expansion which our nation has heretofore followed he endeavors to work in an indirect defense of the policy which the administration has adopted in the Orient. It is evident that his reference to "some abstract shibboleth" is intended as a rebuke to those who insist upon the application of American principles to the Philippine question, and yet the Roman example which he condemns is really like our present Philippine policy.

The expansion of Jefferson was a totally different thing from imperialism. First, it included land not only contiguous to the United States, but so situated that its occupancy by an unfriendly nation would have seriously hampered the growth of our country. Second, it was a sparsely settled and uncultivated territory. Third, it was to be settled by our own people, and made a part of the United States. The Philippine islands are not only not near us, but are so remote from us and so situated as to be a source of weakness rather than a source of strength. Instead of being sparsely settled the population per square mile is greater in the Philippine islands than in the United States, which means that if we add the Philippines to our land, and their people to our people, there would be fewer acres for each citizen than there are today. Third, and most important, the Philippine islands are not to be settled by Americans, as the Louisiana territory was, but, if imperialism is to prevail, to be ruled by the Americans as Rome ruled her subjects. It will never be possible to make eight millions submit willingly to the government of a few thousand. At least, there is not a single example in history to justify the belief that they will welcome a foreign ruler. Canada, Australia and New Zealand can not be cited in defense of our present policy in the Philippines, first, because the inhabitants of these English colonies are largely descendants of Englishmen, and therefore attached to England by ties of blood, and, second, because England does not attempt to make their laws for them or to tax them. If England attempted to do in Canada, Australia or New Zealand what we are now doing in the Philippines, she would not hold the colonies long, notwithstanding the blood relationship.

The president persistently refuses to consider the real

question involved in the Philippine policy, namely, the theory of government to be applied. Is this an "abstract shibboleth?" Our home government rests upon the theory set forth in the Declaration of Independence, our colonial policy rests upon the European theory of government which our revolutionary patriots successfully resisted. A colonial government would ultimately destroy the doctrine of self-government in the United States, for we could not permanently assert the principles of the Declaration of Independence here and deny them abroad. If, on the other hand, the present policy in the Philippines is only intended to be temporary, if the purpose is to make the Philippine islands a part of the United States as the Louisiana purchase was made a part, and the Filipinos citizens, as the inhabitants of the Louisiana territory were made citizens, then while avoiding danger to our theory of government we would encounter another danger which is appalling, namely, the demoralizing influence of Filipino states upon our government and destiny. The Filipinos are separarated from us by an ocean which places them in another hemisphere and adjacent to other nations. Their history, race and language, make it impossible for them to act intelligently upon our affairs, or for us to act intelligently upon their affairs, and the objections to incorporation are so great that nearly all the republicans who voted for the ratification of the treaty voted for a resolution which declared that the Philippine islands were not to become an integral part of the United States.

While the president talks of expansion and intimates that a nation must continue to grow in territory if it is to be a great nation, he avoids the vital questions raised by his Philippine policy. His argument in regard to the necessity of continuing expansion is absurd, for it means that the United States must continue to take in new territory until it has all there is in the world, and then must die because there are no more worlds to conquer. Constant expansion is not essential to greatness.

Every proposed extension of our territory must rest upon its own merits, and in deciding whether it is wise or unwise, we must consider both the wishes of our own people and the wishes of the people to be incorporated. Our system of national unity, combined with local self-government, makes it possible for the United States to include an indefinite area of land so long as the people are homogeneous, but it is essential that the national unity shall be not merely a unity in government, but a unity in sympathy and in purpose. Jefferson regarded the North American continent as the natural home of the American republic. He believed that we could extend our borders throughout North America without endangering our form of government. Our theory of government is applicable to all the world, but it is far better that there should be several separate republics administering their own affairs and arbitrating their differences, than one republic with elements so antagonistc as to be warring with each other.

Our nation has demonstrated the correctness of our theory of government and it has inspired other nations to attempt the same experiment. It ought never to weaken its influence by a policy that casts suspicion upon its faith in equal rights and self-government. Our nation is under no compulsion to sacrifice its own ideals, even if by doing so it could hope to force undesired blessings upon a resisting people. Experience shows, however, that you can help people by raising their ideals, not by crushing their aspirations. The expansion of Jefferson was democratic and entirely in keeping with our form of government; republican imperialism is antagonistic to every principle of a republic and a menace to the nation's welfare.

DOES IT DARE ANSWER?

The Nashville *American* seems to resent the suggestion made by THE COMMONER that it is a republican paper in disguise. It responds in the following choice language:

Yet there is a wild ass of the Nebraska plains who with the practiced ease of an untruthful pen and a slanderous lip denounces as republican organs and subservient tools of monopoly those newspapers which have the intelligence and the courage to declare against a continuation of the absolute folly which has led the party into such disaster. The unfairness, the injustice, the downright falsehood of such charges ought to condemn their author to the perpetual and profound contempt of the general public.

If THE COMMONER has done the *American* injustice it will be glad to acknowledge the same, but it does not believe that the *American* has been misrepresented. To settle the question the following offer is made: If the *American* will publish upon its editorial page the names of its three largest stockholders, with the amount of their holdings, their business and sources of income, and state how they voted in the national elections of 1896 and 1900, and will also give the names of its three most prominent editorial writers, and state how they voted in those elections, THE COMMONER will be glad to republish such an editorial and withdraw its charges if the *American's* own statement shows that those who control its policy and speak through its columns are really democrats and in sympathy with the general public. Surely the *American* ought not to be ashamed to reveal the identity of those who own it and speak for it.

WHY SILVER IS COINED.

A reader of THE COMMONER asks by what law silver is coined since the repeal of the Sherman law. The government is now coining (has almost finished) the seigniorage that accumulated under the Sherman law. The Sherman law provided that silver should be bought at the market price and certificates issued therefor. The difference between the market price and the coinage price was called seigniorage and was held as silver bullion. The Sherman law also provided that so much of the purchased silver should be coined as was necessary to redeem certificates presented. The act of 1898 required the coinage of the seigniorage and also the coinage of the silver held for the redemption of the Sherman certificates.

When this silver is coined coinage will cease, as there is now no provision for the purchase of further silver except for subsidiary coinage. A bill passed the lower house of the last congress authorizing the recoinage of silver dollars into subsidiary coin. If this bill ever becomes a law it will make it unnecessary for the government to buy silver for a century to come, and at the same time the volume of standard money will be reduced to the extent that the silver dollars are recoined into fractional currency.

THREE QUESTIONS ANSWERED.

A reader of THE COMMONER asks three questions:

First—What provision is made to insure retirement of national bank notes when the bonds upon which they are issued have matured or have been redeemed?

Second—Can any state bank issue notes for circulation within the borders of the state?

Third—Would it be possible for the banks to organize a boycott against silver and silver certificates in case silver was restored?

Answer to the first: If the bank is using bonds at the time of the maturity of the bonds it can withdraw them and substitute other bonds. As bank notes today rest upon bonds they would have to be retired if all the bonds were redeemed and cancelled.

Answer to the second: A state bank can issue notes, but those notes are subject to a 10 per cent tax. It was intended to be prohibitory and has proven so.

Answer to the third: The banks would not find it to their interest to boycott silver. The banks are so dependent upon the government that they could not afford, and would not attempt, to oppose the policy of the party in power.

GOOD ROADS.

Speech Delivered by Mr. Bryan, April 28, 1903, at the Good Roads Convention, Held at St. Louis, Missouri.

I desire, in the first place, to acknowledge my obligation to your president, Mr. Moore, for his efforts to enlighten me on this subject. He came out to Nebraska some three or four weeks ago and urged upon me the importance of attending this meeting. I have learned more about good roads from him and from the literature that he has brought to my attention, than I ever knew before.

I have become exceedingly interested in this subject, as I have studied it. In fact, I have been thinking how many questions there are that enlist the thought and arouse the interest of those who seek to do something for their fellowmen. If we attend a meeting of home missionaries, we are surprised to find how much need there is in this country for home missionary work; and after we have listened to the speeches made at such meetings we make up our mind that the work of the home missionary is an exceedingly important work. If we attend a meeting of the foreign missionary society we are amazed to find what a large world this is, how much sacrifice has been made by foreign missionaries, and how extended is their field of labor. If we attend an educational meeting, and hear great educators speak, we wonder that we could have been so ignorant of the great forces at work for the uplifting of our people, and we are astonished to find how many people there are, with all our schools, public and private, who are yet illiterate. And then, if we go to a prison congress and hear people talk about the various means of reforming people, why, we find that there is another wide field for energy. And so with many other kinds of work, not to speak of political work. And as I have gone from one of these meetings to another I have been more and more impressed with the largeness of the vineyard in which people can work if they really want to work. And then, when I read in the paper that someone has committed suicide because there was nothing for him in the world, I cannot help thinking that if one has a proper conception of life and measures it by its outflow and not by its income, he will find so much to do that he will never despair.

They tell us about the wonderful improvement in shipping. I was interested this morning when I heard of the launching of a boat that would carry eight thousand tons more than any other boat ever built. It gives us some idea of the magnitude of our foreign commerce. I was glad to hear them talk of the railroads; for in this country we have wonderful railroad development. But, my friends, nothing I have turned my attention to in the last few years has seemed to me to come nearer to the people than this question of good country roads. I find that there is a new field there, and I have already advanced so far that I have made up my mind to build a little road out near my farm, as an object lesson; and not only that, but to do what I can to get my county and my state to do something in the matter of roads.

I confess to you that this subject, this great subject, is one that I had scarcely thought of until Mr. Moore called it to my attention. And you know how a person's attention will be attracted to a thing—I might tell you the first thing in regard to it that challenged my attention; I asked him about how wide these roads ought to be? He said that about sixteen feet was the ordinary width—I remember that; that attracted my attention—sixteen feet to one road. When I got to reading up on the subject, I found it was not sufficient to have a road wide enough for one wagon; it had to be wide enough for wagons to pass; there must be room enough for two wagons to pass—a double standard road, so to speak. You can imagine how intensely interested I became in the matter.

Then I began to investigate, and I found a political reason for interesting myself in these roads that I have not heard mentioned by any speaker today—and, my friends, that is not a reflection upon the gentlemen who have spoken, because they have covered a wide range, and have said about all on this subject, it seems to me, that could be said. But, you know, our ideas become larger with our experience, and a thought has come to me in regard to these good roads that probably has not occurred to any of the rest of you. I do not claim any special originality in thinking of it, it simply shows that we learn from experience. In two campaigns I noticed that a great many of our people did not get out to vote, and it occurred to me that it might have been because the roads were not good enough. I have such confidence in the doctrines that I have been advocating that I am satisfied if the people had not been stuck in the mud they would have gone to the polls and voted for our ticket; and, therefore, I think I must commence a little further back. I think before trying to show people how they ought to vote, I must show them how they can get to the polls to vote. I have come to the conclusion that next to getting into the right road, it is important to have roads passable. I had to prepare this speech before I had time to read what others had said. And then, having prepared the speech, I was at liberty to read and find out what I ought to have said in the speech. I felt a little like a young man I knew in Southern Illinois: He studied medicine awhile and then quit and began practicing; he said he thought he would practice while he was young, and study when he was old and could not practice. I feel a good deal in the same position.

In going over this subject I jotted down certain things I wanted to submit for your consideration, and I assure you I am more interested in getting before you certain ideas, than I am in the manner of presenting those ideas. In fact, I have been so busy trying to present ideas that I fear I have neglected the matter of ornamentation.

The expenditure of money for the permanent improvement of the common roads can be defended, first, as a matter of justice to the people who live in the country; second, as a matter of advantage to the people who do not live in the country, and, third, on the ground that the welfare of the nation demands that the comforts of country life shall, as far as possible, keep pace with the comforts of city life.

It is a well-known fact, or a fact easily ascertained, that the people in the country, while paying their full share of county, state and federal taxes, receive as a rule only the general benefits of government, while the people in the cities have, in addition to the protection afforded by the government, the advantage arising from the expenditure of public moneys in their midst. The county seat of a county, as a rule, enjoys the refreshing influence of an expenditure of county money out of proportion to its population. The capital of a state and the cities where the state institutions are located, likewise receive the benefit of an expenditure of public money out of proportion to their population. When we come to consider the distribution of the moneys collected by the federal government we find that the cities, even in a larger measure, monopolize the incidental benefits that arise from the expenditure of public moneys.

The appropriations of the last session of congress amounted to $753,484,018, divided as follows:

Agriculture	$ 5,978,160
Army	78,138,752
Diplomatic and consular service	1,968,250
District of Columbia	8,647,497
Fortifications	7,188,416
Indians	8,512,950
Legislative, executive and judicial departments	27,595,958
Military academy	563,248
Navy	81,877,291
Pensions	139,847,600
Postoffice department	153,401,409
Sundry civil	82,722,955
Deficiencies	21,561,572
Permanent annual	132,589,820
Miscellaneous	3,250,000

It will be seen that the appropriation for the agricultural department was insignificant when compared with the total appropriations—less than one per cent. The appropriations for the army and navy alone amounted to twenty-five times the sum appropriated for the agricultural department. An analysis of the expenditures of the federal government will show that an exceedingly small proportion of the money raised from all the people gets back to the farmers directly; how much returns indirectly it is impossible to say, but certain it is that the people who live in the cities receive by far the major part of the special benefits that come from the showering of public money upon the community. The advantage obtained locally from government expenditures is so great that the contests for county seats and state capitals usually exceed in interest, if not in bitterness, the contests over political principles and policies. So great is the desire to secure an appropriation of money for local purposes that many will excuse a congressman's vote on either side of any question if he can but secure the expenditure of a large amount of public money in his district.

I mention this because it is a fact that I have not heard referred to. The point is, that the farmer not only pays his share of the taxes, but more than his share, yet very little of what he pays gets back to the farmer.

People in the city pay not only less than their share, as a rule, but get back practically all of the benefits that come from the expenditure of the people's money. Let me show you what I mean when I say that the farmer pays more than his share: The farmer has visible property, and in every form of direct taxation visible property pays more than its share. Why? Because the man with visible property always pays. If he has an acre of land the assessor can find it; if he has horses, they can be counted; his cattle can be enumerated. If he has pigs, they begin to squeal when the assessor approaches; he cannot hide them. The farmer has nothing that escapes taxation; and in all direct taxation, he not only pays on all he has, but the farmer who has visible property has to pay a large part of the taxes that ought to be paid by the owners of invisible property, who escape taxation.

And when we come to indirect taxation, the farmers' share is even more, because, when you collect taxes on consumption, you make people pay, not in proportion to what they have, but in proportion to what they need. And God has so made us that the farmer needs as much as anybody else, even though he may not have as much as other people with which to supply his needs. In our indirect taxation, therefore, for the support of the federal government, the farmer pays even more out of proportion to his wealth. And then, when we remember that when we collect taxes on consumption, we make the farmer pay not only on that which is imported, but upon much of that which is produced at home, we find that the farmer's burden is not measured by what the treasury reecives, but is frequently many times what the treasury receives. While in indirect taxation the burden upon the farmer is far greater than it ought to be, yet when you trace the expenditure of public moneys distributed by the federal government, you find that even in a larger measure special benefits go to the great cities and not to the rural communities. This point I desire to emphasize and make clear.

The improvement of the country roads can be justified also on the ground that the farmer, the first and most important of the producers of wealth, ought to be in position to hold his crop and market it at the most favorable opportunity, whereas at present he is virtually under compulsion to sell it as soon as it is matured, because the roads may become impassible at any time during the fall, winter or spring. Instead of being his own warehouseman, the farmer is compelled to employ middlemen, and share with them the profits upon his labor.

I believe as a matter of justice the farmer ought to have roads that will enable him to keep his crop and take it to the market at the best time; and not place him, as he is placed today, in a position where they can run down the price of what he has to sell just when he must sell, and then, when he has disposed of it, run the price up and give the speculator what the farmer ought to have.

The farmer has a right to insist upon roads that will enable him to go to town, to church, to the school house, and to the homes of his neighbors, as occasion may require, and with the extension of rural delivery he has an additional need for good roads in order that he may be kept in communication with the outside world.

A great deal has been said, and properly so, in regard to the influence of good roads upon education. In the meeting held at Raleigh, N. C., last year, the speeches which I had the pleasure of reading placed great emphasis upon the fact that it is impossible to have a school system such as we ought to have, unless the roads are in condition for the children to go to school. And Professor Jesse, in the excellent speech to which you listened this morning, also took this position. I hardly know whether to feel grateful to him or indignant that he presented one of the thoughts that I intended to suggest, yet, he presented it so much better than I could, that I think my gratitude overcomes my indignation.

I was thinking this morning, before I reached here, that while we are building great libraries in the cities, we do not have libraries in the country, and there ought to be a library in every community. Instead of laying upon the farmer the burden of buying his own books, we ought to make it possible for the farmers to have the same opportunity as the people in the cities, to use the same books, and thus economize on the expense of a library. But Professor Jesse brought that out, and not only spoke of the library that ought to be connected with the school house, but also mentioned another thing which I feel to be important, namely, the country high school. Have you ever thought what an advantage the child in a city has over the child in the country? Our country school houses teach the lower grades, but it is impossible in any community to have a high graded school with only a few students, except at great expense. In cities, when a child gets through the graded school, still living at home and without expense to himself or his parents, he is able to go on through the high school. But if the country boy or girl desires to go from the graded school to the high school, as a rule it is necessary to go to the county seat and there board with someone; so the expense to the country child is much greater than to the child in the city. I was glad, therefore, to hear Professor Jesse speak of such a consolidation of schools as will give to the children in the country advantage equal to those enjoyed by the children of the city.

And as you study this subject, you find it reaches out in every direction; that it touches us at every vital point. What can be of more interest to every parent than bringing instruction within the reach of every child? It does not matter whether a man has children himself or not. He may have a small family, like the graduates of Yale and Harvard are said to have (they average about three), or he may have a family large enough to excite the admiration of the president. No matter whether he has few children or many; every citizen of a community is interested in the intellectual life of that community. Sometimes I have heard people complain because, having few children, they thought themselves overburdened with taxes for the education of other people's children. My friends, the man who has no children cannot afford to live in a community where there are children growing up in ignorance; and the man with none has the same interest as the man with many, barring the personal pride of the parent.

Anything, therefore, that contributes to the general diffusion of knowledge, anything that makes more educated boys and girls throughout our country is a matter of intense interest to every citizen, whether he be the father of a family or not; whether he lives in the country or in the town.

And ought not the people to have an opportunity to attend church? Why, my friends, I am coming to believe that what we need in this country even more than the training of the intellect, is the development of the moral side of our natures. I believe with Jefferson, that the church and the state should be separate. I believe in religious freedom, and I would not have any man's conscience fettered by act of law. But I do believe that the welfare of this nation demands that man's moral nature shall be educated in keeping with his brain and his body. In fact, I have come to define civilization as the harmonious development of the body, the mind and the heart. And we make a mistake if we believe that this nation can fulfill its high destiny and mission, either with mere athletes, or even with scholars. We need the education of the moral sense. And if these good roads will enable men, women and children to go more frequently to church, and there hear expounded the gospel, and there receive the inspiration that comes from the holding up of the life of the Man of Gallilee, that alone is reason enough for good roads.

Then, too, I am satisfied that the people of the country do not have enough of social life. It is one of the things that we all should regret, that the extremes of society have been pushed so far apart, that some who think themselves at the top know nothing but society, while those who are declared to be at the bottom, know nothing of society.

Again, the people of the towns, especially the rural towns, are interested in making it possible for the people in the country to reach their local market or trading place during all times of the year, for, throughout the agricultural portion of the country, at least, the villages and the cities rest upon and derive their support from the farms.

I think I ought to make this plain. I once said in a speech (1896): "Burn down your cities and leave our farms, and your cities will spring up again as if by magic. But destroy our farms and grass will grow in the streets of every city in the country." I thought I was stating a truth; I never supposed it could be distorted, but when the election was over I received a dodger which had been circulated just before the election, saying in big letters: "Burn the cities," without anything else, and it was declared to be the utterance of "Anarchist Bryan." So I think it is necessary to qualify the statement a little and assure you that I do not want to destroy the cities; I simply want to remind you of a very patent fact, and that is, that the cities rest upon the country. That the farm is the life of the cities, and that especially in the agricultural communities the people in the cities are intensely and vitally interested in enabling the people of the country to get into the towns to do their trading. Sometimes I have heard country merchants express dissatisfaction because the people of the country sometimes buy of the mail order houses. If the country merchant wants to keep the trade at home let him help to make roads good between the patron and his store. That is the best way. He cannot expect that people who are prevented from going to town will refuse to utilize the best means of supplying their needs. I repeat that people in the town are interested in making it possible for the people of the country to get into town.

There is a broader view of this question, however, that deserves consideration. The farm is, and always has been, conspicuous because of the physical development it produces, the intellectual strength it furnishes and the morality it encourages. The young people in the country find health and vigor in the open air and in the exercise which farm life gives; they acquire habits of industry and economy; their work gives them opportunity for thought and reflection; their contact with nature teaches them reverence, and their environment promotes good habits. The farms supply our colleges with their best students and they also supply our cities with leaders in business and professional life. In the country there is neither great wealth nor abject poverty—"the rich and the poor meet together" and recognize that "the Lord is the Father of them all." There is a fellowship and, to use the word in its broadest sense, a democracy, in the country that is much needed today to temper public opinion and protect the foundations of free government. A larger percentage of the people in the country than in the city study public questions, and a smaller percentage either corrupt or are corrupted. It is important, therefore, for the welfare of our government and for the advancement of our civilization that we make life upon the farm as attractive as possible. Statistics have shown the constant increase in the urban population and the relative decrease in the rural population from decade to decade. Without treading upon controversial ground or considering whether this trend has been increased by legislation hostile to the farm, I may suggest that the government is in duty bound to jealously guard the interests of the rural population, and as far as it can, make farm life inviting. And it may be added, comfort is a relative rather than a positive term. Transportation by wagon did not seem slow until the steam engine made more rapid travel possible. The tallow candle seemed bright until it was dimmed by oil, gas and electricity; the flint and the steel were convenient enough until the friction match displaced them. In the employment of modern conveniences the city has considerably outstripped the country, and naturally so, for in a densely populated community the people can by co-operation supply themselves with water, light and rapid transit at much smaller cost than they can in a sparsely settled country. But it is evident that during the last few years much has been done to increase the comforts of the farm.

In the first place, the rural delivery has placed millions of farmers in daily communication with the world. It has brought not only the letter, but the newspaper to the door. Its promised enlargement and extension will make it possible for the wife to order from the village store and have her purchases delivered by the mail carrier.

The telephone is also a great boon to the farmer. It lessens by one-half the time required to secure a physician in case of accident or illness—an invention which every mother can appreciate. In a hundred ways it saves time and steps.

The improvements in the methods of manufacturing gas, and the invention of machines suitable for family use, must not be overlooked. It is now possible for every farmer to install at a small expense a gas plant sufficient for the production of the light necessary for his house. While the extension of the system of private water plants has not been quite so rapid, it is still very marked. Probably no one modern convenience enjoyed in the cites is more missed in the country than the water system that supplies the kitchen and the bath-room. No woman who lives, or visits awhile, in the city can return to the country without noticing the difference between the faucet and the pump.

The extension of the electric car line also deserves notice. It is destined to enlarge the limits of the city and to increase the number of one, two, five and ten-acre farms at the expense of flats and tenement houses. The suburban home will bring light and hope to millions of children.

But after all that has been done and is being done by the improvements above referred to, there still remains a pressing need for better country roads, a need emphasized and made more apparent by the pavement of city streets. As long as mud placed an embargo upon city traffic the farmer could bear his mud-made isolation with less complaint, but with the improvement of city streets and with the establishment of parks and boulevards, the farmers' just demand for better roads finds increasing expression.

Just to what extent action should be taken by the federal government, the state government, the county and the precinct, or in what proportion the burden should be borne is a question for discussion, but that country roads should be constructed with a view to permanent and continuous use is scarcely open to debate.

There must be a recognition of disease before there can be an intelligent discussion of a remedy; but when the disease is once located the people may be depended upon to find not only a remedy, but the right remedy. The people are beginning to realize that bad roads are indefensible and are prepared to consider the remedy. I have discussed simply the disease, and have tried to point out that we are not helping the farmer to keep up with the progress of the towns-people. I have tried to show that from every standpoint, from the farmer's standpoint, from the standpoint of the citizen of the town, and from the broader standpoint of the patriot, the farmer's interests must be looked after. And when this disease of bad roads is once understood, then you can trust the intelligence of the American people to do whatever is necessary. Meetings like this will not only emphasize the fact that bad roads are intolerable, but will bring out men who are interested in these questions, who have studied them, and can present remedies for your consideration. And I have such confidence in the patriotism and intelligence of the American people that I believe that in the clash of ideas and conflict of views, the best will always be triumphant, the people having the benefit of the combined wisdom of all the people.

In some countries the people have not the right to suggest, not even the right to pass upon a suggestion; but under our form of government the people not only have a right to sit in judgment upon every suggestion made, but have the right of suggestion; and in this "multitude of counsel there is safety."

THE PRICE OF SILVER.

The recent rise in the price of silver is being made the subject of discussion by a number of papers. The Chicago *Chronicle* says:

"The price of silver bullion has advanced about 3 cents per ounce during the last three months, and dealers are looking for a still further advance. The rise in the price is attributed in part to the purchases by our government for the Philippine coinage, and in part to a more active demand outside of the

United States. Inasmuch as the purchases for the Philippine coinage are not to exceed a million per month, the rise must be due mainly to outside demand."

The Cleveland *Leader*, speaking of the rise, says:

"The advance is attributed to the short supply and the heavy buying of the United States government, amounting to an average of 550,000 ounces weekly for use in the Philippines. In fact, it is declared, the market is heavily oversold, and there is little spot silver in Europe. Two years ago the decline was due to the heavy sales of silver by China to meet the claims of indemnity demanded by the powers."

The *Leader*, in the same editorial, insists that the price of silver in the markets of the world is regulated entirely by supply and demand, and has no connection with the prosperity of the people, and it asserts that "the theory that whether the people of the country were to prosper depended entirely upon the price of silver, appears to have been abandoned." A reader of the *Leader* having challenged this statement and denied that it ever had been advanced, the *Leader* replied that Mr. Bryan "in 1896 in almost half a thousand speeches, attributed all the financial, industrial and agricultural ills of the people of the United States to the fact that silver had been denied its proper place as one of the money metals of the country." The argument made by Mr. Bryan in 1896 and since did not differ from the arguments made by other bimetallists. It was known, not only by advocates of bimetallism, but by all intelligent advocates of the gold standard, that there had been an era of falling prices, and the English commission appointed to investigate the cause had come to the conclusion that all other students of the subject had reached, namely, that the fall in prices was mainly due to the fact that the supply of money had not increased in proportion to the demand for it. And this was due to the demonetization of silver. Bimetallism was advocated as a means of increasing the volume of standard money, and it was the only means then in sight. The purpose of the increase was not only to stop falling prices, but to raise them up to, and to keep them at, the bimetallic level. The purpose of all the agitation was more money, and bimetallism was the means of securing it. Bimetallism requires the coinage of gold and silver at a fixed ratio into legal tender money. The Chicago platform embodied this demand in specific words and every one who knew anything about the subject knew that bimetallism would increase the volume of money, that an increased volume of money would raise prices, and that higher prices would make better times. The people opposed to bimetallism were divided into two classes—those who wanted dear money and those who, though interested in a sufficient volume of money, were deceived by the financiers and political leaders in whom they had confidence. No one ever argued that bimetallism depended upon any particular ratio, but all bimetallists knew that some ratio must be fixed before silver could be restored. They had found that pretended bimetallists had secured election on ambiguous platforms and then defeated action by objecting to any reasonable ratio. They, therefore, decided to name the ratio so that the advocates of bimetallism might have a rallying point. This ratio was not only the present legal ratio of 16 to 1, but a ratio more favorable to gold than the ratio existing between silver and gold coins of most of the other nations.

Bimetallists planted themselves upon the law of supply and demand, which, although now universally recognized, was at that time disputed. They insisted that the value of a dollar depended on the number of dollars—supply and demand regulating the price. They insisted that an increase in the demand for money or a decrease in the supply of it, would raise the price of the dollar. They recognized that the law of supply and demand also fixed the market price of both gold and silver, and that the supply remaining the same an increase in the demand would increase the price. And they also insisted that the government could create so great a demand for silver as to fix the bullion price at the coinage price, just as the government's demand for gold fixes the bullion price at the coinage price. They pointed to the fact that the Sherman law of 1890, by creating the legislative demand for silver, had raised the price from less than a dollar an ounce to $1.20 an ounce—not only in the United States, but throughout the world, and they argued from this that if the purchase of four millions and a half ounces a month would raise the price of silver to $1.20 per ounce then the law converting into legal tender money not four millions and a half, but every ounce presented, would increase the bullion value to $1.29. This reasoning was sound, and while it was disputed, no one ever brought forth any facts or arguments to shake the faith of bimetallists. The advocates of the gold standard refused to recognize the demand created by the government as an element in fixing the bullion price of silver, just as they refused to recognize the quantitative theory of money. Now, every republican who boasts of the increased quantity of money and points to the benefits flowing therefrom admits the quantitative theory of money—the paramount contention of the supporters of the Chicago platform. And even papers like the Chicago *Chronicle* and the Cleveland *Leader* are admitting another contention of bimetallists, namely, that a demand created by the government raises the price of silver. If the purchase of about two million ounces a month for use in the Philippines raises the price of silver three to five cents an ounce, who can doubt that the free and unlimited coinage of silver would raise the price vastly more—even enough to restore the parity? And yet tomorrow the *Chronicle* and the *Leader* will renew their silly and senseless prattle about a 50-cent dollar and refuse to recognize the influence of legislation upon the market price of the white metal.

Events have fully and completely vindicated the contentions of the advocates of free silver. What though the increase has come from unexpected sources? The question at issue was whether we needed more money, and no advocate of the gold standard would be willing today to wipe out the unexpected increase since 1896 and go back to the volume that we had when the republicans said we had enough. The coinage of silver was never advocated as an end in itself, but merely as a means to an end. No man who advocated the gold standard in 1896 on the ground that we had enough money then can defend his position by showing that gold, afterwards discovered, supplied a need of which he previously denied the existence, and yet the men who mock and jeer at the Chicago and Kansas City platforms have been rescued from the logic of their own position by a supply of money which they did not expect—a supply which has overthrown their theory and demonstrated the correctness of the theory of the bimetallists.

But in spite of the fact that they have been saved from annihilation by an unexpected increase in the supply of gold, the financiers refuse to learn anything and are now blindly calling for more credit money while they violently protest against any further increase in the volume of real money. If the mints of the United States were open to the free and unlimited coinage of silver on equal terms with gold at the ratio of 16 to 1, without waiting for the aid or consent of any other nation the price of silver would not only be raised to $1.29 an ounce, but the quantity of silver thus brought into circulation would not be more than sufficient to keep pace with the increased demand for money. It would give a supply of real money instead of supply of promises to pay money.

Bimetallists pointed out that when our country came into competition with silver-using nations it was at a disadvantage because of the fall in silver. As long as England could buy silver bullion at a low price and exchange it for India wheat our people were compelled to meet a silver price with a gold price. The fixing of a ratio between gold and silver in India, while injurious to the people of India, saved our farmers from a further fall in the price of wheat, although the Indian farmer even now has a 50 per cent advantage over the American farmer.

Secretary Rusk in the Agricultural Report of 1890 pointed to the rise in the price of silver—due to the Sherman purchase law—and declared that the rise in the price of silver had been followed by a rise in the price of farm products. There is no doubt that a permanent increase in the price of silver bullion to $1.29 an ounce would be followed by a material increase in the price of all farm products wherein we compete with silver-using countries, and this increase would enable us to increase the balance of trade in our favor and thus increase our gold supply rather than diminish it.

There is a scarcity of money throughout the world and silver is needed today. Bimetallism has behind it the history of thousands of years. It rests upon a substantial basis, and is supported by arguments that are clear and conclusive, and while the silver question has been temporarily subordinated, first by an extraordinary increase in the supply of gold; and, second, by the importance of other questions, there is no reason to believe that the world has reached a point where it can do without silver as money. There is no reason, therefore, why the advocates of bimetallism should abandon their faith or consent to the leadership of men who advocated the gold standard when the dollar was rising in value and who will, if intrusted with power, legislate entirely in the interest of financiers who would rob the people of the benefits that have accrued from an enlarged production of gold.

The above relates to the silver part of the money question, but aside from the question of metallic money there is the question of paper money which must be considered, even if there were no need of silver. The gold standard plan includes the further degradation of silver, the withdrawal of full legal tender qualities from it and its final retirement. The plan also includes the reciremnet of all government paper and the substitution of bank paper, and with the decrease in the public debt the financiers will insist upon an asset currency resting upon an unsubstantial foundation of bank credits.

It is impossible to retire the money question until the owners of money cease to love it or, loving it, cease to use legislation to enhance its value, but it is gratifying to those who have been fighting for a larger volume of money to know that the gold papers will, in lucid moments, admit the principles for which bimetallists have contended.

REPUBLICAN TARIFF REFORM.

The Des Moines *Capital* is prophesying that the tariff revision sentiment which has manifested itself in the republican party will soon disappear, and it likens it to the free silver sentiment which, it alleges, appeared and disappeared in the republican party. The *Capital* is undoubtedly correct in saying that the tariff revision sentiment is not likely to last long in the republican party. In fact, the tariff reform republicans can be divided into two classes—those who really want tariff reform and those who would like tariff reform provided it could be secured through the republican party. The former, finding that tariff reform through the republican party is impossible, will leave the party in order to get tariff reform; the latter, finding that tariff reform through the republican party is impossible, will give up tariff reform in order to be in harmony with the party. This was true of the republicans who advocated free silver. Those who were in earnest left the republican party; those who were republicans first and silver men afterward, gave up free silver. The same division can be seen among the republican opponents of the trust, and the *Capital* might just as well have mentioned this element as the tariff reform element. Those who want to destroy the trusts will leave the republican party and try to destroy them, while others will quit talking about the trusts as soon as it is evident to all, as it now is to many, that the republican party has no intention of destroying the trusts. A like division will be found among the anti-imperialist republicans. Those who are genuinely attached to the doctrine of self-government will leave the republican party and assist in the overthrow of colonialism. Those who are more attached to their party than to our form of government will stick to the party and risk the growth of imperialism in the United States rather than risk injury to their party.

The *Capital*'s logic is right as far as it goes, but it does not go far enough.

THE ADMINISTRATION'S POSITION.

(Interview given New York Commercial.)

The government's attitude upon the trust question, as disclosed by the conduct and words of the president, together with the action of the house and senate, seems to be this: That a private monopoly is not in itself a bad thing, but that it may become injurious; and that if a private monopoly becomes injurious an effort should be made to curb it, but that this effort should be so cautious and conservative as not to risk the destruction of those aggregations of wealth which do not come within the condemnation of the administration. The administration seems to think that it is better that ninety-nine guilty trusts should escape than that one innocent one should be injured. There are two fallacies, it seems to me, in the administration's position—first, that any private monopoly can be good, and, second, that it is more important to protect a benevolent private monopoly from unjust attack than to protect the public from the evils of monopoly. No progress can be made until the administration recognizes that a private monopoly, no matter where it is found, or how it is conducted, is indefensible and intolerable. Even if it were possible to conceive of a private monopoly so administered as to be beneficial to the public, it could not be defended, both because a monopoly good today may become bad tomorrow under a different management, and also because the principle once admitted would do infinitely more harm than good.

The second fallacy is one to which the supreme court has lent some encouragement in the decisions which protect what are called "innocent purchasers" of railroad bonds. In some instances bonds have been held good which were issued corruptly and through frauds which might, upon reasonable inquiry, have been ascertained. The sacredness of an obligation, honestly entered into, would be increased rather than lessened if the purchaser of the bonds of a corporation was compelled to make some investigation before entering the Elysian fields set apart for "the innocent" and "unsuspecting."

The attempt to protect the holders of watered stocks and bonds of railroads has been carried so far that the rights of the speculator upon the market are sometimes declared paramount to the rights of the patrons of the road to have the services of the roads for reasonable compensation.

And so with the monopolies that are scattering their watered stocks and watered bonds broadcast. We are hearing a great deal more of the "poor widow and orphan" who "innocently and unsuspectingly" purchase stock than of the victims of the extortion practiced by the monopolies.

There is every reason why the legislative and executive departments of the government should give more heed to the people generally and less to men and women who invest in securities which, as they could learn upon slight investigation, must derive their principal value from a violation of rights human and divine. The administration, so far, has failed to show that sympathy with the rights and interests of the masses that is necessary to any effective legislation upon the trust question or to any effective execution of present laws. Not only has the administration failed to enforce the criminal clause of the anti-trust law (save in one case recently decided), but it has given its approval to, and even boasted of, a law drawn by the corporations themselves and intended to relieve the trust magnates of the rigors of the criminal law.

As to the effect of the stock market on general prosperity it is difficult to speak accurately. If transactions upon the stock market were confined to legitimate purchases and sales, the quotations might indicate the prosperity of the corporations listed, but when companies are promoted for the benefit of the promoter and wrecked for the benefit of the wrecker; when conspiracies can be formed to boost one kind of stock or to depress another, the fluctuations of the stock market enable one to form a better estimate of the moral apathy among stock manipulators and the general public than of the state of business.

THE LESSON OF 1894.

THE COMMONER has pointed out the necessity for faithful adherence to the principles of the democratic party. It has insisted that a victory which would betray the people, as they were betrayed by the victory of 1892, would be more disastrous to the party than defeat, because without accomplishing anything for the country it would leave the party weaker for future contests. It has shown that a party must desire something more important than the distribution of patronage to be entitled to public confidence. The last time patronage was dispensed among democrats it corrupted and led out of the party a large proportion of those who received the patronage— the party can well pray to be spared from another distribution of that kind. But the reorganizers are constantly asserting that to win is the important thing to be considered, and that they, the reorganizers, hold the key to success. While this is a low plane upon which to discuss a question, THE COMMONER is prepared to meet them, even upon this plane, and to show by experience—bitter experience—that the Clevelandizing of the democratic party would mean complete disaster rather than victory. Let us review this experience.

In 1892 Mr. Cleveland carried twenty-two states, as follows: Alabama, Arkansas, Connecticut, Delaware, Florida, Georgia, Illinois, Indiana, Kentucky, Louisiana, Maryland, Mississippi, Missouri, New Jersey, New York, North Carolina, South Carolina, Tennessee, Texas, Virginia, West Virginia and Wisconsin, and received eight electoral votes out of nine from California, five out of fourteen from Michigan, one out of three from North Dakota, and one out of twenty-three from Ohio, He had a popular plurality over the republican candidate of 400,000. He went into office on the 4th of March, 1893, and immediately surrounded himself with a gold standard cabinet, largely selected by the great corporations, and began his system of proscription against the democrats who represented their constituents upon the money question. He refused to call congress together in extraordinary session to consider the tariff question—the issue that had been paramount in the campaign—but at the request of the financiers called congress together in August to consider a bill framed by John Sherman a year before—a bill indorsed by Wall street and supported by a larger percentage of the republican party than of the democratic party. To secure the passage of this bill he used promises of patronage, and rewarded with official position those who deliberately betrayed their constituents on this issue.

By this subserviency to Wall street and by his scandalous contracts and negotiations with syndicates, he made the money question the paramount issue, and there is much reason for believing that he advised that attempt at the coercion of borrowers which, carried too far, resulted in the panic of 1893.

In the fall of 1894 we had a congressional election throughout the Union and a state election in most of the state. Mr. Cleveland's administration was the issue in that campaign, and his financial policy was the most important item of his administration. The Wilson bill had been passed (it became a law without his signature) during the summer, but it had not been in operation long enough to become the paramount issue in that campaign. What was the result of the election in 1894? Mr. Cleveland was president; his influence was dominant in the party, in both senate and house, and he had control of the national committee through which he distributed his patronage.

Below will be found the states with the majorities given at that election. The figures are taken from the New York World Almanac of 1895.

State—	Democratic.	Republican.
Alabama	27,582	
Arkansas	48,724	
California	1,206	
Colorado		7,368
Connecticut		17,688
Delaware		1,221
Florida	25,300	
Georgia	21,164	
Idaho		2,375
Illinois		123,427
Indiana		44,673
Iowa		79,396
Kansas		30,368
Kentucky		*1,047
Louisiana	*42,082	
Maine		38,978
Maryland		*2,696
Massachusetts		65,377
Michigan		106,392
Minnesota		60,013
Mississippi	*15,561	
Missouri		3,044
Montana		*12,771
New Jersey		*48,728
New Hampshire		12,532
New York		159,108
North Carolina		**20,751
North Dakota		14,369

Ohio		137,087
Oregon		15,001
Pennsylvania		241,397
Rhode Island		6,307
South Carolina	22,229	
South Dakota		13,833
Tennessee	748	
Texas	53,427	
Utah		1,821
Vermont		28,521
Virginia	39,726	
Washington		*18,995
West Virginia		*13,359
Wisconsin		53,900
Wyoming		3,184
Nebraska (fusion)	3,202	
Nevada (fusion-silver)	1,362	

*On congressional vote.
**Populist and republican fusion.

In eight states where no state election was held the vote on the congressional ticket is taken. From this table it will be seen that only eleven states out of the forty-five—Alabama, Arkansas, California, Florida, Georgia, Louisiana, Mississippi, South Carolina, Tennessee, Texas and Virginia—were carried by the democrats, and of the eleven only one, California, was a northern state, and the democratic majority there was only 1,206. Missouri went republican for the first time since the war; Kentucky, represented in the cabinet by John G. Carlyle, went republican by 1,047 on the congressional vote, and elected five republican congressmen out of eleven. Maryland went republican on the congressional vote. Illinois went republican by a larger majority than it did in 1900. Michigan went republican by over a hundred thousand, and Ohio went republican by a majority of 137,000. Connecticut, the home of Mr. Cleveland's friend, Benedict, went republican by 17,000. New Jersey, Mr. Cleveland's present home, went republican on the congressional vote by 48,000. New York, with Mr. Hilll as the candidate for governor, went republican by 159,000, and Pennsylvania gave a republican majority of 241,000. Iowa gave a republican majority of 79,000, Massachusetts of 65,000, Minnesota of 60,000, Wisconsin of 53,000, Indiana of 44,000 and Maine of 38,000.

The sum of all the majorities cast for the democratic ticket in the eleven states only amounted to 300,744, while the majorities cast for the republican ticket in thirty-two states amounted to 1,383,277. The net republican majority was, therefore, 1,082,533; this was nearly twice as large a popular majority as the republican ticket had in 1896, when Mr. Cleveland helped the republicans, and was about 20 per cent larger than the popular majority of the republicans in 1900.

The crushing character of this defeat can be realized when we remember that it was a change from nearly 400,000 in 1892 to 1,082,533 in 1894.

The fusion majority of 3,202 in Nebraska cannot be considered a Cleveland majority, because the Cleveland democrats ran a ticket of their own against the fusion ticket. Neither can the silver majority of 1,362 in Nevada be counted as a Cleveland victory, for it was antagonistic to Mr. Cleveland. The republican majority in North Carolina was secured by a fusion between the republicans and the populists, but both of them opposed Mr. Cleveland. So much for the majorities cast in the states.

According to the World Almanac, above referred to, the congress elected in 1892 stood 219 democrats to 127 republicans, a majority of 92. The congress elected in 1894 contained only 104 democrats, a falling off of 115, or more than half, while the republicans had 244 members, nearly double what they had in the congress before. There were twenty-four states which did not elect a single democratic representative to congress: Colorado, Connecticut, Delaware, Idaho, Indiana, Iowa, Kansas, Maine, Michigan, Minnesota, Montana, Nebraska, Nevada, New Hampshire, New Jersey, North Dakota, Oregon, Rhode Island, South Dakota, Vermont, Washington, West Virginia, Wisconsin and Wyoming. In fact, outside of the southern states, there were, all told, only eighteen democrats elected to congress (Missouri being counted with the northern states—she elected five democratic members to congress out of fifteen) and of these one came from California, two from

Illinois, one from Massachusetts, five from New York, five from Missouri, two from Ohio and two from Pennsylvania.

The reorganizers think that their cause is popular in New England, New York and New Jersey, and yet when the people had a chance to express themselves on Cleveland's policy the democrats only elected six congressmen (five in New York and one in Massachusetts) in all that territory. If it is thought that Cleveland is popular in the states between the Ohio river and the Missouri, let it be remembered that the democratic party did not carry a single state in that section in 1894, and excluding Missouri, sent only four members to congress, although in 1892 he carried Illinois, Indiana, and Wisconsin, and secured one electoral vote in Ohio and five in Michigan.

On another page will be found a cartoon which appeared about Thanksgiving time in 1894 in Judge and is reproduced by the kind permission of that paper. This cartoon represents Cleveland and Hill as the chief figures at a Thanksgiving dinner of crow and exhibits to perfection the spirit of exultation manifested among republicans at that time. The very papers which are now speaking in such complimentary terms of Mr. Cleveland were then loud in their denunciation.

These figures show the demoralization of the party under Mr. Cleveland's leadership in 1894, and what has been since done to make him popular? If the reorganizers insist that tariff reform is the issue now, why did not tariff reform save the party in 1894? If the people have such a profound reverence for Mr. Cleveland, why did they not show it in 1894? If he is popular now because he helped the republican ticket in 1896, how can that act be expected to make him popular with both republicans and democrats? Why would the republicans support Mr. Cleveland in preference to a republican who agrees with them on every question? And why would the democrats feel more kindly to Mr. Cleveland now, since he has openly helped the republican party, than they did in '94 when they opposed his principles, but still recognized him as a member of the party? If the trust question is to be the issue, how can the reorganizers expect to hold the votes of both the friends and the opponents of the trusts? And if imperialism is to be the issue, how can they expect to poll more votes with a gold bug anti-imperialist who was silent in 1900 than with a silver anti-imperialist who fought imperialism in 1900? How can they expect to come nearer to victory with a man who is in harmony with the democratic position on a few questions than with one in harmony with the democratic position on all the questions?

The reorganizers are always talking about the independent vote, but it must be remembered that the independent vote is of no value unless it is added to the democratic vote. The election of 1894 shows (and it was Mr. Cleveland's last appearance as a democrat) that he could not get enough independents to make up for the democrats who were alienated.

The democrats who think more of "success" than they do of democratic principles can find food for thought in the history above reviewed. If they want victory, let them learn from the failures of the past that right is, after all, expedient. The democratic party was defeated, it is true, in 1896, yet after four years of defeat it was stronger than it was in 1894, two years after a Cleveland victory.

Mr. Cleveland left the party demoralized by his conduct and disgraced by his record. Can the party afford, even as a matter of expediency, to travel again the road that it traveled from 1892 to 1896? Is it not better—aye, is it not necessary—that it should resolutely defend democratic principles and espouse the cause of the people, trusting to the intelligence and patriotism of the people for accession from the ranks of those who really sympathize with the masses, but either have been led into the republican party by misunderstanding or have been held in the republican party by allegiance to the party name?

MEMORIAL DAY.

Memorial Day is here again, and the flowers, fragrant offerings of love and gratitude, will soon make the graves as beautiful as the memory of the soldiers' deeds is precious. Each year diminishes the number of veterans who assemble at the cemetery to conduct the memorial exercises; each year increases the number of mounds to be decorated, but the living may be trusted to perpetuate the custom even when the survivors of our wars have entirely disappeared. Sorrow for the dead is the one sorrow, it has been said, from which the living do not care to be weaned, and this is the more true, when with that sorrow there is mingled the appreciation of patriotic service. The living can rejoice that the animosities aroused by the civil war have been so completely buried that those who wore the blue and those who wore the gray can march together to the "silent city of the dead" and join in showing respect to the valor and sacrifice of those who, in the war between the states, proved the strength of their convictions by the offer of their lives. The living, also, should in the presence of the dead consecrate themselves anew to the work that lies before the nation, to the end that the wise and prompt solution of the present problems may insure permanent peace and prosperity to our beloved land.

CONGRATULATIONS TO CUBA.

One year of successful existence, in spite of the failure of our nation to do its duty toward Cuba, has justified that new republic's claim to a separate government. Cuba has met and overcome the difficult problems incident to a beginning and enters upon her second year, cheered by the congratulations of her friends and inspired by the hopes which her own good conduct has excited. President Palma and his associates in office have shown their ability to deal wisely with public affairs and the people have given new demonstrations of their patriotism. The Cubans have reason to celebrate the 20th of May, 1903—the first anniversary of their independence—and THE COMMONER wishes them many happy returns of the day.

PERSECUTIONS IN RUSSIA.

The persecution of the Jews in Russia, accompanied as it has been by the most terrible atrocities, has shocked the conscience of the civilized world. It is hard to believe that fanaticism and race hatred could make human beings as brutal as the reports show some of the Russians to have been. The secretary of state has even more reason now than he had a few months ago to express national abhorrence of the cruelties which have been practiced against a harmless and helpless race. The fact that Russia has always been friendly to us should hasten rather than delay our protest, for a friend can speak where an enemy's counsel would give offense. The United States should take the lead in the formation of a public sentiment throughout the world which will condemn injustice and promote respect for human rights.

MILES ON THE PHILIPPINES.

General Miles, who went to the Philippine islands to investigate and returned with too much information to suit the imperialists, is disposed to defend his position and in doing so draws a nice distinction between the army as a whole and the officers and soldiers who have been guilty of cruelty. Replying to a criticism in the Army and Navy Journal, he says: "It is most gratifying that the serious offenses have not been committed by the soldiers unless they were under the direction of certain officers who were responsible. Soldiers have withheld fire when ordered to shoot prisoners, protested against acts of cruelty, and written to relatives at home to take action to put a stop to these crimes. It will be one of the glories of the army that such deeds, committed by whatever authority, are abhorrent to the American soldier. There must be a very unmistakable line drawn between the great body of honorable and faithful officers and private soldiers whose records have been commendable and those, of whatever station, whose acts have received and should receive the earnest condemnation of all honorable men."

The general is right. A line must be drawn between the soldier who respects his country's position and always endeavors to so act as to defend the nation's high position among the nations, and the soldier, whether he be officer or private, who permits an inherent brutality to manifest itself in cruelty to the helpless. It is natural for the guilty and for their friends to resent criticism of individual officers as if it were criticism of the whole army, just as the predatory rich seek to make it appear that punishment of them is an attack upon property and property rights. The punishment of the guilty is necessary for the protection of the innocent, for only in this way can the guilty be located and the whole army be exonerated. It is better that the offending member be punished than that whole body suffer.

LEADERSHIP.

Mr. Bryan has not thought it proper to use the columns of THE COMMONER to make answer to criticisms which are purely personal, for he desires to make the paper an exponent of ideas rather than of persons. There would be no room for anything else if he attempted to reply to the many republican and gold papers which contain unkind comments and groundless criticism. He has felt at liberty, however, to take notice of some editorials which, in condemning him, condemn the ideas which he advocates.

On another page will be found an editorial from the Springfield *Republican* which well illustrates one class of papers. The *Republican* opposed the democratic ticket in 1896, but in 1900 supported the ticket because the question of imperialism was made paramount. The editorials of that paper, while they have often found fault with the editor of THE COMMONER, are usually written in a friendly vein and with more fairness than many papers show. Attention is called to this editorial in order to point out a fact which must be borne in mind by the advocates of the Kansas City platform. It will be noticed that the main charge made by the *Republican* is that Mr. Bryan needs "a sane opportunism." It is pained that Mr. Bryan does not bury the silver question and thus become the "leader" of the radical movement. The *Republican's* position is easily explained. Its editor has never shown any comprehension of the real issue between the republicans and the gold democrats on the one side and the Kansas City platform democrats on the other side—namely, the issue between Mammon and man. The *Republican* thinks that the silver question should be buried, but the force of its opinion on this subject is materially weakened by the fact that it thought the same thing in 1896 and the years prior to that. When the dollar was constantly rising in value because of legislation hostile to silver the *Republican* was in no wise alarmed. The appeals of the wealth-producers and the debt-payers never reached its sanctum. It treated the subject in a calmer manner than the ultra-gold standard organs, but it treated it from the side of the money lender and the money changer. It is hardly fair for a paper that could see no life in the money question prior to 1896 to pose as an expert physician and give an opinion upon the vitality of the issue now. The editorial quoted from shows that the editor does not understand today the issue between those who want money scarce and those who want a sufficient quanity; between those who want a financial system, made by the financiers for their own profit, and those who want a financial system made by the people for themselves. The editorial contains not the slightest reference to the gold standard plan, still uncompleted, which contemplates, first, the making of the silver dollar redeemable in gold; second, the withdrawal of full legal tender qualities from it; third, its final retirement; fourth, a branch bank system; fifth, the complete retirement of the greenbacks, and, sixth, an asset currency. These propositions are very important ones, and are being considered by the financiers and will be pushed as rapidly as possible.

If the editor of the *Republican* was as well informed on the subject of money as he is on the subject of imperialism, or if his sympathies were as actively with the masses of America, who are the victims of Wall street's financial legislation, as his sympathies are actively with the Filipinos who are the victims of American exploitation, he would understand that the money question cannot be dropped without a criminal disregard of public interests. If he understood the money questions or if his sympathies were on the right side of the question, he would know that no compromise short of complete surrender can be made with the financiers.

At this moment there is such a scarcity of money in the United States that that very scarcity is being used as a club to beat congress into the passage of an asset currency law. That scarcity is a sufficient reason for insisting upon opening the mints to the coinage of silver. Throughout the world there is a scarcity of standard money and that scarcity is evidence that silver is still needed. These things can be disregarded by those who do not understand the subject or by those who understand the subject, but sympathize with the financiers in their desire for dear money, but they cannot be overlooked by those who are acquainted with the principles of monetary science and whose sympathies are with the people once described by John G. Carlyle as "the struggling masses."

But even if the advocates of the Kansas City platform were willing, for the sake of harmony, to consider the money question as temporarily settled, if they were willing to waive their views on this subject and agree to keep the money question in abeyance for a few years while other questions were considered, they would find that no progress would be made toward harmony, first because the advocates of the gold standard are not satisfied with our money system as it is, but insist upon changes that are inimical to the interests of the public. The honest gold standard leaders would not agree to any proposition that would leave the money question in statu quo for four years, and there is no way by which they could be bound to an agreement, even if they were willing to make it. The advocates of the gold standard have proposed the only terms that they will propose, namely, that the platform shall ignore not only the silver part of the money question, but every part of the money question. Second, that the candidates shall be men who can be relied upon by Wall street to use the entire influence of the government to carry out the plans of Wall street. Third, that the party organization shall be turned over to the advocates of the gold standard to have and hold in perpetuity.

This is the only basis of compromise, and it is not compromise, but surrender, absolute and complete. If the *Republican* does not know this it has not improved the opportunity which it has had to discover what is going on. If the *Republi-*

can, as is more likely, understands this, but can see no harm in it; that fact alone would disclose its bias in favor of the financiers. Like some of the other anti-imperialists, the *Republican* seems to wonder why the democrats who constitute the majority of the party are not disposed to accept an undemocratic man for a place at the head of the democratic ticket. The answer is plain and ought to be known without the necessity of stating it. A man who is undemocratic in his sympathies cannot be trusted with the immense power of the chief executive. The democratic party tried that in 1892, and the result was that the administration became more subservient to plutocratic influences than any republican administration had ever been, and this subserviency alienated an immense number of voters and placed upon the democratic name an odium that it has been difficult to remove.

In 1896 the most potent argument that we had to meet was, "The democratic administration has ruined the country; a republican administration will restore prosperity." Mr. Hanna presented Candidate McKinley as the advance agent of prosperity, and while the democratic party was being held responsible for Mr. Cleveland's administration Mr. Cleveland was helping the republicans to elect their candidate. In 1900, when the democratic party tried to make imperialism the paramount issue, the most potent argument it had to meet was, "The republican party has brought prosperity. Let well enough alone; do not risk a return to the hard times and soup houses of the last democratic administration." While the democratic party was bearing the burden of Mr. Cleveland's administration, he sat silent in his New Jersey home and refused to say one word to assist the party in its fight against the republican party, notwithstanding the fact that he had two years before denounced imperialism as a menace to the country. As soon as the election was over, his voice returned to him, and he has been making the air vocal ever since with his advice to the party that he demoralized.

A man's sympathies control him—"as a man thinketh in his heart so is he." If one sits down in a street car and overhears a conversation between two men he can very soon tell their sympathies, and when he knows their sympathies he can guess the arguments they will use in support of their positions. The trouble with those who lead the reorganizing forces is that their sympathies are wrong; they look at every question from the standpoint of the capitalist. According to their theory society is constructed from the top—the capitalist is the great benefactor and the laborer ought to be in an attitude of thankfulness for the opportunity to work. A man's sympathies control his position on every question which he understands. A man may be misled, and may ignorantly oppose those with whom he sympathizes, but he will not knowingly do so.

While the editor of THE COMMONER appreciates the generous advice given him, his respect for the *Republican* compels him to answer with the same frankness with which it has spoken. He is not seeking leadership. Neither is he concerned about his "political position in future years;" no man is in position to do his duty who is controlled by the ambition to be a leader or who is always looking out for his own political future. Leadership is not secured in that way, neither can one insure his political position in future years by centering his thoughts upon his own interests. Nominal leadership in a party is determined by the action of the convention, but leadership in thought and in political action is entirely independent of caucuses and conventions. He leads who proposes the wisest measures and defends them with the strongest argument. No one can see the truth who constantly gazes at himself. Those find truth who seek for it—who seek not casually or carelessly, but earnestly and constantly. The best evidence that one can give of his faith in a truth is to be willing to suffer for it. Christ gave utterance to a principle of wide application when He said, "He that findeth his life shall lose it, and he who loses his life for my sake shall find it." So it may be said of truth. He whose only object is to save his own political life will lose it, and will deserve to lose it, but he who is willilng to lose his life or the sake of a cause or a principle, triumphs with the cause or principle to which he adheres; he grows with it and enjoys the confidence of those who are wedded to it. The advocates of the Chicago and Kansas City platforms have shown their willingness to suffer for their convictions. Why should they pretend a confession of error when they believe that they were right? Why pretend that the issue is past, when it is still delude ourselves with the belief that a real or even a nominal upon us, and must remain? Why ignore, for the sake of a few offices, a fierce conflict between money and manhood? Why victory can be won by a sacrifice of the people's interest to the cold, cruel and merciless dictation of monopolists, and magnates, in whom love of money has extinguished the feeling of brotherhood.

The *Republican's* reference to Jefferson is an unfortunate one, for no man, not excepting Jackson, was ever more consistent in his course or more tenaciously held to fundamental principles. Jefferson's sympathies were with the people. He was not only the defender of individual liberty, religious liberty and self-government, but he sounded the first note of warning against monopolies, against banks of issue and against the money power. He was assailed by the aristocrats because he was a democrat. He was assailed by those who enjoyed special privileges because he believed in equal rights to all and special privileges to none, and himself said that he was denounced as a maniac by the bankers because he opposed banks of issue.

Gladstone may have changed parties, but that alone would not convict him of changing his principles. The silver men who came to the democratic party in 1896 insisted that they were maintaining the position that the republican party had maintained on the money question, and the anti-imperialists who came to us in 1900 insisted that they were maintaining the principles for which the party had stood.

Opportunism is a good or bad word according to its definition. If it means a willingness on the part of one to change his principles in order to compass individual success, it is a most offensive word; if it means that one employs new facts, new incidents and new conditions to give expression to his principles, it is an entirely proper word. Eevery man and every party must utilize circumstances and conditions to advance principles, but no man or party can justify the abandonment of principles for selfish gain.

MASKED BATTERIES.

In discussing newspapers in a recent interview, Mr. Bryan mentioned some of the papers which call themselves democratic, but which can be relied upon to support any republican policy in which the financiers of the country are interested. He expressed the wish that the law might compel a disclosure of the names of the men who really dictate the editorial policy of papers. Among these papers the New York *Times* was mentioned by name. The *Times* refers to this comment and attempts to defend the papers which speak as corporations without a known personality behind the corporation. It says:

"We regard that, and Mr. Bryan ought to regard it, as a real negligible detail. The vital question is, Do these papers tell the truth; do they preach sound doctrine; and do they, in their daily exhortations, seek to set the feet of the democracy into paths of safety? These are the important things; if a newspaper is sound, then Mr. Bryan may leave the supposed dictator of its policy to his money grubbing in the dust-holes of Wall street, for, though it may cause him daily anguish, how the poor wretch shows his wisdom in committing to more competent hands the filling of its columns!"

The *Times*, instead of disclosing its owner, or the dictator of its policy, presents this puerile defense of the newspaper which fires its daily round from ambush. So it makes no difference at all who controls the paper! Suppose it should appear that the *Times* was owned by John D. Rockefeller (of course, this is only a supposition), would its defence of trusts have as much weight as if it were owned by some one not at all connected with the trusts? Suppose it were owned by the officials of the National City Bank? Would its defence of every Wall street scheme have the same weight as if it were owned by some one who could view the subject disinterestedly? Suppose (and this may not be a supposition) it is owned by a man who habitually votes the republican ticket and is in constant communication with the republican leaders, would its advice to democrats have as much weight as it would if it were owned by a man whose fidelity to democratic principles was unquestioned? If the *Times* was a defendant in a suit at law, would it consent to have the witnesses against it concealed in an adjoining room? Would it allow the witnesses to talk to the court or jury through a speaking tube, relieved from the scrutiny of a cross-examination?

The *Times* says that the vital thing is, "Do these newspapers tell the truth; do they preach sound doctrine; do they, in their daily exhortations, seek to set the feet of the democracy into the paths of safety?" The *Times* talks as if the readers of the newspaper accepted its utterances as if they were utterances of a voice from heaven, whereas a more intimate acquaintance with that editorial oracle might show that the voice was anything but heavenly, and that the inspiration came from an entirely different direction.

The *Times* assumes that the dictator may be "money grubbing in the dust-holes of Wall street," while his agent, the editor, is filling the columns of the paper with competent hands. But suppose the editor is numbered among those who boast that they can write as well on one side of a question as on the other, and suppose he is told to write on the capitalistic side of every question—to defend the gold standard and a bank currency, to argue that trusts are a natural development and necessary to public welfare, to justify imperialism and glorify government by injunction—hasn't the reader a right to know the influences which control and the interests that guide the editorial pencil? The defence made by the *Times* is in itself a sufficient condemnation of the so-called impersonal, but more often subsidized, newspaper representative of some plutocratic interest or group of interests.

DEMOCRACY DEFINED.

Mr. William O. McDowell, of New York, president of the Cuban-American league, was asked at the close of one of his lectures: "What is the correct conception of democracy?" He replied: "It is an aspiration—a determined purpose—hoping for, struggling for, fighting to the death for, Liberty—the equal well-being of all men. It is a religion built upon a creed that asserts the natural dignity and birthright equality of all men. It is the golden rule, the ten commandments, the Sermon on the Mount, and the American Declaration expressed in a single word."

The word "democracy," it will be seen, has a meaning deep and broad. It is derived from the Greek and means the rule of the people, and the rule of the people, resting as it does upon the doctrines set forth in the Declaration of Independence, can only be preserved by the cultivation of a profound and universal respect for human rights.

Both aristocracy and plutocracy are constantly at war with democracy and the democrat must be not only vigilant and active, but he must know that his own security rests upon the protection of the equal rights of all.

THE ORATOR'S PREPARATION.

The editor of THE COMMONER frequently receives inquiries from young men who desire to prepare themselves for an active part in the discussion of public questions, and it is an economy of time to answer all at once.

Webster, the great orator, said of eloquence that it must exist "in the man, in the subject, and in the occasion." And then he proceded to elaborate the statement, showing that it was a combination of high purpose, firm resolve and dauntless spirit, speaking from every feature and reaching the heart of the hearer. There are two things absolutely essential to eloquence. First, the speaker must know what he is talking about, and, second, he must mean what he says. Nothing can take the place of knowledge of the subject and earnestness. To these other things can be added, such a clearness of statement, felicity of expression, aptness in illustration, beauty in ornamentation and grace in delivery.

Eloquence is heart speaking to heart. There is no mistaking the cry of terror or the shout of joy, and so there is no misunderstanding the sincere message that passes from heart to heart.

The young man who would fit himself for real influence in the forum must himself feel deeply upon the subjects which he discusses, and he can not feel deeply without being in full sympathy with those whom he addresses. He must also be able to give them information which they do not possess or to state what they know more forcibly than they can state it themselves.

The young man ambitious to stand as the representative of his people—not as an official nominally speaking for them, but as a man actually voicing their aspirations and giving utterance to their hopes—such a young man is advised to read the address entitled, "The People in Art, Government and Religion," delivered by George Bancroft at Williams college in 1835. (It will be found in Volume VII. of Modern Eloquence, known as Reed's Collection of Speeches). This oration is one of the greatest tributes ever paid to the common people, and it will furnish not only thought, but inspiration to young men. It defends not only the rights of the people, but the capacity of the people for self-government, and declares not that "the people can make right," but that "the people can discern right." This admirable address is referred to because of the sound advice that it gives to young men, advice that is pertinent in this connection.

Bancroft says: "Let the young aspirants after glory scatter seeds of truth broadcast on the wide bosom of humanity, in the deep fertile soil of the public mind. There it will strike root and spring up and bear a hundred-fold and bloom for ages and ripen fruit through remote generations."

The difference betwen a demagogue and a statesman is that the former advocates what he thinks will be popular, regardless of the effect that it may ultimately have upon the people to whom he appeals; the statesman advocates what he believes to be the best for the country, regardless of the immediate effect which it may have upon himself. One is willing to sacrifice the permanent interests of others to advance his own temporary interests, while the other is willing to sacrifice his own temporary interests to advance the public welfare. While the conduct of the statesman may seem unselfish, and is unselfish in the usual acceptation of that term, yet it is really an enlightened selfishness, for no man, when he takes a broad view of his own interests, can afford to accept an advantage which comes to him at the expense of his country. The statesman is building upon a firmer foundation than the demagogue, and in the end will find a more substantial reward for his self-denial than the demagogue will be able to secure for himself.

It has been said that the orator, more than any one else, needs information upon all subjects, for questions that are no longer matters of controversy can be used as matters of argument, and no one can speak so well of the future as he who is well acquainted with the past.

A knowledge of human nature is necessary to the orator. Pope has said that the proper study of mankind is man, and in the study of man the heart is the most interesting as well as the most important subject of investigation. He who would succeed in public speaking must understand that a sense of justice is to be found in every heart, and that that sense of justice is the safest foundation upon which to build a government. Bancroft, in the address above referred to, declares that popular government is the strongest government in the world, because "discarding the implements of terror, it dares to rule by moral force and has its citadel in the heart."

Moral courage is indispensible to the orator. A man can not speak eloquently while he is running from the enemy; neither can he inspire courage if his knees smite each other, and there is a tremor in his voice. Courage rests upon conviction; a man has no convictions to speak of who is not willing to endure suffering in support of them.

The orator must have faith—faith in God, faith in the righteousness of his cause and faith in the ultimate triumph of the truth. Believing that right makes might, believing that every word spoken for truth and every act done in behalf of truth contributes to the final victory, he does his duty, more anxious to help the cause which he espouses than to enjoy the fruits of victory.

And, finally, let the ambitious young man understand that

he is in duty bound to discard everything which in the least weakens his strength, and under obligation to do everything that in any degree increases his power to do good. Good habits, therefore, are always important, and may become vitally so. He can well afford to leave liquor to those who desire to tickle the throat or to please the appetite; it will be no help to him in his effort to advance the welfare of his fellows. He can even afford to put into books what others put into tobacco. The volumes purchased will adorn his shelves for a lifetime, while smoke from a cigar is soon lost to sight forever. He does not need to swear; logic is more convincing than oaths. Let him feed his body with food convenient for it, remembering that food is only useful insofar as it strengthens man for his work; let him train his mind to search for the truth, remembering that his power to discern the truth will increase with the effort to find it. Let him keep his heart diligently, for "out of it are the issues of life." Let him recognize service as the measure of greatness, and estimate life by its out-go rather than by its income. Let him to himself be true, "and it follows as the night the day, he can not then be false to any man."

SUNDAY READING.

The editor of THE COMMONER often receives inquiries in regard to reading of various kinds. Some ask for historical works, some inquire about the best orations, still others are interested in good reading for children, and not a few are desirous of information in regard to subjects of a moral and religious nature, suitable for contemplation on the Sabbath. In this and in an article that will appear later, reference will be made to books that the editor himself has read and which he can commend to those who are intent upon making the most of life and anxious for the help which inspiring books give.

Not many weeks ago Mr. Bryan's attention was called to a book entitled "The Simple Life," written by Charles Wagner, of France, and published by McClure, Phillips & Co., of New York. He secured the book and was not only delighted, but greatly edified by a perusal of it. Wagner is an Alsacian by birth, and after the annexation of his birthplace to German as a result of the war, he removed to France. The book begins with a biographical note by Grace King, who traces the life of the author and shows how the foundations of his later work were laid in the instruction and environment of his youth.

Wagner has become an apostle of simplicity and his little book will bring a restful peace to those who are weary of the superficiality of much of our social life and intercourse. A reproduction of the chapter titles of the book will indicate the scope of the work.

I. Our Complex Life. II. The Essence of Simpliciy. III. Simplicity of Thought. IV. Simplicity of Speech. V. Simple Duty. VI. Simple Needs. VII. Simple Pleasures. VIII. The Mercenary Spirit of Simplicity. IX. Notoriety and the Inglorious Good. X. The World and the Life of the Home. XI. Simple Beauty. XII. Pride and Simplicity in the Intercourse of Men. XIII. The Education for Simplicity. XIV. Conclusion.

He shows that our communion with one another, instead of being a candid exchange of confidence and good will, tends to become stilted and insincere—man becoming the servant of material things and the victim of a changeless routine. He pleads for the development of individuality and the cultivation of a frank sincerity. He points out how the better promptings suffer suppression and how the recreations that should be helpful and invigorating have become too largely dissipations that wear away your strength.

The editor of THE COMMONER would be glad if he could put this unassuming and yet invaluable little volume into the hand of every reader of his paper—yea, into the hand of every citizen.

Another book quite different in its character and yet not less readable, is "The Quiet King," written by Caroline Atwater Mason and published by the American Baptist Publication society of Philadelphia. It is the story of Christ told in narrative form with a few new characters introduced to round out the account presented in the gospels. The character delineation is most excellent and the home life of a number of Bible personages, especially of Mary, Martha and Lazarus, is interwoven with the travels and experiences of the Man of Galilee.

The title, "The Quiet King," is peculiarly appropriate and the book can be read with immense advantage at this time when so many high-minded and well disposed people are intoxicated with the glitter and pomp of imperialism and when some even think they see in a war of conquest a pillar of fire guiding the hosts of a church militant to a broader field of labor.

A study of the gentle and consecrated life and the peacceful methods of the Nazarene will tend to substitute Christian ideals for the brutal conceptions which have glorified national covetousness and covered the earth with bloody foot-prints.

"GET RICH QUICK" SCHEMES.

The guessing contests, which are but lotteries in disguise, the turf companies and the "get-rich-quick" concerns, are giving damaging testimony against the American people. They could not flourish but for the people who are trying to get something for nothing and who adopt gambling methods to carry out their purposes. The turf companies appealed especially to those who bet on horse races. The managers of these companies represented that they had perfected a plan by which they could insure winning on a horse race, and thousands deposited their money and drew their weekly returns until the fraud was exposed. It was easy for a company to pay 3 per cent a week, for the principal invested would pay the dividends for thirty-three weeks, and each dividend excited the depositor to new deposits and interested others through him.

The "get-rich-quick" schemes were worked on practically the same principle. Some alluring promises of rich rewards were circulated among the greedy and the infection spread until the manager of the concern failed to pay. Of course, it is the duty of the government, state and national, to arrest swindlers and punish them for their frauds, just as it is the duty of the government to stop guessing contests run on the lottery principle. But after all it will be difficult for the government, however vigilant, to protect people who have no higher conception of life than to desire a short cut to wealth. The fact that these frauds can be successfully practiced proves the prevalence of a false standard of success. Boys and girls growing up and hearing nothing but money talked about are apt to get the idea that money is the only thing to be desired, and when this belief gets a firm hold upon one, he is not apt to be scrupulous as to the means employed to get the money.

What we need in this country more than anything else is an elevation of the moral standard—a raising of the ideals of the people. Life, instead of being measured by the income, should be measured by its overflow. Man is great, not in proportion as he receives much from the world, but in proportion as he gives much to the world. Success in life is not measured by dollars and cents, but by the contribution which one makes to the welfare of his fellows. The man who is always talking about the world owing him a living is apt to spend most of his time trying to collect the living; the man who recognizes that he owes the world a life of service will always be worthily employed. It is necessary that one should have an income in order to provide for his needs, but he should be careful to give something to society that is at least equal in value to the compensation which he draws from society. Fakes, swindles and confidence games will never make victims of those who seek no reward except that which comes as a reasonable return for services rendered. People will never be immune to the "get-rich-quick" schemes until they adopt worthy ideals and begin to build their lives upon the basis of merit.

EMERGENCY CURRENCY.

The republican financiers are all the time talking about an emergency currency, but the fact is that none of them have proposed a currency that would really be valuable in an emergency. No asset currency meets this requirement, and an asset currency is the only kind that the republicans contemplate. An asset currency must necessarily be a lien upon the assets of the bank, and if it is only to be issued when money is tight it will in all probability intensify the stringency rather than relieve it. The dangerous thing is that depositors will get frightened and commence withdrawing their deposits from the bank and this, of course, embarrasses the banks and compels them to draw in loans, and the contraction of loans embarrasses the business community.

The only proposition looking to an emergency currency worthy of the name was the proposition suggested in an amendment offered by Congressman Clayton of Alabama, when the Fowler bill was under discussion. It reads as follows:

A bill to provide an emergency circulation fund, and for other purposes.

Be it enacted by the senate and house of representatives of the United States of America in congress assembled, That the secretary of the treasury be, and he is hereby authorized and directed to have printed and to keep on hand United States treasury notes under a special account to be called the "emergency circulation fund." Such notes shall be full legal tender. Any citizen of the United States shall have the right to deposit United States bonds, under rules and regulations to be prescribed by the secretary of the treasury, and receive from such fund one hundred per centum of the face value of such bonds in United States treasury notes, and shall have the right at any time within twelve months to redeem such bonds by repaying in United States treasury notes the amount so received by him on account of such bonds, with interest at the rate borne by the bond on such amount. Failure to redeem such bonds within the limit of twelve months shall operate as a forfeiture of such bonds to the United States, and such bonds shall be sold to the highest bidder in the open market, and the balance, after the payment of the principal of the amount advanced, the interest on the same, and the expenses, shall be paid to the former owner of such bonds. Any moneys received from such sale may be exchanged with other moneys in the treasury, so that this fund shall consist alone of treasury notes. The principal of all sums so advanced when repaid shall be returned to the "emergency circulation fund," and all interest upon such sums shall be passed to the credit of the treasury under miscellaneous receipts.

The actual amount of notes held in the "emergency circulation fund" shall never be less than fifty million dollars in excess of any outstanding advances. Said fund shall neither be increased nor diminished except in the manner provided.

This is an emergency currency that helps. It is issued by the government, and is a legal tender, like our present greenbacks. Then, too, instead of being issued to banks to be loaned out at a high rate of interest, it is issued to the holders of government bonds whether they be bankers or not. The government uses its own bonds as collateral, and there can be no loss. It charges a rate of interest equal to the interest it is paying, so that it saves the interest while the loan is outstanding, and as the holder of the bonds can at any time return the money and secure his bonds he will act according to the plentitude or scarcity of money.

From every rational point of view, this would look like a solution of the question of emergency currency, and yet there is one objection to it, and so long as the republican party is in power it is a fatal objection—namely, that it helps the people instead of the banks. The republican leaders can not bring themselves to think seriously of any remedy that does not play into the hands of the great capitalists, but it is only a question of time when the people will get sufficiently awake to their own interests to turn out the worshipers of Mammon and put in authority officials who will solve public questions in the interests of the people rather than in the interests of the capitalists.

GIFTS FROM MONOPOLISTS.

There seems to be a wide difference of opinion as to the propriety of accepting gifts from men like Rockefeller. Those who solicit such gifts start in with the proposition that a worthy object has a right to call upon any one for assistance, regardless of the manner in which he secured possession of his money; and the second argument in such a defense is usually that the individual himself is a man of generous impulses and high character and that even though a part of the income is derived from objectionable sources, the contamination does not extend to that portion of the income derived from legitimate sources.

The subject is worthy of consideration because if private monopolies continue to grow, it is likely to become a more and more important issue. First, can a worthy institution afford to accept money that is wrongfully accumulated? In order to establish the principle, let us take an extreme case and assume that a gang of highwaymen should succeed in accumulating a large sum by robbing travelers and also succeed in so terrifying the authorities as to escape punishment. Would any Christian college or any other worthy institution feel justified in accepting donations from such a group of individuals while they continued in lawlessness? If they repented and as far as they could made return of the stolen goods, and offered to some worthy institution that for which they could not find the real owner, a different question might arise, but who would defend such a donation while disrespect for moral and statute laws continued to be manifested?

Does it really make any difference, from a moral standpoint, whether the sum secured is a small sum and in violation of statute law, or a large sum secured in the absence of law, but in violation of moral rights? In other words, can an institution founded on moral principles hide itself behind mere statutory law and excuse a thing which is wrong, merely because the law does not specifically prohibit, or, if it does prohibit, is not rigidly enforced? A private monopoly has always been an outlaw, and the principle involved can not be defended from a moral standpoint. Not only is a monopoly morally wrong but it is also a violation of statute law. Within the last few days the Federal Salt company has been convicted of maintaining a monopoly contrary to the anti-Sherman trust law, just as the meat packers were found guilty in Missouri of violating a state statute. The Standard Oil company, like several other monopolies, exercises an absolute control over the price of oil. If the manager desires to make a contribution to any fund he has it in his power to raise the price of oil and then collect the amount contributed, and such interest as he may think proper, from the consumers. It is not only an immoral use of the taxing power, but an illegal use, even though these trusts have so far had influence enough to prevent an enforcement of the law.

Can a benevolent enterprise afford to be the recipient of money collected from such a source?

Aside from the moral principle involved, there is another question of scarcely less importance. Can the friends of a benevolent enterprise afford to risk the silencing influence of such a gift? Can they afford to risk the restraining effect of such an acceptance upon their lips? The people who are interested in benevolent enterprises are, as a rule, persons of active mind and of social and political influence. Are they in a position to denounce as strongly and as constantly as they should the conduct of the trusts if they solicit or accept a part of the proceeds of the trust's misconduct?

And what should be said of the responsibility of the stockholder in a trust? Some may attempt to draw a line between the stockholder, and the directors, or manager. Some may say that a stockholder can conscientiously draw dividends from a trust, if in the election of directors he tries to secure men who will deal fairly with the public.

Likewise, some may argue that a man may conscientiously be a director in a trust if, in the selection of its officers, he tries to secure the election of men who will respect the rights of the public. But one who will attempt to defend either a stockholder or a director on the ground that he means well, but is out-voted, will probably defend the manager of the trusts on the ground that he is acting for others and not for himself, and therefore under compulsion to make the most possible for them, regardless of his own conscientious scruples.

This shifting of responsibility is in itself a recognition of the indefensible position of the man who accepts the benefits of immoral transactions. It marks the triumph of a love of money over conscience. A man who buys stock in a trust buys it with the knowledge that it is conducted by human beings; he buys it with a knowledge that he can not control the conduct of those in charge unless he has a majority of the stock, and if he will allow his reason to exercise itself he will soon come to the conclusion that he takes the stock for the purpose of securing for himself the profits that arise from a disregard of human rights.

If it is impossible for a mere stockholder to justify a participation in tainted profits, what shall be said of the director and the manager himself? In the case of Mr. Rockefeller, it is a fact known to all that he not only derives a large part of his present income from the Standard Oil company, but that the dividends of his Standard Oil stock have furnished the money for his other investments. The tremendous pyramid of his fortune rests upon the stock of the Standard Oil company, and it is a matter only too well known that in acquiring his fortune he has resorted to every evil practice known to the trusts. He has forced rivals to sell to him by cutting off their market or source of supply, or both; he has bankrupted men who refused to sanction his business methods. He has voalted the laws of state and nation, and secured not only rebates but a part of the freight paid by others. If but a few of the facts set forth in "Wealth Versus Commonwealth" (by Henry D. Lloyd) are correct, no criminal now incarcerated in the penitentiary for larceny has shown more indifference to human rights and property rights than this same Rockefeller. Does it lessen his sins that he has given liberally to churches and colleges? Nay, it exaggerates them, for he attempts to make others share with him the odium that his conduct merits. He is held up as a Christian, but the test of Christianity is not in profession, but in performance, and a Christian has been too well defined to enable a man like Rockefeller to be mistaken for one. "If a man say I love God and hateth his brothers, he is a liar." This may seem a forcible way of putting it, but who has authority to change the test? And what victim of statute law has ever shown his hatred of his brother more than Rockefeller has in his management of the Standard Oil company? "Thou shalt love thy neighbor as thyself," can not be proved by a distribution of a part of one's income if it is disregarded in the collection of the income.

It is high time that we should have a moral awakening which will condemn both the giver and the gift where the money is accumulated by methods which are repugnant to the conscience. This form of punishment should not take the place of the law; it should rather supplement the law, but it is a form of punishment that might prove effective if the public opinion awakened was strongly and forcibly expressed. After all, the possession of money would lose much of its charm if ill-gotten gains, instead of bringing flattery and praise, brought contempt and universal criticism. It is time worthy enterprises were learning to spurn the blood money offered by trust magnates to relieve their consciences or to purchase immunity.

THE POSTOFFICE SCANDAL.

The evidence shows unexpected rascality and corruption in the postoffice department. The evidence collected against Miller and Machen is conclusive proof that the interests of the public have been shamefully neglected by these officials. The offenses committed by them represent the two popular branches of malfeasance—first, the acceptance of money for official service, and, second, interest in contracts with the government. Mr. Miller is charged with receiving money for official opinions, said opinions being given in behalf of swindling corporations that wanted to use the mails. It will be seen that such conduct is not only a crime against the government, but a crime against thousands of citizens who are taken in by the advertisements sent through the mails.

The fact that the swindling concerns were allowed to use the mails for a consideration suggests the possibility of crookedness in connection with the guessing contests which some of the newspapers have been conducting. These are simply lotteries in a more vicious form. In a lottery there are a certain number of tickets and the prizes bear a fixed and large proportion of the entire money invested by patrons, but in the case of a guessing contest the contestant has no way of knowing what his chances are or what proportion the amount invested bears to the prizes. In a wheel of fortune it is always known that the owner of the wheel has a certain percentage in his favor. For instance, if there are one hundred paddles and the successful paddle carries a hundred-dollar prize, there will be more than a hundred paddles sold, say 110, and the $10 goes to the man who owns the wheel. But in the case of the guessing contest the amount given in prizes may be $40,000 and the amount invested by patrons may be $400,000, so that the "wheel" gets 90 per cent instead of 10 per cent.

On another page will be found a copy of the anti-lottery message submitted to congress by President Harrison, July 29, 1890. All that the president says of the Louisiana State Lottery can be said of the newspaper guessing contests, and they are spreading over the country so rapidly that it is only a question of time when public sentiment will be aroused against them. Let the reader of THE COMMONER show this editorial and President Harrison's message to his pastor and to all the preachers and priests whom he knows, with the request that the matter be given attention.

Mr. Machen's offense is in another line, namely, the receiving of a commission upon sales made to the government. It is not often that an official will risk receiving money directly on such transactions, but it is more often the case that the official will become pecuniarily interested in a company that sells to the government. It is so nearly impossible for a man to deal honestly with the government where he himself is pecuniarily interested that the rule against such transactions ought to be universally and rigidly enforced. The same principle that would be violated by a judge trying his own case, or by a juror acting in a suit in which he is pecuniarily interested, is violated when an official transacts business with a company of which he is a member.

If there is no law making it a penal offense for an official to buy for the government from a firm in which he is interested, there ought to be such a law. It is to be hoped that the investigation now commenced will be continued until every guilty party has been exposed and punished.

It is a short-sighted partisanship that would lead the party in power to hush up such things out of fear of political injury. When an administration punishes the offenders it puts the responsibility where it belongs; when an administration shields the offenders it shares the odium of the individual's crime. If President Roosevelt has the courage that he ought to have, he will allow no friendship or partisanship to stand in the way of a thorough investigation and exemplary punishment.

CORRUPTION IN POLITICS.

While traveling through an eastern state the editor of THE COMMONER had occasion to discuss the political situation with several persons and heard so much of political corruption that he took the pains to inquire for specific instances. At the conclusion of this editorial will be found a summary of the information which he received. It is worthy of the careful consideration of the readers of THE COMMONER. There seems to be a numbness of conscience on this question that bodes evil to the country. Surely the people can not always be indifferent, as they seem to be now, to what is going on.

While corruption is not confined to the republican party, it has been most pronounced in that party because that party has been in power so long that the machinery of the party now completely dominates the voters. To correct this corruption it is not necessary to permanently overthrow the party, but it is necessary that there should be an organzied protest among the members that will inaugurate an era of purer politics.

In some instances it was found that men high in business and high in the church lent themselves to various schemes for the corruption of legislators. There are texts for ministers in the summary as well as for political reformers.

The facts as learned can be briefly stated as follows:

1. In a certain state in a senatorial district composed of three counties, there were to be chosen two state senators, one for the short term of two years, the other for the long term of four years. The short term nomination was conceded to a man in one of these counties without opposition. A certain man in one of the remainnig two counties was indorsed by his county for the long term and he had no opposition in the district until he gave out an interview in which he stated, among other things, he was going to the state senate to fight railroad corporations. The political agents of the railroad corporation which is strong in these three counties, at once set out to find a candidate to defeat this man for the nomination. They picked on a man in the remaining county of the three and he was indorsed by his county. Each of two counties having a candidate for the long term, the balance of power rested with the county in which lived the candidate for the short term. This county was about to hold a primary election for the nomination of a county ticket and it was agreed by all parties concerned that the names of these two candidates for the long term of state senator should be put on the ticket at this republican county primary and the one receiving the larger number of votes, should have the delegates from that county. The candidate selected by the railroad interests went to that county, called together thirty active republicans from all parts of the county and gave them $50 each for their time and expenses to work for him until after the republican primary, which was in five days. He told them that if he were successful, he would give them each $25 after the election. Between that time and the day of the primary election, a circus came to town and he gave away 800 tickets to this circus. When the votes were counted he had a small majority.

2. At a city election in the capital city of a certain state, about 450 negroes were imported from the coal mines in various parts of that county and an adjacent county, all of whom were voted, and some three or four times. About 60 were voted as residents of a certain alley, where but four negroes

lived. Among the republican leaders in this colonization business was a postmaster, a deputy United States marshal, a sheriff and a criminal judge.

3. At a republican primary at which delegates to a senatorial convention were to be appointed from the largest county in the senatorial district, there were two candidates for state senator. The United States senatorship was the issue and there were two avowed candidates for that office; one of whom was the brother of one of the candidates for state senator and the other a United States senator. Several thousand dollars were spent at that primary. Tickets were issued without limit, which were redeemable in any saloon in the city that night at $2.00. Other tickets bearing the names of delegates to be voted for were wrapped in $2.00 bills and handed out as publicly as tickets are sold at a theatre ticket office. A United States marshal was manager for the United States senator.

4. The practice of paying men for the time to go and vote has been carried to such an extent that many men of means who have been regarded as ruggedly honest, are demanding from $1.00 to $2.00 for the day to go and vote. During the last congressional election a farmer with 500 acres of land, unemcumbered, drove fourteen miles to the county seat of his county on the day before the election to tell the manager of the campaign he would not vote at the election on the following day unless he was given $1.50 for his time. His voting precinct was less than two miles from his home. Another farmer went nine miles the day before the election to demand $5.00 and a jug of whisky for himself and four neighbors, stating that unless the money and whisky was furnished, none of them would go to the polls and vote.

5. The citizens of a certain town in a certain state, being desirious of becoming the county seat, undertook to form a new county out of parts of their own county and adjacent counties, with their town as the county seat. Within one day, the citizens of that town (the population of which is less than 3,000) raised by subscription $50,000 in cash, and the cashiers of the two banks in that town carried the $50,000 to the capital of the state where the legislature was in session. A lobby was formed

composed of a number of leading politicians. This lobby was engaged to handle this money in a way that would secure the passage of the bill creating the new county. The effort was defeated only because the county seats of the three counties affected put up a larger fund.

LIGHT OUT OF DARKNESS.

Helen Keller, the blind and deaf girl who has astonished the world by the marvelous progress she has made in spite of the fact that the ordinary sources of information are closed, delivered an address at New York recently in which she said: "I am studying economics this year, and I have learned that it is the condition of social life that people shall work for one another, and it is the interest of society to enable every member to work. A human being who does not work is not a member of society and can have no standing in it."

It is strange that this frail being whose sightless orbs look only "into the darkness which the blind see" and whose ears have heard only "the stillness which the deaf hear," has discovered a truth unseen by countless millions who trample upon each other in their mad effort to secure the lion's share of earth's bounties; strange that the harmony of human life should have penetrated her understanding when it is unheard by multitudes of selfish and self-centered people. Why is it? Either some companion has given her an ideal which shapes her thoughts or, protected from the frivolities of life by the wall which her misfortunes have builded, her heart is open to the highest and the best impulses.

Christ, in the beautiful parable of the sower, explains why some receive truth more readily than others. Some seed, He said, fell where the thorns sprang up and choked it, and interpreting its meaning to His disciples He said that the cares of this world and the deceitfulness of riches, choke the truth. So it has ever been; the cares of this world and the deceitfulness of riches still choke the truth. Helen Keller's heart seems to be the good ground where seed is free to grow and where it brings forth manyfold.

HOW RICH SHOULD ONE BE?

A Missouri reader of THE COMMONER asks, "How rich is it right to be?" He calls attention to some of the Bible references to riches, especially to the one likening a rich man's entrance into the kingdom of heaven to the camel's passage through the needle's eye. As no one is in position to answer the question authoritatively and as it is not likely that there will ever be universal agreement in any answer to the question, those who discuss it are apt to vary widely in the opinions expressed. It ought, however, to be possible to agree upon certain general principles that should govern the solution of the problem. Certain arguments can be drawn from analogy. For instance:

How much food should a person eat? While no one can prescribe a quantity in pounds and ounces, or designate with authority certain kinds of food to the exclusion of others, it is possible to agree, first, that the quantity should be just sufficient, and no more, to give to the body the maximum of strength for the discharge of all of its functions, and, second, that those kinds of food, and those kinds only, should be used which suit the body's needs and add to its efficiency. No one can justify the over-loading of the stomach merely to tickle the palate or to satisfy an unnatural appetite. The welfare of man is above the momentary pleasures of gluttony, and so is the welfare of the body more to be considered than epicurian delights. Bodies differ in the quantity of food that they need and the condition of the body may determine the kind of food required, but no one can justify himself if he either destroys the body by indulgence or occupies all the wakening hours in caring for his stomach. If man has no higher purpose in life than to eat he is lower than the beasts, for he neglects to feed the mind and the soul.

How much clothing should a person wear? Well, no one has authority to prescribe the kind or quality of clothing; but it is not unfair to say that both quantity and quality should be determined by the requirements of the body and the purpose of life. There should be sufficient clothing not only to protect the body from harm, but to bring it up to the point of highest efficiency. It would be inexcusable in a person to wear enough clothing to unnecessarily burden his body or to hamper his movements. A man would be thought beside himself if he taxed all the strength of the body to carry clothing, merely to show how much clothing he could support. Neither would it be easy to defend the wearing of clothes so fine as to make an observer think of the clothing more than of the superior qualities of the head and heart; or to excuse the possession of a wardrobe so varied and extensive as to occupy all of one's time in the changing and fitting of clothes. We would be quick to find fault with Nature if she offered us a nut with gorgeous hull and no kernel.

How much money should a person have? Is it so useful that there can be no limit to the amount that one should possess? If man is the climax of creation and the lord of material things, is not money his servant? If a man has so much money (even though it comes to him by inheritance or in a way considered legitimate) that it requires all of his time to take care of it, has he not too much?

There are things which money cannot buy, and they are the dearest things of life. Money cannot purchase love, but the love of money has sometimes separated the best of friends. If one thinks that money can purchase happiness he is doomed to disappointment. The Creator was not so unkind as to make one's highest enjoyment rest upon so unsubstantial a foundation as dollars, nor does he dole out joy in proportion to one's earthly possessions. Compare, for illustration the joy of the philanthropist (and philanthropy is determined more by the spirit of the giver rather than by the size of the gift) with the joy of the miser (and here, too, it must be remembered that the miser is distinguished by his avarice rather than by the amount of gold that he clutches). Compare the happiness of the virtuous cottage-covered couple whose souls are held together by the indissolube bonds of a holy love with the estranged occupants of a palace. Compare the uplifting delights of one who follows, even though unshod, the path of duty, with the revelries of the profligate with inherited millions at his disposal.

Man needs money for the purchase of clothing, for the

securing of an education, for the procuring of books and for the gratifying of his spirit of benevolence. He can justify the expenditure of money, if honestly acquired, for travel, if travel contributes to his higher self; for recreation, insofar as it is strengthening, and for social intercourse insofar as it is helpful. But no one can afford to cultivate that love of money which, if not the root of all evil, is the root of far too much of evil, or even to possess so much money that the mere care of it will absorb energies that are deserving of better employment.

The highest purpose that man can have is the betterment of the human family, all other things are secondary; even the improvement of himself—if it has no higher end than self, it is unworthy. The marble statue may be more nearly perfect in feature and in form than any living creature; its hands do no mischief; its feet run on no errands of evil and its lips speak neither lie nor blasphemy. No human being with passions and frailties can approach in harmlessness the product of the artist's chisel, and if he could, of what value would his life be? It is a low measure of man that estimates him by his negative qualities. He must be positively good to be respected. His back even though it bend, must help to bear his brother's load; his hands, though sometimes idle or worse than uselessly employed, must have a part in the shaping and molding of the world; his tongue, though it may stammer or sometimes utter what the heart would fain retract, must be the vehicle of a higher and a broader truth than can be found within selfish limits.

As the ship's captain throws over any cargo that endangers the safety of the passengers, so man must be willing to sacrifice anything and everything—yea, even money—if it impedes his progress or prevents the highest possible achievements. Some men can carry a larger load of money than others. Some may run with a burden that would bear others to the ground, but there is a limit to the strength of all, and each must, at his own risk, find the limit for himself.

The ideal wisely chosen and conscientiously followed offers the surest protection against overloading with money, for the ideal will first prevent the accumulation of any money at all except as it comes as a fair remuneration for services rendered to society; second, it will lead to such a use of the money as will be most helpful to the individual and to society; and, third, it will develop impulses that will themselves overmaster and regulate the desire for lucre.

* *

A FALLACIOUS DEFENSE.

The Ohio *Farmer* of recent date publishes an article by a citizen of Ohio, an ex-member of the legislature, on the election of senators by the people. He starts out by saying that the present method of electing United States senators by legislatures was a compromise. That is true. There were men of the Jeffersonian school who believed in the people and were willing to trust them, and there were men of the Hamiltonian school who were afraid of popular government and sought to hamper it by every possible restriction, but certainly a hundred years of experience ought to be worth something. That experience has shown that the government is best when it is nearest to the people, and it is high time for an amendment that will give the people power to elect their representatives in the senate.

The second argument made against the change is that it would lead to the destruction of the equality of the states in the senate. There is no force in this argument. The state's representation has nothing whatever to do with the manner of election, and the state's equality in the senate is more likely to be made sure by an amendment which would relieve senatorial elections of the suspicion that now attaches to them than by a blind disregard of present defects. Unless a state is something different from the people of the state, there is no reason why the sovereignty of the state could not be represented by senators elected by the people as well as by senators chosen by the legislature.

The Ohioan above referred to then attempts to answer the charge of corruption by saying that it is possibly true, but that "purchase of seats in legislative bodies is not a new thing." He quotes the corrupt election of members of parliament and cites a case in 1831 where 489 members out of 659 "were elected by 144 peers and 123 commons." He quotes Macauley as an authority on the corruption that existed, but he neglects to add that it was because of the rotten borough system that the representation in parliament was changed and that Macauley was one of the advocates of the change.

It is true that the election of senators by the people would not absolutely prevent corruption, but it would work a great improvement over the present method. It is easier to purchase an election from a few representatives to whom large sums can be paid than to secure an election by buying a majority of the people.

It is no answer to the almost universal demand for the popular election of senators to say that the voter ought to be more careful about the selection of representatives in the legislature. That is true, but there is no reason why those who do use care in the selection of legislators should be left at the mercy of legislators who, although with a good private record, yield to the temptations that beset a legislator when great corporations are interested in selecting a senatorial agent to carry out their purposes.

SAVED BY THE ELKINS LAW.

The New York *American* calls attention to the testimony of Mr. Baer which casts some suspicion upon the good faith of the republican party in the enactment of the Elkins law. The interstate commerce law as it existed prior to February 19 last, contained the following provision:

"Any person who shall neglect or refuse to attend and testify, or to answer any lawful inquiry, or to produce books, papers, tariffs, contracts, agreements and documents, if in his power to do so, in obedience to the subponena or lawful requirement of the commission, shall be guilty of an offense, and upon conviction thereof by a court of competent jurisdiction shall be punished by a fine of not less than one hundred dollars nor more than five thousand dollars, or by imprisonment for not more than one year, or by both such fine and imprisonment."

The Elkins law which the president has pointed to as a partial fulfillment of his promise of anti-trust legislation contains the following:

"In all convictions occurring after the passage of this act for offenses under said acts to regulate commerce, whether committed before or after the passage of this act, or for offenses under this section, no penalty shall be imposed on the guilty party other than the fine prescribed by law, imprisonment wherever now prescribed as part of the penalty being hereby abolished."

A comparison of these extracts will show that the Elkins law repealed so much of the interstate commerce law as prescribed imprisonment as a part of the penalty, and it will be noticed that it is retroactive to the extent of relieving from imprisonment even when the criminal act committed was committed prior to the passage of the Elkins act. This makes it possible for an official to refuse to attend and testify, to answer any lawful inquiry or to produce books, papers, tariff contracts, agreements and documents, even though it is in his power to produce them. The only punishment for such refusal is a fine of not less than $100 nor more than $5,000. Under no circumstances now can the official be imprisoned. What is a fine of $5,000 to a corporation that may make a hundred thousand or even a million by violating the law? It would seem that the real purpose of the Elkins law was not to prevent discrimination so much as to prevent the punishment of officials who are guilty of violation of the law.

More than four months prior to the passage of the Elkins law Mr. Hearst called the attention of the president to the fact that the coal trust was violating the interstate commerce law, and urged the enforcement of the law. Nothing has been done so far, and the Elkins bill makes it more difficult than before to enforce the interstate commerce law. In the hearing before the interstate commerce commission on the 29th of April last, Mr. Clarence J. Shearn, attorney for Mr. Hearst, called Mr. Baer's attention to an official bulletin of the department of labor, in which a statement made by Mr. Baer to Mr. Wright relative to the miners' strike in 1900 was quoted. The following is taken from the *American's* report of the testimony.

Mr. Shearn (to Mr. Baer)—Did you say as follows, referring to the preceding strike, that:

"Shortly after this strike was inaugurated, Senator Hanna met a number of gentlemen and insisted that if the strike were not settled it would extend to Ohio, Indiana and Illinois, and the election of Mr. McKinley and Mr. Roosevelt would be endangered. He insisted that he was authorized to settle the strike, through Mr. Mitchell, if the operators would agree to a 10 per cent advance in wages. After a great deal of pressure had been brought to bear upon the presidents of the coal companies and positive assurances were given that the situation was really dangerous, President McKinley sending me personally a gentleman to assure me that Ohio and Indiana were in danger unless some adjustment was made, we agreed to put up a notice which was prepared, we understood, at Indianapolis and furnished by the united mine workers. The private operators absolutely refused to join in this advance, and instead of the strike being ended as promised, it continued on for some time, and it became necessary, in order to relieve the situation, to call a meeting of the private operators with the presidents of the coal companies and to agree with them that if they would put up notices to pay 10 per cent increase we would meet a committee which they should appoint and endeavor to increase, if possible, the price of coal. They agreed to this, a committee was appointed by the private operators, and we sat two or three days a month for three months to reach an agreement with them. That agreement involved a heavy compensation to the private operators from the coal companies. The coal companies had agreed to change the basis of coal purchased from the private operators from a basis of 40 per cent and 60 per cent to a basis of 35 per cent and 65 per cent. In other words, we had to decrease 5 per cent and they increased 5 per cent."

Mr. Shearn: You stated that to Mr. Wright?

Mr. Baer: I did, I assume; it sounds all right—if you have read it correctly.

Mr. Shearn: That is the fact, is it not, anyway?

Mr. Baer: Yes, sir. It is the fact.

It seems from Mr. Baer's testimony that the republican candidate for the presidency personally sent word to Mr. Baer to assure him that Ohio and Indiana were in danger unless the strike could be settled, and Mr. Baer and his associates, desiring to help the republican ticket, agreed to a settlement by which the operators were to have 10 per cent increase in wages, and the coal trust, in order to secure this, had to compensate the private operators. Here we have it—the republican candidate appealing to the trusts to help him at a heavy loss to themselves and now the administration that came into power by the aid of the trusts puts through a bill that relieves Mr. Baer, among others, from the possibility of imprisonment for the violation of the law.

Does this not prove that the democratic charges against the republican party were well sustained? Does it not prove that the republican party is in close affiliation with the trusts and obligated to them? It will be remembered that Mr. Baer is the president of a railroad, besides the president of the trust. How long will the republican farmers, laboring men and business men be blind to their party's subserviency to the trusts? How long will the rank and file of the democratic party be blind to the fact that the reorganizers would, if possible, put the democratic party in exactly the same position that the republican party now occupies in regard to the trusts?

SQUEEZED BY THE TRUSTS.

It seems that those makers of farm implements who are outside of the implement combination have petitioned President Roosevelt for relief from more than thirty institutions which are denounced as trusts. The petitioners make about 10 per cent of the farm machinery, but are subject to extortion in the purchase of raw material and other things that go into the manufacture of implements. Several of the corporations are specifically named, among them the Standard Oil company, the United States Steel company, Tube, Leather, White Lead and Pig Iron trusts. One of the republican papers, in speaking of the petition, says, "If there is any ground for government interference the attorney general will undoubtedly take action," but it insists that the case of every trust must be tried separately, and that a "long time must necessarily elapse before relief can be given, if any is needed." The International Harvester company, it is stated, manufactures 90 per cent of the farm implements used, and it is able to avoid the hardships from which the independent manufacturers suffer. The circumstances in this case, and the arguments made by the republican papers, show that the republican position is not one of opposition to the trusts in general, but to particular features of the trusts. In other words, the republicans do not denounce the private monopoly as a bad thing, but assert it to be the duty of the government to interfere in case a monopoly misuses its power, but as it takes a long time for investigation and a long time for action, it will be seen that this remedy is really no remedy at all.

LAZINESS.

With the coming of spring there is apt to be the languor sometimes called spring fever which attacks the boys who are old enough to work. It is so pleasant to rest under the shade of the tree or stroll along the stream with hook and line that where some necessity does not assist it requires some effort to throw off the feeling and undertake work with energy. Laziness is the weed that grows where industry is not seduously cultivated—to use the comparison that some one has employed to describe the weed and the plant—laziness seems to be the child of Nature while industry is the step-child. A little reasoning would teach the boy verging upon manhood's estate that laziness is a physical condition to be shunned while industry is a physical habit to be cultivated. All that it requires to convert a lazy boy into an industrious boy is the stimulus of the will and the habitual triumph of the will over the inclinations of the body will permanently transform a sluggish and slothful creature into one alert, quick and active. And what will stimulate the will? Give the boy a true conception of life and let him understand that God has linked enduring enjoyment with uprightness and honest toil. Let him learn that those are not only most useful, but most happy who have something to occupy their hands, their heads and their hearts.

The body needs exercise and without sufficient exercise it finds itself less capable to resist the inroads of disease and the advances of age.

The mind needs exercise. Unless it is employed the faculties are dulled and the mental perceptions grow less acute. The heart, too, needs exercise; unless it is frequently employed in deeds of kindness and benevolence it will shrivel up.

While recreation and amusement have necessary places in furnishing variety and elasticity, the boy should learn that amusements have to be the seasoning of his work, not the entire food of his life.

Habits of industry formed in youth made labor easy in after years. Laziness in youth is apt to blight the mature years. Very few can expect to go through life without labor. Many who expect to inherit wealth lose it because they lack the habits of those who acquired it. The young man who is diligent has, other things being equal, the best chance of finding leisure to rest as he grows old, while those who waste the morning hours of life are most apt, other things being equal, to find it necessary to work when their strength is declining and when the shadows are falling to the east.

EXPANSION VS. IMPERIALISM.

In discussing the Louisiana purchase recently ex-Secretary Charles Emory Smith attempted to use the act of Jefferson as a precedent for the Philippine policy of the McKinley administration, but the distinction between Jeffersonian expansion and republican imperialism is so clear that it would be a reflection on a man's intelligence to say that he could not see it.

The land purchased by Jefferson was contiguous, the islands, forcibly taken by the republican administration, are in another hemisphere and are separated from us by the Pacific ocean. The Louisiana territory was sparsely settled; the Philippine islands are more densely populated than our own country. (If we take the Filipinos and their land we will have less land per capita than we have now.)

The scattered inhabitants of the Louisiana territory came in as citizens; the Filipinos come in as subjects.

The Louisiana territory was settled up by people who located on the land for the purpose of living upon it and cultivating it; the Americans who go to the Philippines go there to work the natives and to carry away all the wealth that is movable.

The settlers in the Louisiana territory formed self-governing communities, the people who go to the Philippines go almost wholly as carpet-bag officials or as exploiters of the helpless.

The Louisiana territory was carved into states; the Philippine islands are to form a colony.

The people who live in the states made out of the Louisiana purchase share in the guarantees of our constitution and in the destinies of our nation; the Filipinos have no protection from our constitution, and no voice in our government, or even in their own.

The people who live on the land purchased by Jefferson participate in the levying of the taxes which they pay; the Filipinos are taxed without representation and shot down if they object to the exercise of arbitrary power by an alien government.

These are some of the distinctions.

To use the purchase of the Louisiana territory as an excuse for a colonial policy in the Orient is as absurd as it would be to use the kindness of the Good Samaritan as a justification of the criminal conduct of Cain.

ORGANIZED WEALTH.

The Wall Street *Journal*, which may fairly be considered one of the ablest representatives of the money worshiping portion of the nation's population, rushes to the rescue of "organized wealth." It begins by attempting to misunderstand the phrase, and then endeavors to throw upon legitimate business the odium that ought to be reserved for predatory wealth. It would be a reflection upon the intelligence of the editor of the paper to suppose that he does not understand of the financiers and trust magnates to control the government in their own private interests, corrupting voters, coercing business men, and even threatening panics whenever such threats are thought to be useful.

There is a clear line of demarkation between those, on the one hand, who as individuals, partners or stockholders in a corporation, are attempting to add to the nation's wealth by the development of industry and commerce, giving to society a full return for the money they receive, and those, on the other hand, who attempt to destroy competition and extort from their victims such bounties as greed and avarice may dictate.

It is one of the tricks of the fox, when hotly pursued, to rush through a flock of sheep or a herd of cattle in order that those who pursue may lose the scent, and so the monopolies that prey upon the public are always sure to run to cover behind legitimate and honorable organizations in order to avoid those who endeavor to punish them. It is a confession of cowardice, and an admission that the institutions thus defended cannot be defended upon their merits.

A recent issue of the *Journal* illustrates the methods employed by organized wealth and those who speak for it. It seems that the eastern capitalists are not pleased with the democratic administration in Chicago. That administration, although evidently satisfactory to the people of Chicago, is not acceptable to the New York financiers. The Wall Street *Journal*, therefore, reads the people of Chicago a lecture on their duty, and winds up with this warning:

"We know the pulse of eastern capitalists toward investments in Chicago about as well as anybody, and we have not hesitated to say that disgust with Chicago has been evident among them all, and it will take very attractive offerings to get investment capital from the east to Chicago again."

The people of Chicago are advised that "the terminal charges of the railroads in Chicago should be carefully scrutinized," and that "capital should be encouraged to come to Chicago." It will be remembered that Mayor Harrison has opposed the ninety-nine-year street railway lease, and insisted upon giving the people of Chicago a chance to speak on the subject of franchises; even the legislature of Illinois was finally compelled to indorse the position taken by Mayor Harrison and his supporters. Having failed to coerce the city, the capitalists now seek to intimidate it with the threat of withdrawing capital. If the New York financiers are not willing to loan money to Chicago, Chicago might issue the bonds in small denominations and sell them to the people of Chicago. It would not be difficult to find a demand for all the bonds that Chicago is compelled to issue, and it would be just as well for those bonds to be held by the people as to have the people's money deposited in savings banks. Whenever any state attempts to reduce the rate of interest or to legislate for the protection of its people, it is always warned, as Chicago is now being warned, that capital must be tenderly dealt with, and laws made for foreign investors rather than for the benefit of the citizens of the state.

If the Wall Street *Journal* wants to find a legitimate field the difference between the legitimate business enterprises with which no one finds fault and the arrogant and insolent attempt for its energies let it turn its attention to the watered stock that is being palmed off upon the public and made valuable by extortion practiced on the public; let it arraign the street speculators who are shocked at small gambling, but swindle the public with corners, raids and concerted manipulation of stock. If the people outside of New York were as careful to protect their own interests as the Wall street financiers are to advance theirs, those who are now the masters of commerce would find their power for harm greatly curtailed.

ROCKEFELLER'S PRAYER.

A reader of THE COMMONER sends a clipping containing a dispatch from New York reporting a speech made by John D. Rockefeller, Jr., to his Bible class. The dispatch stated that Rockefeller "practically stated today that the Standard Oil company was under divine guidance." In the quotation from the speech young Rockefeller is represented as saying: "In one important matter involving big money I prayed every night and morning to God to direct me. The matter was so big it seemed beyond me. Suddenly one day light came, and I saw the proper path clear. God answered my prayer. The consciousness that we are divinely directed gives comfort, courage, strength, and then the way brightens."

Mr. Rockefeller is to be commended for his trust in God, and he is right also in saying that there is comfort and courage in faith. But the fact that he prays is not in itself conclusive evidence that his business is under divine guidance. It is not necessary that all Christian people shall sanction the Rockefeller method of making money merely because Rockefeller prays. In every great war in which Christians have been engaged on both sides, prayer has been offered on both sides, and men of both sides have believed themselves justified in appealing to the God of Battles. In every persecution that has been carried on in the name of religion both those who persecuted and those who were victims, lifted up their voices to God and prayed for help. Mothers have sacrificed their children to appease or to propitiate idols, and mothers have protected their children to please God. There must be intelligence as well as zeal, and the zeal must be directed to righteous ends before it can be condemned. Lincoln drew the proper distinction; when asked if he was not anxious to have God on his side, he said that he was anxious rather to be on God's side. Mr. Rockefeller must make the same distinction. He may think that he is doing his full duty when he prays that the Lord will help the Standard Oil company to make an enormous profit by the practice of extortion, but millions of people believe that his prayer would be more in keeping with holy writ if he prayed for strength to resist the temptation to use trust methods—methods which differ in form, but not in principle, from the methods of the robbers upon the highway.

PICAYUNE WRONG AGAIN.

The New Orleans *Picayune* now admits that the supporters of the Chicago and Kansas City platforms only asked for the reinstatement of the law which Andrew Jackson signed, but it attempts to dodge the issue by complaining that conditions are different. It says:

"Today silver is worth per ounce in London, the greatest silver market of the world, about 50 cents, so that our silver dollar would be worth about 38 cents. If we had the free coinage of silver, anybody could go into the market and buy silver at, say 50 cents an ounce, and have it coined and pay it out at the rate of 129 cents an ounce."

The position taken by the *Picayune* is absurd. It is strange that a man who has enough intelligence to occupy a position on the editorial staff of any paper should be guilty of so ridiculous a statement. Why would any man sell his silver at 50 cents an ounce and let another man make the profit on it? We do not sell hogs or corn, cotton or cattle, in that way. The moment the price goes up in New York it goes up all over the country, and so when a man can go to the mint and coin an ounce of silver into $1.29 he will not sell it to the editor of the *Picayune* for 50 cents or for anything less than $1.29.

The argument of the *Picayune* recalls the story told by Ignatius Donnelly. It ran like this: Two men were discussing the money question in a sleeping car, and as they talked others came up and asked questions. Finally one man asked the silver man if he thought it was right for the government to pass a law that would enable a person to buy silver for 50 cents and coin it into a dollar and make the difference (the same argument advanced by the *Picayune*). The silver man explained that under free coinage any man in the world could take an ounce of silver to the mint and convert it into $1.29, and then asked if, under such a law, anybody in the car would sell an ounce of silver for less than $1.29 and let some other person make the profit. There was silence for a moment, and then a voice in a remote corner said: "I would." The silver man went to see from what source the voice came, and found that it came from a young man who was sitting by his mother, and the mother said: "Don't pay any attention to the boy. He is an idiot, and I am taking him to the asylum."

If the editor of the *Picayune* would not sell his silver for less than its market value, why does he suppose any one else would; and if nobody would sell his silver for less than it was worth at the mint, how could anybody buy an ounce for 50 cents and coin it into $1.29.

The trouble is that the editor of the *Picayune*, like other goldites who discuss the question without understanding it, then talks about coining it after the free coinage law passes, without considering the influence of a law-created demand upon the price of silver.

ARGUMENTS AGAINST SECOND TERM.

A reader of THE COMMONER asks whether Mr. Cleveland did not in his first campaign use language condemning a second term. Yes; he said in his letter of acceptance, given to the public August 18, 1884:

"When we consider the patronage of this great office, the allurements of power, the temptation to retain public place once gained, and, more than all the availability a party finds in an incumbent whom a horde of office-holders, with zeal born of benefit received and fostered by the hope of favors yet to come, stand ready to aid with money and trained political service, we recognize in the eligibility of the president for re-election a most serious danger to that calm, deliberate and intelligent political action which must characterize a government by the people."

It will be seen that Mr. Cleveland at that time fully recognized "the serious danger" of a second term, but the knowledge of this danger did not prevent his being a candidate for re-election in 1888; neither did it prevent his accepting the service of a "horde of office-holders, with zeal born of benefits received and fostered by the hope of favors yet to come." He was not only willing to use a "horde of office-holders" for his own benefit in 1888, but he was willing to use the ex-office-holders for his own advantage in 1892, and in 1896 he used the office-holders, as far as his influence extended, to defeat the democratic party.

There is, however, supporting Mr. Cleevland a more dangerous horde than the horde of office-holders. It is the horde of plutocrats—the predatory rich, the beneficiaries of class legislation, the exploiters of the public. These have found in Mr. Cleveland a man who can be trusted to do their bidding.

HISTORY DISTORTED.

A Kansas reader of THE COMMONER quotes a magazine writer as saying that the gold standard was adopted by the United States in 1834 under the leadership of Andrew Jackson and Thomas Benton. It is strange that any one could be so ignorant of history or so devoid of conscience as to make such an assertion. The law of 1834 merely reduced the size of the gold dollar, so as to make it weigh one-sixteenth as much as the silver dollar, it having weighed one-fifteenth as much from 1792 down to that year.

Free and unlimited coinage at the ratio of 16 to 1 continued to 1873, and every holder of gold or silver bullion could have his bullion converted into unlimited legal tender money at the established ratio. Prior to 1834 the gold dollar was undervalued at the mint, and was therefore at a premium. Between 1834 and 1873 the silver dollar was undervalued at the mint, and therefore at a premium.

When in 1896 and 1900 the gold standard advocates declared that the gold standard was adopted in 1834 the advocates of bimetallism answered them conclusively by offering to accept as a settlement of the question, the very law which Jackson signed, but as that law provided for the free and unlimited coinage of gold and silver at the ratio of 16 to 1, without waiting for the aid or consent of any other nation, it was of course not acceptable to the gold-bugs. All that bimetallists ask for today is the re-enactment of the very law of 1834 to which Andrew Jackson affixed his signature.

NOT YET ENOUGH MONEY.

Who would have thought it? Harper's Weekly, that thick and thin exponent of scarce money, dead dollars, cheap goods and plutocracy in general, has at last recognized that we need more money! It says:

"The vision of financial reform and of a much needed elasticity of currency, held out before American business men, has passed in a political wrangle in which jealousy and the spite of factions have unfortunately figured. It was hardly to be expected that a short session of congress could have passed a measure of so much moment and one so radical in comparison with our own antiquated system. But the crisis of last fall demanded that legislative precedent be set aside in the universal clamor for ways and means of conducting the business of a constantly expanding nation."

Financial reform is needed and an elastic currency! There is a "universal clamor" for ways and means of conducting the business of a "constantly expanding nation." What are the measures advocated by Harper's Weekly? First, an asset currency. This is defended on the ground that we need an elastic currency, one that the banks can let out and draw in at pleasure, a currency that will put the people still more at the mercy of the financiers than they are today. If an elastic currency is needed why do they not provide that any person having a government bond shall be permitted to deposit it and draw the money, foregoing the interest while he uses the money? This would give instant relief in case of stringency. It would simply convert an interest-bearing non-legal tender obligation into a non-interest-bearing legal tender obligation. Nobody would deposit the bond unless the money was needed worse than the bond, and he would withdraw the bond as soon as money became easy.

According to the republican plan the banks are to issue the money when money gets scarce and then they loan it out to the people at the high interest rate which a money stringency makes.

The democratic plan allows a person having a government bond to obtain relief without the aid or consent of any banker. No advocate of asset currency will claim that an asset currency is as safe as greenbacks, or as convenient or as certain in its automatic action. Why, then, is an asset currency favored? Because the bankers want it.

Harper's Weekly also wants the Aldrich bill, which provides

for the loaning of government money to the banks. Why? Because we need the money in circulation, is the reply. It is less than seven years since we were told, in the campaign of 1896, that we had plenty of money in the country and did not need any more. Since that time the volume of money has been increased over five hundred millions, and yet money is still so scarce that the financiers insist upon the loaning of all surplus money to the banks in order to keep business going—this, in addition to the asset currency defended by the same arguments. If we need more money, as we certainly do in spite of the enormous increase since '96, why not use good money instead of bad money? A Nebraska banker who went over to the republican party in 1896 to save the country, as he declared, from "a depreciated currency," made a speech at a banquet recently and denounced the asset currency. He said: "The silver dollar which we condemned had nearly fifty cents worth of silver in it, but the asset currency which they propose may be absolutely worthless. I left the democratic party to protect the country from bad money. Is the republican party going to reward me with an asset currency, which is infinitely worse than silver?" He ought to sue the republican party for breach of promise.

The democratic party believes that more money is needed and it believes in supplying that need with standard money— money that has been used for thousands of years. The republican party first denied that we needed more money and now it sets up a "universal clamor" for an increase of the banks' promises to pay. How long will it be before the people of the country recogize the irreconcilable contradiction between the arguments made against an increase of good money in 1896 and the arguments made in favor of a lot of bad money now?

ANOTHER NEGRO BURNED.

The burning of the negro school teacher at Belleville, Ill., recently, is the latest, if not the most forcible evidence that has been given in this country of race prejudice. The victim was not a low or brutal representative of his race, but, on the contrary, one of the more intellectual of his people. He had sufficiently advanced to enable him to become a school teacher.

The burning did not occur in a southern state where the race question is constantly present in the minds of all, but in one of the largest northern states, and under the administration of a republican governor.

The crime which led to the lynching and burning was not an assault upon a woman—the revolting crime that has usually led to burnings in the south, but an assault upon a republican official. It seems that County Superintendent Hertel had, for reasons which to him seemed sufficient, refused to renew Wyatt's certificate. There is nothing to indicate that the refusal to issue the certificate was due to race prejudice, and certainly republicans will not claim that the superintendent in the discharge of his official duty gave any just cause for offense. Angered by the refusal, Wyatt drew a revolver and fired upon the superintendent. He was arrested and taken to the jail, but as soon as the news of the attempted murder became known a mob gathered at the jail, took the negro out, and hung him to a telegraph pole. That not being sufficient, a fire was kindled and the man cut down and burned. Even the burning did not satisfy the vengeance of his executors. According to the account published in the New York *World* "they fell upon him with clubs and knives, and cut and beat the burning body almost to pieces, and not until every sign of life had departed did they desist and permit the flames to devour the body."

It is needless to say that a white man would have been differently dealt with. Shocking as is the teacher's assault upon the superintendent, it did not differ materially from the tragedies that occur only too frequently in all parts of the country. Sometimes the perpetrator of such an act is hanged by a mob, but there was nothing in this case to justify the belief that a frenzied mob would have acted as they did had Wyatt been white instead of black. We may say what we please in condemnation of race prejudice, but it is a thing that must be considered—it cannot be ignored—and there is no doubt that the prejudice has been growing during the last few years.

Can its growth be traced to any source? Is it unreasonable to suppose that the effort on the part of some of the republican leaders to force the appointment of colored men upon protesting white people has had something to do with it? These appointments have embittered the whites and the protests made by the whites have embittered the negroes, and the two races are more hostile than at any time since the war. Is it not time to discuss this subject soberly and seriously, with a view to arriving at some honest understanding? Is it not time to lay aside the political phases of the subject and seek a solution that will render it possible for the two races to develop and make progress without constant and increasing friction?

CLEVELAND AND FRANCIS.

Labor Compendium of St. Louis criticises the World's fair management for inviting Cleveland to speak at the dedication exercises. What it says in regard to Mr. Roosevelt's use of the occasion to make a republican speech is just. The president was guilty of a gross breach of propriety in practically ignoring Jefferson's part in the acquisition and in attempting to build a republican argument upon the purchase of the Louisiana territory. Mr. Cleveland's appointment, however, was perfectly natural when all the circumstances are considered. Mr. Francis is at the head of the exposition and is devoting his time to it. Having been a member of Mr. Cleveland's cabinet he, of course, feels under obligation to the ex-president, and having deserted the democratic party at the time that Mr. Cleveland did, he would very naturally prefer his brand of democracy to the Kansas City platform brand.

Then, too, Mr. Francis is conspicuous among the reorganizers, and desires to give them all the prestige and advantage he can. It was hardly to be expected that he would consult the democrats of Missouri or of the section of the country immediately tributary to St. Louis. The selection of Mr. Cleveland was not only more pleasing to the republican members of the national commission, and to the republicans generally than the selection of any democrat could have been, but, as he belongs to no party, it made the occasion non-partisan. Mr. Bryan was invited along with other visitors to occupy a seat upon the stand, but he feared that his presence there, even as an invited guest, might inject that partisan element which the management had so studiously avoided.

ORGANIZED AGAINST LABOR.

The National Manufacturers' association, of which Mr. D. M. Parry of Indianapolis is president and Marshall Cushing of New York secretary, has sent out a letter signed by the secretary in which the association makes the following claim:

"We beat the eight-hour bill in the last congress and have evidently got to do it in the next; for already the labor leaders are having an eminent lawyer draw a new eight-hour bill which shall be constitutional, if possible, and if possible, shall pass muster with the committee on education and labor of the senate, and the senate itself, and even with the president, who is to be urged, through all the pressure that can be brought to bear by the American federation of labor, to indorse this measure in his next annual measure."

In the declaration of principles the association makes no mention of its opposition to an eight-hour day. It starts out by declaring in favor of "fair dealing," but it seems that its idea for fair dealing is to attack a proposed law which is in the interest of fairness. The letter then proceeds:

"Our association must also be prepared to beat the anti-conspiracy bill—which would legalize the free picket around your plant. But that proposition also can be beaten—if we have the help of all who are naturally our friends."

The association seems to be getting into politics fast. The next thing that the association has to deal with is the new department of commerce and labor. The letter says: "There will also be, during the fall and winter, very much of assistance that will have to be given to the new department—which our association can give all the better because it was the chief influence creating that department. This new branch of the government hasn't merely the labor question to deal with, but also all the questions relating to the big combinations and the continuing expansion of our export trade." So it seems that the department of commerce and labor was not after all in the interest of labor, but in the interest of commerce, and the national association of manufacturers is to occupy itself getting the new department started. It more and more clearly appears that the measures of the republican party are all of the same kind, in the interest of capital rather than in the interest of those whose labor creates capital. We shall see whether the association will be able to control congress as other capitalistic associations have.

THE NATIONAL CITY'S SCHEMES.

The Boston *Transcript* has the following in regard to the scheme which the National City Bank worked on the other banks. It just slipped in and used the government to send its letters to the holders of bonds. Of course the secretary would show the same favor to other banks, after it had given the inside to the National City Bank, but would it have given the other banks the start, or could it have given to all the same opportunity?

"The National City Bank of New York has addressed a circular letter to every registered holder of United States government bonds offering to buy their bonds at the highest current quotations or exchange other securities for them. The bank sent their letters through the United States treasury, where the addresses and stamps were put on the envelopes by the treasury clerks, the bank paying for the labor and postage. In this way the addresses of the holders of the bonds were not secured by the bank nor otherwise made public. In reply to a complaint for permitting the circulars to be sent to holders of bonds, Leslie M. Shaw, secretary of the treasury, said that the same favor would be granted to any reputable bond firm or to any bank, especially when the object was, as in this case, to further the government's plan for refunding some of its bonds. The National City Bank's circular letter was signed by Frank A. Vanderlip, one of its vice presidents. He pointed out that at present prices the 4 per cent bonds of 1907 return the investor only 1 1-5 per cent, while the 4s of 1925 can be bought on a 2 per cent basis."

SELECTING CANDIDATES.

Mr. Hamilton Holt, New York Independent, New York City.—My Dear Sir: I have been trying to get time to send you the article which you desire, but so far have not found leisure for it. I can answer your question in a very few words. The real issue between the democratic party and the republican party is whether the government shall be based upon the doctrine that all men are created equal and so administered as to recognize the rights of man, or built upon an aristocratic foundation and administered in behalf of the few at the expense of the many. In all the republican policies you will find that what are called "property rights"—and the phrase simply means superior consideration for those who

On the tariff question the manufacturers are singled out for benefits at the expense of the consumers; on the money question the financiers are singled out and their interests advanced at the expense of the producers of wealth; on the trust question the comparatively few who are endeavoring to monopolize the industries of the country are singled out and protected as against the many who must buy of them; and on the question of imperialism the syndicates organized to exploit the islands are given greater consideration than the taxpayers of this country or the victims of our benevolent assimilation.

You ask whether the candidate of 1904 should be "a compromise between the gold and silver democrats, a silver democrat or a gold democrat." This depends entirely upon what the democratic party wants to do. If it wants to bid for the support of the plutocratic element, it will nominate a gold democrat; if it wants to bid for the support of the masses, it will nominate a silver democrat. If it does not want any support at all and does not care to take part in the contest between man and Mammon, it will find a man who lacks either the brains or the heart to take a position. There is no possibility of compromise; if the party is to be an effective force in politics it must go in one direction or the other, and the direction cannot long be concealed.

The difference upon the money question, among those who understood it, was not so much a difference of opinion as a difference in sympathies and that difference exists today as it did then. A man whose sympathies are with organized wealth has no claim to leadership in the democratic party unless the party intends to become the exponent of organized wealth. The money question is not a matter of gold or silver; it is whether there shall be a sufficient volume of money or an insufficient volume of money. Gold and silver together furnish more money than gold alone, and the same reasons that led some to favor the gold standard as against the double standard will lead the same persons to favor some limitation upon gold coinage if the quantity of gold ever becomes sufficient to maintain the level of prices.

In 1891 Mr. McKinley denounced Grover Cleveland and declared that during his first administration he was discriminating against one of the money metals of the country; "trying to make money scarcer and therefore dearer—money the master and all things else the servant." No one has ever stated the issue more clearly than Mr. McKinley did in those words, and no one ever brought a more severe arraignment against a public man than Mr. McKinley brought against Mr. Cleveland. The issue still exists and in the nature of things must ever exist; and it makes a great deal of difference to the democratic party whether its candidate wants to make "money the master and all things else the servant," or desires rather to make man the master and all things else the servant. It makes a great deal of difference to the people of the country, too, whether it has a president who recognizes the true relation which should exist between the man and the dollar.

Very truly yours, W. J. BRYAN.
(Letter to the New York Independent.)

GOV. BLACK'S STRONG WORDS.

Governor Chauncey F. Black, recent president of the National Association of Democratic Clubs, sent to the Crescent Democratic club at York, Pa., on Jefferson's Day, a letter which deserves consideration. Mr. Black comes from sturdy democratic stock, being a son of the famous Judge Jerry Black. The governor's labors in behalf of democratic principles and his prominence in party work give an emphasis to his comments upon the attempted reorganization. The following extract will be of interest to the readers of THE COMMONER:

"We read a good deal in republican newspapers about a variety of schemes for the reorganization of the democratic party. We never see in connection with these remarkable projects the names of any regular and reliable democrats. The engineers are all well known republicans, who helped, directly or indirectly, to beat down the democracy and put the trusts in power in 1896, and to keep them in in 1900. They are insignificant in numbers. They describe themselves as 'leaders,' but point to no followers. Now it strikes me that where a hundred democrats disagree, in sentiment, and ninety-nine are found on one side and one only on the other side, ninety-nine ought to have their way. But if besides it appears that the one obstinate fellow is not a democrat at all, but an interloping republican, who has come back simply to boss matters, on the ground that at some remote period he pretended to be a democrat, but deserted at the pinch, the claim of the ninety-nine just democrats to run their own party, as against this self-sufficient agent of the enemy, detailed to regulate democratic affairs for the time being, would seem to be pretty clear.

"The democratic party in the national field is at present very well and satisfactorily organized. The masses who voted its tickets in 1896 and 1900, are more than content with it, and have no desire to have it republicainzed or reorganized in the interest of the trusts. And the plans with that object in view are pure wind. They have no substance. There will be no reorganization. The democratic national convention will be democratic; it will nominate a democrat on a democratic platform. He will poll the democratic vote, with its natural increase, possibly more, according to circumstances then existing, and he may be elected. But with any other kind of a platform or candidate, it is hard to conceive how, with the most efficient organization imaginable, and any amount of money contributed by special interests concerned, one-third of the honest democrats of the country could be brought to the polls. Such an experiment would make a wreck only less complete and contemptible than that of the shameless republican side show—the Indianapolis sham gold 'democratic' affair of 1896. And that is precisely the result the reorganizers propose to themselves and are expected by the republican managers to accomplish!"

ROOSEVELT'S "MASTERLY RETREAT."

At a time when it was apparent that anti-trust legislation was at an end so far as the recent session of congress was concerned, Attorney General Knox gave out an interview in which he said:

"On the whole, the situation is eminently satisfactory, and is the result of concessions, modifications of views and forms of expressions on the part of many earnest and thoughtful men who have endeavored within a very brief session to meet a rational public demand in a rational and effective way."

"Concessions" is good, and "modifications" even better. No wonder the same paper which contained the Knox interview announced that Mr. Morgan called at the White house. Surely the meeting must have been a pleasant one after so amicable a settlement of trust questions. If anything more is necessary to prove that the president has obeyed—it sounds harsh, but obeyed is the word—the commands of the trust magnates it is found in the following editorial which appeared in the New York Sun (reported to be owned by Mr. Morgan):

THEODORE ROOSEVELT'S GREATEST SERVICE TO HIS COUNTRY.

"What is now called 'the president's program' of legislation for federal suppression of business appears to be nothing more or less than this:

"The rejection of all the more radical measures proposed by senators or representatives or judiciary committees or unofficial sociologists, or even by Attorney General Knox.

"The elimination of every plan or proposal which by the utmost strain of courtesies of language can be described as a real sure-enough trust-buster.

"The progressive refinement of the original demands of strenuous conviction down to the point where the passage of the Elkins anti-rebate bill and the enactment of the department of commerce bill, with its mildly statisical bureau of information, are regarded as 'satisfactory' by the president.

"Let no candid person withhold from Mr. Roosevelt the immense credit that belongs to him for his present efforts, between eleven o'clock and noon, to undo as far as possible the mischief wrought in the darkness and unwisdom of the early hours of the morning. Consider what it is he is now doing for the cause of sanity and constitutional government! He had delivered on the stump a series of speeches which could scarcely be distinguished from Mr. Bryan's utterances on the same subject. He had inspired by suggestion the great mass of incendiary measures that are piled high in the document room of the capitol, like a harmless monument in memory of his initial mistake. He had spurred on Mr. Littlefield to a rivalry which resulted in that stateman's discomfiture and disgust. He had even set ablaze the sociological imagination of the venerable Mr. Hoar. He had carried the white plume of Rooseveltian leadership far to the front of the attack on the foundations of business confidence and national prosperity. He had done all this and much more in the emotional earnestness of his misunderstanding of his mission and duty at Washington.

"But as soon as the president clearly perceived the disastrous potentialities of the forces he had invoked and the true direction and significance of the movement he had inaugurated—and he has apparently had the wit to perceive the same before it was too late—no foolish consideration of personal consistency or pride of individual opinion prevented him from facing squarely about and bracing himself with all the force of his will to withstand the onset of the revolutionists.

"We accordingly find him now employing the enormous power of his office to check the raid upon the United States constitution; to allay the dangerous sentiment aroused by the speeches of last summer; to defeat the plans of the radical experimenters and innovators. The measure of the conservative influence Mr. Roosevelt is now exerting may be found in the circumstance that his program includes even the repudiation, as unconstitutional, of the bill drawn by poor Mr. Littlefield to meet the suggestions so elaborately conveyed to the judiciary committee by the president's legal adviser, the attorney general.

"May it prove that Mr. Roosevelt is not too late in his revised conception of the presidential mission!

"More power to his elbow! He is now attempting, under disadvantageous conditions, the greatest service it has yet been his privilege to render the nation. The ride up San Juan Hill was nothing to this masterly retreat to the cover of common sense."

DR. HIRAM K. JONES.

On another page will be found a copy of the resolutions prepared by Rev. A. B. Morey and others of the Literary union of Jacksonville, Ill., on the occasion of the death of Dr. Hiram K. Jones, also an abstract of the address delivered at the funeral by Dr. W. F. Short. I add a brief comment, impelled by a profound appreciation of the uprightness, modesty, wisdom and greatness of the man and by a deep sense of personal obligation to him for the stimulating and strengthening influence he exerted upon me during my college days when I was for six years a member of his family. While he was a distant relative, the connection was so remote that I can speak of him without reserve. No one within the range of my acquaintance or observation more nearly approached the ideal in all that goes to make up the highest type of manhood. He inherited a strong constitution and preserved his vigor by a regular and temperate life. The environment of his youth was such as to give him a broad view of life, implant lofty purposes and encourage him to great endeavor. Early taught the advantage of mental discipline, he prepared himself for his work by a thorough and liberal education. He chose the medical profession and applied himself to it so diligently that he soon rose to eminence. Simple in his life and economical in his tastes, he gradually accumulated a sum sufficient to keep him in comfort during his later years, but his accumulations were a scant return for the vast service, which he rendered to society. Even while he was laying aside for old age, he responded generously to the demands of the church, charity and education, and after giving with increasing liberality as his own needs grew less, he remembered in the final disposition of his estate the institution that most appealed to him. He was a thinker of national fame and delivered lectures at the Concord School during its existence. His philosophy was all-comprehending, and his conception of life included both the here and hereafter. Heaven was as real to him as earth and death but the entrance to immortality. Like Socrates, he spent his time in the search for truth, determined to follow where it led. To him preparation for the present life was likewise preparation for the life beyond, and he went to his rest "like one who wraps the drapery of his couch about him and lies down to pleasant dreams."

Dr. Jones was fortunate in the choice of a wife who proved to be a congenial companion as well as a helpmeet and who was his intelligent and devoted co-laborer in every good work. Their home from its first establishment became a center of virtue, purity, love and light—a center from which eminated helpfulness and inspiration. The influences which they thus set in motion, transmitted from generation to generation, will be more valuable to the world than money and more enduring than marble. If service is the measure of greatness and example the method by which service can best be rendered, then Dr. Jones and his wife deserve to be numbered among the really great and their lives were knit together by a love that spanned the grave.

As the body of the sage, flower-covered and enshrouded in the affection of mourning friends, lay in the library where he had studied, for half a century, Dr. Hayden read Longfellow's tribute to Bayard Taylor—and it seemed a fitting conclusion of the funeral exercises:

> Dead he lay among his books;
> The peace of God was in his books;
> And those volumes from their shelves
> Watched him, silent as themselves.
> Ah! his hand will nevermore
> Turn their storied pages o'er;
> Nevermore his lips repeat
> Songs of theirs, however sweet.
> Let the lifeless body rest!
> He is gone, who was its guest;
> Gone as travelers haste to leave
> An inn, nor tarry until eve.
> Traveler! in what realms afar,
> In what planet, in what star,
> In what vast aerial space
> Shines the light upon thy face?
> In what gardens of delight
> Rest thy weary feet tonight?
> Lying dead among thy books,
> The peace of God in all thy looks.

THE PEOPLE IN ART, GOVERNMENT AND RELIGION.

The following address was delivered by George Bancroft, historian and statesman, before the Adelphia society of William's college, in August, 1853.

(See Reed's Modern Eloquence.)

It would be well if every American citizen could read and re-read this splendid speech. Its reproduction is at this time particularly pertinent to the celebration of July 4. The lessons

Bancroft sought to convey are now more important to the welfare of the American people than they were in 1835. The men of today should know just as the men of Bancroft's early days were told that "no principle once promulgated has ever been forgotten. No 'timely tramp' of a despot's foot ever trod out one idea. The world cannot retrograde; the dark age cannot return. Truth is immortal; it cannot long be resisted. Wherever moral truth has struck into being, humanity claims and guards the greatest bequest." When you have read the Bancroft address, ask your neighbor to read it and to seriously consider the pertinent truths therein presented.

Mr. Bancroft's address:

Gentlemen of the Adelphi Society: The material world does not change in its masses or in its powers. The stars shine with no more lustre than when they first sang together in the glory of their birth. The flowers that gemmed the fields and the forests before America was discovered, now bloom around us in their season. The sun that shone on Homer shines on us in unchanging lustre; the bow that beamed on the patriarch stilll glitters in the clouds. Nature is the same. For her no new forces are generated; no new capacities are discovered. The earth turns on its axis, and perfects its revolutions, and renews its seasons without increase or advancement.

But a like passive destiny does not attach to the inhabitants of the earth. For them expectations of social improvement are no delusion; the hopes of philanthropy are more than a dream. The five senses do not constitute the whole inventory of our source of knowledge. They are the organs by which thought connects itself with the eternal universe; but the power of thought is not merged in the exercise of its instruments. We have functions which connect us with heaven, as well as organs which set us in relation with earth. We have not merely the senses to open to us the external world, but an internal sense, which places us in connection with the world of intelligence and the decrees of God. There is a spirit in man— not in the privileged few, not in those of us only who by the favor of Providence have been nursed in public schools, it is in man; it is the attribute of the race. The spirit, which is the guide of truth, is the gracious gift to each member of the human family.

Reason exists within every breast. I mean not that faculty which deduces inferences from the experience of the senses, but that higher faculty which, from the infinite treasures of its own consciousness, originates truth and assents to it by the force of intuitive evidence; that faculty which raises us beyond the control of time and space and gives us faith in things eternal and invisible. There is not the difference between one mind and another which the pride of philosophers might conceive. To them no faculty is conceded which does not belong to the meanest of their countrymen. In them there cannot spring up a truth which does not equally have its germ in every mind. They have not the power of creation; they can but reveal what God has implanted in every breast. The intellectual functions by which relations are perceived are the common endowments of the race. The differences are apparent, not real. The eye in one person may be dull, in another quick; in one distorted and in another tranquil and clear; yet the relation of the eye to light is in all men the same. Just so, judgment may be liable in individual minds to bias the passion, and yet its relation to truth is immutable and uinversal.

In questions of practical duty conscience is God's umpire whose light illumines every heart; there is nothing in books which had not first, and has not still its life within us. Religion itself is a dead letter wherever its truths are not renewed in the soul. The individual conscience may be corrupted by interest or debauched by pride, yet the rule of morality is distinctly marked; its harmonies are to the mind like music to the ear; and the moral judgment when carefully analyzed and referred to its principles is always founded in right. The eastern superstition which bids its victims prostrate themselves before the advancing car of their idols springs from a noble root, and is but a melancholy perversion of that self-devotion which enables the Christian to bear the cross and subject his personal passions to the will of God. Immorality of itself never won to its support the inward voice; conscience if questioned never forgets to curse the guilty with the memory of sin; to cheer the upright with the meek tranquility of approval. And this admirable power which is the instinct of Deity is the attribute of every man; it knocks at the palace gate, it dwells in the meanest hovel. Duty, like death, enters every abode and delivers its message. Conscience like reason and judgment, is universal.

That the moral affections are planted everywhere needs only to be asserted to be received. The savage mother loves her offspring with all the fondness that a mother can know. Beneath the odorous shade of the boundless forests of Chili the native youth repeats the story of love as sincerely as it was ever chanted in the valley of Vaucluse. The affections of family are not the growth of civilization. The charities of life are scattered everywhere; enameling the vales of human being as the flowers upon the meadows. They are not the fruit of study, nor the privilege of refinement, but a natural instinct.

Our age has been a revolution in works of imagination. The poet has sought his theme in common life. Never is the genius of Scott more pathetic than when as in the "Antiquary" he delineates the sorrows of a poor fisherman, or as in the "Heart of Mid-Lothian," he takes his heroine from a cottage. And even Wordsworth, the purest and most original poet of the day in spite of the inveterate character of his political predilections, has thrown the light of genius on the walks of commonest life; he finds a lesson in every grave of the village churchyard; he discloses the boundless treasures of feeling in the peasant. The laborer and the artisan, the strolling peddler, becomes through his genius a teacher of the sublimest morality; and the solitary wagoner, the lonely shepherd, even the feeble mother of an idiot boy, furnishes lessons in the reverence for humanity.

If from things relating to truth, justice, and affection, we turn to those relating to the beautiul, we may here still further assert that the sentiment for the beautiful resides in every breast. The lovely forms of the external world delight us from their adaptation to our powers.

"Yea, what were mighty Nature's self,
Her features, could they win us,
Unhelped by the poetic voice
That hourly speaks within us?"

The Indian mother on the borders of Hudson Bay decorates her manufactures with ingenious devices and lovely colors prompted by the same instinct which guided the pencil and mixed the colors of Raphael. The inhabitants of Nootka Sound tattooes his body with the method of harmonious Arabesques. Every form to which the hands of the artist have ever given birth, sprung first into being as a conception of his mind from a natural faculty which belongs not to the artist exclusively, but to man. Beauty like truth and justice lives within us; like virtue and like moral law it is a companion of the soul. The power which leads to the production of beautiful forms or perception of them in the works which God has made is an attribute of humanity.

But I am asked if I despise learning. Shall one who has been much of his life in schools and universities plead the equality of uneducated nature? Is there no difference between the man of refinement and the uneducated savage?

"I am a man," said Black Hawk nobly to the chief of the first republic of the world; "I am a man," said the bartarous chieftain, "and you are another."

I speak for the universal diffusion of human powers, not of human attainments; for the capacity for progress, not for the perfection of undisciplined instincts. The fellowship which we should cherish with the race receives the Comanche warrior and the Caffre within the pale of equality. Their functions may not have been exercised, but they exist. Immure a person in a dungeon; as he comes to the light of day, his vision seems incapable of performing its office. Does that destroy your conviction in the relation between the eye and light? The rioter over his cups resolves to eat and drink and be merry; he forgets his spiritual nature in his obedience to the senses; but does that destroy the relation between conscience and eternity? "What ransom shall we give," exclaimed the senators of Rome to the savage Attila. "Give," said the barbarian, "all your gold and jewels, your costly furniture and treasures and set free every slave " "Ah," replied the degenerate Romans, "what then will be left to us?" "I leave you your souls," replied the unlettered invader from the steppes of Asia, who had learned in the wilderness to value the immortal mind and to despise the servile herd that esteemed only their fortunes, and had no true respect for themselves. You can not discover a tribe of men but you also find the charities of life, and the proofs of spiritual existence. Behold the ignorant Algonquin deposit a bow and quiver by the side of the departed warrior, and recognize his faith in immortality. See the Comanche chieftain, in the heart of our continent, inflict on himself the severest penance; and reverence his confession of the needed atonement for sin. The barbarian who roams o'er the western prairies has like passions and like endowments with ourselves. He bears with him the instinct of Deity; the consciousness of a spiritual nature, the love of beauty; the rule of morality.

And shall we reverence the dark-skinned Caffre? Shall we respect the brutal Hottentot? You may read the right answer written in every heart. It bids me not despise the sable hunter that gathers a livelihood in the forests of southern Africa. All are men. When we know the Hottentot better we shall despise him less.

If it be true that the gifts of the mind and heart are universally diffused, if the sentiment of truth, justice, love, and beauty exists in every one, then it follows as a necessary consequence that the commonest judgment in taste, politics, and religion is the highest authority on earth, and the nearest possible approach to an infallible decision. From the consideration of individual powers I turn to the action of the human mind in masses.

If reason is a universal faculty, universal decision is the nearest criterion of truth. The common mind winnows opinions; it is the sieve which separates error from certainty. The exercise by many of the same faculty on the same subject would naturally lead to the same conclusions. But if not, the very differences of opinion that arise prove the supreme judgment of the general mind. Truth is one. It never contradicts itself. One truth can not contradict another truth, Hence truth is the bond of union. But error not only contradicts truth, but may contradict itself, so that there may be many errors and each at variance with the rest. Truth is thererfore of necessity an element of harmony; error as necessarily an element of discord. Thus there can be no continuing universal judgment but a right one. Men can not agree in an absurdity; neither can they agree in a falsehood.

If wrong opinions have often been cherished by the masses, the cause always lies in the complexity of the ideas presented. Error finds its way into the soul of a nation only through the channel of truth. It is to a truth that men listen; and if they accept error also it is only because error is for the time so closely interwoven with the truth that the one can not readily be separated from the other.

Unmixed error can have no existence in the public mind. Wherever you see men clustering together to form a party you may be sure that however much error may be there truth is there also. Apply this principle boldly, for it contains a lesson of candor and a voice of encouragement. There never was a school of philosophy nor a clan in the realm of opinion but carried along with it some important truth. And therefore every sect that has ever flourished has benefitted humanity; for the errors of a sect pass away and are forgotten; its truths are received into the common inheritance. To know the seminal thought of every prophet and leader of a sect is together all the wisdom of mankind.

"By heaven there should not be a seer who left
The world one doctrine, but I'd task his lore,
And commune with his spirit. All the truth
Of all the tongues on earth; I'd have them all,
Had I the powerful spell to raise their ghosts."

The sentiment of beauty as it exists in the human mind is the criterion in works of art, inspires the conceptions of genius and exercises a final judgment on its productions. For who are the best judges in matters of taste? Do you think the cultivated individual? Undoubtedly not; but the collective mind. The public is wiser than the wisest critic. In Athens the arts were carried to perfection when the "fierce democracy" was in the ascendant; the temple of Minerva and the works of Phidias were planned and perfected to please the common people. When Greece yielded to tyrants, her genius for excellence in art expired, or rather the purity of taste disappeared, because the artist then endeavored to gratify a patron and therefore humored his caprice, while before he had endeavored to delight the race.

When after a long eclipse the arts again burst into a splendid existence it was equally under the popular influence. During the rough contests and feudal tyrannies of the middle age religion had opened in the church an asylum for the people. There the serf and the beggar could kneel; there the pilgrim and the laborer were shrived, and the children of misfortune not less than the prosperous were welcomed to the house of prayer. The church was consequently at once the guardian of equality and the nurse of the arts; and the souls of Giotto, of Perugino, and Raphael, moved by an infinite sympathy with the crowd, kindled into divine conceptions of beautiful forms. Appealing to the sentiment of devotion in the common mind, they dipped their pencils in living colors to decorate the altars where man adored. By degrees the wealthy nobility desired, in like manner, to adorn their palaces; but at the attempt the quick familiarity of the artists with the beautiful declined. Instead of the brilliant works which spoke to the soul a school arose which appealed to the senses; and in the land which had produced the most moving pictures addressed to religious feeling and instinct with the purest beauty, the banquet halls were covered with grotesque forms such as float before the imagination when excited and bewildered by sensual indulgence. Instead holy families the ideal representations of the virgin and the godlike Child, of the enduring faith of martyrs and the blessed benevolence of evangelical love, there came the motley group of fauns, and satyrs of Diana stooping to Endymion, of voluptuous beauty and the forms of licentiousness. Humanity frowned on the desecration of the arts, and painting no longer vivified by a fellow-feeling with the multitude, lost its greatness in the attempt to adapt itself to personal humors.

If with us arts are destined to a brilliant career the inspiration must spring from the vigor of the people. Genius will not create to flatter patrons or decorate saloons. It yearns for larger influences, if feeds on wider sympathies, and its perfect display can never exist except in an appeal to the general sentiment for the beautiful.

Again. Italy is famed for its musical compositions, its inimitable operas. It is a well-known fact that the best critics are often deceived in their judgment of them, while the pit, composed of the throng, does without fail render a true verdict.

But the taste for music, it may be said, is favored by natural organization. Precisely a statement that sets in a clearer light the natural capacity of the race, for taste is then not an acquisition, but in part a gift. But let us pass to the works of literature.

Who are by way of eminence the poets of all mankind? Surely Homer and Shakespeare. Now Homer formed his taste as he wandered from door to door a vagrant minstrel paying for hospitality by song, and Shakespeare wrote for an audience composed in a great measure of the common people.

The little story of Paul and Virginia is a universal favorite. When it was first written the author read it aloud to a circle in Paris, composed of the wife of the prime minister and the choicest critics of France. They condemned it as dull and insipid. The author appealed to the public, and the children of all Europe reversed the decree of the Parisians. The judgment of children, that is the judgment of the common mind under its most innocent and least imposing form, was more trustworthy than the criticism of the select refinement of the most polished city in the world.

Demosthenes of old formed himself to the perfection of eloquence by means of addresses to the crowd. The great comic poet of Greece, emphatically the poet of the vulgar mob, is distinguished above all others for the incomparable graces of his diction; and it is related of one of the most skillful writers in the Italian that when inquired of where he had learned the purity and nationality of his style, he replied; from listening to country people as they brought their produce to market.

At the revival of letters a distinguished feature of the rising literature was the employment of the dialect of the vulgar. Dante used the language of the populace and won immortality. Wycliffe, Luther, and at a later day Descartes, each employed his mother tongue and carried truth directly to all who were familiar with its accents. Every beneficent revolution in letters has the character of popularity; every great reform among authors has sprung from the power of the people in its influence on the development and activity of mind.

The same influence continues unimpaired. Scott, in spite of his reverence for the aristocracy spurned a drawing-room reputation; the secret of Byron's superiority lay in part in the agreement which existed between his muse and the democratic tendency of the age. German literature is almost entirely a popular creation. It was fostered by no monarch; it was dandled by no aristocracy. It was plebian in its origin and therefore manly in its results.

In like manner the best government rests on the people and not on the few, on persons and not on property, on the free development of public opinion and not on authority; because the munificient Author of our being has conferred the gifts of mind upon every member of the human race without distinction of outward circumstances. Whatever of other possessions may be engrossed the mind asserts its own independence. Lands, estates, the produce of minds, the prolific abundance of the seas may be usurped by a privileged class. Avarice assuming the form of ambitious power may grasp realm after realm, subdue continents, compass the earth in its aggrandizement, and sigh after worlds, but mind eludes the power of appropriation; it exists only in its own individuality, it is not a property which can be confiscated and cannot be torn away. It laughs at chance, it bursts from imprisonment, it defies monopoly. A government of equal rights must, therefore, rest upon mind, not wealth, not brute force; some of the moral intelligence of the community should rule the state. Prescription can no more assume to be a valid plea for political injustice; society studies to eradicate established abuses and to bring social institutions and laws into harmony with moral right; not dismayed by the natural and necessary imperfections of all human effort, and not giving way to despair because every hope does not at once ripen into fruit.

The public happiness is the true object of legislation and can be secured only by the masses of mankind, themselves awakened to acknowledge and care of their own interests. Our free institutions have reversed the false and ignoble distinctions between men; and, refusing to gratify the pride of caste, have acknowledged the common mind to be the true material for a commonwealth. Everything has hitherto been done for the happy few. It is not possible to endow an aristocracy with greater benefits than they have already enjoyed; there is no room to hope that individuals will be more highly gifted or more fully developed than the greatest sages of past times. The world can advance only through the culture of the moral and intellectual powers of the people. To accomplish this end by means of the people themselves is the highest purpose of government. If it be the duty of the individual to strive after a perfection like the perfection of God, how much more ought a nation to be the image of duty. The common mind is the true Parian marble fit to be wrought into the likeness of a God. The duty of America is to secure the culture and the happiness of the masses by their reliance on themselves.

The absence of the prejudices of the old world leaves us here the opportunity of consulting independent truth, and man is left to apply the instinct of freedom to every social relation and public interest. We have approached so near to nature that we can hear her gentle wispers; we have made humanity our lawgiver and our oracle; and therefore the nation receives, vivifies and applies principles which in Europe the wisest accept with distrust. Freedom of mind and of conscience, freedom of the seas, freedom and industry, equality of franchise—each great truth is firmly grasped, comprehended and enforced, for the multitude is neither rash nor fickle. In truth it is less fickle than those who profess to be its guides. Its natural dialectics surpass the logic of the schools. Political action has never been so constant and so unwavering as when it results from a feeling or a principle diffused through society. The people is firm and tranquil in its movement and necessarily acts with moderation because it becomes but slowly impregnated with new ideas, and effects no changes except in harmony with the knowledge which it has acquired. Besides where it is permanently possessed of power there exists neither the occasion nor the desire for frequent change. It is not the parent of tumult; sedition is bred in the lap of luxury, and its chosen emissaries are the beggared spendthrift and the impoverished libertine. The government by the people is in very truth the strongest government in the world. Discarding the implements of terror it dares to rule by moral force and has its citadel in the heart.

Such is the political system which rests on reason, reflection, and the free expression of deliberate choice. There may be those who scoff at the suggestion that the decision of the whole is to be preferred to the judgment of the enlightened few. They say in their hearts that the masses are ignorant; that farmers know nothing of legislation; that mechanics should not quit their workshops to join in forming public opinion. But true political science does indeed venerate the masses. It maintains not as has been perversely asserted that "the people can make right," but that the people can discern right. Individuals are but shadows, too often engrossed by the pursuit of shadows, the race is immortal; individuals are of limited sagacity, the common mind is infinite in its experience; individuals are languid and blind, the many are ever wakeful; individuals are corrupt, the race has been redeemed; individuals are time-serving, the masses are fearless; individuals may be false, the masses are ingenious and sincere; individuals claim the divine sanction of truth for the deceitful conceptions of their own fancies; the Spirit of God breathes through the combined intelligence of the people. Truth is not to be ascertained by the impulse of an individual; it emerges from the contradictions of present opinions; it raises itself in majestic serenity above the strifes of parties and the conflict of sects; it acknowledges neither the solitary mind nor the separate faction as its oracle, but owns as its own faithful interpreter the dictates of pure reason itself proclaimed by the general voice of mankind. The decrees of the universal conscience are the nearest approach to the presence of God in the soul of man.

Thus the opinion which we respect is indeed not the opinion of one or of a few, but the capacity of the many. It is hard for the pride of cultivated philosophy to put its ear to the ground and listen reverently to the voice of lowly humanity, yet the people collectively are wiser than the most gifted individual for all his wisdom constitutes but a part of others. When the great sculptor of Greece was endeavoring to fashion the perfect model of beauty he did not passively imitate the form of the loveliest woman of his age, but he gleaned the several lineaments of his faultless work from the many. And so it is that a perfect judgment is the result of a comparison where error eliminates error and truth is established by concurring witnesses. The organ of truth is the invisible decision of the unbiased world; she pleads before no tribunal but public opinion; she owes no safe interpreter but the common mind; she knows no court of appeals but the soul of humanity. It is when the multitude give counsel that right purposes find safety; theirs is the heart of which the largeness is as the sand on the seashore.

It is not by vast armies, by immense natural resources, by accumulations of treasure, that the greatest results in modern civilization have been accomplished. The traces of the career of conquest pass away, hardly leaving a scar on the national intelligence. Famous battle-grounds of victory are most of them comparatively indifferent to the human race; barren fields of blood, the scourges of their times, but affecting the social condition as little as the gaging of a pestilence. Not one benevolent institution, not one ameliorating principle in the Roman state was a voluntary concession of the aristocracy; each useful element was borrowed from the democracies of Greece or was a reluctant concession to the demands of the people. The same is true in modern political life. It is the confesion of an enemy to democracy that "all the great and noble institutions of the world have come from popular efforts."

vate and bless humanity. The exact measure of the progress of civilization is the degree in which the intelligence of the

It is the uniform tendency of the popular element to elevate and bless. The exact measure of the progress of civilization is the degree in which the intelligence of the common mind has prevailed over wealth and brute force; in other words, the measure of the progress of civilization is the progress of the people. Every great object connected with the benevolent exertions of the day, has reference to the culture of those powers which are alone the common inheritance. For this the envoys of a religion cross seas and visit remotest isles; for this the press in its freedom teems with the productions of maturest thought; for this philanthropists plan new schemes of education; for this halls in every city and village are open to the public instructor. Not that we view with indifference the glorious efforts of material industry, the increase in the facility of internal intercourse, the accumulations of thrifty labor, the varied results of concentrated action. But even there it is mind that achieves the triumph. It is the genius of the architect that gives beauty to the work of human hands and makes the temple, the dwelling, or the public edifice an outward representation of the spirit of propriety and order. It is science that guides the zeal of cupidity to the construction of the vast channels of communication which are fast binding the world into one family. And it is as a method of moral improvement that this swifter means of intercourse derives its greatest value. Mind becomes universal property; the poem that is published on the soil of England finds its response on the shores of Lake Erie and the banks of the Missouri, and is admired near the sources of the Ganges. The defense of public liberty in our own halls of legislation penetrates to the plains of Poland, is echoed along the mountains of Greece and pierces the darkest night of eastern depotism.

The universality of the intellectual and moral powers and the necessity of their development for the progress of the race proclaim the great doctrine of the natural right of every human being to moral and intellectual culture. It is the glory of our fathers to have established in their laws the equal claims of every child to the public care of its morals and its mind. From this principle we may deduce the universal right to leisure; that is, to time not appropriate to material purposes, but reserved for the culture of the moral affections and the mind. It does not tolerate the exclusive enjoyment of leisure by a privileged class, but defending the rights of labor would suffer none to sacrifice the higher purposes of existence in unceasing toil for that which is not life. Such is the voice of nature, such is the conscious claim of the human mind. The universe opens its pages to every eye, the music of creation resounds in every ear, the glorious lessons of immortal truth that are written in the sky and on the earth address themselves to every mind and claim attention from every human being. God has made man upright that he might look before and after, and He calls upon every one not merely to labor, but to reflect, not merely to practice the revelations of divine will, but to contemplate the displays of divine power. Nature claims for every man leisure, for she claims every man as a witness to the divine glory manifested in the created world.

> "Yet evermore, through years renewed
> In undisturbed vicissitude
> The seasons balancing their fight
> On the swift wings of day and night,
> Kind nature keeps a heavenly door
> Wide open for the scattered poor,
> Where flower-breathed incense to the skies
> Is wafted in loud harmonies;
> And ground fresh cloven by the plow
> Is fragrant with a humbler vow;
> Where birds and brooks from living dells
> Chime forth unwearied canticles,
> And vapors magnify and spread
> The glory of the sun's bright head;
> Still constant in her worship, still
> Conforming to the Almighty will,
> Whether men sow or reap the fields,
> Her admonitions nature yields;
> That not by bread alone we live,
> Or what a hand of flesh can give;
> That every day should leave some part,
> Free for a Sabbath of the heart;
> So shall the seventh be truly blest,
> From morn to eve with hallowed rest."

The right to universal education being thus acknowledged by our conscience not less than by our laws, it follows that the people is the true recipient of truth. Do not seek to conciliate individuals, do not dread the frowns of a sect, do not yield to the prescription of a party, but pour out truth into the common mind. Let the waters of intelligence like the rains of heaven descend on the whole earth, and be not discouraged by the dread of encountering ignorance. The prejudices of ignorance are more easily removed than the prejudices of interest; the first are blindly adopted, the second wilfully preferred. Intelligence must be diffused among the whole people, truth must be scattered among those who have no interest to suppress its growth. The seeds that fall on the exchange or in the hum of business may be choked by the thorns that spring up in the hotbed of avarice; the seeds that are let fall in the saloon may be like those dropped by the wayside which take no root. Let the young aspirant after glory scatter seeds of truth broadcast on the wide bosom of humanity, in the deep fertile soil of the public mind. There it will strike deep root and spring up and bear a hundredfold and bloom for ages and ripen fruit through remote generations.

It is alone by infusing great principles into the common mind that revolutions in human society are brought about. They never have been, they never can be affected by superior individual excellence. The age of the Antonines is the age of the greatest glory of the Roman empire. Men distinguished by every accomplishment of culture and science for a century in succession possessed undisputed sway over more than one hundred millions of men, until, at last, in the person of Mark Aurelian, philosophy herself seemed to mount the throne. And did she stay the downward tendencies of the Roman empire? Did she infuse new elements of life into the decaying constitution? Did she commence one great beneficent reform? Not one permanent amelioration was affected. Philosophy was clothed with absolute power; and yet absolute power accomplished nothing for humanity. It could accomplish nothing. Had it been possible, Aurelian would have wrought a change. Society can be regenerated, the human race can be advanced, only by moral principles diffused through the multitude.

And now let us take an opposite instance; let us see if amelioration follows when, in despite of tryanny, truth finds access to the common people. Christianity itself shall furnish me the example.

When Christianity first made its way into Rome the imperial city was the seat of wealth, philosophy, and luxury. Absolute government was already established; and had the will of Claudius been gained or the conscience of Messalina been roused, or the heart of Narcissus, once a slave, then prime minister, been touched by the recollections of his misfortunes, the aid of the sovereign of the civilized world would have been engaged. And the messenger of divine truth making his appeal to them—was his mission to the emperor and his minions? To the empress and her flatterers? To the servile senators? To wealthy favorites? Paul preserves for us the names of the first converts; the Roman Mary and Junia, Julia and Nerea, and the beloved brother, all plebeian names unknown to history. "Greet them," he adds, "that be of the household of Narcissus." Now every Roman household was a community of slaves. Narcissus, himself a freedman, was the chief minister of the Roman empire; his ambition had left him no moments for the envoy from Calvary; the friends of Paul were a freedman's slaves. When God selected a channel by which Christianity should make its way in the city of Rome, and assuredly be carried forward to acknowledged supremacy in the Roman empire, he gave to the apostle of the Gentiles favor in the household of Narcissus; he planted the truth deep in the common soil. Had Christianity been received at court it would have been stifled or corrupted by the prodigal vices of the age; it lived in the hearts of the common people; it sheltered itself against oppression in the catacombs and among tombs; it made misfortune its comfort and sorrow its companion, and labor its state. It rested on a rock, for it rested on the people; it was gifted with immortality, for it struck root in the hearts of the million.

So completely was this greatest of all reforms carried forward in the vale of life, that the great moral revolution, the great step of God's providence in the education of the human race, was not observed by the Roman historians. Once indeed at this early period the Christians are mentioned, for, in the reign of Nero, their purity being hateful to the corrupt, Nero abandoned them to persecution. In the darkness of midnight they were covered with pitch and set on fire to light the streets of Rome, and this singularity has been recorded. But their system of morals and religion, though it was the new birth of the world, escaped all notice.

Paul, who was a Roman citizen, was beheaded just outside the walls of the eternal city; and Peter, who was a plebeian and could not claim the distinction of the ax and block, was executed on the cross, with his head downwards to increase the pain of the indignity. Do you think the Roman emperor took notice of the names of these men when he signed their death warrants? And yet, as they poured truth into the common mind, what series of kings, what lies of emperors, can compare with them in their influence on the destinies of mankind?

Yes, reforms in society are only effected through the masses of the people, and through them have continually taken place. New truths have been successively developed and are being its condition. This progress is advanced by every sect precisely because each sect obtained vitality, itself of necessity embodied a truth; by every political party, for the conflicts of party are the war of ideas; by every nationality, for a nation cannot exist as such until humanity makes it special trustee of some part of its wealth for the ultimate benefit of all.

The irrestible tendency of the human race is therefore to advancement, for absolute power has never succeeded and can never succeed in suppressing a single truth. An idea once revealed may find its admission into every living breast and live there. Like God, it becomes immortal and omnipresent. The movement of the species is upward, irrestibly upward. The individual is often lost; Providence never disowns the race. No principle once promulgated has ever been forgotten. No "timly tramp" of a despot's foot ever trod out one idea. The world cannot retrograde; the dark ages cannot return. Dynasties perish, states are buried, nations have been victims of error, martyrs for right; humanity has always been on the advance, gaining maturity, universality and power.

Yes, truth is immortal; it cannot be destroyed; it is invincible; it cannot long be resisted. Not every great principle has yet been generated, but when once proclaimed and diffused it lives without end in the safe custody of the race. States may pass away, every just principle of legislation which has been once established will endure. Philosophy has sometimes forgotten God, a great people never did. The scepticism of the last century could not uproot Christianity because it lived in the hearts of the millions. Do you think that infidelity is spreading? Christianity never lived in the hearts of so many millions as at this moment. The forms under which it is professed may decay, for they, like all that is the work of men's hands, are subject to changes and chances of mortal being, but the spirit of truth is incorruptible; it may be developed, illustrated, and applied; it never can die, never can decline.

No truth can perish, no truth can pass away; the flame is undying, though generations disappear. Wherever moral truth has struck into being, humanity claims and guards the greatest bequest. Each generation gathers together imperishable children of the past, and increases them by new sons of light alike radiant with immortality.

THE AMERICAN COMMONS.

(Poem Read by Hon. Howard S. Taylor at the Fourth of July Celebration at Fairview under the Auspices of the Fairview Jefferson Club.)

When Liberty, wounded, betrayed and oppressed
By the insolent, tyrannous kings of the world,
Fled over the sea to the ultimate West
And, here, in her refuge her banner unfurled;
When the hopes of mankind in the balances lay,
And the unborn, wondering centuries stood
To witness America's Passover Day

And the sign of her door-lintels sprinkled with blood,
Then Liberty, menaced by envy and hate,
From the seats of the mighty, the thrones of the great;
  With tocsin and summons
   Called forward her commons
And marshaled and made them her Pillars of State.

They were men from the mines, from the shops, from the farms;
They were hunters and herdsmen and fishermen, bold;
They were homespun minute-men, springing to arms,
With a faith that could neither be bought nor be sold—
And these were the paladins, nobles and knights
Who conquered King George and his hireling host;
Who penned with their weapons our charter of rights,
And made our republic humanity's boast.
Who gave to posterity riches untold—
A heritage greater than mountains of gold.
  It is no man's nor woman's.
  It was won by the commons,
For them and their children to have and to hold.

A blend of all races, in many creeds bred,
They were fused in the white-heated furnace of war.
United, they followed where Liberty led
As the wise men once followed the Bethlehem star.
Go question the flag—it will tell in a breath
How its tri-color hues by their spirit were planned;
That the white is their honor, the blue is their faith,
And the red is their valor on ocean and land.
Go search through the myths of the ancients in quest
Of their builders of empire, their bravest and best;
  But Grecians and Romans
   Are dwarfed by the commons
Who founded the Great Commonwealth of the West.

The fathers are gone—has their faith perished, too?
Has the spirit that moved them declined and decayed?
Have their lofty ideals grown dim and untrue
In the hurrying scramble of pleasure and trade?
Have the fanes of our patriot altars and graves
Sunken downward to mix with insensible clods?
Are we parting our race into masters and slaves
With only fierce Mammon and Moloch for gods?
Ah, no. By our bells and our jubliant guns,

By the stars and the stripes where our proud story runs!
    By a score of good omens
    We still have our commons!
And the hearts of our Fathers still throb in their Sons!

ADDRESS TO THE CZAR.

President Roosevelt has decided to forward to the government of Russia the petition addressed to the czar and signed by many well known American citizens protesting against the treatment of the Jews in the czar's dominion. This petition was prepared under the direction of the executive council of the B'nai B'rith. It was submitted to the president and he agreed to transmit the same to the Russian government.

The Washington correspondent for the Chicago *Record-Herald* says that though the document which the American government is to send to St. Petersburg is in the form of a petition signed by leading citizens of the United States, its moral effect is that of a protest sanctioned by this government. This correspondent explains:

"It is very unusual for one government to transmit such a petition to another government. According to precedents, if the rights and interests of American citizens are involved, our government acts directly in their behalf. If American citizens are not directly involved, our government ignores the case. In this instance, it is not pretended that American citizens have been maltreated in Russia and yet the American people are so deeply concerned that our government, breaking precedents, consents to forward their petition with what must to Russia and the world appear the stamp of the approval of the government of the United States."

A copy of the petition that will be forwarded to the czar appears in another column of this issue. The president is to be congratulated upon his determination to forward this protest. Unquestionably, "Russia and the world" will understand that this petition has the approval of the people of the United States and it will be just as well for "Russia and the World" to recognize the stamp of the approval of the United States government.

If the czar is all that he pretends to be, if the several worthy movements led by the czar and toward a higher civilization have been undertaken with good motive, then he cannot find anything objectionable in the protest that is soon to be forwarded to him by American citizens. Lovers of humanity have the right to hope that "he who led his own people and all others to the shrine of peace will add new luster to his reign and fame by leading a new movement that shall commit the whole world in opposition to religious persecutions."

THE FOURTH AT FAIRVIEW.

All nature smiled on the Fourth of July and the celebration at Fairview was a great success. The members of the Fairview Jefferson club are entitled to great credit for the completeness of the arrangements and the congratulations of those who attended fully repaid them for the efforts put forth. The crowd was variously estimated at from 5,000 to 10,000 and would have been larger if the street car service had permitted. The tent used for the speaking was loaned by the Monroe club of St. Joseph, Mo. The stage was draped with American and Cuban flags and ornamented with the pictures of Washington and Lincoln. The Jefferson picture was an excellent portrait in oil on white silk and was painted by Mr. William Homer Leavitt of Newport, R. I., and presented to the club.

The following program was presented, Mr. Bryan presiding:

10:00 a. m.—Music, Hagenow's Band.

11:00 a. m.—Reminiscences by Pioneers, conducted by Hon. J. V. Wolfe and Mr. J. W. Crist.

12:00 m.—Intermission for Lunch.

Music—Hagenow's Band.

1:30 p. m.—Invocation, Rev. Harry Huntington.

Song—America, Commoner Choir.

Reading the Declaration of Independence, William W. Bride, Esq., Washington, D. C.

Address—Louis F. Post, Esq., Chicago.

Song—The Star Spangled Banner.

Address and Poem—Hon. Howard S. Taylor, Chicago.

Music—Hagenow's Band.
Address—Hon. Tom L. Johnson, Cleveland.
Song—Culumbia, the Gem of the Ocean.
Music—Hagenow's Band.

The Poem, The American Commons, written for the occasion by Mr. Taylor, will be found on another page. The speeches will be discussed in the next issue. It was an old-fashioned celebration and everybody felt better for having participated. The only change in the program from that printed in former issue was the substitution of Mr. Louis F. Post of Chicago for Col. R. S. Wynne, of Ft. Worth, Tex., who was unavoidably detained.

AN INQUIRY ANSWERED.

The following is an answer to an inquiry:
Money, except where made a legal tender by the law of some other country, passes by weight when it leaves its own country. This is true of gold as well as silver. The Mexican silver dollar is, therefore, only worth in this country the same as the same weight in bullion. Mexico cannot maintain the parity between gold and silver at her ratio of 16 1-2 to 1 because her commercial strength is not sufficient. It all depends upon the demand which the nation can, by its coinage law, create. International bimetallists contend that all of the nations together or several of the leading ones, could, by joining in free coinage, create a demand for silver which would maintain the parity between that metal and gold at the legal ratio. Independent bimetallists believe that this nation alone could, by the opening of its mints, create a demand for silver which would be sufficient to maintain the parity here and throughout the world. This is a contention which cannot be proved with mathematical certainty except by experiment. But the same can be said of the opposite contention of the advocates of the gold standard. Those, however, who deny the ability of this nation to maintain the parity, are as a rule persons who would not want silver coined even if they were certain that the parity could be maintained. The fact that Mexi-

co cannot maintain the parity does not disprove our nation's ability to maintain the parity. Our nation is greater than Mexico, both in population and commerce, and can do what Mexico cannot do.

THE PRICE OF SILVER.

A reader referring to the article in THE COMMONER entitled "The Price of Silver," asks why, if the demand of the government raised the price of silver in 1890, the price of silver afterwards fell? And why silver went down between 1878 and 1890? The questions are easily answered. The price of silver fell between 1878 and 1890 because the demand created by the government was not sufficient to take all the silver that was available for coinage, and the surplus silver dragged down the market price. The increased demand created by the Sherman law in 1890 raised the price of silver immediately, and it was at first thought that this demand would be sufficient to utilize all the silver available for coinage, but it was found, in a short time, that there was still a surplus, and this surplus again depressed the market price. Under the Bland-Allison act and the Sherman act, the government purchased a certain limited amount of silver; under free coinage the government offers to convert into legal tender money, not a certain limited amount, but all of the silver presented. This leaves no surplus to depress the price. If the production of silver was unlimited it would be impossible for the government to fix the price of it by a coinage law, but gold and silver are called precious metals because they are limited in quantity, and being limited in quantity the government by offering a demand greater than the supply, can fix the price.

SUNDAY READING.

In a recent issue of THE COMMONER reference was made to two books, suitable for Sunday reading, which had come to the attention of the editor of this paper, and been enjoyed by him. Attention is now invited to two more. The first is entitled, "What All the World's A-Seeking," or "The Vital Law of True Life, True Greatness, Power and Happiness," By Ralph Waldo Tryne, author of "In Tune With the Infinite." The book is published by Thos. Y. Crowell & Co., of New York. The author opens the volume with several questions:

"How can I make life yield its fullest and best? How can I know the true secret of power? How can I attain to a true and lasting greatness? How can I fill the whole of life with a happiness and peace and joy and satisfaction, that is ever rich and abiding, that ever increases, never diminishes, that imparts to it a sparkle, that never loses its luster, that ever fascinates, that never wearies?"

A complete and satisfactory answer to these questions should certainly be of interest to all, for who has not asked them? The author then proceeds to elaborate his answer. He presents the Bible measure of greatness, namely, service: "He that is greatest among you shall be your servant." He also contends that this is the measure of happiness as well as greatness. The entire book is an argument in defense of the proposition that "Love is the greatest thing in the world"—that love is the controlling force in the world, and that it enriches the giver while it helps the one on whom it is bestowed. It is a plea for that unselfishness which might after all be called the broadest selfishness, because it is really productive of greater and more permanent good than the short-sighted selfishness that sacrifices others for one's own benefit.

The second book to which attention is called at this time is entitled "Jesus, the Jew, and Other Addresses," by Harris Weinstock, and published by Funk & Wagnalls, New York. This book presents a Jewish view of Christ. It claims Christ for the Jewish race and shows how the Jewish race has influenced the entire world through the system of religion founded by the Nazarene. As a discussion of the Jew's debt to Christianity and Christianity's debt, it is both instructive and interesting. It also contains a masterly discussion of Moses, his work and the system of ethics developed under his leadership. The spirit manifested by the writer is so broad and kindly and the argument so forcible that the book must exert a powerful influence in increasing the harmony between the Jew and the Gentile.

TO P. O. DEPARTMENT.

Postmaster General Payne, Washington, D. C.—Dear Sir: I enclose a circular sent out by a St. Louis company which is conducting a guessing contest based upon the number of admittances to the Louisiana Purchase Exposition. You will see that the sum of $75,000 is offered in prizes, the estimates being sold for 25 cents each, or five for a dollar. The company is soliciting the aid of newspapers throughout the country to advertise the contest. It is apparent from the advertisement that this is even more demoralizing than the ordinary lottery, because the low price of the ticket and the large capital prizes promised are more alluring to those who are susceptible to the temptations offered by a lottery. It is also less fair than the ordinary lottery, because the contestant has no way of knowing how many competitors he has. In the public lottery the prizes usually bear a fixed and known proportion to the amount received for tickets, but in this case the company may take in ten or a hundred times the amount paid out in prizes. The concluding paragraph of the advertisement discloses the gambling character of the institution. It reads as follows:

"A good investment. Better than stocks and bonds. We are receiving from shrewd business men from the large trading centers, monthly orders for certificates, they claiming that the investment is safer and the possibility of large gain greater than investment in bonds, life insurance or any of the speculative stocks offered on the boards of trade in the various commercial centers. Most of them purchase certificates systematically, that is, send in every month for from one to five dollars' worth. Almost every one can economize a few cents a day, and the funds thus saved can be invested in certificates, and with a hundred or more certificates in your possession you are likely to wake up some morning and find yourself the lucky possessor of an independent fortune. It hardly seems reasonable that with a hundred certificates one could miss ALL of the 1,889 prizes."

Please let me know whether the department has issued any order on the subject and whether or not such a contest is regarded as a violation of the anti-lottery laws. Yours truly,

W. J. BRYAN.

FROM P. O. DEPARTMENT.

Office of the Assistant Attorney General for the Postoffice Department, Washington, D. C., June 23, 1903. Your communication of the 10th inst. addressed to the postmaster general, submitting a circular of the World's Fair Contest company, Saint Louis, Missouri, and expressing the view that the prize scheme advertised therein is a lottery, has been referred to this office.

It is unquestionable that the effect upon the public of these so-called guessing contests—considering the elaborate plan upon which they are operated, the very large prizes offered, etc.—is almost as pernicious as that of ordinary lotteries, and it is the disposition of the postoffice department to scrutinize very carefully all such schemes and to deny them the use of the United States mails where authority of law can be found for so doing. You, of course understand, however, that in all such cases the department must be governed by decisions of the federal courts and opinions of law officers of the government.

In this connection your attention is directed to the opinion of Attorney General Miller, 19 Opinions of Attys-Gen. 679; opinion of Attorney General Griggs, 23 Opinions of Atty-Gen. 207; opinion of Attorney General Knox, 23 Opinions of Atty-Gen. 492; and to the decision of the United States circuit court for the southern district of New York, in United States vs. Rosenblum, set forth in the inclosed circular.

From a consideration of the authorities above cited you will observe that the scheme to which you call attention is beyond the reach of the postoffice department, unless it shall develop that fraud is being practiced in its operation. Very respectfully, C. H. ROBB,
Assistant Attorney General for the Postoffice department.
To Hon. William J. Bryan, Lincoln, Neb.

AN INTERESTING DISPUTE.

Rev. Newell Dwight Hillis of the Plymouth church, Brooklyn, and Senator Chauncey Depew are engaged in an interesting dispute as to the effect of great wealth. Dr. Hillis said in a sermon recently:

"I want to say that we will all go to the devil on $50,000 a year—at least a great many men I know are going to the devil on that sum—and very few are escaping it. Once a man has an income of that much money a year, he is apt to forget, in the same way that a man forgets to say grace after he has dined.

"Today we are raising pampered sons and daughters, surrounding them with every luxury and idle satisfaction of the decade and they are rotten before they are ripe. I repeat it—they are rotten before they are ripe—and the boys in many cases are sinful before they are bearded.

"They practice the ten commandments with the 'shall nots' left out and I warn them that in the future they will find that God and nature practice the ten commandments, but the 'shall nots' are left in.

"I cannot pick up a paper, but that I see the '400' of this city engaged in divorce suits.

"I tremble for my country when all the work the preacher does at one end in marrying the judge undoes at the other end in the divorce court.

"If the women of my congregation who are suffering with nervous prostration had the will power to take nine out of every ten of their frocks into the back yard and burn them, I do not think they would longer be troubled with their nervous prostration."

This is pretty strong language for the pastor of a prominent New York church, and no one who is familiar with the situation can doubt that there is truth in what he says.

Now comes Senator Chauncey Depew with his reply. He says:

"It all amounts to this: Whether a man has, first, an inclination to go to the devil; or, secondly, will power enough to resist the temptations to take him there. If a man possesses the first or lacks the second condition, he can just as well go to the devil on $10,000 a year as on $50,000."

He then goes on to argue that the sons of the very rich are less liable to dissipation than the sons of families of moderate means who come in from the country. The trouble with Senator Depew's argument is that he does not give enough consideration to his second proposition. Very few men have an inclination to go to the devil; the great trouble is that they yield to temptation, and the temptations that come to those who are idle are greater than the temptations that come to those who are necessarily occupied.

The divorce suits that seem to be so frequent among the "400" are largely due to the fact that having no useful employment and spending their time in the search of pleasure they fail to find any real enjoyment at home or anywhere else. The temptations of such a life are not only greater than the temptations that come to those whose hands and thoughts are occupied, but the strength to resist temptation is also weakened by high living.

THE TARIFF LOGICIANS.

The St. Louis *Star* has attempted to explain how a tariff on manufactured products makes manufactured products cheaper by stimulating competition and at the same time makes wheat dearer by preventing competition. But its explanations are as lame as the explanations of the protectionists usually are. The price of wheat is fixed abroad. Whether the farmer sells to the miller in his home state or to the miller in Europe he gets the foreign price less carriage and commissions. The republicans try to show that a tariff on wheat raises the price of the farmer's wheat and then they try to show the farmer that a tariff lowers the price of manufactured products. They make the same argument in regard to wool. They do not put the arguments side by side, but in the course of the same speech they will assert that a tariff on wool raises the price of wool and that a tariff on the goods made out of the same wool lowers the price of the goods. They make these contradictory arguments not because there is any truth in them, but because they have to deceive the farmer. The manufacturers understand the necessity for such arguments and overlook them, but republican farmers are expected to accept them at their face value.

SLAVERY IN THE PHILIPPINES.

The Buffalo *Express* comments upon the new government to be established among the Moros and says that "the new council will be authorized to abolish slavery," and it adds: "This is not only a confession that slavery has continued to exist under the American flag, but apparently there has not even been authority to abolish it hitherto." The *Express* then proceeds to quote the constitution on the subject and says:

"Not all the advantage which the possession of the Philippines can possibly bring to the United States could offset the harm done by this demonstration that the military power can violate the most explicit and essential clauses of the constitution with impunity."

The *Express* ought to have learned before this that colonies are governed outside of the constitution and that it is this very thing that the democratic party has been objecting to.

MR. BRYAN'S DEMOCRACY.

The gold democrats, unable to make a successful attack upon the principles for which Mr. Bryan stood as the nominee of the party, and which he now defends, are attempting to question his right to membership in the democratic party. Three points are urged against him. First, he is quoted as saying at some time (the date is not fixed) prior to 1896, that he was not a democrat, but a bimetallist. Second, that he voted for General Weaver in 1892; and, third, that he advocated principles which are not democratic.

The first charge is entirely without foundation. Mr. Bryan never at any time or place denied his political affiliation with the democratic party or permitted it to be questioned. His parents were democrats before him, and he counted himself a democrat in his youth because his parents were, and after he was grown, was a democrat because of his belief in democratic principles and policies. He made democratic speeches in 1880, before he was old enough to vote, and has made democratic speeches in every campaign since. He has attended democratic conventions for about twenty years, and has never been a delegate to a convention of any other party. He has favored fusion with the populists in Nebraska for the reason that upon the questions immediately before the country the populists and democrats agree, their differences being as to questions not reached.

In 1890 Mr. Bryan was nominated for congress by a democratic convention and was elected, defeating both the republican candidate and the populist candidate. He was renominated for congress in 1892 and again elected, defeating this time also a populist as well as a republican. In 1894 he was the nominee of the democratic state convention for the United States senate, but was not indorsed by the populist state convention. While he would probably have received the votes of the populist members of the legislature if their votes could have elected him, just as Senator Allen had received the democratic votes in the legislature two years before, the republicans had a majority in the legislature elected in 1894—the year in which Mr. Cleveland's administration was so overwhelmingly condemned. Nearly all of the populists voted for a member of their own party.

At the close of the 53rd congress, in March, 1895, Mr. Bryan joined with Mr. Bland in preparing and circulating an appeal to the democratic believers in bimetallism to organize and secure control of the democratic organization. From that date on to the meeting of the Chicago convention, he visited all parts of the country, attending democratic meetings and conventions and giving whatever assistance he could to the democratic believers in bimetalism. There was never any question raised as to his party relations.

In 1894 a few democrats left the democratic state convention and nominated what they called "a straight democratic ticket." This ticket received about five thousand votes in the state.

The bolting organization was maintained until after the election of 1896. In 1895 the organization secured for this ticket an unfair advantage by collusion with the republican judges. In 1896 both organizations sent delegates to Chicago, and the national committee, by a strict gold and silver vote, gave temporary credentials to the bolting organization. The credentials committee of the convention, however, after a full hearing, decided in favor of the regular delegation, headed by Mr. Bryan, and the testimony before this committee was so clear and convincing that the minority did not present a report.

During all this period it will be seen that Mr. Bryan was active in party work and gave no excuse for any one to doubt his party connections.

Congressman O'Farrall, afterwards governor of Virginia, has stated that Mr. Bryan in the fall of 1894 intended to speak in favor of the populist candidate for governor in Virginia, but was persuaded not to do so by Mr. O'Farrall, then the democratic candidate for governor. Mr. O'Farrall may have been so informed, but if so his informant was in error, for Mr. Bryan never contemplated any such thing. The criticism, however, comes with poor grace from Mr. O'Farrall, for while asserting that he prevented Mr. Bryan's speaking against him when he was a candidate for governor, he bolted the national ticket when Mr. Bryan was a candidate for the presidency. Certainly his fight against a national candidate nominated by the aid of Virginia's votes was a more serious breach than the failure to support a gubernatorial candidate, even if Mr. Bryan had opposed Mr. O'Farrall, which he did not do.

The charge that Mr. Bryan voted for Mr. Weaver has already been explained and the facts have been presented so often that one must confess himself misinformed if he circulates the charge as an evidence of Mr. Bryan's abandonment of the democratic party.

As the election of 1892 approached it became evident that it was impossible for the democrats to carry several of the western states, but that it was possible for the democrats to assist the populists in carrying them. This situation having been fully discussed, the democratic national committee, of which Mr. Harrity was chairman and Mr. Whitney the controlling spirit (if the word "spirit" can properly be used of the Whitney type) instructed to urge the democrats of Kansas Colorado and a number of other western states, to support the Weaver electors for the purpose of taking those states out of the republican column and throwing the election into the house of representatives where the democrats had a majority. The evidence of this is conclusive, and has been published time and again. The following letter from James E. Boyd, then the governor of Nebraska and the Nebraska member of the national committee, ought to set this fact at rest:

LINCOLN, Neb., Oct. 17.—(Personal and confidential.)—Dear Sir: I have just returned from the east where I was honored by a consultation with the national committee and leading men of our party, with regard to the best policy to be pursued in Nebraska this fall in dealing with the electoral ticket; and they agreed with me, that the wisest course would be for democrats to support the Weaver electors; the object being to take Nebraska out of her accustomed place in the republican column.

Information has reached me that a number of independents who were formerly republicans contemplate voting for the Harrison electors. With the republican strength thus augmented it would be impossible for the democrats to carry their own electors' ticket to victory. It is therefore the part of good judgment and wise action for democrats to support the Weaver electors in as large numbers as possible. For democrats to do this is no abandonment of principle; on the contrary, it is a definite step toward victory, and the ultimate triumph of Cleveland and Stevenson, and the principles they represent. JAMES E. BOYD.

Mr. Bryan was then a member of congress as well as a candidate for re-election, and announced that if the election was thrown into the house he would vote for Mr. Cleveland, the democratic nominee, as against Mr. Harrison, the republican nominee. Mr. Bryan may be justly criticised for having known so little of Mr. Cleveland as to prefer him to Mr. Harrison, but from the standpoint of democratic regularity he can not be criticised for obeying the democratic national committee, and voting for General Weaver in order to help elect Mr.

Cleveland. In the election of 1896 Mr. Weaver was one of the most active supporters of Mr. Bryan, while Mr. Cleveland turned to republican advantage the influence which the democratic party had given him. When Mr. Bryan became personally acquainted with the two men, he found that General Weaver was infinitely more democratic than Mr. Cleveland in environment, principles, purpose and method.

As to the policies which Mr. Bryan has supported, only a word need be said. On the tariff question no one will dispute his orthodoxy. He helped to prepare the Wilson bill, which was much more acceptable even to Mr. Cleveland, than the senate bill after Mr. Gorman and Mr. Hill got through with it. The free list of the Wilson bill was practically identical with the free list set forth in the platform upon which Mr Bryan was elected in 1890, four years before. The democrats of the 52nd and 53rd congresses favored the election of United States senators by direct vote of the people, and this was made a part of the democratic platform of 1900. This demand will be found in the democratic platform upon which Mr Bryan ran in 1890. The Wilson bill contained an income tax, and this was supported by a large majority of the democrats of the senate and house. The income tax was also demanded in Mr. Bryan's congressional platform of 1890. Mr. Bryan's first congressional platform also contained a plank in favor of the free coinage of silver, and during that year the democrats of the house by an overwhelming majority voted to recommit the Sherman law with instructions to the committee to bring in a free coinage bill (16 to 1 being the only ratio then considered). For twenty years the democrats of the senate and house had been voting for bills embodying exactly the coinage provisions that the platform of 1896 contended for. There was not a plank in the Chicago platform that was inconsistent with the record of the party on questions dealt with, and that platform was prepared by a committee selected from all the states of the Union, and was reported to the convention before Mr. Bryan's nomination was considered probable by any considerable number of the convention.

The money plank of the Chicago platform, while identical

with the plank adopted by the democrats of Nebraska in 1894, had been indorsed by the democrats at the primaries in almost all the states and no one can say that its adoption was not the free and voluntary act of the rank and file of the party. At Kansas City the only controversy was over the money plank. No other plank of the Chicago platform was questioned or opposed, and the dispute over the money plank was as to whether it should be reaffirmed or reiterated.

Mr. Bryan has defended the Chicago platform and the Kansas City platform, and if his democracy can be questioned because of his advocacy of those platforms, then the same objection must be made to the democracy of the millions who belive in those platforms as firmly as he and have advocated them as earnestly.

Space has been given to the above not because Mr. Bryan's conduct or views ought to influence others, but because the reorganizers are seeking to make the fight a personal one against Mr. Bryan, whereas it is and ought to be made upon principles. A principle is neither good nor bad because it is advocated by any man; it is good or bad in itself, and this discussion of Mr. Bryan's personal connection with these questions would not appear here but for the fact that the friends of the Kansas City platform are continually annoyed by the misrepresentations that are made by the gold democrats and by the republican papers which take great delight in assisting the gold democrats.

ON MAMMON'S SIDE.

The Milwaukee *Sentinel* seems anxious to earn a front place among the champions of organized wealth. It recently published an interview with Mr. Bryan and then quoting a part of the interview proceeded to make an ultra-corporation argument on the questions referred to. Here is what the *Sentinel* quoted:

"The money question must be an issue so long as the money changers attempt to run the treasury department in their own interests, and the labor question must also be an issue, involving as it does both arbitration and government by injunction."

And this is what the *Sentinel* says:

"The peculiar genius for politics possessed by Mr. Bryan is admirably illustrated by the paragraph quoted. He had previously opened the way for these two issues by lining up 'the people'—a title which he gives to those who agree with him or who accept his doctrines without amendment—against the corporations. Having brought this happy business disturbing and calamity breeding matter to a focus, he would make sure of accomplishing his purpose by attacking the integrity of the national currency, and the grand climax would be reached when he brought out his labor issue.

"Just at this time, when leading union men and employers, as well as economists of national reputations, are working night and day with the hope of finding a solution of the labor problem that will insure the rights of both employers and employes, of organized labor and organized manufacturers, Mr. Bryan comes forward with the cheerful suggestion that the matter be treated as a political issue. He would adopt the policy that has brought disaster to Australian industries—compulsory arbitration—and he would abolish 'government by injunction,' which means that in cases of rioting the protection of the courts is to be withdrawn from the employers of labor until after the damage is done and the property destroyed. Even labor leaders who are entitled to respect for having accomplished something of substantial benefit for organized labor do not make these demands.

"On the whole, it may be said that Mr. Bryan's program is about the most complete and promising one that could be devised for bringing about industrial chaos. It would be difficult to improve upon it in any particular or at any point. It would not be necessary to add shotguns, dynamite, and red flags in order to round it out, for they would all come in due course of time."

This reveals the viewpoint from which the *Sentinel* surveys the political field.

Those who object to having the treasury department run by the money changers in their own interests are, according to its logic, "attacking the integrity of the national currency," and those who prefer arbitration to strikes and who condemn government by injunction are denounced as disturbers of the peace.

Mr. Bryan has never advocated compulsory arbitration, as the *Sentinel* might have known, and would have known if it had placed a proper estimate upon accuracy of statement.

Both the Chicago and Kansas City platforms demanded arbitration and while the republican leaders steadfastly refuse to consider the question, the sentiment in favor of voluntary arbitration is growing and will ultimately triumph.

If, in the meantime, there are disturbances, lockouts, boycotts or bloodshed, the responsibility will not rest upon those who seek to establish just and peaceable means for the adjustment of differences, but upon those servile and sycophantic worshippers at the shrine of Mammon who insolently assault all remedial legislation.

The *Sentinel* will praise the president for suggesting the arbitration of one strike after the loss of one hundred millions of dollars, but it condemns Mr. Bryan for advocating arbitration as a means of settling all labor disputes without the necessity for a strike.

The *Sentinel* boldly defends government by injunction and it does so with full knowledge that the purpose of this extraordinary writ is to deny the laboring man the right of trial by jury. If the editor of the *Sentinel* were charged with a libelous assault upon the reputation of a citizen or a murderous assault upon his employer or even with converting a subscription to his own use, he would be entitled to a trial by jury and no court could deny it to him; but he is so soaked and steeped in prejudice for the great corporations that he would rob the wage-earners of this invaluable safeguard.

Of all the forces in society no one force is doing more to create class hostility than plutocratic newspapers like the *Sentinel* that blindly follow at the heels of the money magnates and bark at all who plead for justice and fair play.

THE WORLD MOURNS.

The universal sorrow evinced at the death of Pope Leo shows the willingness of the people of all denominations to lay aside their prejudices and do honor to those who really deserve well of their fellows—and he has earned this. In his selection there was a fortunate conjunction of the man and the opportunity. His mental and spiritual traits admirably fitted him for the eminent place which he filled and his position as the head of the great Catholic church gave him a large sphere in which to act. While he was the highest representative of one branch of the Christian church and passionately devoted to his task he took an active part in all that concerned humanity and his mighty influence was ever thrown upon the side of peace and justice.

The valiant fight which he made for life aroused profound sympathy and the prolonged struggle gave an opportunity for his admirers to lay their tributes at his feet.

His successor, while inspired by his lofty example, will find it difficult to live up to the pattern set by the recent occupant of the vatican.

THE JEWISH PETITION.

The action of our government in offering to forward a petition of American Jews and others asking the czar to afford protection to Russian Jews, has had the desired effect, even though our government was notified that the petition would not be received. It has called public attention to the cruelty practiced in Russia and has helped to create a public sentiment that will make for righteousness and humanity. Mr. Leon N. Levi, of New York, well expresses it in the following interview:

"The answer made by Russia to Secretary Hay's note is no surprise to me. The movement, however, has had all the good effects that were in contemplation and even more. It has enabled the American people and the government to make an enduring record of their view on the Kishineff horror.

"The petition, being now an official document, will be preserved in the archives of the United States and will forever testify to the lofty humanity of the people, which is splendidly represented by the signers and of the president and his official advisers. I am convinced, too, that the influence in Russia of the petition and of the agitation which preceded it has been powerful and good.

"The precise method of conveying the petition was never regarded by the United States as of controlling importance, and when Russia indicated, semi-officially, that it would be unacceptable, we deemed it best for the interests of this country and of the Jews in Russia to avoid a course that would produce unnecessary friction. It was therefore that we, upon our own initiative, and without any suggestion whatsoever, besought President Roosevelt to alter his decision to send the signed petition, and to transmit its text instead."

THE COMMONER is pleased to be able to commend the part taken in the matter by President Roosevelt and the secretary of state.

FOREIGNERS IN CHINA

At the Christian Endeavor Society meeting, held in Denver recently, a Mr. Beach, described in the press dispatches as a missionary in China for six years, declared that foreign syndicates had secured every available railroad concession or business enterprise in that country and that the greed of these foreign operators had brought about an industrial revolution in that country.

"If the Chinese had the spirit of the men of 1776," he added, "there would not be a foreigner or missionary left in China." This explains the anti-foreign sentiment which is to be found in the countries that are being "developed." The "civilized nations" are engaged in commercializing the world. The business men of these nations obtain concessions and monopolize trade, and then the home government is expected to back up the demands of the traders with armies and navies.

Money! money! money! Human rights are being subordinated to it; nations are being embroiled in it, and Christianity is being retarded on account of it. Until within a few years America was free from suspicion and her representatives could go anywhere, but now that we have joined other nations in land-grabbing we must expect to meet the same opposition and, if we are going to get our share of the plunder, we must leave a trail of blood as other exploiting nations have done. Imperialism must be abandoned or it will work a complete change in the ideals and methods of our government.

CAN NOT KEEP IT DOWN.

They say that the money question is settled, and yet the president is conferring with republican leaders about financial legislation and the money magnates are preparing to squeeze the public into submission to their demands. Speaker Cannon was called to Oyster Bay and urged to assist in carrying out the schemes of Wall street, but he could not be enthused. He was willing to allow congress to pass such a bill, but he would not promise to help. His assistance, however, will hardly be needed, for the financiers will bring the necessary influence to bear on republican members and Speaker Cannon would find it quite difficult to prevent the passage of any bill that Rothschild and Morgan agreed upon. It might be well, though, for the republicans to pause long enough to consider what Mr. Cannon says about the increase in the currency. He boasts that the volume of money has increased $126,000,000 in the last year and he does not favor tinkering with the currency. The quantitative theory of money has been vindicated and still the republicans refuse to make permanent provision for an adequate supply of real money.

The fight that is coming up in congress over the currency measure will give the democrats a chance to call public attention to the manner in which the monied element controls the republican party.

THE MELTING POT TEST.

On another page will be found an editorial from the New York *World* discussing "intrinsic value." The editorial was called out by an inquiry from Hon. Charles A. Towne and the *World* makes the absurd mistake so commonly made by the worshippers of the gold standard. It relies upon the melting pot test to determine intrinsic value, when a moment's reflection would convince the editor that "melting without loss" is a law made characteristic and nothing else. If, for instance, our law fixed a mint charge of 1 per cent for the coinage of gold the dollar would lose one cent by melting because the owner would have to pay one cent to have it recoined. If the charge was five cents the loss would be five cents. When silver was given free and unlimited coinage silver coins could be melted without loss and the same would be true again under free and unlimited coinage. Bimetallists believe that the parity could and would be maintained under free coinage, but even if the parity was not maintained the silver dollar could be melted without loss just as the gold dollar can be now.

The *World* also overlooks the fact that what it calls intrinsic value is in part, at least, value created by a law-made demand. The monetary use of gold is its principle use and if this use were withdrawn the market price would necessarily fall.

The *World* and those who like it ignore reason and common sense in the discussion of the money question give gold credit for all that law bestows upon it and then blame silver for all that law takes from it. The editorial reproduced is a fair illustration of the lack of logic which characterizes the *World's* utterances upon the money question.

ANOTHER WALL STREET DEMAND.

Wall street has been demanding an elastic currency for some time, but now comes the demand from the Wall Street *Journal* for an elastic anti-trust law. It says that the decision of the court in the merger case "calls loudly for remedial legislation." It says: "The law must be made, if possible, more elastic so as to permit of such combinations as are beneficial even though technically in restraint of trade." Elasticity seems to be popular in Wall street—elasticity of conscience, elasticity of law, elasticity of currency, and elasticity even of the Declaration of Independence. It would seem that we need less elasticity instead of more.

MISINTERPRETING PROVIDENCE.

A reader of THE COMMONER has sent in a pamphlet printed by the Missionary Society of one of the protestant churches which sets forth a doctrine that is as un-Christian as it is un-American.

The pamphlet describes the conversion of a Filipino some sixteen years ago and the evangelistic work of his son, and concludes as follows:

Is this not one evidence that God was preparing a man to preach the truth as soon as political and religious liberty was given to the Philippine islands, and a new evidence that God is using the wars of our times for the evangelization of the nations?

The person who forwarded the pamphlet takes exception to THE COMMONER'S position on imperialism and declares his belief in the doctrine that God uses the thirteen-inch gun to spread his Gospel, and no one can read the pamphlet without feeling that the writer of it is a believer in the doctrine that wars can be justified as a means of extending the Christian religion. Not only that, but the pamphlet shows that the main work of this protestant preacher is to convert Filipinos from Catholicism to Protestantism. Americans being believers in religious liberty recognize and defend the right of a Catholic to convert a protestant to his faith and the right of a protestant to convert a Catholic to his faith, but to justify a war on the ground that it is a divinely appointed means which enables one part of the Christian church, or to enable any part of the Christian church, to proselyte among unbelievers, is totally at variance with our theory of government and our ideas of religion. Some have vaguely hinted that our Philippine policy can be defended as a missionary policy, but so far as the editor of THE COMMONER knows this is the first written argument prepared for circulation which attempts to justify imperialism on the ground that it is a divinely appointed system.

It certainly does injustice to the members of the great ciyuIcfHwowa-fir p lfiWb$. EJH" olj etaoi etaoin etaonnu protestant denomination responsible for the pamphlet for the members of its church have given as conclusive proof, as the members of any other church, that they believe in the power of the Christian religion to propagate itself by appeals to the heart. The very fact that one of the Filipino missionaries described in the pamphlet was converted sixteen years ago is evidence that even under Spanish rule it was possible for the protestant religion to make a convert. The fact that the convert was banished not only did not injure his cause, but really gave it prominence. "The blood of the martyrs is the seed of the church," is an old saying and its truth has been shown many and many a time. Persecution never destroys an idea. The very fact that a man is willing, if necessary, to die for an idea is the most potent argument that can be made in defense of that idea.

The pamphlet assumes that American rule in the Philippine islands is necessary to religious liberty. For it says: "During the year of 1898 in the provision of God for the religious liberty of the Philippine people three events occurred, (1) Paulino Zamora returned to Manila; (2) Nicholas Zamora, his son, graduated with honors for the priesthood from a Roman Catholic college, and, (3) the American flag floated over Manila."

It is a gratuitous assumption to say that American rule in the Philippines is necessary to religious liberty. If any reader of THE COMMONER doubts that religious liberty is possible under a Philippine republic, let him visit Mexico, a Catholic country, and he will find that the Mexicans, without the aid of any outside influence, have secured and are enjoying absolute religious freedom. Protestant churches can be found in Mexico; while they are not numerous and while they are not large in membership, they enjoy all the rights and privileges enjoyed by the Catholic church or any other church, and the protestant missionaries who go to Mexico are just as free to preach their doctrines in Mexico as a Catholic priest is to present his views and the beliefs of his church to protestants in the United States. The same can be said of Cuba, which is also a Catholic country.

The doctrine that "God is using the wars of our times for the evangelization of the nations" is not only an assumption, but it is an exceedingly dangerous doctrine. If those who believe in the protesant form of the Christian faith have the right to wage war against a Catholic country for a religious purpose, then the people of a Catholic country have a right to wage war against a protestant nation for a religious purpose. Who will defend such a barbarous doctrine? If the United States can justify the subjugation of a Catholic country for a religious purpose, then is there not danger that people who apply that doctrine to our nation's dealing with other nations, may apply the same doctrine in the United States, and attempt to justify the forcing of one form of religion upon those of another denomination or religion?

Christ's gospel was a gospel of peace. While its introduction creates a contest between the Christian ideals and the ideals of Mammon, it does not justify the use of force in the propagation of that gospel. If there is not something in the heart to which the religion of Christ can successfully appeal there is certainly no way in which it can be introduced into man by a surgical operation.

A line must be drawn, and it is a distinct line, between the utilization of an existing condition and the creation of that condition. No one would attempt to justify the burning of a town, and yet after the town is burned people, accepting the situation, may take advantage of the burning to improve the town in a way that they might not have been able to do before the fire. Instances have been known where a disastrous season has turned attention to new crops that have proved greatly beneficial to the people of that section, and yet no one should justify the sending of a drouth or a flood in the hope that good might come out of it. So with wars. It is proper to make the most of the condition which follows a war, and yet no one could afford to assume responsibility for a war in the hope of producing the condition. It is proper for the representatives of all branches of the Christian church to present their ideas and to give expression to their beliefs, but no one can justify a colonial policy on the ground that it may be utilized to advance any form of religion.

Those who attempt to interpret Providence often make the mistake of considering the good that comes out of evil, without considering the good that might have been done without the evil. In order to make a fair comparison one must understand what can be done peacefully as well as what is done violently. It is impossible to see both what has been done and what might have been done, and, therefore, comparison is difficult. The only sound method of argument is to reason from the individual to the collection of individuals. We can understand a thing when we see it emphasized in an individual better than when we attempt to look at it as exemplified in a nation. If an individual went about with a club beating people and bruising them and commanding them to live in a certain way, inspiring not love, but terror, we would describe him as a bully and as a braggart. If he acted thus merely because he found pleasure in it, we would condemn his disposition, but if he made money out of his brutality we could call him a robber. No pretense that he was benevolently inclined or that he was only exacting a reasonable compensation for the good that he was doing, would palliate his crimes. If he did this in the name of Christianity we would accuse him of adding hypocrisy to his other sins. But when a nation acts upon the principle of a bully or a highwayman it is sometimes applauded as a world power by those who desire to exercise the power. Sometimes the action is applauded as Providential if a grain of good can be found in a bushel of evil.

We have no difficulty in contrasting the example of an upright man with the example of an evil doer. We recognize the virtues of the man, we recognize the good influence which he exerts upon his community, and we know that the benefits flowing from such a life go on increasing with each new generation forever. Can we doubt that a nation which applies its measure of individual worth to its national greatness does more good than a nation which risks the corruption of its individual ideals by brutalizing its national purpose?

Imperialism strikes at the principles of our religion as well as at the principles of our government. Love, not force, is the foundation of our religion—love that sacrifices and persuades, not that robust selfishness which boasts of its brute force or hides its mailed hand in the glove of benevolent assimilation. Our missionary societies should study the gospel of the Prince of Peace.

MAKING THE ISSUE PLAIN.

The decisions rendered in the two merger cases present the issue very clearly. Judge Thayer in deciding the case in which the United States government was prosecuting said that the merger—

"Destroyed every motive for competition between two roads which were natural competitors for business by pooling the earnings of the two roads for the common benefit of the stockholders of both companies, and, according to the familiar rule that every one is presumed to intend what are the necessary consequences of his own acts, when done willfully and deliberately, we must conclude that those who conceived and executed the plan aforesaid intended, among other things, to accomplish these objects."

In the case in which the state of Minnesota was plaintiff, Judge Lochren said:

"I am compelled to reject the doctrine that any person can be held to have committed or to be purposing and about to commit a highly penal offense merely because it can be shown that his pecuniary interests will be thereby advanced and that he has the power either directly by himself or indirectly through persuasion or coercion of his agents to compass the commission of the offense."

It will be noticed that in the Thayer decision a monopoly is condemned because the influence of selfishness was recognized, while in the Lochren decision the court refused to recognize the bias which one naturally has in favor of his own interests. The democrats take the view expressed by Judge Thayer and say that "a private monopoly is indefensible and intolerable," while the republicans insist that there are good trusts and bad trusts and that only the bad ones should be disturbed. This is the point on which the fight will turn and the people might as well acquaint themselves with the issue. To make it plain, let us take a familiar case. Suppose Judge Lochren was trying a jury case, and suppose a juror admitted that he had a large pecuniary interest in the result of the suit, would the judge say: "I refuse to believe that the juror will disregard his oath merely because it can be shown that his pecuniary interests will be thereby advanced." There would be just as much sense in allowing a biased juror to serve and then put on the injured party the burden of proving his injury as to permit the trusts to be formed and then throw upon the victim the burden of protecting himself from trust exactions. A private monopoly is a highwayman and it is not sufficient to say that it shall be moderate in its exactions—it must be exterminated. Extermination of trusts does not mean that all corporations should be attacked or that all combinations of capital should be prohibited, but it does mean that the line should be drawn against every attempt to monopolize any article of merchandise. It means that the fight must be made against all private monopolies everywhere.

GENERAL MILES RETIRES.

At noon, August 8, Lieutenant General Nelson A. Miles ceased active connection with the regular army and went upon the retired list. As a soldier General Miles has served his country well and faithfully. He won his way from the ranks to the position of lieutenant general by force of his ability as a leader and his prowess as a soldier. He enlisted as a private in the Fifty-first Massachusetts volunteers, and was successively promoted until he became a major general of volunteers. At the close of the civil war he was made a colonel in the regular army. As an Indian campaigner he attracted the attention and won the admiration of the whole people, and was promoted through different ranks until he became senior major general. Upon the death of Lieutenant General Schofield he was promoted to the highest rank in the army. During the later years of his active service General Miles was bitterly assailed by many who either could not or did not care to conceal their ulterior motives, but he gave his attention to the duties of his high office and deported himself as a gentleman and a soldier.

THE MONEY QUESTION.

In its issue of Friday, July 31, the Wall Street *Journal* said:
"As it was in the beginning of the year, is now, and is likely to continue to be during all of 1903, the money question is the one of most vital importance. There is nothing in the business situation as it presents itself at this time, to prevent a continuance of our national prosperity, except the congestion of the money market, due to its inability to expand as rapidly as the trade and industries of the country."

The *Journal* addresses the bankers when it reminds them that "the money question is the one of most vital importance."

When other representatives of Wall street address the people, the people are assured that the money question is a dead issue.

From the standpoint of these men the people should not tamper with the money question. They should not discuss it. They should not insist upon having a part in the arrangement of our monetary system.

But with the bankers it is different. They are to be reminded that "the money question is the one of most vital importance," and they are to be counseled to urge senators and representatives in congress to see that this question is disposed of entirely in line with the vital interests of the financiers.

But when the Wall Street *Journal* admits that "the money question is the one of most vital importance," with what reason does it assume to draw the line where the discussion of this question may terminate?

Does it object to the bimetallists urging their method of providing the country with what they believe to be a sound monetary system? Or does it insist that all discussion with respect to this question of "most vital importance" be limited to a consideration of the currency system proposed by the financiers and that participation in that discussion be confined to the financiers themselves?

The Wall Street *Journal* has made a most intersting confession. Whatever men may say about the "dead and buried past," whatever men may say about "worn-out issues," the indisputable fact remains that in the discussion of our financial system the "money question" can not be separated from the money question.

A NEWSPAPER LOTTERY.

The Nashville *American* is not only republican in its views, but it is willing to demoralize its readers by cultivating the gambling spirit among them. A reader of THE COMMONER has sent in a letter issued by the *Weekly American*, April 4, inviting subscribers to enter into a guessing contest—the thing guessed upon to be the amount of cotton received at all United States ports between September 1, 1902, and May 1, 1903, (the time is now past). As there was no way of ascertaining the exact amount of bales it was so largely a guess that the contest does not differ essentially in principle from the old lottery or wheel of fortune. It is not strange that a paper that supports a Wall street financial policy should urge its subscribers to speculative money-making rather than stimulate them to the honest accumulation of money by legitimate means. The *American* offered a number of free estimates to agents on terms stated in the letter. When it can spare time from the denunciation of Mr. Bryan as a disturber of harmony, will it give a few words in defense of its lottery, from a moral standpoint?

THE RACE PROBLEM.

On another page will be found a letter recently written by President Roosevelt to Governor Durbin on the subject of lynching. Forgetting for the present the failure of the president to enforce the law against the trust magnates and Governor Durbin's refusal to deliver to Kentucky authorities a republican ex-governor charged with murder, let us consider the subject of mob law as it is related to the race question. The president is right in protesting against mob law—it can not be defended. It is a reflection on the people if legal means of punishment are inadequate and ineffective, and it is a reflection on the government if the people have reason to distrust its ability to enforce the law. All will agree with the president that punishment should not only be sure, but should be as swift as a due regard to the rights of the accused will permit. Whatever punishments are sanctioned by public opinion should be embodied in the law and in the case of crimes against women the laws should be such—even though a constitutional amendment were necessary to secure it—that the victim of the outrage will be protected from the humiliation of having to give testimony before a crowd of curious, but disinterested, persons.

The president is also to be commended for having coupled a denunciation of rape with a condemnation of lynching. Too many cry out against the lawless punishment without saying anything against the horrible crime which arouses the anger of the people. If some of the enthusiasm that is spent in passing resolutions denouncing mob law was employed in condemning the unspeakable beastiality that provokes summary punishment there would be fewer instances of mob law.

The fact that the president did not specifically mention southern lynching shows that the lynchings and burnings in northern states have convinced him that race prejudice is as strong in Illinois, Indiana, Delaware, and Kansas as in Mississippi, Georgia, Alabama or Texas.

It may be well in this connection to consider race prejudice for a moment in connection with mob law. That there is such a thing must be admitted. It is written on every page of history and is not likely to disappear soon. It must be remembered, too, that the negro has as much prejudice against the white man as the white man has against the negro, and if the reason to doubt that the white man would have reason to complain. This was apparent in the carpet-bag days and is apparent today wherever it can find expression. negro was in a position to rule the white man there is no

A sense of justice, however, restrains this prejudice and it is not often that either the white man or the negro says anything in the presence of the other that is calculated to offend. Color is not a matter of choice, neither can it be changed by will or by law. It is, therefore, as unkind to taunt a man with being black as it is unreasonable for a black man to be angered by such a taunt.

A man is to be praised or blamed according to the use he makes of his talents or opportunities, not by his inherited advantages. The fact that a negro is lynched by a mob because of an outrage upon a woman ought not to increase the race prejudice that exists. White men are lynched for the same crime. Neither must the white man's feeling toward the negro be judged by his conduct when under great excitement. Man mad is an entirely different creature from man deliberate. Men in anger have killed fathers, wives, brothers, sons and friends —they have broken every tie of love and kinship.

Suffrage qualifications can not be attributed entirely to race prejudice for suffrage qualifications are to be found in nearly all countries and have been employed in many of our own states. They have been employed by white men against members of the white race and by people of every color against people of their own color. Woman suffragists complain that women are disfranchised and such disfranchisement can not be explained on the ground of race prejudice either, for husband and wife, mother and son, are not only of the same race, but are linked together by the strongest bonds known.

The suffrage amendments in the south, so much complained of by republican politicians, are not nearly so severe as the republican colonial policy in the Philippines.

First—In every southern state some of the negroes can vote now, and all others can qualify themselves for suffrage; in the Philippines the inhabitants are permanently disqualified.

Second—The negroes in the south, even when they can not vote, have the protection of federal and state constitutions; the Filipino has no constitutional protection whatever.

Third—The negroes in the south live under the laws that the white man makes for himself; the Filipino lives under laws that we make for him and would not live under ourselves.

While the brown man of the Orient is faring worse than the black man in the south, the republican leaders are stirring up race antagonism in this country in order to keep the colored vote solid for the republican party. Even the president has contributed more than his share to the agitation. When he has appointed a colored man to office he has done it with a flourish of trumpets and a brass band accompaniment that the world might know that the "door" was wide open. When a colored postmistress was objected to he refused to allow her to resign and closed the office—and did it allay race prejuice? No; it did more to excite race prejuice than any ten colored appointments that President McKinley made.

The Booker T. Washington dinner at the White house did even more than the Indianola postoffice incident to excite race prejudice.

The president surely did not intend to inject the question of social equality into politics, for on that issue he could not carry a state in the Union; then why arouse the colored people to expect social equality or agitate the whites with the fear of it? It is a grievous mistake to turn the negro's thoughts from the substantial advantages of industrial, intellectual and moral progress to the unsubstantial promises of social recognition. The amalgamation of the races is not the solution of the race question, and that would be the logical result of social equality. In their natural right to life, liberty and the pursuit of happiness the white man and the black man are equal and these rights should be protected with jealous care. Educational advantages should be open to both races and both should be encouraged to secure all the mental discipline possible.

Whether the more advanced race should fix suffrage qualifications for the less advanced is a question to be determined by the facts in the case, but it is safe to say that on this subject the people of the north would be much like the people of the south if they were compelled to meet the same conditions.

As to social equality there should be a frank and candid understanding. There is no difference on this subject between the white people of the north and the white people of the south. The color line is drawn by republican families as distinctly as it is by democratic families, as distinctly by northern families as by southern families. There is more friendliness and helpfulness where this is recognized than where it is left in doubt and uncertainty.

The white race ought to recognize the rights of the black race and lend it every possible assistance. The whites of the south are taxing themselves to educate the children of darker skin, while republican politicians in the north are riding into office on black votes and, while they exclude the colored people from their social functions, are constantly trying to array the southern negro against the southern white man.

There is another aspect of the question. The promise of social equality—false as it is—encourages the educated negro to hope to get away from his race and thus the race loses the benefit that the more progressive negroes might bring to it. Instead of trying to bleach the face or to take the kink out of the hair let the colored man recognize that he is black by nature and set to work to show what one of his race can accomplish. No upright, intelligent and law-abiding colored man ever gets into trouble himself or involves his people in a race war. After the colored man has established a reputation for virtue, sobriety and good sense, let him devote himself to the building up of a society that will satisfy his needs. If he has daughters let him make them worthy of the best young men of his race; if he has sons, let him make them examples of industry and good habits. To deserve respect and not enjoy it is better than to enjoy respect without deserving it, but to deserve respect is the best and surest way to secure it.

A good character is more valuable and more permanent than a postoffice, and nothing will do more to kill race prejudice than the building up of character.

The white man needs to be reminded, as the president suggests, that lawlessness is dangerous and torture demoralizing to those who practice it, but the black man must also be cautioned not to judge the white man's life purpose by the passions of an hour and he should be warned not to allow the vices and lusts of the most abandoned of his race to provoke hostility between himself and the whites.

The race question is here and it will require the intelligence and the patriotism of the people north and south to settle it aright. It has too long been used for political advantage.

PHILO SHERMAN BENNETT.

Mr. Bryan has been called upon to mourn the death of another close personal and political friend—Mr. Philo Sherman Bennett of New Haven, Conn. He was senior member of the New York wholesale firm of Bennett, Soal & Co., and was one of the few prominent business men of the east who refused to be intimidated by the financiers in 1896. He began at the bottom of the ladder and worked his way up to a commanding position in the commercial world, and yet he never lost his sympathy with the struggling masses.

The address delivered at the funeral by Rev. Artemus J. Haynes, pastor of the United church, so accurately described the controlling purpose of Mr. Bennett's life that it is given in full:

"The most appropriate words on such an occasion as this are the words of the Holy Scripture, leading our thoughts and feelings out into some simple utterance of prayer. It were better under ordinary circumstances to withhold our testimony of praise until some hour when the mind could dwell more calmly upon the character and achievements of him who has gone. But the circumstances of this occasion are not ordinary; the man whom we honor today was no ordinary man. He was unique by virtue of the opinions which he held, the ideals which he followed, and the type of manhood which he exemplified. Such a life calls for some direct and simple word of appreciation. To go out from this service without voicing the sentiments that have moved you to come to this house today were to tempt the very stones in the street to render tribute to him whom you have known and loved.

"Even had I been well acquainted with Mr. Bennett, it would hardly be fitting that I should enter into the intimacies of his life and character. He whose personality was made beautiful by the rarest modesty, would shrink, I am sure, from having his private virtues shown forth for the admiration of the crowd. The sacredness of personality is not destroyed by the death of the body. In every man's life is a holy of holies; and God alone has the right to enter that inner sanctuary. Of that religious life which is the expression of a man's sense of relationship to his brother the world has a right to take note, but of that life which is hidden with Christ in God the world can know nothing, and into the secret workings of that life no man should attempt to intrude. Jesus spoke to his disciples of their obligations to the brotherhood—that was one side of the religious life, but when he would worship, he went apart into the mountain that he might be alone. Of that side of Mr. Bennett's life which, as I believe, was profoundly religious, that side which had to do with his relation to God, I shall say nothing. The life of faith and aspiration and prayer—only God knows that life, knows its sweetness and beauty. Concerning the other side of his personality, that side which was open to all the world, his relation to the men and women about him, the great brotherhood—concerning that side of his life I would venture to say a few words.

"And that which I would say has defined itself very clearly to my thought. It is not of a general character—the ordinary commonplaces which may be attached to every good man who dies—but something definite and distinct. May I come to my thought by way of a much slighted word of scripture? I can not help feeling that if Mr. Bennett had chosen a text it would have been this: 'He that loveth not his brother whom he hath seen, how can he love God whom he hath not seen?'

"Brotherhood! that was the great word in the language to him. He believed in the democracy of religion and in the religion of democracy. Laws, customs, institutions—nothing was sacred to him only as it ministered to human life. He hated shams of every sort, because he saw that they separated men; he despised conventionalities, for he knew they were as fetters on the souls of his brothers. In his boyhood he experienced the bitterness of struggle. The battle of life sharpened his intellect, but did not dull his sensibilities. By sheer force of ability, honestly applied, he won a large measure of success, even as success is estimated in our commercial age. And this brings me to the definite thing I would say. Mr. Bennett did not forget his past; his heart, to the very last, was with the people. The burning sin among our strong and successful men lies in the fact that they forget their past. Sprung from the people they forget the people. In many instances those who are most bitter against the great masses of laboring men are the very ones who have risen from the ranks of labor. As I study men I find that worldly success has a way of changing their sympathy. It was not so with Mr. Bennett. The cause of the people, those who could not speak for themselves, those who were doing the world's hard work—the cause of the people was nearer his heart than the interests of his own affairs. Simple, modest, unassuming—no man, however humble his labor, but found in him a brother. He believed in Chirst, and in Christ's idea of brotherhood. How devotedly he gave himself—his time, his strength, his means, to the realization of this dream of brotherhood is known to you far better than to myself. His whole life was a valiant service in the interests of justice and mercy and truth. On every hand men are saying of him that he could not rest until he got to the bottom of things; and I firmly believe that we honor one today whose heart was set, above everything else, on reality.

"Reality! how this word brings us back to the sacred mystery of the hour. 'If a man die shall be live again?' It is a question old as the world. And to that question there is only one answer: It is the answer of the good life. In the hour of supreme sorrow all our arguments and speculations crumble into nothingness. The soul must be a witness to itself of its own eternal nature. If you would believe in the immortal life, go live as though you were immortal. Face your life as this man faced his, and the future need hold no fears for you. Wealth, fame, honor—all these sweep by and on; the love of God that bindeth men together in brotherhood—this is the undying reality."

The floral tributes were numerous and beautiful, the most conspicuous being an elaborate wreath from the employes in the store.

Mr. Bryan interrupted his Chautauqua work long enough to attend the obsequies. His remarks at the grave were as follows:

"At another time I shall take occasion to speak of the life of Philo Sherman Bennett and to draw some lessons from his career; today I must content myself with offering a word of comfort to those who knew him as husband, brother, relative or friend—and as a friend I need a share of this comfort for myself. It is sad enough to consign to the dust the body of one we love—how infinitely more sad if we were compelled to part with the spirit that animated this tenement of clay. But the best of man does not perish. We bury the brain that planned for others as well as for its master, the tongue that spoke words of love and encouragement, the hands that were extended to those who needed help and the feet that ran where duty directed, but the spirit that dominated and controlled all rises triumphant over the grave. We lay away the implements with which he wrought, but the gentle, modest, patient, sympathetic, loyal, brave and manly man whom we knew is not dead, and can not die. It would be unfair to count the loss of his departure without counting the gain of his existence. The gift of his life we have and of this the tomb can not deprive us. Separation, sudden and distressing as it is, can not take from the companion of his life the recollection of forty years of affection, tenderness and confidence, nor from others the memory of helpful association with him. If the sunshine which a baby brings into a home, even if its sojourn is brief, can not be dimmed by its death; if a child growing to manhood or womanhood brings to the parents a development of heart and head that outweighs any grief that its demise can cause, how much more does a long life full of kindly deeds leave us indebted to the Father who both gives and takes away. The night of death makes us remember with gratitude the light of the day that has gone while we look forward to the morning.

"The impress made by the life is lasting. We think it wonderful that we can by means of the telephone or the telegraph talk to those who are many miles away, but the achievements of the heart are even more wonderful, for the heart that gives inspiration to another heart influences all the generations yet to come. What finite mind, then, can measure the influence of a life that touched so many lives as did our friend's?

"To the young, death is an appalling thing, but it ought not to be to those whose advancing years warn them of its certain approach. As we journey along life's road we must pause again and again to bid farewell to some fellow traveler. In the course of nature the father and the mother die, then brothers and sisters follow, and finally the children and the children's children cross to the unknown world beyond—one by one 'from love's shining circle the gems drop away' until the 'king of terrors' loses his power to affright us and the increasing company on the farther shore make us first willing and then anxious to join them. It is God's way. It is God's way."

THE WAGES OF SIN.

Those who are opposed to imperialism doubtless read with great interest the concluding paragraph of Mr. Roosevelt's letter to the governor of Indiana. In that paragraph Mr. Roosevelt said:

"The nation, like the individual, cannot commit a crime with impunity. If we are guilty of lawlessness or violence, whether our guilt consists of active participation therein or in mere connivance or encouragement, we shall assuredly suffer later on because of what we have done. The cornerstone of this republic, as of all free governments, is respect for, and obedience to, the law. Where we permit the law to be defied or evaded, whether by rich man or poor man, by black man or white man, we are by just so much weakening the bonds of our civilization and increasing the chances of its overthrow and the substitution therefor of a system that shall be violent alternations of anarchy and tyranny."

Mr. Roosevelt here stated a proposition that has frequently been put forth by those who criticise the republican party's policy toward our new possessions. Yet republican orators and republican organs have had many sneers for such statements as these when they were made by those who do not subscribe to republican doctrine.

Jefferson wrote: "I know but one code of morality for men, whether acting singly or collectively."

Franklin wrote: "Justice is as strictly due between neighbor nations as between neighbor citizens. A highwayman is as much a robber when he plunders in a gang as when he plunders singly, and a nation that makes an unjust war is only a great gang."

Men may dare to do in crowds what they would not dare to do as individuals, but the moral character of an act is not determined by the number of those who join it. Force can defend a right, but force has never yet created a right. If it was true as declared in the resolution of intervention that the Cubans "are and of right ought to be free and independent," it is equally true that the Filipinos "are and of right ought to be free and independent."

As Mr. Roosevelt says: "The nation, like the individual, cannot commit a crime with impunity." To be sure, the nation like the individual, can commit a crime. It can by its acts repudiate its best traditions and it may violate the great principles to which its founders successfully appealed for their own liberties; but just as Mr. Roosevelt says, "We shall assuredly suffer later on because of what we have done."

The young man upon reaching his majority, can do what he pleases; he can disregard the teachings of his parents; he can trample upon all that he has been taught to consider sacred; he can disobey the laws of the state, the laws of society, and the laws of God; he can stamp failure upon his life and make his very existence a curse to his fellowmen, and he can bring his father and mother in sorrow to the grave, but he cannot annul the sentence "the wages of sin is death."

And so with this nation. It is of age and it can do as it pleases; it can spurn the traditions of the past; it can repudiate the principles upon which the nation rests; it may employ force instead of reason; it can substitute might for right; it can conquer a weaker people; it can exploit their lands, appropriate their money and kill their people, but it cannot repeal the moral law or escape the punishment decreed for the violation of human rights.

In the concluding paragraph of his letter to the Indiana governor, Mr. Roosevelt but stated in another way a principle treated in pleasing verse by a well-known American poet:

> Would we tread in the paths of tyranny,
>   Nor reckon the tyrant's cost?
> Who taketh another's liberty
>   His freedom is also lost.
> Would we win as the strong have ever won,
>   Make ready to pay the debt,
> For the God who reigned over Babylon
>   Is the God who is reigning yet.

BRIBING CONGRESSMEN.

In last week's COMMONER was some correspondence given to the public by Congressman Baker of Brooklyn. It shows that the railroads are issuing passes to congressmen in spite of the Elkins law, and it must also be evident to any reasonable person that the railroads do not issue passes for the pleasure of issuing them.

Washington is so far away from the average constituent that the congressmen can help the railroads without detection, and evidence is not lacking to show that both the railroads and many congressmen understand this.

In the last congress a large sum was given to both the Baltimore & Ohio and the Pennsylvania railroads to aid in the construction of depots and the representatives of the road were hanging about the capitol freely using passes. One of the lobbyists had a record of the vote and rewarded those who voted for the appropriation and refused passes to those who voted against the company's demands.

Governor La Follette might add a paragraph to his Chautauqua lecture and show how the pass is used to bribe congressmen and representatives.

Mr. Baker, who calls attention to the pass custom, is from the state of New York. It is an encouraging sign that the protest comes from the east and it is to be hoped that it will be taken up by the congressmen from the west and south.

LEGISLATION, NOT PETITION.

On another page will be found a *Courier-Journal* editorial which illustrates the servile attitude of the gold bug papers toward the trusts. The *Courier-Journal* shows how the tobacco trust controls the market and is able to fix the price; it shows how the trust has watered its stock and made huge dividends on fictitious capital, and then instead of urging legislation that will make a private monopoly impossible it petitions the trust to deal mercifully with the tobacco growers. On bended knees it begs the trust to consider the poor farmer who makes it possible for the trust magnates to grow rich. While it intimates that "a mighty power" may teach the trust a lesson if it does not look out, it assures the trust that "a recognition of the rights of producers will further good feeling."

Brother Watterson ought to know enough about human nature to know that it is not safe to leave the producers of wealth at the mercy of the trusts, relying only on persuasion and such mild threats as a corporation-controlled organ dares to make. He ought to know also that the trusts cannot be killed so long as each class of producers is willing to "further good feeling" with some particular trust in return for a little consideration. If the trusts are to be overthrown the principle of private monopoly must be attacked wherever it manifests itself. There can be no compromise and no flirting with a trust merely because it happens to be near at home.

PLAYING FOR TRUST SUPPORT.

Every republican who imagines that Mr. Roosevelt is really determined to "shackle cunning as in the past we have shackled force," and that he is willing to stand for the people's interests against the schemes of the financiers and the trust magnates, should read the interesting dispatch printed in the Chicago *Record-Herald* of Monday, August 24, from Walter Wellman, its Washington correspondent.

Mr. Wellman says: "The important point and the new point is that President Roosevelt is behind this currency reform scheme pushing as only he knows how to push. He organized and promoted the effort." And then Mr. Wellman asks: "Why is President Roosevelt so much interested in currency reform?"

Mr. Wellman's reply to his own question is so interesting that it deserves the widest possible publication. He says:

"Mr. Roosevelt's masterly skill as a politician has been employed so successfully that no one suspects he is a politician—the best test in the world. Having become the most popular man in the United States and having won the enthusiastic approval of the masses by his fight upon the trusts and the corporations, Mr. Roosevelt not long ago began to cast about for methods by which he might even up. He had the people with him, but the trusts, the corporations, the financial leaders, the bankers were hostile. This hostility was centered in New York. It chanced that in New York and among these very people there was a general and earnest desire for a reformation of our currency system. The president has gone in for that reformation with his accustomed ardor and energy, and it will not be his fault if the financial people of New York do not soon look upon him with more favor."

It is generally understood that Mr. Wellman is nearer to the Roosevelt administration than any other newspaper correspondent. Certainly no correspondent is more friendly to that administration than is Mr. Wellman; and it is interesting to be told by this administration correspondent that feeling that he has the people with him because of his "fight upon the trust and the corporations;" Mr. Roosevelt proceeds to display his "masterly skill as a politician" by seeking to win over to him the representatives of the trusts and the corporations.

According to this administration correspondent, Mr. Roosevelt discovered "that in New York and among these very people (the trusts and corporations) there was a general and earnest desire for a reformation of our currency system," and also that "the president has gone in for that reformation with his accustomed ardor and energy and IT WILL NOT BE HIS FAULT IF THE FINANCIAL PEOPLE OF NEW YORK DO NOT SOON LOOK UPON HIM WITH MORE FAVOR."

A very frank and candid confession, indeed, and perfectly in line with the idea which democrats generally have entertained of Mr. Roosevelt's disposition to "shackle cunning as in the past we have shackled force."

DEMANDING ARMY INCREASE.

At a banquet given at St. Paul, Minn., in honor of Col. George E. Pond, Mr. James J. Hill, the great railroad magnate, came out boldly for a large army. He said:

"It was not many years ago that everyone thought we needed but a small standing army. This feeling has changed. The transition was sudden and complete. The belief is now general, and I am glad to see the time come when it is acknowledged, that if we are to be a member of the great family of nations we must have absolute and undisputed power to enforce respect for our flag and for our commerce, both on land and on the high seas.

"I am not overrating the demand when I say that it is imperative that the United States maintain the nucleus always and the organization and the officers for an army of 200,000 men. With our varied interests, with our expanding commerce, and with our crowning and ever-increasing power, this strength is not more than sufficient for our uses in times of stress and danger. However that may be, I am thoroughly convinced that the United States should maintain at all times an army of 100,000.

"The people of the United States are the government, their own words dictate. But they are a people of peace, and there is no way so sure to maintain and promote peace as to be prepared to fight for it. We must have peace for our industrial and commercial growth, and peace we will have if we have to fight for it. Therefore, I say that 100,000 men should be always at hand to take the field, with the knowledge always that 200,000 men can be at once brought forward should the need arise."

This can only be explained on one of two theories; either he thinks that imperialism requires an army four times as large as we had before 1896, or he is looking forward to labor troubles and wants a large army to enable the administration to enforce government by injunction at the request of the corporations.

Are the republicans ready for this situation? Have they counted the cost in money? Have they considered its effect on the national welfare? When the plain people of the United States come to consider the purpose of the republican leaders and the natural effect of their policies there will be a revolt that will shake that party to its foundation. The democratic party only needs to maintain its integrity, stand by the people on all questions and await a vindication of its position.

SPECULATION IN STOCKS.

The bank embezzlements which have come to light since the slump in stocks emphasize the necessity for a law that will make it a penal offense for a bank officer to speculate on the market. The gambling mania is so strong when one once yields to it that trust funds are always in danger if the holder of such funds is speculating. A law to prevent such speculating by a bank officer would not only protect the public, but would be a protection to the official as well.

THE "HARD UP" DISEASE.

"I assert without fear of intelligent contradiction that the new Fowler bill for asset currency to be issued by thousands of banks, large and small has no parallel in any progressive country; that it is a discarded, unsuccessful experiment of the past; that it is unsound and gives privileges to picayune creditors as against larger creditors, the millions of depositors."

These statements were made by Andrew J. Frame, president of the Waukesha, Wis., National bank, in an address delivered before the Wisconsin state banking association. Mr. Frame is an advocate of the single gold standard, but unlike many other advocates of monometallism, he does not take kindly to the proposed asset currency scheme. In his address before the Wisconsin bankers, Mr. Frame said that the disease to be treated might be diagnosed as "hard up," but he said that issuing I. O. U.'s would not cure the malady. He declared that the advocates of asset currency proposed "to undermine our present foundation by the injection of an additional quantity of inferior currency;" and he concluded: "From a careful survey of the world's history of banking, I believe asset currency as the cure-all for economic troubles is a fraud, a delusion and a snare. The remedy is worse than the disease."

RACE QUESTION AGAIN.

In a recent issue of THE COMMONER there appeared an editorial entitled "The Race Problem," in which a contrast was drawn between the action of the republican party in the Philippine islands and the action of some of the democratic states of the south. The Inter-Ocean criticises some of the statements made and calls upon Mr. Bryan to tell the truth about the matter. In order that the Inter-Ocean's criticism may be understood, the entire editorial is reproduced:

In THE COMMONER W. J. Bryan writes on "The Race Problem," and commends the president's recent letter to Governor

Durbin against lynching. He gives, also, some very sensible advice to white and black men as to their relations.

But Mr. Bryan could not, of course, treat such a subject without defending his party in the south and without some reference to colonial conditions. He says:

"The suffrage amendments in the south, so much complained of by republican politicians, are not nearly so severe as the republican colonial policy in the Philippines.

"1. In every southern state some of the negroes can vote now, and all others can qualify themselves for the suffrage. In the Philippines the inhabitants are permanently disqualified.

"2. The negroes in the south, even when they cannot vote, have the protection of federal and state constitutions. The Filipino has no constitutional protection.

"3. The negroes in the south live under the laws that the white man makes for himself. The Filipino lives under laws that we make for him and would not live under ourselves."

Here are three positive statements about the condition of the Philippines, every one of which is an absolute falsehood. What is the truth?

1. No law "permanently disqualifies" Filipinos for the suffrage. They vote in local affairs now. They will soon vote for an insular legislature. As to voting for congressmen and president, they are in exactly the same condition as the residents of the District of Columbia. The latter are not even permitted to vote in local affairs. Are they therefore slaves?

2. The Filipino has every constitutional protection that Mr. Bryan himself has—every personal and civil right. He has not certain political privileges, but he is no more deprived of hope of them than are the people of Alaska.

3. Filipinos and white men in the Philippines live under exactly the same laws. Filipinos are helping now to make these laws. They will soon help still more. Perhaps Mr. Bryan would not live under these laws, but white men are living under them and are not complaining of them more than they complain everywhere.

Of the justice and expediency in theory of the suffrage laws of the south nothing need be said here, though a great deal might be said of the unfairness of their application in practice. It is enough to say that the laws which have to be defended by manifest lies, such as Mr. Bryan puts forth in defense of his party's suffrage legislation in the south, must be suspected to be neither expedient nor just.

If Mr. Bryan's party has a good defense for its southern suffrage legislation, why should its advocate defend it with falsehoods? Why not tell the truth?

The editor of THE COMMONER reiterates the three propositions and unqualifiedly asserts the truth of each. The colonial system permanently disqualifies the subjects living thereunder. No matter what local self-government may be permitted, the subject in a colony has no part in the government of the country of which he is a subject. The Filipino today has nothing whatever to say in regard to the policy of the United States or in regard to the appointment of the executive authority in the Philippines. Even if hereafter the Filipino is given a voice in the selection of a local legislature, the fact that he will have nothing to say in regard to the selection of the executive who enforces the laws, (and in a colonial system has an absolute veto), is complete and conclusive proof that he is disqualified for suffrage in the sense in which the term is used in this country. In every state of the south there are negroes who vote for state officers and for national officers, and have every political right that a white man has. No Filipino today, no matter how intelligent he may be or how much property he may have, is able to enjoy the suffrage privileges that are enjoyed now by those negroes in the south who are able to come up to the qualifications for suffrage there. The Inter-Ocean must admit, then, that its criticism of the first proposition is unfounded and that the republican party is doing much worse in the Philippines than the democratic party has done in the south.

As to the second proposition, the Inter-Ocean says that "the Filipino has every constitutional protection that Mr. Bryan himself has—every personal and civil right." That is palpably false. The constitution does not apply in the Philippine islands. Congress can extend to the Filipinos such privileges as congress wishes, but these are not guaranteed by the constitution; they are simply conferred by congress and can be taken away by congress. If the editor of the Inter-Ocean will read the latest Philippine legislation, he will find that there are many rights guaranteed to the citizens of the United States that are not guaranteed to the Filipinos. For instance, the right to trial by jury, which is one of the most sacred rights that there is. Neither is the right to free speech guaranteed there as here, and an editor, although an American, has already been deported for criticising public officials. The democratic party insists that the constitution follows the flag. The republican party takes the position that the constitution does not follow the flag, and two decisions of the supreme court "each rendered by a majority of one," support the republican position. On the second proposition, therefore, the Inter-Ocean must admit that The Commoner is right and the Inter-Ocean is wrong.

Now as to the third proposition, the Inter-Ocean says that "Filipinos and white men in the Philippines live under exactly the same laws." This is dodging the question. It is a cowardly evasion of the proposition. The white people who live in the Philippine islands have no part in the making of the laws of the Philippine islands. Those laws are made by the people of this country, and the few white people who live in the Philippine islands are there not as permanent residents, but merely as visitors and temporary sojourners. The United States congress exercises supreme power over the Filipinos and over the white people who go there to trade and traffic. The laws for the Filipinos would not be permitted in this country, and the editor of the Inter-Ocean knows it; and he also knows that they would not be made by the Filipinos if they had a voice in the making of them. The distinction pointed out by the editor of THE COMMONER is one of very great importance. It is the very essence of imperialism when you come to consider the probable effect of the laws. The interest that the white people of the south have in the making of the laws under which they themselves live is a protection to the black man where the black man does not vote—a protection the value of which cannot be overestimated. This protection is entirely withdrawn with the people of this country making laws relating to the Filipinos while they themselves are exempt from the operation of the laws. It is fortunate that the *Inter-Ocean* ventured upon the criticism above referred to, because it calls the attention of its readers to the principal points in the colonial question, and the editor of THE COMMONER takes pleasure in pointing out the gross and inexcusable error into which the editor of the *Inter-Ocean* has fallen.

The *Inter-Ocean* also refers to the District of Columbia and says that "as to voting for congressmen and president, the people of the Philippines are in exactly the same condition as the residents of the District of Columbia;" and adds; "The latter are not even permitted to vote in local affairs." It is an unfortunate reference for the *Inter-Ocean*, because the right to vote was taken away from the people of the District of Columbia by the republican party and taken away solely for the reason that there were so many colored people in the District of Columbia that even white republicans preferred to rely upon congress rather than a local legislature. The case, however, is not at all analogous with the situation in the Philippine islands. The residents of the District of Columbia are largely temporary residents, and many of them still hold their citizenship in their states and go home to vote. Then, too, the sessions of congress are held in the District, and the members of congress are in close and constant touch with the people, and as the population of Washington is largely made up of people who hold official position and receive their appointment from the federal authority, there can be no similarity between their condition and the condition of the Filipinos ten thousand miles away, who must depend upon an American congress for everything in the form of legislation.

Neither is it fair to compare the condition of a territory like Alaska or Oklahoma with the condition in the Philippines, for the territorial state under our republican form of government is a temporary state. It lasts only while the people are preparing themselves for citizenship. If wrongs are endured, they are only for a season, and the people look forward with patience to the time when they shall enjoy all the rights and privileges of citizenship in the states. It must be remembered, too, that the inhabitants of the District of Columbia, and of all the territories that lie between the Atlantic and Pacific, enjoy all the guarantees of the constitution. They are also under the operation of the same general laws as the people of the states. The more the *Inter-Ocean* discusses this question, the more apparent will become the fact that the republican party in its Philippine policy is not only defying the principles of self-government, but criticising a condition in the south which from every standpoint of government is infinitely superior to the condition of a colony. If the *Inter-Ocean* will publish this editorial and answer it, THE COMMONER will be glad to reproduce the answer for the benefit of the readers of this paper.

THE STRONG AND WEAK.

In addressing a religious society, Mr. Roosevelt said: "I want to see every man able to hold his own and be strong and also ashamed to oppress the weak. I want to see him too strong of spirit to submit to wrong; and on the other hand ashamed to do wrong to others."

That is a very good sentiment, indeed; and it should apply as directly to nations as it does to individuals.

Civilization advanced materially when men learned to die rather than surrender their rights; but that advancement was inconsequential compared wtih the mighty progress that will be made when men shall learn to die rather than trespass upon the rights of others.

Mr. Roosevelt could make valuable contribution to his country's history, as well as to his country's progress, if in doing his part in shaping republican policies, he would apply to nations the rules he lays down for the guidance of individuals.

THE DEFEAT EXPLAINED.

The editor of THE COMMONER has run across a new argument against free silver, which may explain the violent opposition to bimetallism manifested in some quarters. The following dialogue took place in 1896 between a Kentucky democrat and an old colored man, who worked for him:

Democrat: "Are you going to vote this year, Uncle Abe?"

Uncle Abe: "O, yes; that is what they fit for, and that is what they freed me for."

Democrat: "What candidate will you vote for?"

Uncle Abe: "I'll vote for Mr. McKinzie and against that young man Byron, of course."

Democrat: "Well, what do you know about the issues?"

Uncle Abe: "I've heard them talking on the street and I know all about the money question."

Democrat: "What do you know about the money question, Uncle?"

Uncle Abe: "I know that I want round money. I've always carried round money and I don't want any three cornered money. Why, three cornered money would wear a hole in your pocket. No, sir, I want round money."

Now, this misunderstanding of terms may account for the large republican vote in 1896. The republicans may have mistaken "sound" money for "round" money and "free coinage" for "three cornered" money. Next time we must be more careful to explain the words used.

TO SECRETARY SHAW!

To Secretary Shaw: You are reported as advocating the passage of a law that will enable national banks to issue emergency currency based upon their capital or assets. As this would be an innovation, here are several questions that ought to be carefully considered before such a law is enacted.

First—Why let the relief of the public in money matters be left to the whim, caprice or interest of those who are in charge of national banks? If more money is needed, is it not safer and better to allow that money to be issued by the government which acts in the interest of all the people and is directly responsible to the people? Experience has shown that the banks are governed entirely by their pecuniary interests in increasing or decreasing their circulation. During the panic period following 1893 when more money was badly needed, the banks defended their refusal to materially increase their circulation by saying that it was not profitable; after 1896 when there was a large increase in the volume of money from other sources, the banks defended a considerable increase in the bank note currency by saying that the reduction in the tax on circulation and the increase in the limit had made the issue profitable. Today, while you are depositing government money with the banks to relieve a stringency the banks are trying to retire circulation because they think they can make a profit on their bonds. You are certainly aware that the banker's speculative interest in the market is different from, and often antagonistic to, his interest in serving his patrons and the country.

Second—Why do you single the banks out for the special and valuable privilege which the issue of money confers? Even at present, when money is issued upon government bonds, the bank has a great advantage over the ordinary individual. If a farmer or a merchant or a laboring man purchases government bonds he is out the use of the money invested and must be content with the interest, but a bank can purchase the same bonds and by depositing them receive the face value in notes, upon the payment of half of 1 per cent interest. The bank thus has the use of its money (for this insignificant interest) and draws interest on the bonds besides. This is a pecuniary advantage granted to the banking class and denied to others. Just how much profit there is in it can be seen from the following statement: If a bank purchases one hundred thousand dollars' worth of 2 per cent bonds at $1.09 and deposits those bonds it receives back one hundred thousand in bank notes and as these bank notes serve the same purpose as the money paid for the bonds, the bank has invested in the bonds only $9,000. The $5,000 retained at Washington, as a reserve fund for the redemption of the notes, is constructively in the vaults of the bank and is as useful to the bank as if it were actually in the vaults, because that sum can be counted in the bank's legal reserve and the bank is thus enabled to use that much more of the money on hand. Having invested this sum of $9,000 in the bonds the bank pays half of 1 per cent tax to the government, or $500 a year. It lays aside a small sum to retire the premium, pays another small sum for the printing of the currency, and draws two thousand dollars interest from the government. After deducting the tax and all other expenses, the bank makes a net profit of between 10 and 15 per cent on the money actually invested, namely, $9,000.

Statistics show that the farmers of the United States do not make anything like that interest upon the investment which they have in farm property, and yet they take risks far greater than the bank takes, for there is no risk to the banker at all in this transaction.

Statistics also show that in banking the percentage of failures is smaller than in merchandising. Why this valuable privilege to the banks?

Third—In what respect is a bank note better than a greenback? During the war when gold and silver were at a premium the bank note and the greenback kept company because the bank note was redeemable in lawful money and the bankers used the cheapest lawful money they could find. It is worthy of note that the bankers, while insisting that other people shall pay them in the dearest money, always exercise the right to redeem their bank notes in the cheapest money. Even today when there is so much talk about gold and about the government paying debts in the best money, the bankers are not willing to have a law passed compelling them to redeem their bank notes in gold. The bank note is good because it has a greenback behind it; why is the greenback not good without any bank note in front of it? The bank note is not a legal tender; the greenback is a legal tender. Which is the better money? If you are afraid that the volume of government money might be unwisely increased or decreased, do you not find a lesson in the fact that for thirty years the volume of greenbacks has remained stationary while the volume of bank notes has constantly fluctuated? Would you not rather risk the decision of congress, the secretary of the treasury or the president to determine when the volume of paper money should be increased or decreased, than to leave that matter to be determined by a coterie of bankers?

Fourth—If this emergency currency is a lien upon the assets of the bank, will not the issue of it be an announcement to the public that the bank is in difficulty? Will not the issue of such currency frighten depositors, and make probable a run on the bank? The rate of interest has not been decided upon, but it is evident that the scare will be somewhat in proportion to the rate. If a bank has to pay 6 per cent interest, the public will know that it is in greater financial difficulty than if it issued currency at 3 per cent. If it issues at 3 per cent, it will be known to be in greater financial difficulty than if it issued at 1 per cent.

How can you keep an emergency issue from aggravating the very conditions which it is intended to relieve? Is there not danger that with an asset currency, a bank official may run away with the assets and leave the currency outstanding? If you find any pleasure in the contemplation of a currency system under which the bank would still owe for the currency even when its assets had disappeared, you will relish the story that is told of a man who carried contentment so far that when he traded off his coat for a loaf of bread, and a dog then snatched the bread, he thanked God that he still had his appetite left, even though he no longer had the means of satisfying it.

If emergency currency is issued with the knowledge of the public it is apt to frighten the public; if it is issued without knowledge of the public, is it fair to the depositors? If it is intended to make all of the banks liable for the emergency currency issued by each bank, it imposes an unjust burden upon the well conducted banks for the benefit of the poorly conducted ones. If the government is to guarantee this currency, is it not unfair to give the bankers the benefit and make the public pay the expenses?

Fifth—Does the issue of an emergency asset currency contemplate a restriction upon the interest to be charged by the banks which issue it? Will the government issue at a low rate to the banks and then permit them to loan it at a high rate? If this is solely in the interest of the banks, it would be natural to allow the banks to make as much out of the privilege as possible, but if it is done in the interest of the public, ought there not to be some relation between the interest paid by the bank to the government and the interest charged by the bank to the people? And if this legislation is intended for the benefit of the public, why is the benefit given by indirection? If a bank in time of emergency is allowed to issue money on its assets, why not allow people engaged in other business to issue on their assets in an emergency? Most of the banks loan money to farmers, and the notes given by the farmers are good because the farmer has land or personal property of value. Now if the government is going into the business of helping people in an emergency why not loan the money to the farmer directly, and take a mortgage on his property? If the government can loan to the banker because the farmer's note is good, why can it not loan to the farmer and save him the interest that he would have to pay to the banker? Why help the banker out of an emergency by loaning him money at a low rate of interest merely that he may turn around and help the farmer out of an emergency by loaning him the same money at a high rate of interest? And what is said of the farmer may be said of the merchant, and men engaged in other occupations. The bank's assets are composed to a large extent of the notes of business men. Now if the bank is good it is because the business men are good. If the notes of business men are good enough to make the bank good for a government loan, why are not these notes good enough to loan on directly? Why should the government turn the money over to the banker and then permit him to profit by the merchant's embarrassment? It is not contended here that the government should loan to the farmer or to the merchant, but attention is called to the discrimination which your system makes between the banker and the rest of the people, and you are asked to explain why the administration should always yearn for the financier and yet be indifferent to the manner in which the financier treats his customer.

Sixth—Have you ever read Jefferson's opinion of a bank currency? He declared that banks of issue were more dangerous than standing armies. He pointed out that their power to contract and expand the currency enabled them to increase or decrease prices at will. When you know the speculative tendency of the day—and the embezzlements which appear after every marked fall in stocks always reveals this—how can you doubt that this power to change the volume of currency and thus effect prices will be seized upon by those who stand at the head of the banking interests? If you say that the law can reduce to narrow limits the power of the banks to expand or contract the currency, does that not destroy the flexibility that those prate about who want a rubber currency? How can you have flexibility without vesting somewhere the power to contract and expand? Is it not dangerous to vest this power in the banks, and allow them to use it for their own profit? And if authority is given to the secretary of the treasury to control them, can you explain why it is safer to allow this official to control the volume of bank currency than it would be to control the volume of greenbacks?

Metallic money is a flexible currency. The amount can be increased by coinage or import and it can be decreased by melting or export. The paper portion of the currency must be either fixed in amount or flexible. If it is flexible there must be a power somewhere which will determine the conditions upon which it can be expanded or contracted. If in your next report you advocate a flexible paper currency would it be out of place to ask you to give your reasons for trusting this almost omnipotent power to those frail and human members of society who engage in the banking business and who are as constantly tempted to look after their own interests, as those engaged in any other business?

Seventh—In what respect would an asset currency, such as you have advocated, be superior to an emergency currency issued by the government to any one who would present a government bond and indicate a willingness to forego the interest on the bond while the currency was outstanding? In this way the government would loan upon its own obligations to any one who had a government obligation; it would save interest upon the bond while the currency was outstanding and the man who drew the currency would be interested in returning it when the stress was over. Such a plan would give relief to the public directly without the intervention of bankers. It is true that business men might be tempted to put their accumulations in bonds which could be thus utilized when needed instead of in the banks, but unless the government is being run in the interest of the bankers this ought to be no objection to the plan. Greenbacks thus issued would be a legal tender, would not increase the obligations of banks, and would not shake credit.

When the debt is paid off the government can still issue an emergency currency if desired.

If the asset currency is safer and better for the people, you are the proper one to point it out.

The case may be stated in a few words. There is a grave suspicion that the asset currency, now called an emergency currency, is merely the forerunner of a permanent asset currency, and this suspicion is increased by the fact that you in your last report announced that the time had come when the people had to decide whether they would have a permanent national debt as a basis for bank notes, or provide some other basis. The advocates of a bank currency recognize that it would be difficult to defend a permanent national debt upon which the people would pay interest merely to give the banks a chance to issue notes upon which they (the banks) would draw interest.

Is not this emergency currency the "nose of the camel?" Or, if that illustration has a foreign flavor, is it not the edge of the wedge? Is it not intended to establish the principles of an asset currency upon which the banks can expand later?

If you believe in the right of the people to self-government, will you not admit that they have a right to know the purpose of the asset currency bill? If you believe in the capacity of the people for self-government, do you not believe that they are capable of considering and deciding this question after a fair understanding of all the matters connected with it? If such a currency is wise, how is it and why is it that no republican convention outlines a plan or specifically indorses the principle? And in this connection it may not be out of place to ask why it is that the republican party has not for the last twenty-five years stated specifically in advance of an election the financial policy which the leaders of the republican party intended to pursue after the election?

If you, Mr. Secretary, will answer the questions above submitted either in a speech—and I read your many speeches with pleasure—or in an interview—and you are frequently interviewed—or in a government report—THE COMMONER will be glad to publish your answer and to give it the consideration which, because of your official position, your utterances deserve.   THE COMMONER.

SELFISHNESS ADMITTED.

Those who are in favor of turning the currency of the country over to national banks assume, as a rule, that the banks will exercise in a patriotic way the authority conferred upon them. Occasionally a republican paper is candid enough to admit that the banker acts purely from selfish motives, and such an admission is worth reproducing for the benefit of those who may ignorantly hold a different opinion.

The Lincoln (Neb.) *Daily Star* is one of the most candid of republican papers, and in a recent issue it had the following in regard to banks:

"But a man who engages in banking, the same as those who engage in farming, merchandizing, manufacturing, etc., does so for the purpose of making money for himself. That is why he puts up United States bonds as security for circulation—because he expects to make a profit on the bank notes. When he can make a distinctly greater profit by recovering the bonds and selling them he will ordinarily do it. If a farmer could secure from the government circulating notes on the security of warehouse receipts for his stored grain, and if the price of grain should subsequently rise so that he could make much greater profit by recovering his warehouse receipts and selling the grain, he would certainly do it. That is to say, he would do just what the banker is doing—all within his legal rights.

"It is a simple plain matter of business. There is not a particle of sentiment in it. The banker and the farmer act on the same general considerations of interest and upon the same conditions of human nature."

The *Star* is correct, in saying that "is a simple, plain matter of business," but if the banker is going to exercise the power for his own advantage, why give him a power that can be used against farmers and merchants, and people in other occupations? If he is going to sell his bonds, and withdraw circulation every time he can make a profit by selling the bonds, will not the currency fluctuate in such a way as to jeopardize the interests of the public? Must the security of the people be endangered whenever the bank has a chance to speculate and make more that way than in ordinary banking? If the public generally understood that the banker is as selfish as other people, and that he will use for his own advantage power put into his hands, there would be few outside of the bankers' association who would be in favor of turning the financial system of the United States over to the financiers.

LAW-MADE VALUE.

In an editorial recently printed in THE COMMONER and entitled, "The Monetary Peril," it was said that: "The monometallist overlooks the fact that what is at once intrinsic value is in part the metal value created by law-made demand. The monetary use of gold is its principal use and if this use were withdrawn, the market price would necessarily fail."

An El Paso, Tex., reader of THE COMMONER says that "this paragraph points out an argument against the single gold standard that is not, I think, sufficiently emphasized by the advocates of bimetallism. That gold is not principally valuable on account of any intrinsic value inherent with the metal itself does not seem to enter the mind of the average monometallist while they are continually harping upon the law-made value of silver. It occurs to the writer that converts from the single gold standard might be made among the honest and patriotic portion of our opponents by proving to them that a great part of what they are taught to consider intrinsic value of gold is only law-made value and would disappear at once if the nations of the world should unite in depreciating that metal as they have done in the case of silver. What would gold be worth now if it should immediately be demonetized by all the nations that have demonetized silver? The champions of bimetallism have been thrown upon the defensive to such an extent that in trying to teach the people what would happen to silver if its free and unlimited coinage should be enacted, they have not laid sufficient stress upon what would happen to gold if its free and unlimited coinage should be curtailed or entirely suspended."

EYES ARE OPENING.

The Sioux City *Tribune*, a newspaper that in recent years has supported the republican party, has concluded that "the banks that are on the inside of Wall street financiering are now asking for flat money, but under the control of the banks." And the *Tribune* has come to the conclusion that "the country will probably decide on two things at an early day; to abolish a tariff so high that monopoly may find shelter behind it, and to curtail the privileges of the national banks."

The Sioux City *Tribune* seems to have reached this conclusion because as it explains: "The Chicago *Tribune*, a newspaper owned and edited by multi-millionaires, is responsible for the statement that the recent tremendous slump in Wall street was the direct result of a policy inaugurated by the great financiers, and managed by J. Pierpont Morgan, for the purpose of reducing prices. Prices were pounded down, lower and lower, until solid railroad stocks were bought on less than a 6 per cent basis. Then they took an upturn of 10 to 20 points. Many of these stocks were loaded on the public by Mr. Morgan. Steel stock was sold to employes of the steel trust at more than double the price it now brings. This was done ostensibly for the benefit of the more than 300,000 employes. History will judge it differently."

CLEVELAND AND THE INCOME TAX.

A reader of THE COMMONER has called attention to a publication which claims that Mr. Cleveland secured the adoption of the income tax feature of the Wilson bill. As the editor of THE COMMONER was then a member of the ways and means committee and assisted in preparing the income tax measure he knows whereof he speaks when he says that Mr. Cleveland was not only not responsible for the income tax, but that his influence was cast against it.

Mr. Cleveland's closest friends on the committee were opposed to the income tax, and the committee learned that Mr. Cleveland himself objected to a tax on individual incomes. When the matter came up for final action among the democrats of the committee, the advocates of the income tax had just one majority in favor of the bill, and that one voted with the opponents of the bill when the friends of the tax attempted to attach it to the Wilson bill. The friends of the measure then circulated a petition and called a democratic caucus. At this caucus a resolution was passed uniting the income tax bill with the Wilson bill, but the effort was opposed by most of Mr. Cleveland's friends. The main reason urged by the advocates of the income tax for making it a part of the Wilson bill was that if it passed separately it would run the risk of a presidential veto. It will be remembered that Mr. Cleveland refused to sign the Wilson bill, but allowed it to become a law without his signature. It is not impossible that the income tax portion of the bill was as much responsible for the president's refusal to sign it as the senate's failure to allow iron and coal to be placed on the free list.

ANOTHER GOLD BUG FALLACY.

An Illinois reader of THE COMMONER says that the gold bugs are asserting that England is buying up silver at a low price with the expectation of making a profit if the United States restores silver. This is on a par with the arguments that are generally used to support the Wall street system of finance. There is no considerable amount of silver bullion held either by individuals or by governments, and England least of all would be benefited by the rise in silver. When silver is cheap she can purchase silver at a low price and send it to India for cotton and wheat (not the English government, but the English traders). With silver at $1.29 per ounce, England would have to pay more for her wheat and her cotton, and our producers would reap the benefit. The argument made by the more conscienceless of the gold papers that the mine owners are the only people who would profit by bimetallism and that those who advocate it are in the employ of the mine owners, is an insult to the intelligence of the readers of those papers. Bimetallism is a system of finance, and those who advocate it are interested in silver as money, not in silver as merchandise. We have already had four international conferences to deal with the money question, and have a commission abroad now. If it is only a matter of interest to the mine owners, why have all the nations in the world been considering it for twenty-five years? The editor who attempts to put aside the money question by abusing the producers of silver writes himself down as an ignoramus or a knave. He lacks either brain capacity or conscience.

RACE PROBLEM DISCUSSED.

Editor *Evening Post*, New York City.—Dear Sir: The pressure of other work has delayed an answer to your inquiry. The questions which you ask are predicated upon the assertions of the appellant in the case referred to, and it is hardly necessary to discuss the subject until the case is decided. You say, "Granting the authority of these statements and failing intervention by the supreme court, has congress any duty in the premises?" The first thing to do is to ascertain the truth of the statements, and the second is to learn whether the court will intervene. It will then be time for congress to act, and in acting it will have before it the facts as ascertained and the reasons as given by the court.

The second question also begins with an "if" and is based upon an assumption.

The third question begins with an "if" and the answering of it would require a prophecy, and as Speaker Reed once said, "It is never safe to prophesy unless you know."

The suffrage question is one of the most important ones that can come up for consideration, and if by your inquiries you mean to raise that question, I take pleasure in submitting the following:

Conditions are imposed upon suffrage everywhere. Age is always made a condition. It is also required that the voter shall be present at the polls, and this excludes any one who may be necessarily away from home, or who may be unable on account of ill health to leave the house. This provision has sometimes been suspended in the case of soldiers, but it is generally made one of the prerequisites to suffrage. In cities registration is often required, and sometimes it is necessary for the voter to be at a certain place on a day previous to the election as well as at the polls on election day.

Communities differ also on another phase of the suffrage question. Most of the states limit suffrage to men, while in other states men and women vote on exactly the same terms. Some of the states give to women a limited suffrage, that is, a suffrage on certain questions. Often the payment of a poll tax is made a condition to manhood suffrage and a criminal conviction is usually a bar to suffrage. Many of the states have at one time or another had educational qualifications, and some of them have had property qualifications. In view of the experience through which we have passed in this country, it is difficult to lay down a rule upon this subject that can be applied everywhere. We ought to start with the proposition that universal suffrage is the thing to be desired, and where a limitation is placed upon it there must be a satisfactory reason to justify it. That is to say, the presumption is in favor of suffrage and the burden of proof is upon those who would limit it.

An educational qualification is less objectionable than a property qualification, because knowledge is more needed than the possession of property for the proper performance of one's civic duty. An educational qualification is easier to surmount than a property qualification, and then, too, those who prescribe an educational qualification are not so apt to be influenced by purely selfish reasons as those who prescribe a property qualification. Sometimes the property qualification is made to relieve the educational qualification rather than to aggravate it, that is, one possessing a certain amount of property can vote even without complying with the educational provisions and vice versa.

As the race question in the south has given rise to the present controversy, it is sufficient for the present to consider it alone, and the arguments made upon the race question as it now appears could not be used in discussing the suffrage question unless the same principles were involved and the same conditions had to be met.

Whether or not a given state should adopt a qualification

aimed at the black race is a question which must be decided upon the facts in the case, and no person whose judgment is worth considering would announce a decision without knowing the facts. The race question does not present itself to the people of the north as it does to the people of the south. The colored population of the north is small compared to the white population, and therefore white supremacy is never menaced. Very few colored men hold elective offices in the north, although the colored votes help to elect a great many republicans. Negroes do not hold offices even in the north in proportion to their voting strength, and much less in proportion to their voting strength in the party with which they usually cast their votes. Even where a colored man holds office in the north, it is a colored man who has commended himself to the white people of the community, because in no instance is there a colored majority in any considerable territory in the north.

It is different in the south. In many sections the black population outnumbers the white and, if every male adult voted, the colored population could fill all the offices with negroes selected by the colored population regardless of the opinions of the whites. It is hardly fair for a man who lives where white supremacy is not menaced, and who has never lived or visited the black sections to state dogmatically what ought to be done by the white population who have lived under the reign of the carpet bag legislatures. The administration of government during the reconstruction period just after the war took on a somber hue that the people of the south still remember, and they have reason to dread a return to it. The question which the white people of the south have to meet is whether the white race, with its more advanced civilization and its higher ideals, shall permit its progress to be turned backward by the dominance of the black race. This is the question which the citizen of the north has never had to contemplate.

The republican officeholder who is drawing a salary given to him by colored voters is hardly in a position to set himself up as an impartial judge as to what should be done by the people of the south who live under the shadow of the race problem. It is no reflection upon the black man to say that he is behind the white man in progress. It would be a miracle, indeed, if in a period of forty years the slave could become the intellectual equal of his former master. For centuries the white race has been toiling up the hill and it has not by any means reached the top. However rapidly the black man may have advanced, who is so blind as to say that the Caucasian is not in front? This question can not be settled by comparing a few individual cases; it must be judged by the mass. If the black man was inhabiting this country and a few white men without invitation and without necessity entered his domain, attempted to bring him into subjection and then to exploit him, the case would be different. That condition we have now to meet in the Philippine islands, but not here. Here the white man and the black man are living together, and while they live together one race must be dominant. Lincoln expressed what every white man must feel when he said that as the two races could not live together on terms of perfect equality, he was in favor of the race to which he belonged "having the superior position."

Unless all arguments in favor of civilization are without foundation, the superior race, if dominant, would be more considerate toward the inferior race than the inferior race would, if dominant, be toward the superior race. A superior race, when dealing with an inferior one (where it is necessary that one shall be dominant), is restrained, first, by its conscience, and, second, by its view of its own interests; and it is only fair to assume that the superior race will be more responsive to the dictates of conscience and will take a broader view of its own interests, than an inferior race will. To make the application, the white people of the south, if in control, will be more apt to deal justly with the blacks than the blacks would be, if in control, to deal justly with the whites. And the whites, if in control, will be more amenable to public opinion and will take a more comprehensive view of their own interests than the blacks would if in the same position. People differ not so much in the possession of a selfish spirit as they do in their breadth of view when they consider their own interests. The man who steals is selfish, and yet the man who refrains from stealing takes better care of his own interests than the man does who steals. If the white people of the south make laws that are unjust to the blacks, the more intelligent blacks will leave the south, and the whites of the south will suffer because of the absence of a refining and elevating element among the blacks. The provision which the white people of the south have, at heavy expense, made for the education of the negro, shows that they realize that it is to their interest to raise the standard and elevate the condition of the black man. The excesses of the black legislatures after the war show, on the other hand, the indifference of the blacks to their own interests as well as to the interests of the white people.

I am sure that you will pardon me, my dear sir, for putting aside the hypothetical and one-sided questions which you submitted, and taking up the principles which are involved in this subject. If I lived in the south and had to act upon the question, I would act upon it in accordance with the principles which I have suggested, favoring such qualifications as seemed to me necessary to protect the interests of all, making those qualifications as easy as conditions would permit, and doing justice to the black man and the white man both according to my best judgment.

As a citizen of the north, practically unacquainted with the conditions that the southern whites have to meet, I would refuse to express an opinion without first informing myself more fully. I might favor a qualification if I lived in one state and oppose it if I lived in another, being governed entirely by the conditions that had to be met.

The position which I take does not in the least controvert the principles set forth in the Declaration of Independence. A qualification for suffrage does not deny the natural and inalienable rights of the black man. The negro in the south, as I have frequently pointed out, has the same constitutional guaranties as the white man, and lives under the law that the white man makes for himself. If he can not vote today, he can look forward to the time when he may vote. The subject, on the other hand, who lives under a colonial system is denied constitutional protection, can not look forward to citizenship, and lives under a law passed by the dominant power, a power which itself escapes the burdens that it imposes upon the subject.

Where two races must live together under the same government, the superior race, as a matter of self-preservation, will impose conditions upon the inferior, just as the individual may defend himself even to the point of taking life in the protection of his own life, or he may put a dangerous enemy under bonds to keep the peace. It is not a denial of the equal rights of others to protect one's own right, but as it is always necessary for one to show that he acted for the protection of himself, so at the bar of public opinion those who fix suffrage qualifications upon others must show that it is done in self-defense and for self-preservation. Yours truly,
W. J. Bryan.

THE PHILIPPINE QUESTION.

A reader of The Commoner asks whether the republican party has done anything in the Philippine matter that would prevent the carrying out of the democratic policy. It has done nothing and it can do nothing that would make it unwise to carry out the democratic platform on this subject.

The democratic party contends that title to people can not be obtained by conquest or by purchase, and that no lapse of time can validate a title gained by force and held by force. If a man makes a note while under duress no continuation of the duress can make the note good. The democratic platform announces a permanent policy. It denies that this country can exist half republic and half empire, and it insists that the right of the Filipinos to independence should be recognized. If that right had been recognized in the Paris treaty it would have saved the expenditure of millions of money, and the loss of thousands of lives. If it is recognized now it will save future loss and bloodshed, although it can not repair the loss already suffered or restore the lives already sacrificed.

A long continuance of the colonial policy simply means a continuation of sacrifice of life and money, but no amount of wrong-doing can commit this country permanently to a wrong policy or make it dishonorable to do right. From the beginning the democratic position has been that the nation should immediately declare its purpose, first, to establish a stable form of government in the Philippine islands in the place of the government overthrown; second, to recognize the independence of the Filipinos as soon as the stable government is established, and, third, to protect the Filipino government from outside interference as we have protected the republics of Central and South America. That policy was right when it was adopted; it is right now, and it will be right when the opportunity comes to put it into practice, whether it is this year or next year, or farther in the future.

The democratic position on this question can not be abandoned without an abandonment of our principles of government. It can not be revised, because there is no other course that is democratic. To recognize the right of this country to administer a colonial system is to impeach the foundation principles of our government. To advocate the incorporation of the Filipinos as embryo citizens to participate in the election of members of congress and senators and presidents, is not to be thought of, for it would involve this country in a race question even more difficult to handle than the tremendous race problem with which the nation is now grappling.

No democrat need fear to defend the position of his party on the Philippine question. No republican with prominence enough to be considered a leader dares to outline the policy of the republican party and as long as the republicans have no position that they are willing to announce there is no reason why a democrat should be afraid of the discussion of the Philippine question.

WORTH REMEMBERING.

Dr. Howard S. Taylor, city attorney of Chicago, when he was in Nebraska on the occasion of the Fourth of July celebration at Fairview, quoted in private conversation some lines, the authorship of which he did not know. But the lines are so excellent and the sentiment so patriotic that they were written down for the benefit of the readers of THE COMMONER. They are worth remembering. Sentiments like these, so beautifully expressed, are good to carry in one's mind. There is frequent occasion to use them, for they ornament and strengthen a speech. Those who are preparing themselves for the discussion of public questions are especially interested in gathering together everything that can illustrate or enforce an argument. The words are as follows:

"O, 'tis a goodly heritage, this noble land of ours!
It boasts, indeed, not Gothic fame nor ivy mantled towers;
But, then, its interlinking lakes, its forests wild and wide,
Its streams, the sinews of its strength, which feed it as they glide,
Its rich primeval pasture lands, fenced by the sloping sky,
Its mines of wealth, as yet undelved, which 'neath its surface lie,
Surely a great destiny which we alone can mar
Is writ upon the horoscope where shines our risen star!"

DODGING THE ISSUE.

On another page will be found an editorial from the *Register and Leader* of Des Moines, Ia. It is reproduced because it presents a good specimen of the reasoning used to support an asset currency. It will be noticed that the Des Moines paper starts out with a denial that there is likely to be an asset currency measure enacted. It denies that there is any expression of public sentiment that would justify the expectation of the passage of such a bill. It then suggests that congress is likely to make provision for an emergency currency. It will be noted that the *Register and Leader* avoids a general discussion of the principle and hides behind an exigency. It quotes, however, with approval an argument made in behalf of an asset currency by the United States *Investor*, and it is to this argument that attention is now directed. The *Investor* takes the total amount of assets and the total amount of liabilities of the national banks, and from that constructs an argument in favor of a currency based on assets. And note the argument. We are gravely told that there would still be a margin of $483,000,000 between the assets and the liabilities, but as the liabilities are $4,386,000,000, it would seem that the margin of assets would only be a little more than 10 per cent above the liabilities. Would any bank be willing to loan a merchant $9,000 if his total assets were only $10,000? In loaning on real estate, the most permanent form of property, the money loaners insist that the loan shall not be more than two-thirds of the present market value of the property, and yet we are told that an asset currency is safe if the liabilities are nearly 90 per cent of the face value of the assets.

The weakest point in this argument is that it is based on averages, whereas the currency would be issued by individual banks. Nothing is more deceptive than an "average." Those who apologize for any evil condition always hide behind an average. If you point out to them that an increasing number of people are being endangered by a bad system, they tell you that "the average" wealth of the United States is increasing. While money is being taken from the many and put into the pockets of the few, the apologists for the system use the average to return in figures what the poor lose in fact. Those who study social and economic conditions must consider not merely the total accumulation of wealth, but the equity of its distribution. So, in considering an asset currency. It is not sufficient to take the total assets of the banks, and their total liabilities, and insist that there is a sufficient margin to permit the issue of an asset currency (even upon this basis the margin is not sufficient to cover the dangers of a panic or of an industrial depression), we must remember that an asset currency is issued by individual banks and the value of such a currency depends, not upon the margin between the total assets of all the banks and the total liabilities of all the banks, but upon the margin between this particular bank's assets and liabilities. If a bank issues an asset currency and then its officials embezzle the money, what is to become of the currency? A few failures of this kind would soon throw discredit on the entire system and currency issued by good banks would share the odium with the currency issued by bad banks.

The present bank currency, while obnoxious to democratic principles and gross favoritism to the banking element, has at least the merit of being secure The government holds the bonds and the currency is therefore safe, but an asset currency is not safe and could not be made safe for, if the bank had to put up security the very purpose of the emergency currency would be defeated. If, for instance a bank had to put up any kind of bonds it would have to first buy the bonds, and probably at a premium, so that it would obtain in currency less money than it paid for the bonds. Such a currency could not, therefore, be of any assistance in an emergency. If the currency is unsecured it might possibly relieve the bank in one way, but it would be almost sure to embarrass it in another, for while it might give it more ready money today it would be likely to deprive it of deposits tomorrow.

The Des Moines *Register and Leader* is wise in avoiding any general discussion of the asset currency, for it can not be defended, but it is a little inconsistent to dodge the question itself and, while protesting that the enactment of an asset currency is improbable, yet at the same time present by indirection an argument in favor of such a departure from sound finance.

THE ALDRICH BILL.

To Secretary Shaw: You are quoted as having expressed yourself in favor of the Aldrich bill or of some measure of like character. The object of this bill is to enable the government to deposit in the national banks a much larger sum than it has been in the habit of depositing. It has been estimated that according to the provisions of the Aldrich bill something like three hundred millions of government money could be deposited with various national banks. Notwithstanding the fact that the republican national platform of 1888 condemned the loaning of the government's money "without interest to pet banks," you have loaned more money to pet banks without interest than any former secretary of the treasury, and the purpose of the Aldrich bill is to still further increase these loans.

There are certain objections to the Aldrich bill, and you ought to be prepared to meet them before you urge such a measure upon congress. In the first place the loaning of government money to the banks is an act of favoritism. The secretary of the treasury has to select the banks. Whether he selects justly or unjustly is a question which the public can not pass upon, because it has not the facts before it. It is a fact that one of the New York city banks urged its claim to consideration on the ground that its directors rendered valuable assistance to the republican party in the preceeding campaign. The power of the government to thus reward political friends and to withhold deposits from political opponents is a tremendous power in the hands of an administration that is disposed to use it for personal or party advantage. What has happened since 1888 to make the loaning of government money to pet banks less reprehensible than it was then?

Second—The loaning of government money to the banks makes the government dependent upon the banks. If it loans a large sum (as it is doing now) it is hardly at liberty to withdraw the money, for the withdrawal of a considerable sum would disturb business and threaten a panic. If the government goes into the business of loaning money to the banks it will be difficult to withdraw deposits, and what is therefore regarded as an emergency deposit is very apt to grow into a permanent deposit.

Third—By loaning the government's surplus to the national banks these powerful institutions are given a pecuniary interest in the maintenance of high taxes and in the collection of large revenues, for the more money the government collects the more it has to deposit. It is evident that every banker who has a large government deposit is permanently interested in preventing any reduction of taxation, however onerous the burden may become to the people. Can we afford to array so potent an interest against a reduction of taxation? Is it not difficult enough now for the taxpayer to secure a hearing? Will it not be more difficult when the national banks profit largely by heavy taxation? Can the people afford to use their own money to hire the national banks to work against them.

Fourth—The Aldrich bill provides for the payment of interest at the rate of 1½ per cent. Some opposition has been expressed to this provision, and until the measure is finally enacted it is impossible to know what compensation, if any, will be fixed. But whether the money is loaned at 1½ per cent or is loaned without interest, it is evident that the banks receiving the money can make a large profit by loaning it. If, for instance, $300,000,000 is loaned to the banks at 1 1-2 per cent the amount paid to the government would be four millions and a half. If this money is loaned out at 3 per cent, the banks' profit is four millions and a half. If it is loaned at 4½ per cent the banks make a profit of $9,000,000; if it is loaned at 6 per cent the profit is $13,500,000.

The banks that receive the benefit of these deposits can well afford to contribute to the campaign fund of the party that continues them. At the lowest rate suggested above the banks would make four millions and a half. If they can make this sum each year for four years, can they not afford to give one year's profit to insure four years more? Is it not apparent that the Aldrich bill lays the foundation for an enormous corruption fund? At the lowest possible rate at which any one will calculate the profit to the banks, the national banks can afford to contribute more to the campaign fund of the party that favors them than can be collected from all the people by any party that opposes special privileges and seeks merely the equal rights of all.

It may be added that the Aldrich bill is objectionable because it permits the deposit of miscellaneous assets, as a security for the loan of government money. First mortgage railroad bonds under certain conditions are declared by the bill to be sufficient to secure the deposit of money. Heretofore the government has protected itself by taking its own bonds as security for deposits. While all the other objections made to this system are good against deposits, even when government bonds are given as security, still the government is protected, but in the case of the deposit of miscellaneous securities the government may or may not be secure. It is apparent that the designation of bonds as suitable for security must have a powerful influence upon the stock market. Is it wise or safe that the government should thus connect itself with the stock exchange?

The congestion of money in the treasury is due to the collection of more taxes than the government needs. Why not reduce taxation? That would be a protection against any future surplus. The surplus now on hand can be used buying up the government's obligations. The purchase of government obligations would not only stop the interest, but would relieve the government of the embarrassment which it finds in having on hand so large a sum of money. But the surplus on hand would not bother the government so much but for the fact that there is a scarcity of money in the country. Whenever we attempt to increase the quantity of real money we are told that we do not need any more money. As soon as this argument is forgotten the banks begin clamoring for an opportunity to use the government surplus and alleging as an excuse that the money is needed in the channels of trade. It is possible to have enough money to do business with and thus enable the government to keep in the treasury whatever money it has on hand. This is not only possible but it is desirable, for it avoids the various questions which arise in connection with the loaning of government money. Then, too, if the money is locked up in the treasury the people who need more money will be interested both in increasing the volume of money and also in reducing taxation. Where the money is held in the treasury powerful interests are brought to the support of the people in their demand for a sufficient volume of money and for an economical government, whereas these same interests are arrayed against the people when unnecessary taxes can be collected and the unncessary surplus loaned out to financiers. The republican policy is to take from the people money that ought to remain in the people's pockets and then loan the money to the banks on the ground that the people need it. The democratic policy is, first, to have a sufficient volume of money to do business with; second, to collect only so much as is needed for the economical administration of the government, and, third, to keep the government money in the government vaults, and avoid the evils that follow the loaning of government funds. By the way, are you not now doing without legal authority what the Aldrich bill is intended to authorize? THE COMMONER.

MANANA.

After apologizing for the removal of Miss Todd, the postmistress at Greenwood, Del., Walter Wellman, the Washington correspondent for the Chicago *Record-Herald*, says:

"At the same time the comment of the press generally, now that the affair has attracted attention in all parts of the country, is so unfavorable to the huckstering of politicians in postoffices that it is regarded as quite probable President Roosevelt will soon—that is, after the presidential election—take steps to revolutionize the system and have the fourth-class postoffices placed under the civil service."

It is interesting to be assured by Correspondent Wellman that "it is regarded as quite probable President Roosevelt will soon—that is, after the presidential election—take steps to revolutionize the system and have the fourth-class postoffices placed under the civil service."

Manana, manana, manana, seems to be a very popular cry under the republican administration.

"After the presidential election," the republicans will revise the tariff.

"After the presidential election," the republicans will amend the currency laws.

'After the presidential elction," the republicans will establish the merit system to which Mr. Roosevelt and the republicans generally have professed devotion.

"After the presidential election"—but "after the presidential election" there may be no republican party.

MR. SHAW AS A LEGISLATURE.

Secretary Shaw has deposited the sum of $2,500,000 in the national banks of St. Louis, the same to be secured by the deposit of state and municipal bonds rather than by government bonds.

The purpose of the Aldrich bill was to substitute for government bonds, as security for government deposits, state bonds, municipal bonds, or first mortgage bonds of railroads. By accepting state and municipal bonds in lieu of government bonds, for the deposits at St. Louis, Secretary Shaw has practically put in operation the provisions of the Aldrich bill, a measure that has not yet been passed and against the passage of which many republicans are protesting.

The Washington correspondent for the St. Louis *Republic* points out that Secretary Shaw's action in St. Louis differs in several respects from his action last year in accepting such security for public deposits. This correspondent analyzes Mr. Shaw's action in this way:

"A year ago the secretary was anxious to obtain an increase in the national bank circulation, and he did so by allowing depository banks to substitute state and municipal bonds for part of the United States bonds they had on deposit to secure public moneys held by them, and they were then required to take out circulation based on the United States bonds thus released. The state and municipal bonds were then accepted as security for deposits to an amount equal to three-fourths of their par value.

"In making the St. Louis deposits the secretary does not require the banks to substitute the state and municipal bonds for United States bonds already deposited by them with the treasury. If he had done so, the result would not have been to afford security for any additional amount of deposits, but there would have been a simple changing of one form of security for another. Neither does he require the banks to take out additional bank-note circulation."

If, without the authority of law, Secretary Shaw may substitute state and municipal bonds for government bonds, he may also substitute first mortgage railroad bonds; and when he has done that he will have carried out, practically, the provisions of the Aldrich bill. But we are told that in accepting state and municipal bonds, as substitutes for government bonds, Mr. Shaw does not require the favored bankers to take out circulation based on United States bonds thus released. We are reminded that that was the policy adopted by Mr. Shaw last year. Is it not strange that Mr. Shaw abandons that policy this year at the very time when the newspaper dispatches reveal the fact that national banks are retiring their bank notes in such large amounts and numbers that the limit of the amount retired within any one month—$3,000,000 —is very nearly reached during this period.

If while the financiers are clamoring for an increase in the volume of currency through the asset currency route, they retire the bank note circulation on the government bond plan to such an extent that business men will become so embarrassed that they may be persuaded to urge their congressmen to vote for the asset currency scheme for the sake of "business interests"—then it may be possible for the asset advocates to work up quite a sentiment in favor of their unholy scheme.

The retirement of the bank notes issued on government bonds may have large effect in pushing through the asset currency measure; and if that shall be the result Secretary Shaw, who seems to have great legislative powers within himself, will doubtless be able to look after the Aldrich bill by arbitrarily putting into effect the provisions of that measure.

THE BEGINNING OF EVIL.

There is perhaps no more important lesson that young or old can learn than that evils are more easily resisted in the beginning than after they have been allowed to develop. Take, for instance, disobedience to parents It usually begins in some small matter when the child feels that the parent has required an unnecessary thing, or refused to permit something that the child desires to do. If it were in an important matter the child would shrink from an act of disobedience, but it seems so small that the wish of the child triumphs over the will of the father or mother, and that act of disobedience becomes the precedent for others until disobedience is easier than obedience.

Disobedience usually leads to other offenses; untruthfulness, especially, is apt to follow in the wake of disobedience, being resorted to as a means of avoiding punishment or even reproof.

From disregard of parental authority it is an easy step to the disregard of the authority of government, and the disobedient child not unnaturally develops into the lawless citizen until finally the downward course leads to the door of some institution established for correction and reform. Disobedience to authority is more easily checked when it first begins to manifest itself than after the habit has grown strong by indulgence.

So, too, with the liquor habit. The taste for intoxicating liquor is far more easily avoided than it is overcome when once it is established. The moderate drinker has not only to risk the strength of the liquor habit when it once gets a hold upon him, but if he drinks at all he must defend his refusal to drink either on the ground that he is going to change his course, a thing which implies an acknowledgement of previous error, or he must give a reason that fits the particular case in hand. If he drinks with one it is difficult to refuse to drink with others, and if he accepts invitations to drink he must give invitations or seem stingy. There is less difficulty and more safety, therefore, in not commencing.

It is the same with gambling, and it is hard to conceive of a more demoralizing vice. If one gambles at all it is not easy to limit the things gambled for or the amount wagered. If one bets at all and refuses to back up his opinion with money, his opinion is, in the minds of some, discredited. If he does not bet at all, that is a sufficient reason why he should not be called upon to put up money in support of his opinion on any subject. Then, too, the gambling habit weakens a man's energies. Money won on a bet or in a lottery seems to be much more easily obtained than money secured by industry of any kind, and after one has obtained his living for awhile from games of chance he becomes practically incapacitated for any legitimate effort, and is not content with the slow accumulation that generally accompanies the ordinary forms of industry. It is the part of wisdom not to gamble at all. Where one resolutely refuses to begin he is not worried about a stopping place. And so with other evils into which the individual is likely to fall.

The experience of the state is not essentially different from the experience of the individual. As a rule the first departures from the right path are slight and scarcely observable, but they become precedents for more and more serious departures, until the country is imperceptibly committed to policies which can not be endured and hardly remedied. Every one recognizes in the abstract the evil of class legislation and the granting of special privileges to a favored few, and yet it is difficult to apply the Jeffersonian principle of equal rights to all and special privileges to none. Some powerful interest asks the government to suspend the principle in its favor, and the principle once suspended for one is suspended again and again with increasing frequency.

There is no reason why the financiers should determine the financial policy of the government, and yet concession after concession has been made to the financiers until they not only run the government in their own interest, but resent any interference with the prerogatives which they have assumed.

The same is true of the class legislation which has grown

up under the guise of a protective tariff. Each new industry that desires an indirect bonus out of the pockets of the people claims as an excuse that others have been given a like privilege. The party that grants the privilege calls for a campaign fund in return, and as a result is re-obliged to the protected interests.

The monopolies that today menace the industrial independence of small producers would not be permitted for a moment if they had sprung up full-fledged. The public would have been alarmed at once, but they began one at a time and grew little by little until many good citizens have been made impotent to strike at the general principle involved because they have given countenance to the principle as manifested in some particular direction. Those who defend a cracker trust can not consistently oppose a sugar trust or an oil trust. Those who think that their community will be benefited by the location of some particular trust are powerless to attack other kinds of trusts, and thus the system of private monopoly has grown until it will take a gigantic effort to rid the country of the full grown evil.

The encroachments of the judiciary through what is known as government by injunction illustrate the tendency of an evil to grow. One judge begins by issuing a restraining order so mild that public attention is not attracted to it. Judge after judge enlarges upon it until now some of the federal judges assume to issue orders declaring to be unlawful that which has never been prohibited by law, and if laboring men are accused of violating this judge-made law the judge who made the law deals with them summarily without giving them the protection of trial by jury, a right guaranteed to the meanest criminal.

Gradually the jury system is being undermined, and if present tendencies continue it is only a question of time when we may expect some open attack to be made upon this ancient form of trial. In fact, even now with increasing frequency contempt is expressed for it as a part of our judicial system. The sooner government by injunction is abolished the better; the sooner the courts are prohibited from making penal laws and the sooner the people are restored to the protection of a jury trial, the safer will be the liberties of the citizen.

Perhaps in no other respect has the slow and constant growth of an evil been more clearly shown than in the country's dealings with the Philippine islands. No one would have been foolhardy enough to propose an imperial policy at the time of the making of the treaty with Spain. The argument then was that the war must be ended and Spain driven out of the Philippines as well as out of Cuba, and everybody acquiesced in this purpose. The means of accomplishing it were not so closely scrutinized as the thing to be accomplished. If the administration had, as it should have done, provided for the independence of the Philippines when it provided for the independence of Cuba, the question of imperialism would never have been raised; but instead of that the islands were ceded to the United States. But even the ceding of the islands to this country would not have caused any trouble if the administration had immediately upon the ratification of the treaty announced its purpose to give independence to the Filipinos as soon as a stable government was established. But instead of that those in control of the government have studiously avoided any declaration of purpose or policy, while they have, step by step, adopted imperialistic methods. At first they said that it was too early to make any statement of the nation's purpose; they then said that no purpose could be announced until the Filipinos laid down their arms; and then when Aguinaldo was captured (by artifice) they announced the insurrection over and declared that the possession of the Philippine islands had become permanent. The republican leaders today ignore the question so far as the principles involved are concerned, and without attempting to defend the acquisition of people either by conquest or by purchase, assert that it is impossible for the nation to honorably withdraw. The defense of a government emanating from without and resting upon force is already sowing the seeds of imperialism in this country. From a denial of the right of the Filipinos to control their own government it is an easy step to the position now taken by republican leaders in Ohio, and elsewhere, namely, that the people of the larger cities are incapable of governing themselves. The attempt to transfer to the state authorities the power to control city fire and police departments is consistent with our policy in the Philippines, but not consistent with the doctrine of local self-government, which has for a hundred years been a fundamental tenet of government in this country. From the transfer of the government of cities to the state capital it is not a long step to the transfer of state governments to the national capital, and this was really a part of the Hamilton idea which seems to be growing among republicans. It is impossible for any one to foresee the results of imperialism, but every one who studies public affairs must know that in government as in nature growth is a universal law. Those who plant corn can expect to gather corn; those who scatter thistle seed must expect a harvest of thistles. It is written that the wise man foreseeth evil and hideth himself, while the foolish pass on and are punished. The power to reason from what is to what shall be marks the difference between the wise and the foolish. Whether we are considering the individual or a nation composed of individuals we must expect that those will fare best who watch the beginning of evil and apply a remedy while the remedy is easy. Many an individual has died from a disease which might have been checked if treated in time, and nations suffer grievously because they fail to act in time. If our people possess the intellectual superiority of which we are prone to boast, they ought to watch every development of government with constant vigilance to the end that only right principles shall be applied or if mistakes are made that they be corrected at once.

THE SILVER DOLLAR.

An East Oakland, Cal., reader of THE COMMONER writes: "It is asserted with emphasis by republicans on the Pacific coast that every silver dollar (which, of course, includes silver certificates) issued by the government is guaranteed by the gold behind it. What is the status of silver money; and if secured by gold, why does the custom house require payment of duties to be made in gold exclusively? If the silver dollar is made equal to a gold dollar by law, can anybody truthfully claim the former to be worth 50 cents? Prior to 1873, was not gold and silver on a parity and good enough for Americans until the nobility of England were permitted to plow with the republican heifers?"

The silver certificate is redeemable in the silver dollar. The silver dollar is irredeemable money. There is no gold dollar behind it. The silver dollar is made legal tender for all debts, public or private, except where otherwise stipulated in the contract; therefore, it can not be possible that the custom houses require payment of duties in gold. The silver dollar is just as good for the payment of duties as the gold dollar. The act of March, 1900, gave the secretary of the treasury authority, if in his opinion it was necessary to maintain the parity of all money, to exchange one kind of money for another; but so far the secretary of the treasury has not accepted the act of March, 1900, as justification for the redemption of the silver dollar in gold; and one of the provisions of the Fowler bill, now being agitated by the financiers, is that all money, including the silver dollar, shall be redeemed in gold. The status of the silver dollar, so far as redemption is concerned, is the same today as it was at the beginning of this government. It is irredeemable money. Some men refer to it as a "50-cent dollar" because the commercial value of the bullion in the silver dollar is not equivalent to the value of the coin as "current money with the merchants." But it is not a 50-cent dollar because men are fighting for it and dying for it, and children are crying for it. Every one is willing to accept it for 100 cents on the dollar knowing that it will pay every debt, public or private, except where otherwise expressly stipulated in the contract.

Prior to 1873, the commercial ratio of gold and silver kept pace with the coinage ratio, and bimetallists believe that a restoration of the coinage conditions that existed prior to 1873 would raise the bullion value to the coinage value. The recent advances in the price of silver, owing to the Philippine coinage, provide an interesting object lesson. If the purchase of 1,750,000 ounces of silver for the Philippine coinage could make such marked difference in the price of silver, what will the effect be when the Philippine coinage is well under way and several hundred million ounces are required in order to sustain the Philippine system? Is it not, also, reasonable to believe that the effect on the price of silver by the mere purchase of a few ounces of metal for Philippine coinage would be incomparable with the effect upon the price of silver if the United States mints were open to free and unlimited coinage?

ANOTHER ANTI-PASS CONGRESSMAN.

The Commoner called attention some time ago to the correspondence which passed between Congressman Baker of Brooklyn, N. Y., and the legal adviser of the Baltimore & Ohio Railroad company. The Detroit *Times* reports Congressman Alfred Lucking of the First Michigan district as taking a similar position. Congressman Lucking said that he had been offered passes, but that he had declined them because he could not look at the offer as purely disinterested kindness. It will be easier to secure needed legislation when all the congressmen and senators look at the matter as Baker and Lucking do, and free themselves from all obligations to the corporations that are constantly seeking aid at the hands of the government.

"GRAFT."

The word "graft" has been so frequently employed of late that it has come to have a technical meaning. It is used to describe the illegitimate profit which a corrupt public servant makes out of his office. The most common form of graft is in the form of a rebate on contracts made by the official for the public. The postoffice investigation shows that several employes were interested in contracts made in their departments. Of course, it is plain, bare-faced stealing, for the official acts for the people as a whole, and to pay a high price for supplies with the understanding that a part of the price will be returned to him personally is only an indirect method of converting government money to his own use. All purchasing agents are tempted to misuse their positions and public opinion ought to be such as to restrain and strengthen those who hold such positions of trust. Even school boards sometimes become venal and sell their decisions to the book company that offers the largest cash bonus to the board. What a sad commentary on public morals to say that men especially selected to supervise the instruction of the young should become purchaseable. In the cities another form of graft is to be found in the selling of immunity. Saloonkeepers, gamblers and keepers of houses of ill-fame, are sometimes allowed to violate the law, provided a stipulated sum is paid to officers whose duty it is to enforce the law. This form of crime should be made so odious that every party organization would, for its own protection, unrelentingly punish its own members when found guilty of trafficking in police authority, but back of all this misuse of official power stands the commercialism—the sordid, greedy commercialism which is stimulating the love of money and condoning the offenses against law and good morals. The only permanent remedy is to be found in purifying public thought and raising the ideals of the people.

THE IDLE RICH.

The Chicago *Tribune* of recent date contains a special dispatch from New York which purports to give an interview with Mr. Henry Dexter, who is described as "many times a millionaire." It seems that Mr. Dexter's son was recently assassinated near his home in the Adirondacks and Mr. Dexter is quoted as saying:

"The United States is no place for a man of wealth who does not strive for more wealth. The personal danger for every man of wealth has grown greater here every year.

"They have killed my son and they will kill others in the Adirondacks because the ignorant natives regard the newcomers of wealth who have bought up the lands as interlopers and tyrants; as men who are malignantly arrayed against the guides and woodsmen. Here in this city the incessant denunciation of wealthy employers is bound to rouse some fanatic in the laboring classes to murder.

"I have seen this awful, un-American sentiment grow year after year.

"Forty years ago, when I had won the aim of my business life, having founded and started toward prosperity the American News company, I was satisfied with my wordly wealth and I invested it securely. The income was more than sufficient for the most extravagant style of living I and my wife cared for. To be comfortable, I looked for a home amid men similarly situated, expecting to find worthy occupation and healthful amusement in the class of which I found myself a member.

"But I found I practically was alone; those who had prospered in the same measure as myself were not content—they wanted more wealth and more power.

"I have found this is true of all Americans. There is no leisure class here; even the wealthiest are actively interested in commercial enterprises or in speculation. I do not know of a single wealthy American who is seeking rest with honor from business. If there be such he is alone in a strange land.

"If I had made England my home I could have surrounded myself with men and women who enjoy worthy leisure. When by God's will my wife had left me I had not lost my son by the bullet of a savage, worked into frenzy by class feeling, deciding in his own ignorance that a condition of affairs that has existed as long as mankind is unjust and a denial of his personal rights."

Mr. Dexter's opinion is worth considering because it represents the opinion of many of his class. If there is in this country any real hostility to wealth honestly acquired and rightly used, then the condition is indeed a serious one. But is there such a hostility? There is no evidence of it. In the first place, no one can defend the possession of wealth that is not honestly acquired, and how can wealth be honestly acquired? Aside from wealth acquired by gift, there is just one way, namely, by the giving of an equivalent for what one receives. If a man, either by his brain or by his muscle, contributes to the welfare of the world, he is entitled to a recompense. The laborer, whether on the farm or in the work-shop or in the mine, is worthy of his hire, and his hire ought to be proportionate to the value of his work. The person who makes an intellectual contribution to the welfare of the world, whether it be in teaching or in writing, or in any other legitimate way, is entitled to a reward commensurate with his work. The same is true of the merchant, the manufacturer and the middle man, provided always that each is rendering actual service and performing for society a real and necessary work.

The man who overreaches his neighbor or who by craft or cunning accumulates money dishonestly, must not be permitted to throw upon honest wealth the odium which his dishonesty has brought upon his particular accumulation. There is a feeling in this country that the great fortunes which are made by watering stock, by running corners, by conducting private monopolies and by bankrupting corporations merely to give those who are manipulating the markets a chance to buy the stock at a low price, are illegitimate, and that the methods employed are as offensive to good morals as they are dangerous to the government. While this hostility may sometimes manifest itself in individual acts of violence, public attention must not be entirely diverted from the wrong-doing of the victims of violence. Every good and patriotic citizen will condemn and help to punish all acts of lawlessness and violence, but patriotic citizens must also be interested in preventing those larger acts of lawlessness which incite desperate men to violence. To apply remedial and restraining legislation to those who are acquiring money dishonestly it is not necessary to either excuse or defend those who, despairing of legal remedies, take the law into their own hands. A man who has been driven into bankruptcy by a trust or who has suffered great pecuniary loss by the manipulations of speculators, is not in a frame of mind to be lectured on contentment and respect for wealth accumulated by wrong-doing. Those who are interested in the preservation of liberty and in the supremacy of the law must devote themselves to the elimination to the causes of ill-feeling—it is not sufficient that they devote themselves merely to the suppression of manifestations of discontent.

The second means by which wealth can be honestly acquired is by gift. The right of a parent to give money or property to his child is everywhere recognized, and the right of a friend to give to a friend is also admitted. The right of the parent to accumulate for the child furnishes a stimulus that is probably equal, if not superior, to any other incentive to earnest and constant endeavor. The receipt of money, however, from parent or relative to friends not only implies that the recipient has in some way earned the money, but also imposes upon the recipient a responsibility for the proper use of the money. Society has always recognized, and often exercised, its right to discriminate against inheritances. At the present time states like New York and Connecticut have an inheritance tax, and the manner in which the tax is graded shows that the people, speaking through the legislatures, have the power to discriminate between beneficiaries. For instance, in the state of New York property received by a child from a parent, by a parent from a child, or by husband or wife from the other, pays a tax of 1 per cent, while property willed, or descending by law, to other relatives or non-relatives, or to organizations of any kind, pays a tax of 5 per cent. In Connecticut the same distinction is observed, but the rates are half of 1 and 3 per cent.

Not only must wealth be legitimately acquired, but it must be rightly employed, although there is probably less disposition to criticise the improper use of honestly acquired wealth than there is to criticise the employment of improper methods in the accumulation of wealth. But even honestly acquired wealth can be so used as to excite just criticism. For instance, if a person, having wealth, is lavish in the expenditure of money for his own enjoyment and disregards the claims of worthy enterprises and the needy he can properly be charged with being selfish and self-centered. If he spends his money in high living he not only excites criticism from without, but he arrays himself against himself, for his health will soon be impaired by his excesses. If he uses his wealth to gratify his vanity; if he flaunts his wealth in the face of those who have to struggle for bare existence, he can fairly be accused of being inconsiderate and lacking in sympathy.

It is possible for one to acquire wealth honestly and it is also possible for one to so employ his wealth as to satisfy even the most exacting public opinion, and that, too, with advantage to himself. There is no more reason why a rich man should have public or personal enemies than there is for a poor man to have enemies. Goldsmith, in "The Deserted Village," points out one source of hostility to the rich. He shows how land that ought to have been employed for the sustenance of the people was converted into hunting preserves and play-grounds for the rich, and he sums up the evil of the system in the following strong lines:

"Ye friends to truth, ye statesmen who survey
The rich man's joys increase, the poor's decay,
'Tis yours to judge how wide the limits stand
Betwixt a splendid and a happy land."

There is no place in this country for the idle rich, if by that term we mean people who, having acquired money, have no other purpose than to secure all the selfish enjoyment they can out of the use of their money. But there is not only a place, but a crying demand in this country for those who, having acquired enough to relieve themselves from want, will devote themselves to public affairs and to works of charity and benevolence. Our cities would be better governed if in every city we had a group of men who, after securing a reasonable competency, would cease from money-making and devote themselves to public affairs. It would not be necessary for all of them to hold office. They could contribute their heads and their hearts to their country's service in many ways. They could study public questions and throw their influence upon the side of good government; they could investigate all improvements in the administration of government, and give to the public through addresses and in other ways the benefit of their investigations. The man who cares for no one but himself, who spends all his money on himself, and puts in all his time pleasing himself, must expect to be lonesome in any country where there is a healthy public sentiment, but the man who is anxious to contribute a dollar's worth of service to society in return for every dollar that he draws from it—the man who uses his money to better equip himself for service and who, when he is free from the necessity of accumulating, devotes his time to work that is beneficial to his fellows, such a man will find in America a congenial home, and a wide field for the employment of his energies. And, surely, if the experience of the race counts for anything there is more happiness to be secured by helpful service than by the greedy and grasping policy of those who live solely for themselves and then abuse all who condemn selfishness and indifference to the public weal.

ANOTHER ARGUMENT GONE.

"I can stand it as long as I can get a good price for hogs," said a republican farmer in 1900 to a democrat who had pointed out the dangers of imperialism, the trusts and republican financiering; and this argument has been the main reliance of republican speakers. Instead of attempting to defend the policies of their party, republican orators and editors have seized upon every transient circumstance that could be turned to their party's advantage, regardless of its cause. When in 1897 wheat went to a dollar because of a short crop abroad, the republican leaders claimed credit for it; when the price of cattle went up they became cowboys and rode bronchos, and when porkers went up they took off their hats to every passing hog. But when wheat dropped, they dropped wheat; when cattle fell in price, they forgot how a steer looked, and now that hogs are "off" they will no longer imitate the grunt and squeal. The following dispatch, which appeared in the Chicago *Tribune*, tells the story and ought to be interesting to those whose political opinions change with the market quotations:

"Lincoln, Neb., Oct. 11.—(Special.)—By reason of the slump in the price of hogs in the last week, Nebraska farmers stand to lose $3,000,000 to $5,000,000. They figure their losses already at $3,000,000, and if the prices continue to recede, as they believe they certainly will, $2,000,000 more can be checked to the wrong side. According to reliable and conservative figures there are 3,000,000 marketable hogs in the state. Farmers have been fattening their swine on 30-cent corn, and the decline means that some hogs must be sold at an actual loss. The farmers are indignant, and charge the packers with causing the slump, at the same time keeping up the prices of the product. In Lincoln the price of pork at the butcher shops has not changed from a week ago."

"NON-PARTISAN" REPUBLICANS.

An association known as the Institute of Social Economics is sending out circulars and representing itself as "a permanent non-partisan institution for the education of the people along the lines conducive to public welfare," and it asserts that it is "indorsed by leading statesmen, educators, business men and philanthropists." On the board of counsellors are Senator Hanna, Senator Lodge, Senator Depew, ex-Secretary Bliss, ex-Vice President Morton, ex-Secretary Gage, ex-Secretary Long, ex-Bank President Hendricks, ex-Secretary Smith, and Senator Burrows. Two or three college presidents are thrown in, but no democrat is to be found on the board.

There is no objection to the organization of any association for the purpose of advancing any line of political thought, but a republican association ought to be known as republican, and not as non-partisan.

On the 19th of September, 1903, Secretary Gunton of the institute above mentioned sent out some letters appealing to persons who were supposed to be interested in this so-called non-partisan work in behalf of the republican party. The letter says: "It is felt that the strong and convincing writings of President Gunton will be of great value in the present campaign in Ohio, and arrangements have been made to send many thousands of bulletins and leaflets into that state." As Mr. Hanna is one of the high priests of the institute and indorses the work of the institute in a letter dated September 4, 1903, it is hardly probable that the institute will do any really non-partisan work in Ohio this year. The writer of the letter referred to seems to be afraid that "yellow journalism," "erratic ideas," and "doctrines detrimental to all sound business conditions" may "obtain too strong a hold among the masses."

The Institute of Social Economics is evidently a dishonest organization, because if it were honest it would not claim to be non-partisan. If any democrat has been led to give his support to this institute under the belief that it is non-partisan, he has a right to resent the deception, and if republicans who support it are not ashamed to make an open fight they ought to insist that the disguise be removed and that the Institute of Social Economics appear in its true light and advocate republican policies openly and above board.

In the campaign in Ohio this year Tom Johnson and his associates are making a fight for just taxation and home rule. If the Institute of Social Economics were non-partisan it would certainly be in sympathy with Mr. Johnson's purpose, but as it is a republican affair it is using false pretenses to secure votes for Mr. Hanna.

DROPPING THE MASK.

Although many republican leaders have insisted that the ship subsidy bill is not a party measure and that there is little reason to believe that that measure may pass, it is now dawning upon many people who have heretofore been deceived that the ship subsidy scheme comprises a very important part of the republican program.

Already there are indications showing a disposition on the part of the Roosevelt administration to come out openly in favor of the ship subsidy.

It is announced that the bureau of statistics of the department of commerce and labor is preparing tables for the purpose of showing the effect of foreign subsidies upon the merchant marine of the world. A Washington dispatch to the New York *World* says that "these tables are to be used at the coming session of congress in behalf of the ship subsidy bill which is now thought to be needed and which the friends of the measure have no doubt is going to be passed."

In his speech delivered at Toledo, O., October 13, Secretary Shaw came out boldly in defense of Mr. Hanna's ship subsidy bill and said that it was the only measure by which the American merchant marine could be built up. He complimented Mr. Hanna on the "statesmanship" that induced him to introduce the bill and said that "its results would be the carrying of American products in American vessels."

The conduct of the republican leaders with respect to the ship subsidy bill is in keeping with their conduct toward all measures of that class. In 1896, the republican leaders declared in favor of international bimetallism and then after they had won their victory, they interpreted the result as an indorsement of the single gold standard. Four years later they boldly declared for the single gold standard. Nearly every republican orator in the country has assured us for a number of years that there was no danger whatever of the passage of any measure like the Fowler bill. They hooted at the idea of asset currency and yet we find today that republican leaders very seriously suggest some form of an asset currency.

The republican habit is to keep these measures before the people, denying responsibility for them for a time and finally, when they think it opportune, they boldly embrace the plan, seeking to justify their position on the ground of "great national necessity."

So it is with the ship subsidy bill. Although republican leaders have for years protested that their party was not the champion of that iniquitous measure, we are now told by Mr. Roosevelt's secretary of the treasury that its introduction by Senator Hanna showed the highest form of statesmanship on the part of that gentleman and no effort is made to conceal the fact that the measure is to be seriously pushed at the coming session of congress.

AFRAID OF 16 TO 1.

Mr. Bryan had an interesting experience recently. He was leaving New York and fell in with three residents of that city. Two were democrats and one a republican, but they agreed on one thing, namely, that Mr. Bryan would have been elected if he had given up free silver. After explaining to them how the silver question strengthened the party instead of weakening it, he told them that most of the opponents of bimetallism did not understand the subject. To prove it, he questioned the three men—men above the average in experience and business ability—and none of them knew what 16 to 1 meant. One of them—the republican—thought he knew and said it meant that the government would coin 16 silver dollars every time it coined 1 gold dollar. It almost surpasses belief that intelligent men should fear free silver and yet be ignorant of the meaning of the simplest terms employed in the discussion of the subject.

Sixteen to one, as readers of THE COMMONER know, describes the ratio existing between the silver and gold dollars when measured by weight—that is, the silver dollar weighs sixteen times as much as the gold dollar. The silver dollar contains 412 1-2 grains of standard silver, while the gold dollar contains only 25 8-10 grains of standard gold. The exact ratio is not quite 16 to 1, but the difference is so smalll that it is always spoken of as 16 to 1. If, as the republican above referred to thought, the government would, under free coinage, coin sixteen silver dollars every time it coined one gold dollar, we would have to coin sixteen billion silver dollars to offset the billion dollars in gold coin, but if we coined all the silver held by all the people in the world, we could not coin more than about four billions. As a matter of fact, free coinage would not so much increase the number of silver dollars as it would restore to the silver coin already in existence throughout the world full faith and credit and end the war which has been made against one of the money metals. The United States and Mexico produce the great bulk of the silver produced in the world and silver would be exported from the United States under free coinage, but England would have to pay $1.29 per ounce for it instead of the present price and that would not only lessen the power of India to compete with us in wheat and cotton, but would broaden the base of the world's financial structure. In dealings with gold-using nations the balances would be paid in gold; in dealings with silver-using nations, the balances would be paid in silver, and our nation would maintain the parity between the two metals as the Latin union formerly did.

BUT HE FORGOT MILES.

When an order was issued transferring Gen. H. C. Corbin from the war department to the command of the eastern division, Mr. Roosevelt took occasion to pay a high tribute to Corbin.

Recently Captain R. B. Bradford, chief of the bureau of equipment of the navy, gave up his bureau position to go on sea duty, and Mr. Roosevelt took occasion to pay Captain Bradford a high and doubtless entirely deserved compliment.

But when General Nelson A. Miles retired from the head of the army after forty years of faithful service, he was permitted to go into private life without one word of commendation from the president. He was dismissed with a cold-blooded order issued and signed by one of General Miles' discredited subordinates. It is not surprising that Mr. Roosevelt is being severely criticised even at this day for his evidently deliberate snub to one of America's greatest soldiers. It is strange that Mr. Roosevelt places so small a premium upon the intelligence of the American people that, after his friends had undertaken to explain the Miles' snub on the ground that the customary order had been issued, the president goes out of his way to pay a high tribute to two other officers neither one of whom performed service at all to be compared with that rendered by General Miles.

It is not difficult to understand the statement made by one Washington correspondent, who said: "Among old soldiers the language used in criticising Mr. Roosevelt is bitter. They regard the Bradford incident as proof that it was personal enmity alone that prevented the president from saying something commendatory to General Miles when the latter gave up command of the army after forty-two years of honorable and distinguished service."

THE BENNETT WILL.

On another page will be found a copy of Mr. Bennett's letter to Mrs. Bennett, establishing a trust in favor of Mr. Bryan or such educational or charitable institutions as he should select, together with a copy of Mr. Bennett's letter to Mr. Bryan, on the same subject. These letters will be found following Mr. Bryan's argument delivered before the probate court of New Haven, Conn., Monday evening, October 26. As he in that argument could only deal with the facts as they had been brought out in the evidence, this additional statement is given to the readers of THE COMMONER in order that they may be able to consider the case on its merits and not be compelled to rely on the misrepresentations of unfriendly newspapers.

Mr. Philo Sherman Bennett, of the New York wholesale firm of Bennett, Sloan & Company, lived at New Haven, Conn., and was a democratic elector in the presidential campaigns both of 1896 and 1900. Just before the election of 1896 Mr. Bennett wrote a letter (which Mr. Bryan did not receive until after the election) telling of his deep interest in the campaign just drawing to a close, expressing gratitude to Mr. Bryan for his work and saying that he desired to give him $3,000 in case of his defeat. Before answering Mr. Bryan inquired whether he was interested in any silver mines, and finding that he was not, accepted the su,m which was paid, $1,000 in 1897, $1,000 in 1898, and $1,000 in 1899. In 1900 Mr. Bennett voluntarily gave $800 more, of which sum $300 was given at the time of the drawing of the will. After this manifestation of friendly interest (begun when his acquaintance with Mr. Bryan was so slight that the latter could not have identified him on the street) they met and corresponded, and Mr. Bennett proved himself to be in full sympathy with the democratic platform of 1896 and with the efforts put forth by Mr. Bryan in defense of the principles set forth in that platform. The acquaintance ripened into a close personal as well as political friendship, and Mr. Bennett always met Mr. Bryan when the latter thereafter had occasion to visit New York. Their conversations and letters covered a period of nearly seven years. In April or May of 1900 Mr. Bennett made an appointment to visit Lincoln, Neb., and when he arrived, produced a former will and certain memoranda to be used in the drawing of a new will. He desired to incorporate in this new will a bequest of $50,000 to Mr. Bryan. The campaign of 1900 was just opening, and as it was certain that Mr. Bryan would be renominated and, as he thought that it was probable that he would be elected, he told Mr. Bennett that he would not need the money in case his candidacy was successful. The latter suggested that he would probably need the money more if elected than if defeated. He was informed that Mr. Bryan did not desire to accumulate money beyond an amount sufficient to protect himself against want in old age and to protect his family in case of a breakdown in his own health, and knowing that Mr. Bryan would not accept the money unless at the time of his (Mr. Bennett's death) he needed it, he requested Mr. Bryan to distribute among educational and charitable institutions any part of the sum that he did not care to accept. At Mr. Bryan's suggestion the money was given to Mrs. Bennett in trust for him instead of being given direct to him, and that provision is now being contested by the widow and other residuary legatees. If the sum had been given directly, as Mr. Bennett intended when he proposed it, there would be no ground for contest, but an attempt is being made to take advantage of the indirect form of the bequest. If the $50,000 clause is invalid as a trust, one-half of the sum will go to Mrs. Bennett, one-fourth to Mr. Bennett's sister, and one-fourth to Mr. Bennett's half-brother—these being the residuary legatees.

The contest was not mentioned to Mr. Bryan until nearly two months after the death of the testator, and the widow and heirs were at once informed that Mr. Bryan would not accept the money without the widow's consent, but that in case of objection from her, he would distribute the sum according to the expressed wishes of Mr. Bennett. While the question involved in the case is purely a legal one, and a very technical one at that, namely: whether under the Connecticut decisions the will and the letter together establish a trust, yet hostile newspapers, for political purposes, have sought to attack Mr. Bryan's connection with the will as viewed from the standpoint of morality. It has been charged that Mr. Bryan is trying to cheat a widow and other relatives out of their rights. Now, what are the facts? According to the will the widow is to receive $75,000 as a specific bequest, and as residuary legatee is to receive an additional sum estimated by Mr. Bennett at $25,000. This Mr. Bennett declared in his letter to her would give her a larger income than she could spend and enable her to make bountiful provision for those whom she desired to remember in her will. Mr. Bennett's sister is to receive a specific bequest of $20,000, and her part in the residuary sum is estimated at $12,500. The sister's only daughter received a specific bequest of $1,000. A half-brother is to receive a specific bequest of $12,500, and his part in the residuary sum is estimated at $12,500, while his wife received a specific bequest of $3,000—$161,500 thus going to the persons who are contesting the will.

The sum left to Mr. Bryan, on condition that he would accept it, was not taken from any of the relatives nor are they the poorer for his being named in the will. If the sum had not been given to him, the testator would have distributed it among public institutions. Mr. Bennett made it clear in his will and in his letter to his wife that he had given to his relatives all that he intended them to have. That he acted within his legal rights in not giving all of his money to his relatives is not disputed; whether he treated his relatives fairly or not is a question which he could decide better than anyone else, because no one knew as well as he the relations existing between him and his kinfolks or could estimate as well as he the use they would make of money left to them.

The unfriendly newspapers have also intimated that Mr. Bryan secured the bequest by exerting an undue influence over Mr. Bennett. This would be a serious charge if true, but the evidence shows that Mr. Bennett traveled fifteen hundred miles on his own initiative for the purpose of having the will drawn and that the proposed bequest came as a surprise to Mr. Bryan. The evidence also shows that the will, while drawn in Nebraska, was executed in the city of New York at least two days after Mr. Bennett had departed from Nebraska. Mr. Bennett, after executing the will, deposited it in a vault in New York where it lay for more than three years, Mr. Bennett alone having a key to the vault-box. During this period Mr. Bennett referred to the will but once by letter (the letter will be found quoted in the argument) and never otherwise so far as Mr. Bryan can recall. During that period of more than three years Mr. Bryan did not see Mr. Bennett more than two or three times a year on an average, while Mr. Bennett was with his wife constantly and with his relatives frequently. No one can say with any truth that injustice is being done to the widow or relatives, neither can it be doubted that Mr. Bennett's act was free, voluntary and deliberate.

The only question of a moral character which can arise is: Should Mr. Bryan have given a conditional acceptance (as he did) to the proposed bequest, or should he have refused it absolutely? To decide this question intelligently the reader must know all the facts, and those that would assist one in reaching a decision are presented herewith:

Mr. Bennett, a childless man, had by his industry, ability and integrity accumulated a fortune of about $300,000—$100,000 more than he desired to leave to his widow and relatives; he was and had been for years deeply interested in political questions and earnestly devoted to democratic principles; after distributing $30,000 among educational institutions and giving more than $20,000 for other purposes of a public nature, he set apart $50,000 for the advancement of his political principles through Mr. Bryan if the latter would accept it, otherwise for educational and charitable institutions.

Mr. Bennett knew that Mr. Bryan was devoting his life to the study and discussion of questions of government and was endeavoring to secure the triumph of the political principles that were dear to Mr. Bennett's heart; Mr. Bennett knew that Mr. Bryan, because of his presidential campaign, was in position to labor in a wider field than Mr. Bennett could hope to do, although Mr. Bryan could not surpass him in zeal or earnestness. Mr. Bennett also knew that Mr. Bryan's political work not only placed him under obligations that compelled a large annual outlay of money, but at the same time restricted his power to accumulate. Mr. Bennett was aware that the money, if accepted by Mr. Bryan, would enable the latter to devote a larger part of his time to unremunerative labor of a public character. Was it, under the circumstances, wrong for Mr. Bryan to accept the bequest conditionally?

Since 1896 Mr. Bryan has given nearly as much, if not quite as much, time to work that brought no compensation as to work for which he received pay, and a large part of his expense account is chargeable to the public nature of his work. During the nearly seven years that have elapsed since 1896, he has given in cash more than $20,000 to political organizations and more than $12,000 to education, charity and religion, while his net savings amount to something like $45,000, more than half of which sum is invested in his home and household goods and is therefore not income-bearing. With the exception of the campaign year of 1900 and the war year of 1898 (during nearly half of 1898 he was in the army) there has not been a year since 1896 when he could not have made more than the Bennett bequest had he abandoned political questions and devoted himself entirely to money-making. His failure to make as much as he might have made is not a matter of regret to him, because he has derived more satisfaction from his political work than he could have have done from a course which, however remunerative, would have taken him away from the consideration of public questions, but reference is made to the matter for the purpose of showing why Mr. Bennett desired to make this bequest and why Mr. Bryan felt constrained to accept it on condition that he needed it at the time of the testator's death.

Before there was any intimation of a contest, Mr. Bryan had notified Mrs. Bennett of his intention to regard the sum as a fund for the payment of work to be done for the public, his plan being to deliver without compensation enough lectures in college towns to make up the sum of $50,000 at the price which he usually receives from lecture bureaus, and this plan will be carried out whether the money is received or not, because Mr. Bennett did his part, and if the bequest fails, it will not be through any fault of the testator.

If the readers of THE COMMONER are surprised that Mr. Bryan's savings have not amounted to more during the last seven years, they must remember that the republican papers have had a political motive for attempting to exaggerate his income and his possessions. THE COMMONER itself has been described as a bonanza, whereas owing to the low subscription price and the exclusion of trust advertisements and other objectionable advertising, the income from the paper has been considerably below what it might have been had it been run with an eye single to profit. During the nearly three years covered by the existence of the paper, Mr. Bryan has not felt justified in drawing out more than about $5,000 a year, the balance being held in THE COMMONER'S reserve fund as a guarantee that each subscriber will receive his paper during the period covered by the subscription.

As Mr. Bryan stated in the argument before the court, he has no choice left him but to carry out the wishes of the testator even though to do so he must come into conflict with the relatives of the deceased and with an attorney who is not in sympathy with the political views held by Mr. Bennett while he lived and still entertained by Mr. Bryan.

TELL THE SENATE.

Senator Redfield Proctor delivered an address at the fortieth annual reunion of the Vermont Civil war veterans. Referring to the colonial policy of the United States, he said: "The government of a people of a country not contiguous is at the best experimental and temporary."

Senator Proctor declared that—

"Such a condition may last a long time, but it can not be permanent with training and development It is the God-given human nature of all people to wish to govern themselves and not owe allegiance across a sea.

"If I could make the future geography of the American Union I might be a little uncertain about the nation's northern boundary, whether to make it Canada or the Arctic ocean —preferably the last, in God's good time—but the proper lines would be fixed east by the Atlantic, west by the Pacific and south by the republic of Mexico and the gulf, and within those boundaries may the future government of our country remain."

Mr. Proctor, as an American statesman, may have something to do with the making of "the future geography of the American Union." If he would boldly take a stand against the policy of imperialism which his party has foisted upon this government, if in the senate chamber he would speak as boldly as he spoke before the civil war veterans, at Rutland,

Vt., then it may not be doubted that his words would have great effect in hastening the day of readjustment of the nation's policy with respect to the Philippine islands. If Mr. Proctor was sincere in his statements at Rutland, and we have no reason to doubt his sincerity, he should, at the earliest opportunity, express similar sentiments in the United States senate.

EX-SECRETARY LONG ON ROOSEVELT.

Ex-Secretary Long of Massachusetts has written for *The Outlook* an article that can not be considered otherwise than as an unfriendly attack on the president. The following is an extract:

"WASHINGTON, D. C., Oct. 11.—(Special.)—Frank and unreserved comment on the services of Theodore Roosevelt as assistant secretary of the navy characterizes an article by John D. Long, former secretary of the navy, in the the current issue of *The Outlook*. The government officials and navy officers familiar with the sometimes tense relations between Secretary Long and Assistant Secretary Roosevelt in the trying period preceding the Spanish-American war have displayed the keenest interest in the article of Mr. Long, who left the cabinet not long after Mr. Roosevelt entered the White house as president. Here is an extract from the article:

"'In May, 1897, on the retirement of Mr. McAdoo, I selected Mr. Roosevelt, who had had a hearty interest in the navy. His activity was characteristic. He was zealous in the work of putting the navy in condition for the apprehended struggle, and his ardor sometimes went faster than the president or the department appreciated.

"'Just before the war he was anxious to send a squadron across the ocean to sink the ships and torpedo boat destroyers of the Spanish fleet while we were yet at peace with Spain, frequently incorporating his views in the memoranda, which he would place every morning on my desk.

"'Most of his sugestions, had, however, so far as applicable, already been adopted by the various bureaus, the chiefs of which were leaving nothing undone. When I suggested to him that some future historian, reading his memoranda, would get the impression that the bureaus were inefficient he accepted the suggestion with the generous good nature which is so marked in him.'"

Here is strenuousness in the extreme! Mr. Long was secretary of the navy at that time and Mr. Roosevelt was assistant secretary, and now comes the chief and accuses the subordinate of desiring to sink the ships of Spain "while we were yet at peace" with that country. President Roosevelt told the students at West Point that a good soldier "must not only be willing to fight, but anxious to fight," but does that mean that a good commander must slip up and destroy another nation's fleet before war is declared? It seems, too, that the secretary became weary of having his assistant make suggestions that had already been carried out and finally the secretary told the subordinate, in substance, to attend to his own business. The rebuke was even more severe—he was informed that some future historian reading his numerous memoranda might get the impression that the bureaus were inefficient. This is a remarkable criticism, coming at this time and from such a source. What is its meaning? Can it be intended to array the friends of President McKinley against his successor? Is it the beginning of an anti-Roosevelt crusade?

A CONSCIENCE CAMPAIGN.

The elections of 1903 are past and the campaign of 1904 is upon us. What shall the democratic party do? Experience has shown that compromises and evasions are as useless from the standpoint of expediency as they are vicious from the standpoint of principle. And, moreover, a defeat which follows evasion and compromise leaves the party weaker for future conflicts, while a fight for principles scatters seed which will bring a harvest later. In 1896 the democratic element in the democratic party, after a fair and honest contest at the primaries, won a decisive victory and obtained control of the party organization. The plutocratic element of the party deserted and ever since that time has been plotting against the party. It threatens defeat if its dictation is resisted and is powerless to give victory when the party yields to its demands. It is planning now to give the democratic nomination to a representative of corporate wealth whose campaign would be made on money furnished by the trusts and whose administration, if he won, would be controlled by Wall street, as Mr. Cleveland's last administration was. To defeat this scheme and keep the party true to the interests of the people will require another contest, but this effort is worth making. In the campaigns of 1896 and 1900 the party had to bear the sins of the Cleveland administration and another surrender would increase the odium and postpone the day of reform. The party must be saved from humiliation and disgrace. Six millions of voters, if fearless and aggressive, will soon win a victory for good government and they can only be made fearless and aggressive by the resolution that comes from deep convictions and high purpose. The democratic party can not win a democratic victory by the use of money, even if it were base enough to try it, for such a victory would not be democratic if by any possibility it was achieved. If the people are to secure needed reforms they must conduct a conscience campaign; they must use honest methods and appeal to honest men who desire honest government. There is far more hope of success if the time is spent explaining democratic principles to conscientious republicans than there is if the time is frittered away in quarreling with men who call themselves democrats, but whose sympathies are with organized greed. Votes that are for sale go to the highest bidder, and democracy's puny purse can not measure itself against the overflowing chest of the republican party. But in an appeal to the higher and better elements of the human heart the democratic party would have little competition from the republican leaders.

The time is ripe for the conscience campaign. Will you enlist? Can you be counted on, not for a year, but until our nation is redeemed from plutocracy and made "a government of the people, by the people, for the people?"

A RISE IN SILVER.

The Portland *Oregonian* has the following to say in regard to a probable rise in silver:

"But the operation of natural laws alone will bring about the rise. Silver can not profitably be produced as a cheap by-product. The low price destroyed silver mining as such in almost every country in the world except Mexico. There is always a certain demand for silver in the arts as well as for subsidiary coinage. The continued shortage of the supply will sooner or later be felt and when the demand comes within sight of the supply mere men and governments may arbitrarily say it shall go no higher, but nature's law will have its way and the price will go up just the same."

The trouble with the *Oregonian* is that it apparently fails to comprehend the fact that a demand created by legislation has the same effect upon the price of silver as a demand arising from any other source. The demand for silver to be used in the Philippine coinage was a demand created by the government. If a demand for a limited amount of silver would raise the price a few cents, would not the free coinage of silver have a far greater effect? In buying for Philippine coinage the government went into the market and bid for silver with other competitors, but under free coinage the government offers to coin into legal tender money all the silver brought to the mint. Why would any one sell silver for less than $1.29 so long as the government will coin it into money at that price? The fact that Mexico has not been able to maintain the parity is not a conclusive argument against free coinage in this country, because the United States is far greater in population and in commercial strength. The international bimetallist recognizes that the United States could do something, but insists that the assistance of other nations would be required to maintain the parity. The advocate of the gold standard, on the other hand, seems blind to the effect that the government demand has upon the price of the precious metal, and some gold standard advocates go so far as to say that all the nations in the world could not, by restoring bimetallism, increase the price of silver or by demonetizing gold decrease the price of that metal. The absurdity of such a statement ought to be recognized by any one who considers the matter at all, but it is no more absurd than some of the other positions taken by the advocates of the gold standard.

A BLACK SPOT.

In the public statement issued by the state department, Secretary Hay placed great emphasis upon the fact that in the treaty between this government and that of New Granada (now Colombia) in the year 1846, the latter government guaranteed the right of way across the isthmus of Panama. Mr. Hay says that "this is the right which we acquired by the treaty for an important compensation."

It will be interesting to examine the treaty of 1846. In that treaty, after New Granada had guaranteed to the government of the United States the right of way across the isthmus and certain other privileges which the representatives of our government eagerly sought for, it was provided:

"And in order to secure to themselves the tranquil and constant enjoyment of these advantages, and as an especial compensation for certain advantages, and for the favors they have acquired by the fourth, fifth and sixth articles of this treaty, the United States guarantee positively and efficaciously to New Granada, by the present stipulation, the perfect neutrality of the before-mentioned isthmus, with the view that the free transit from one to the other sea may not be interrupted or embarrassed in any future time while this treaty exists; and, in consequence, the United States also guarantee in the same manner the rights of sovereignty and property which New Granada has and possesses over the said territory."

It will be seen, therefore, that the Roosevelt administration is very particular with respect to the obligations which Columbia owes the United States, but is not at all particular as to the solemn pledge the United States made to Colombia.

In order to secure to themselves the tranquil and constant enjoyment of certain important advantages and as an especial compensation for these advantages and favors, the United

States guaranteed "the right of sovereignty and property which New Granada has and possesses over the said territory." And yet instead of fulfilling this guarantee, instead of standing by this pledge in an honorable way, there is ample evidence that representatives of the United States deliberately encouraged a scheme to destroy the sovereignty, which this government was pledged to maintain, and gave encouragement to a secession movement among the citizens of a South American republic, with which we were under treaty agreement.

However popular Mr. Roosevelt's filibustering expedition against Colombia may be, it is safe to say that our connection with the Panama revolt will be regarded as one of the black spots in American history.

BENNETT'S BEQUEST TO COLLEGES

The multitude of letters received since the publication of the Bennett will would indicate that many do not understand the nature of the bequests. The will provides that $10,000 shall be distributed by Mr. Bryan among twenty-five institutions of learning. The $400 given to each institution is to be invested by such institution, and the proceeds used for an annual prize for the best essay on "The Science of Government." The institution, of course, determines the terms upon which the prize will be awarded, as it does in case of other prizes.

Another ten thousand dollars is to be distributed among colleges and institutions of learning, and is to be used for the aid of poor and deserving young men who are endeavoring to obtain an education. A similar amount is to be divided among colleges and institutions of learning by Mrs. Bryan and is to be used to aid poor and deserving young women to obtain an education. No attempt will be made by Mr. or Mrs. Bryan to select the persons to be benefited. Their duty is ended when they select the institutions to which the money will be given. A great many letters have been received from students who desire aid, who, not understanding the nature of the bequest, supposed that Mr. or Mrs. Bryan would attempt to select the individual students who were to be aided.

It will be some months before the estate is settled up, and no attempt will be made to select colleges or make a distribution of the fund until the estate is settled up and the money turned over to the trustees. The letters already received have been answered, and this notice is given for the information of those who may have been misled by the newspaper reports that have appeared in regard to the matter.

DECISION IN BENNETT CASE.

District of New Haven—ss. Probate Court, November 6, 1903. Estate of Philo S. Bennett, late of New Haven, in said District, deceased.

Memorandum of Decision: This is a contest over an application to admit to probate a paper purporting to be the last will of Philo S. Bennett of New Haven, in this district, and to probate in connection therewith, and as a part thereof, a certain letter unattested by witnesses, but signed by the deceased, and, it is claimed, referred to in said will.

The 12th clause of said will reads as follows:

"Twelfth—I give and bequeath unto my wife, Grace Imogene Bennett, the sum of fifty thousand dollars ($50,000) in trust, however, for the purposes set forth in a sealed letter which will be found with said will."

The letter, which was found after Mr. Bennett's death in the vaults of the Merchants Safe Deposit company of New York City, in the same safe deposit box with the will, but enclosed in a separate sealed envelope, reads as follows:

"Bennett, Sloan & Co., Importers and Jobbers, Teas, Coffees and Spices, Canned Goods, Flavoring Extracts, Hudson and Franklin Street, New York, May 22, 1900.—My Dear Wife: In my will, just executed, I have bequeathed to you seventy-five thousand dollars ($75,000) and the Bridgeport houses, and have in addition to this made you the residuary legatee of a sum which will amount to twenty-five thousand more. This will give you a larger income than you can spend while you live and will enable you to make bountiful provision for those you desire to remember in your will. In my will you will find the following provisions:

"I give and bequeath unto my wife, Grace Imogene Bennett, the sum of fifty thousand dollars ($50,000) in trust, however, for the purposes set forth in a sealed letter which will be found with this will. It is my desire that the fifty thousand dollars conveyed to you in trust by this provision shall be by you paid to William Jennings Bryan of Lincoln, Neb., or to his heirs if I survive him. I am earnestly devoted to the political principles which Mr. Bryan advocates and believe the welfare of the nation depends upon the triumph of these principles. As I am not as able as he to defend those principles with tongue and pen, and as his political work prevents the application of his time and talents to money making, I consider it a duty, as I find it a pleasure, to make this provision for his financial aid, so that he may be more free to devote himself to his chosen field of labor. If for any reason he is unwilling to receive this sum for himself, it is my will that he shall distribute the said sum of fifty thousand dollars according to his judgment among educational and charitable institutions. I have sent a duplicate of this letter to Mr. Bryan and it is my desire that no one excepting you and Mr. Bryan himself shall know of this letter and bequest. For this reason I will place this letter in a sealed envelope and direct that it shall be opened only by you and read by you alone. With love and kisses.
"P. S. BENNETT."

The indorsement on the envelope reads as follows: "Mrs. P. S. Bennett. To be read only by Mrs. Bennett and by her alone after my death. P. S. BENNETT."

No objection has been made to the probate of the will either on the ground of mental incapacity or improper execution, but the widow, next of kin, and residuary legatees object to the probating of the letter contained in the sealed envelope and to the 12th section of the will referring to such letter, on the ground of undue influence claimed by them to have been exerted over the testator by William J. Bryan of Lincoln, Neb., who benefits by the provisions of said letter and said 12th chapter of said will. They further object on the ground that this unattested letter can not be incorporated into the will, even if no undue influence was exerted in procuring it. No evidence was offered by the contestants except a letter written by Mr. Bryan after the will had been filed in court The proponents' evidence consisted of the testimony of the attesting witnesses, the testimony of Mr. Bryan and of ex-Lieutenant Governor James D. Dewell, and certain letters written by Mr. Bennett.

The question of undue influence will be first considered.

It appears that while Mr. Bennett was doing business in New York city, being a member of the firm of Bennett, Sloan & Company, he resided in New Haven. Mr. Bennett's acquaintance with Mr. Bryan began during the presidential campaign of 1896, Mr. Bryan being a candidate for president of the United States and Mr. Bennett having been nominated for presidential elector on the Bryan ticket in Connecticut. The origin and character of that acquaintance is indicated by the following letter:

"NEW YORK, Oct. 30, 1896.—Hon. William J. Bryan, Lincoln, Neb.—Dear Sir: The betting is three to one against you in this state at the present time; but, notwithstanding that, I am impressed with a feeling that you will win, and if you are defeated, I wish to make you a gift of $3,000, and if you will accept the same, it will be a genuine pleasure to me to hand it to you any time after the 10th of next March.

"You have made one of the most gallant fights on record for a principle, against the combined money power of the whole country, and if you are not successful now, you will be in my opinion, four years later.

"The solid press of the east and all the wealth of the country have, ever since the canvass opened, concealed the truth and deceived the people regarding the whole question. They have suceeded in making 25 per cent of them believe that if you are elected the country will be governed by a lawless, disorganized mob. If you are elected I trust that you will, as soon as you can, issue a letter or make a speech, assuring them that the great body of the people are honest and can be trusted.

"This letter is intended only for yourself and wife to ever see. A feeling of gratitude for what you have done in this canvass for humanity, for right and justice, prompts me to write and make this offer.

"I am one of the electors at large on the silver ticket in the state of Connecticut, and accompanied you from New York to New Haven, and rode in the carriage with you and Mr. Sergeant from the station to the hotel.

"Hoping for your victory, and with kind regards, I am, sincerely yours,   P. S. BENETT."

The friendship thus begun continued up to the time of Mr. Bennett's death. The evidence shows that from the date of this first letter Mr. Bryan never visited New York without seeing Mr. Bennett who, except on a single occasion, always met him at the train. The correspondence continued until Mr. Bennett's last letter to Mr. Bryan, dated July 24, 1903, just before starting west upon the trip ending in his death.

Mr. Bennett invited Mr. Bryan and family on two or three occasions to spend the summer with him in Maine. In a letter written in 1899 extending such an invitation, Mr. Bennett writes: "Perhaps you can accept my invitation to come this way in August, with your family, and take a vacation upon the Maine mountains with Mrs. Bennett and myself." And he then added that Mrs. Bennett and he would meet the family at the station on their arrival in New York. None of these invitations, however, were accepted. A final indication of the high regard which Mr. Bennett had from the first cherished for Mr. Bryan is shown by his call, in the summer of 1903, a few days before his death, at Mr. Bryan's home in Lincoln, Neb.

So much for the preliminary facts. Now as to the circumstances attending the drawing of the paper propounded as Mr. Bennett's will as related by Mr. Bryan.

After inquiry by letter in the spring of 1900, whether Mr. Bryan would be home at a certain time, Mr. Bennett journeyed from New York city to Lincoln, Neb., a few days before the execution of the will in question in New York city, and informed Mr. Bryan that he desired to draw his will. He took with him to Nebraska an old will and various memoranda indicating how he desired to dispose of his property. He conferred with Mr. Bryan who then dictated the will to Mrs. Bryan who wrote it out on the typewriter. Mr. Bennett asked Mr. Bryan whether he would be wililng to act as executor. Mr. Bryan consented, and accordingly he and Mr. Alfred F. Sloan of New York city, Mr. Bennett's partner in business, were named in the will as executors. Most of the individual bequests were copied from the earlier will. The amounts of the bequests to Mr. Bryan and to Mrs. Bryan, in trust for educational institutions, were communicated to Mr. Bryan by Mr. Bennett, and the general provisions as to how these amounts should be given, were matters of discussion between them; the bequest for the founding of the Bryan-Bennett library at Mr. Bryan's birthplace, to which they were jointly to contribute, being the only bequest suggested by Mr. Bryan.

Mr. Bennett proposed to give Mr. Bryan $50,000 direct. Mr. Bryan suggested that the bequest be given in the way it was finally attempted to be given by the 12th section of the will referring to the sealed letter, and in connection with the drafting of the will a typewritten draft was made of the proposed letter to Mrs. Bennett to be enclosed in a sealed envelope and filed with the will, and of a letter to be written by Mr. Bennett to Mr. Bryan, enclosing a duplicate of the contents of the sealed envelope and indicating how he wished Mr. Bryan to divide the $50,000 between himself and family; the proposition being that, upon Mr. Bennett's return to New York, he should execute his will and mail to Mr. Bryan a duplicate of the letter which he was to place in a sealed envelope and deposit with the will, and that in connection with sending the duplicate of the contents of the sealed envelope he was to write Mr. Bryan a letter copying the form prepared by them in Nebraska.

This course was pursued, Mr. Bennett left Mr. and Mrs. Bryan in Nebraska, and returned to New York where, after executing his will in his own store among his business associates, he deposited it together with a letter enclosed in a sealed envelope, as arranged for in Nebraska, in a safety deposit vault of his own selection.

Do these facts warrant the court in finding that the testator was unduly influenced by Mr. Bryan?

While the general rule is that the burden of proof is upon those alleging undue influence, the rule is otherwise when the gift is to one who sustains the relation of attorney to the testator, and draws the will under which he takes the benefit. But this is a mere presumption which the law raises and which may be rebutted by evidence. St. Leger's Appeal, 34 Conn., 434; Dale's Appeal, 57 Conn., 127; Richmond's Appeal, 59 Conn., 226; Livingston's Appeal, 63 Conn., 68.

The testimony of Mr. Dewell, who had known him for a quarter of a century, shows that the testator was a sharp, able business man, a man of decided opinions from which he was not easily turned aside. But whatever presumption, if any, might be raised by reason of Mr. Bryan's drafting the will, has been, in the opinion of the court, abundantly overcome by the evidence. Mr. Bryan testifies that the idea of a bequest in his favor, so far from being suggested by him or Mrs. Bryan, was a complete surprise to both; a statement in which the court has entire confidence in view of Mr. Bryan's frankness on the witness stand and his evident desire to fully disclose all his relations with the testator and all the circumstances surrounding the drafting of the will. It must also be remembered that the testator had ample opportunity to change his will at any time during the last three years of his life and without the knowledge of Mr. Bryan.

Mr. Bennett did not in his will forget his heirs-at-law and made ample provision for the support of his wife. Taking the total amount of the specific legacies in connection with his estimate of the residue as expressed in the sealed letter, he evidently thought he was giving his wife $100,000 or more, absolutely, out of an estate which he apparently thought would approximate $300,000. The Bryans were not the only legatees outside of the widow and his heirs-at-law, but the testator, besides making liberal public and charitable bequests, made generous provision for relatives who would have received nothing but for the will.

Measured by Mr. Bennett's devotion to Mr. Bryan and to the principles for which both had contended, the bequest of $50,000 to the Bryans, to take effect after the testator's death, does not seem more unusual than the gift of $3,000 offered to Mr. Bryan while they were comparative strangers and actually paid during Mr. Bennett's life.

This court finds that neither the 12th clause of the will, nor the letter therein referred to, was procured by undue influence.

The other question to be considered is whether the letter contained in the sealed envelope, and referred to in the 12th clause of the will, was so incorporated by reference as to be made a part of the will. Much emphasis has been placed on the obiter remarks of the court in Phelps vs. Robbins, 49 Conn., 250, 271, seriously questioning whether in this state papers referred to in a will, containing instructions disposing of property, can be incorporated into a will. Whatever our highest court might decide, if the question was squarely presented to it today, it is not necessary to consider in order to pass on the questions before this court. Even though the law in this state is, as it seems to be in most jurisdictions, that such a paper, under certain conditions, may be incorporated by reference, this letter is objected to on other grounds. Even if it be conceded that the 12th clause in this will refers to the extraneous paper as being in existence at the time of the execution of the will, the authorities agree that the paper referred to must in fact be in existence at the time of the execution of the will.

Was the letter in the sealed envelope in existence at the time of the execution of the will? This question is answered by the first sentence of the letter itself. It reads, "In my will, just executed, I have bequeathed to you," etc. There is no ambiguity about the meaning of these words. They say, if they say anything, that the letter was not in existence until after the will was executed. It is not necessary to inquire how the obvious meaning of these words would have been affected if evidence had been offered to indicate that the sealed letter was in fact prepared before execution of the will, because no such evidence was offered. True, the typewritten draft was prepared in Nebraska two or three days before the execution of the will, and is still in existence; but it was found in a safe in the store of Bennett, Sloan & Company after the testator's death, and not with the will, which was found in a safe deposit box of the Merchants Safe Deposit Co., in which box was also found the sealed envelope. This typewritten draft was not designed to be the letter to be referred to in the will, and can not be considered as such.

Page, in his work on Wills, 165, states the law as follows: "The reference in the will to the document as already in existence is not conclusive. It must be shown further that the document sought to be incorporated was, in fact, in existence at the time of the execution of the will. . . . Where the document referred to is written after the will is executed, even if immediately after, and on the same day, it can not be regarded as part of the will." So in Underhill on Wills, 280, it is said: "It must be proved (and this of course can only be done by parol evidence) that the writing was in fact in existence at the date of the will." See also Jarman on Wills, 99, Schouler on Wills, 282; Woerner on Administration, 485; Phelps vs. Robbins, 40 Conn., 250, 272; Newton vs. Beaman's Friend Society, 130 Mass., 91; Shillaber's Estate, 74 Cal., 144; 5 Am. St. Rep., 433; Vestry vs. Bostwick, 8 App., D. C. 452.

In view of the plain recital in the letter itself, it is difficult to see how, without an utter disregard of the authorities, this letter can be incorporated into the will, and this court therefore finds that the sealed letter can not be admitted to probate as a part of the will. It is not, however, the province of this court in probating a will to construe its provisions. Hence the 12th clause, whether operative or not, will be admitted to probate as a part of the will; and in thus refusing to probate the sealed letter as a part of the will, this court does not wish to be understood as expressing any opinion as to whether the letter, without being probated, can have any legal effect as a declaration of the trust attempted to be created by the 12th clause of the will.

LIVINGSTON W. CLEVELAND, Judge.

A SLUMP IN STOCKS.

Since the election of 1900 there has been a slump in the market value of stocks amounting to more than $1,750,000,-000. If the democrats had been successful in the last presidential election the republican papers would have charged this tremendous slump in stocks to the democratic administration. How will they explain it now? When it is referred to at all it is described as a matter of small importance, and often defended as a really desirable thing. We are told that it was a "natural liquidation," an elimination of "speculative values," a "settling down to a solid basis."

The readers of THE COMMONER are asked to remember that this slump in stocks indicates one of two things. If the slump means that the water is being squeezed out of the stocks, that fictitious values are being destroyed, and that the industries are simply settling down to an honest basis, how will republicans defend an administration that permits the inflation of values and the watering of stocks?

It can not be denied that many have suffered by the slump. Those innocent purchasers, of whom we hear so much when remedial legislation is suggested, have been suffering. It is said that the steel trust has 98,000 stockholders, and all of these have suffered by the fall in prices. Why should they be exposed to this loss? Many of the holders of this stock are employes who took the stock more to encourage the idea of co-operation in industry than to make a profit out of it. They wanted to show their appreciation of what they regarded as a generous offer on the part of the company. Was it not a little cruel to thus reward their confidence? When will "confidence" be restored among these people? What about the widow who put her scanty savings in preferred or common steel? We always hear of the widow when we discuss the money question or attempt to curb corporate rapacity, why is she kept in the background now? The Kansas City platform proposed a remedy that, if adopted, would have made it impossible for an interstate commerce corporation to have watered its stock. This tremendous loss would have been prevented if that remedy had been adopted before the steel trust was organized. What remedy have the republican leaders for the situation which now confronts them? What is the president doing, what is the republican congress doing to protect the public from watered stock?

If to escape this dilemma the republicans insist that the shrinkage in stocks does not indicate a squeezing out of water, but a loss in actual and honest values, what will they say about an administration that results in such a blow to industry? Can the country be said to be prosperous if honest stocks have suffered a shrinkage of nearly two billions of dollars in three years? Is the industrial condition a satisfactory one?

The fact is that the republican leaders have permitted the government to be run in the interest of organized wealth. They have permitted the exploitation of the public. They have not only permitted, but encouraged, the issuing of stock and bonds that represent, not existing values, but future power to extort through the power of monopoly. The producing masses are regarded as legitimate objects of prey, and gigantic corporations are created for the purpose of robbing those who toil. Whether in peace or in war, those who earn their living by labor on the farm and in the shop, are the nation's reliance. Why should these, the bone and sinew of every land, be despoiled by the speculators who reap a rich harvest in times of peace and shirk every national duty in time of trouble?

The republican party stands today for plutocracy and all that plutocracy desires. Its policies give prominence to the dollar and leave man in the background. It ought not to require a slump in stocks or a fall in prices or a run on the banks to open the eyes of the people to what is going on, but if any object lesson is necessary it is furnished by present conditions.

We have been passing through a period of bountiful harvests, a period during which the people, recovering from a prolonged depression, have been making up for lost time. Production and consumption have been abnormal, but there are evidences that we have passed the high water mark and are on the down grade. Employers are organizing to resist the claims of employes; corporations are meeting the demand for shorter hours and better wages with threats of a reduction in the number of men employed. The steel trust cuts a dividend on common stock in two, and announces that the orders on hand are less than this time last year. Some of the banks and trust companies have not been able to get new securities as rapidly as old securities have fallen in value. All indicate that the cry of "prosperity" will be uttered with less and less emphasis by the republican party.

Senator Hanna, in his anxiety to be re-elected, threatened that a reduction of the republican majority would result in the closing of many industries. Upon what foundation is republican prosperity based, if it can be shaken by an election in one state? The fact is that Senator Hanna knows that, regardless of the result in any one state, the prosperity argument upon which his party has relied, must sooner or later come to an end, and when it comes to an end, the republican party will have to meet the issues which its riot in power has brought before the American people. It has not attempted to defend imperialism; it has answered every argument against imperialism with the cry of "Prosperity!" It has not attempted to justify a high tariff; it has answered the arguments against tariff schedules by the cry of "Prosperity!" It has not even attempted to defend the gold standard; it has simply claimed that prosperity has justified the gold standard. And its only argument on the trust question is that we can not deal harshly with the trusts without jeopardizing prosperity.

The slump in stocks is an indication that the trusts have overestimated their power to squeeze the people, and that the squeezing process must therefore be applied to the stocks.

Will the republican leaders take warning and address themselves to remedial legislation, or will they blindly refuse to protect the public? There is already evidence that they have been frightened away from the asset currency. They may not even dare to make a beginning by providing for an emergency asset currency, but it is not sufficient to refrain from further bad legislation. What we need now is good legislation, and the Kansas City platform points the way.

THE PRESIDENT'S MESSAGE.

The president's message is remarkable for what it does not say. That portion of the message devoted to Panama is the only really interesting feature.

So far as the administration's Panama policy is concerned, Mr. Roosevelt does not hesitate to accept the responsibility, making it very plain, indeed, that he is proud of his achievements with respect to the new republic on the isthmus. Sifted down, Mr. Roosevelt's defense of his Panama policy is that "the end justifies the means," although he makes an effort, and a feeble one, to show that there are precedents for his course, and that he is sustained by the interpretation which several distinguished secretaries of state, during the earlier days, placed upon the treaty of 1846.

Aside from its reference to Panama, the message is one of the strangest documents that was ever sent from the White house. It reads more like the report of a department chief, who understands that he is expected to go into details, but who is very reluctant to express an opinion concerning any of the policies with which he deals.

The president ignores altogether the tariff question.

In treating the financial situation, the president says that the same liberty should be granted the secretary of the treasury to deposit customs receipts as is granted him to deposit all receipts from other sources. He then dismisses the financial question by directing attention to his message of December 2, 1902. He again asks the consideration of congress for the plans then proposed.

It will be remembered that in his message of December 2, 1902, the president said that "it is necessary that there should be an element of elasticity in our monetary system." In that message he said: "Banks are the natural servants of commerce and upon them should be placed as far as practicable the burden of furnishing and maintaining a circulation adequate to supply the needs of our diversified industries and our domestic and foreign commerce, and the issue of this should be so regulated that a sufficient supply should be always available for the business interests of the country." He suggested "the use of such instrumentalities as will automatically supply every legitimate demand of productive industries and commerce not only in the amount, but in the character of the circulation; and of making all kinds of money interchangeable and at the will of the holder convertible into the established gold standard."

Since the message of December, 1902, was delivered, we have been told that Mr. Roosevelt meant "automatic currency;" and from the definitions we subsequently received, we have learned that Mr. Roosevelt's "automatic currency" or Mr. Shaw's "emergency currency" means nothing more nor less than asset currency.

The president refers to the merchant marine in a way to justify the impression that he is in favor of a ship subsidy, although he does not seem to be willing to state his position clearly. It may not be doubted that when the commission, the creation of which is recommended by the president, shall make its report, it will present a subsidy scheme.

Even upon the question of abolishing the tariff between the United States and the Philippines, the president treads very lightly. He points out that "congress should ever keep in mind that peculiar obligations rest upon us to further in every way the welfare of these communities;" and he adds: "The Philippines should be knit closer to us by tariff arrangements," but he leaves congress to guess whether he is in favor of abolishing the Philippine tariff or making a marked reduction in that tariff.

The president seems to have a weakness for commissions and so he announces that he has appointed a commission whose duty it will be to investigate the operation of existing land laws and recommend whatever changes may be desirable. On this subject, the president says that his purpose is "to effect the largest practicable disposition of the public lands to actual settlers who will build permanent homes upon them," and it is safe to say that a very large majority of the American people are heartily in sympathy with that purpose.

It will be observed that while the president reiterates the recommendations made in his message of December, 1902, with respect to the currency question, he does not take the trouble to reiterate his statements with respect to the tariff question. Many people will wonder how the president could persuade himself to ignore altogether the tariff question just at this time when that question is being more generally discussed among the people than for several years.

The president touches very lightly upon the trust question, speaks enthusiastically of the new department of commerce, says that the work of the bureau of corporations will be productive of great good, emphasizes the plan of "publicity," leaving the impression upon his reader that that is the sole thing to be desired in treating the great trust evil. In fact, the president seems to regard the trust question, concerning which there is large discussion among the people, as of comparatively little importance. So anxious does he seem to be to avoid giving the slightest offense to the trust magnates that the word "trusts" is not at all conspicuous and is used in an incidental way perhaps in half a dozen places.

Altogether, the message must be unsatisfactory, even to republicans, because it leaves the impression that it was written not by a man whose greatest anxiety is for the correct solution of public problems, but rather by a man whose largest concern is for a nomination to the office he now holds.

Those who will carefully read the president's message from the beginning to the end will, we think, conclude that it bears the earmarks of an ambitious politician rather than the impress of a great president.

PURE MUNICIPAL GOVERNMENT.

In instructing the grand jury that met to investigate alleged corruption in Kansas City, Kas., Judge E. L. Fisher said:

"In this community there has grown to be a sentiment that pure municipal government is an unobtainable thing; that every man has his price. Such a condition is appalling and demoralizing. Let no bribe-giver, bribe-taker or corrupt public official escape."

It is true that in many communities throughout the country the sentiment to which Judge Fisher refers is all too conspicuous. In spite of our experiments, we have not made the success in municipal government which we should have made, and which we would have made if the people of a community as a whole devoted strict attention to municipal affairs.

The great majority in many communities display an indifferent sort of interest in their municipal government. Men having axes to grind and corporations seeking to avoid the burdens they should properly bear, are keenly alive as to the character of the local government under which they live and do business. So long as the people of a community remain indifferent, the man with the axe and the corporation manager seeking advantages, will have the controlling voice in municipal affairs; and whenever the representatives of special interests control a municipality, however secretly they may wield their power, it may be depended upon that municipal government in that community, at least, is a failure, so far as public interests are concerned.

It is useless for men to say that "pure municipal government is an unobtainable thing." Whenever the people whose sole interest is in securing clean and honest municipal government do their duty in the primaries and at the polls, rejecting the candidacy of unworthy men and repudiating policies advanced by the representatives of special interests, and for their benefit, pure municipal government will be obtained. It is true that in municipal government, as well as in state and national government, eternal vigilance on the part of the citizen is required in order to see to it that public interests are protected.

THE POLITICAL WEEKLY AS AN ADVERTISING MEDIUM.

(Written by W. J. Bryan for "Judicious Advertising," published by Lord & Thomas.)

The political weekly deserves to be considered as an advertising medium for the following reasons:

First—Such a paper is taken mainly by those who believe in the political doctrines which it advocates, and advertisements appearing in the paper commend themselves to the readers. A man's political convictions are, as a rule, deep and lasting, and in every great crisis there are innumerable instances where the individual's views on public questions are stronger than family ties. Those who hold tenaciously to their political opinions naturally prize papers upon which they can rely for the information which they need in the discussion of political questions, and those who advertise in such papers profit by the confidence which the reader has in the publisher.

Second—Political weeklies are not read and thrown away like daily papers, but are laid aside for reference. The advertising matter is, therefore, of lasting value, and it is not uncommon for an advertiser to hear from such an advertisement many weeks after it has ceased to appear in the paper.

Third—The political weekly is growing, and bids fair to occupy an increasing place in the field of journalism. The daily is becoming a great business enterprise whose editorial page is either practically without political color or defends the interests of the corporations with which the owner is connected. The stockholders of the great dailies are generally unknown to the public; neither are the writers known whose pencils supply copy for the editorial page. It is impossible that an intelligent and thoughtful student of public affairs should pay a great deal of attention to editorials written by nobody-knows-who and often with an ulterior purpose.

With the growth of the daily it becomes less and less possible for the same person to be both editor and owner, and if he is employed to do the writing, he must write as the owner desires or forfeit his place. It is likely, therefore, that there will be an increasing tendency to read the daily for its news and the weekly for the thoughtful discussion of the problems of government. A weekly paper can be published without great expense and can be edited by the owner. Its circulation will depend partly upon the popularity of the ideas presented and partly upon the ability with which the paper is edited.

Fourth—The political weekly has a wider field than the daily can possibly have because a daily published in one city can not hope to invade the precincts of another city, but a weekly published anywhere in the United States can find its way into every village and hamlet of the country. Its contents are not valuable because of their freshness as news, but because of their permanent usefulness in the consideration of questions of moment.

Fifth—The political weekly is inexpensive as compared with the daily and reaches those who would not feel able to pay the price of a daily. It may be confidently expected, therefore, that political weeklies will increase in number, in circulation and in influence, and the value of an inch of advertising in such a paper will approximate the value of like space in a monthly magazine of like circulation. W. J. BRYAN.

BIMETALLISM—(ENCYCLOPEDIA ARTICLE.)

Mr. Bryan has written for the Encyclopedia Americana, now being issued by the Americana company of New York, an article on bimetallism. This article gives in condensed form the principles involved in the discussion of the subject and is reproduced in THE COMMONER by courtesy of the publishers. Papers quoting from this article will please give credit to the Encyclopedia Americana.

BIMETALLISM.

Gold and silver have been used as money for thousands of years, both the Old Testament and profane history making frequent reference to such use of the precious metals. (See Money.)

As time went on the metals were coined into convenient pieces, and the weight and fineness of the coins guaranteed by the government. Finally, a legal ratio between the metals was fixed and the coins made a tender in payment of debts.

The term bimetallism is employed to describe a financial system wherein gold and silver are used as standard money and coined without limit at a fixed ratio. Bimetallism proper implies, first, that the money unit shall rest upon two metals; second, that these metals shall enjoy equal and unlimited coinage privileges; third, that they shall be connected by a fixed and definite legal ratio; and, fourth, that the coins made from them shall be a full legal tender.

The term "limping bimetallism" has been applied to systems wherein gold and silver were used as standard money, but in which one of the metals was not coined at all, or not coined on equal terms with the other. The term, free coinage, has sometimes been used to mean unlimited coinage and sometimes to mean gratuitous coinage. Unlimited coinage is necessary to a complete bimetalllic system. When coinage is limited the volume of standard money is regarded by law; when coinage is unlimited the volume depends, first, upon the total accumulation of coin, and, second, upon the annual production of the money metals. This sum is further augmented by the coinage of gold and silver plate when money becomes scarce, or lessened by an increased demand for gold and silver in the arts when money becomes plentiful.

Gratuitous coinage is not necessary to bimetallism, although it usually accompanies it. A charge can be made for mintage without destroying the bimetallic character of the system, but such a charge necessarily creates a difference between the coinage and the bullion value of the metal. When coinage is gratuitous melted coin can be recoined without loss; when there is a mint charge melted coin loses an amount equal to the cost of coinage. The "melting pot test" is, therefore, not a test of honest money.

Bimetallism does not rest upon any particular ratio; the coinage ratio is fixed by law, and can be changed by law. The ratio simply states the proportion existing between the silver dollar and the gold dollar when measured by weight—that is, at the ratio of 16 to 1, the silver dollar weighs sixteen times as much as the gold dollar. While the legal and commercial ratios between the metals have fluctuated from time to time the legal ratio has, as a rule, caused the change in the commercial ratio, and from the beginning of history down to 1873 the fluctuations in the commercial ratio were never as sudden or as great as they have been since 1873. During the 400 years which elapsed between 1473 and 1873 the extreme variation in the commercial ratio was from 14 to 1 to 16 to 1, although during that period there were greater changes in the relative production of the metals than have occurred since. For instance, between 1800 and 1840 the world's production of silver was about 4 to 1 in value, compared with the production of gold; after the new discoveries of gold in 1849 the production of that metal so increased that the annual output of gold was soon more than 3 to 1 in value, compared with the output of silver, and yet during this tremendous change in relative production the commercial ratio was comparatively stable, owing to the fact that all the gold and all the silver could go through the mints into the world's currency. Hostile legislation has driven the metals widely apart since 1873 and it is the contention of bimetallists that friendly legislation will bring the metals together.

The ratio of 16 to 1 is the one advocated by American bimetallists, first, because it was the ratio existing when the crusade against silver began; second, because it is the ratio now existing between the silver and gold coins in circulation in the United States; and, third, because an increase in the ratio, made by increasing the size of the silver dollar, would to the extent that it was joined in by other nations require the recoinage of silver coins into larger coins, and thus reduce the world's volume of standard money. If, for instance, the ratio were changed to 32 to 1 by international agreement, and the silver money of the world, approximating $4,000,000,000, were recoined into $2,000,000,000, it would cause a shrinkage of about 25 per cent in the total volume of metallic money and, as contracts would still call for the same number of dollars, such a change in the ratio would transfer billions of dollars in value from the wealth producers to the holders of fixed investments.

It will be noticed that bimetallism relates to the legal status of the metals rather than to their commercial value, and does not necessarily imply the simultaneous or concurrent circulation of both metals, although American bimetallists contend that the restoration of free coinage at the ratio of 16 to 1 would result in the concurrent circulation of both metals in this country. When the ratio was 15 to 1 in this country gold went to a premium of about 3 per cent because the French ratio was 15½ to 1; when our ratio was changed to 16 to 1, silver, being undervalued at our mint as compared with its value at the French mint, rose to a premium of about 3 per cent.

The Gresham law has often been quoted against bimetallism. That law is merely a statement, made by a master of the English mint of that name, who announced as his observation that the bad coins ran the good coins out of the country—the explanation being that while, to a majority of the people one coin was as good as another so long as it would pass current, the jewelers would melt and the dealers in money would collect and export the heaviest coins (coins passing by weight rather than by legal tender outside of their own country). It can readily be seen that the Gresham law was not intended to apply to the use of two metals, and that it can apply to the use of two metals only when there is difference between government ratios. When, for instance, we had a ratio of 15 to 1 in this country, and the French ratio was 15½ to 1, there was a tendency to send American gold to France and bring French silver to the United States, and yet this tendency did not cause the exportation of all American gold to France or of all French silver to the United States. France, being at that time the stronger nation commercially, fixed the ratio and our gold rose to a premium. In the payment of debts silver was the money employed, and gold, when it was used, was used at its commodity price. After 1834 the situation was reversed and silver went to a premium. Gold was then used for the payment of debts and for general transactions, and silver, when it was used, brought a premium. It is not fair to say, however, that gold went out of circulation entirely during the former period or that silver went out of circulation entirely during the latter period, for a great deal of the undervalued coin remained here and served the purpose of money, and to that extent relieved the pressure upon other kinds of money. That which left our country in exchange for another kind of metal did not reduce our circulation, and the exported coin still remained a part of the circulation of the world and helped to fix international prices.

In bimetallism the debtor always has the option. This is true, not because of a desire on the part of the government to favor the debtor, but because the parity can be maintained in no other way. If the debtor has the option the desire of all debtors to secure that metal which is the cheaper, will in itself, by increasing the demand for the cheaper metal and decreasing the demand for the dearer metal, tend to make the commercial value of the metals identical with the legal value, whereas, through the operation of the same selfishness, the metals would be driven apart if the creditor had the option, because the demand of the creditors for the dearer metal would still further increase its price, while the lessened demand for the cheaper metal would still further decrease its price.

The arguments in defense of the bimetallic system begin with the self-evident truth that stability in purchasing power is the test of virtue or honesty in money—that dollar being the best dollar which changes least from year to year in its command over all articles of merchandise. Stability would not be so important if all transactions were on a cash basis, but with the increase in credits, especially long time credits, it is a matter of vital importance to have the purchasing power of the dollar fluctuate as little as possible. Jacobs, in his work on the precious metals, shows that an increase of 2 per cent a year in the purchasing power of the dollar would amount to an increase of 500 per cent in 100 years. It will be seen, therefore, that the burden of national debts and other long-time securities may be materially increased or decreased by a change in the purchasing power of the dollar.

That the value or purchasing power of the dollar depends upon the number of dollars has been declared to be, and correctly so, the most fundamental principle in the science of money. To illustrate; if the business of the world is adjusted to a certain volume of money, and that volume of money is afterward suddenly doubled, prices will necessarily rise, because there will be more money with which to purchase other things. If, on the other hand, the volume of money is suddenly reduced one-half prices will fall because of the scarcity of money. Next to absolute stability in the purchasing power of the dollar or unit, the most desirable thing is that any necessary change in the purchasing power of the dollar shall be gradual rather than sudden, and a sudden change in the value of the dollar can only be prevented by the prevention of a sudden change in the volume of money. When it is remembered that the money changer and the owner of fixed investments profit by a rising dollar it is easy to understand why they have always led the movements in favor of scarce money.

Dr. Sturtevant in his book, entitled "Economics, or the Science of Wealth," illustrates the gradual change in the volume of metallic money as follows:

"Gold and silver, considered as a standard value, are an ocean flowing around the whole economic world, and very large additions at two or three points are immediately distributed to every part."

The quantity of metallic money is so great that the annual addition to it is small in comparison.

Bimetallism is theoretically better than monometallism (either of gold or silver), because under the double or bimetallic standard the volume of money changes less rapidly and less suddenly than under the single standard. Thus far history has shown no instance of a large simultaneous increase in the production of both gold and silver. There was an enormous increase in the production of silver during the 16th century; then there was a great increase in the production of gold during the year 1849 and the years immediately following. Early in the 'seventies there was another increase in the production of silver and we are just now enjoying a considerable increase in the production of gold. In each instance the increase in the production of one metal has spread itself over the entire volume of money and has, therefore, caused a less proportionate increase than it would have caused had the world been using but one metal, either gold or silver, as standard money.

The superior stability of the bimetallic system over the monometallic system has been shown by many illustrations, the most familiar being that which likens the volume of money to a body of water receiving the inflow from two rivers instead of one.

The practical argument in favor of bimetallism is that neither metal alone furnishes a sufficient quantity of money to support the world's commerce. Bimetallism is, therefore, actually necessary as well as theoretically advantageous. This phase of the question was not much considered until after 1873 because, prior to that date there were sufficient mints open for the coinage of both metals to furnish a monetary use for every ounce produced. When all of the gold and silver available for coinage could go through the mints into the currency, each nation could consider the question from a purely theoretical standpoint, because so long as the commercial world had the benefit of the entire volume of gold and silver, it did not make so much difference how many nations used one metal, or the other, or both. When, however, the crusade against silver began and enough nations joined in it to reduce the demand for silver below the supply available for coinage, then each nation was compelled to consider not only its preference as to a standard, but whether—and it was a vital question—it was always sure of having a sufficient quantity of the chosen metal.

The advocates of bimetallism not only contend that the law of supply and demand regulates the value of the dollar—an increase in the demand, the supply remaining the same, raising the purchasing power of the dollar, and an increase in the supply, the demand remaining the same, decreasing the purchasing power of the dollar—but they also believe that supply and demand regulate the market price of the metals.

The contention of monometallists that it is impossible to fix a relation between two metals is met with the reply that the relation between two things of limited production, such as gold and silver, can be fixed by any nation or group of nations which can furnish a use for so much of both metals as is available for coinage. Gold and silver differ from agricultural products in that they must be found before they can be produced. If gold and silver could be raised from seed and cultivated practically without limit, as, for instance, corn and wheat can be, it would be very difficult if not impossible to fix a relation between them, but they are called precious metals because they are scarce.

The demand created by the government must be considered as added to the demand created by the arts. If the demand created by the government is sufficient to utilize the surplus over and above what the arts require, the commercial value can be kept up to the coinage value for the reason that each owner will seek the highest possible price, and so long as the government stands ready to convert a given amount of metal into a given amount of money, he will not have to dispose of the metal to any one else for less than the government price. If the government, instead of standing ready to convert one metal into money, stands ready to convert two metals into money, it can make the commercial ratio and the coinage ratio identical, if there is a use for the money. The changes in relative production would not affect this condition so long as the government was able to utilize all of the surplus of both metals.

The influence exerted by the legal ratio on the commercial ratio is well described by the royal commission of England, which in its report of 1888 said: "Nor does it appear to us a priori unreasonable to suppose that the existence in the Latin union of a bimetallic system with a ratio of 15 1-2 to 1 fixed between the two metals, should have been capable of keeping the market price of silver steady at approximately that rate. The view that it could only affect the market price to the extent to which there was a demand for it for currency purposes in the Latin union, or to which it was actually taken to the mints of those countries is, we think, fallacious. The fact that the owner of silver could, in the last resort, take it to those mints and have it converted into coin which would purchase commodities, at the ratio of 15 1-2 of silver to 1 of gold, would, in our opinion, be likely to affect the price of silver in the market generally, whoever the purchaser and for whatever country it was destined. It would enable the holder of the silver to stand out for a price approximating to the legal ratio and would tend to keep the market steady at about that point."

Independent bimetallists and international bimetallists agree as to the theoretical and practical benefits of the double standard, but differ as to the ability of the United States to maintain the parity alone, the former believing, and the latter denying, that under conditions as they now exist our nation is able to utilize all the silver that could come to our mint.

If our government offered to coin into money at a fixed ratio every ounce of gold and silver presented at the mint, the supply brought to the mint would necessarily come from one of three sources—that is, from silver bullion already in existence, from silver coin of other countries, or from the annual product of the mines.

As there is no considerable quantity of silver held in the form of bullion, there could be no material increase in our coinage from that source.

Whether silver coin would come to our mint from other countries would depend entirely upon the ratio. The fear that, under bimetallism, our country would be flooded with the coined silver of the world, is entirely without foundation, for the reason that our ratio, 16 to 1, is more favorable to gold than the ratio existing between gold and silver in the nations that have a large quantity of silver coin. France, for instance, is the largest European holder of silver, but as her silver now circulates on a parity with gold at a ratio of 15 1-2 to 1, it could only come here at a loss equivalent to about three cents on the dollar.

Whether the mines would furnish an excessive amount of silver is a question about which no one could speak positively, because no one can foresee new discoveries or estimate the possible exhaustion of mines now being worked. There is, however, nothing in the past to justify a fear of overproduction.

Raising the government price of a precious metal does not necessarily increase the production of it, neither does the lowering of the price necessarily reduce the production. For instance, the law of 1834 reduced the government price of gold, and yet soon afterward there was a wonderful increase in the production of gold. The discoveries of silver following 1870 were not brought about by an increase in the price of silver, and for several years the production of silver increased, even with a falling market. The monetary use of gold and silver is the controlling use. If, by agreement among all the nations, the legal tender function was withdrawn from both gold and silver, and other money substituted for them, both would fall in value, just how much no one knows, because a fall in the price of either of the metals would develop new uses and thus increase the demand, which, in its turn, would act with the supply in determining the ultimate price. While it is probable that a higher price for silver bullion would cause the reopening of some mines which have been abandoned because of the low price of silver, the production of silver would not be likely to be increased to any such extent as has been imagined.

It is not out of place to refer in this connection to another matter which has been the subject of much speculation, namely, the cost of producing gold and silver. The labor cost has less influence on the price of gold and silver than upon products of the soil. In the case of agricultural products, an attempt to raise the price of any kind of crop much above the cost of production would immediately be followed by such an increase in the crop as to at once cause a supply that would reduce the price. If, on the other hand, the cost of producing a particular kind of crop is increased out of proportion to the price, the production will fall off until the scarcity of the article raises the price. In the case of the precious metals, however, the supply cannot be increased at will, and therefore the price does not necessarily vary with the cost of production. If, for illustration, all the gold mines were to be exhausted excepting one, and this one mine began producing just the amount that all the mines now produce, but no more, the price of gold would remain the same whether it was produced at $1 an ounce or at 1 cent an ounce.

We have no means of ascertaining the labor cost of either gold or silver. About 10 years ago the director of the mint was asked for statistics in regard to the labor cost of producing gold and silver, and his reply was that there were no statistics in regard to gold and none of any value in regard to silver, because the statistics were gathered from the mines in operation and did not include the money expended in prospecting and in mines that had ceased to produce. No two mines in the world have produced either gold or silver at the same cost for any considerable period. If we take into account the money spent in prospecting and the money spent in the purchase of claims that have proven worthless, as well as the money invested in machinery and other appliances, it is probable that more than $1 has been expended for every dollar of either gold or silver taken out of the earth, and it is also probable that, dollar for dollar, it has cost less to produce gold than silver, first, because gold is ofen found in nuggets, while silver is found in veins, and, second, because gold is often found on the surface, while silver is, as a rule, a deep-mine product.

Space does not permit a history of the conflict between the standards in Europe. England has maintained the gold standard for about a century and has exerted a controlling influence on several other European nations. During this period France, although free coinage is now suspended, has been the most loyal supporter of bimetallism and as late as 1897 offered to join the United States in the restoration of coinage, provided England and Germany would do likewise.

After the gold discoveries of 1849, the European fiananciers became alarmed lest the increased production of the yellow metal would largely aid debtors, and there was quite a sentiment in favor of the demonetization of gold. Writers like Crevalier were complaining that holders of fixed investments were in danger of suffering from a cheap gold dollar. It was exactly the same argument that was made against the white metal a little later when the Comstock lode and other rich deposits of silver were discovered.

Bimetallism in the United States—The bimetallic standard was recommended by Jefferson and Hamilton, and adopted by our government by a statute approved by George Washington April 2, 1792. This law provided for the free and unlimited coinage of silver and gold at the ratio of 15 to 1, the coins being equally a legal tender for all debts, public and private. The Spanish milled dollar then in use in this country contained the same amount of pure silver as our present silver dollar and, the ratio of 15 to 1 having been adopted, the gold dollar was made to weigh one-fifteenth as much. The silver dollars then coined (many of which are now in existence) are sometimes called the "unit dollars," because they have on the edge the following inscription: "Hundred cents, One dollar, or Unit."

In 1834 (June 28) the ratio was changed from 15 to 1 to 15.988 to 1, which for convenience has been called 16 to 1 The change was made for the purpose of checking the exportation of gold, but as the new ratio undervalued silver it made gold the money in general use. This law supported by Thomas H. Benton, and approved by Andrew Jackson, provided for the free and unlimited coinage of gold and silver into full legal tender money at the new ratio. In 1873 (January 28) the alloy in the dollar both gold and silver, was changed from one-twelfth to one-tenth, making the weight of the standard silver dollar 412 1-2 grains, nine-tenths fine, and the weight of the standard gold dollar 25 8-10 grains, nine-tenths fine.

As the law of 1834 undervalued silver and led to the exportation of considerable quantities of it, it became difficult to keep fractional currency in circulation, and to remedy this the law of 1853 was enacted. By the terms of this law subsidiary silver (that is, coins of less denomination than $1), were reduced from full weight to light weight and made token money with limited legal tender, instead of standard money. This law, however, did not change the provision in regard to the standard silver dollar, the free and unlimited coinage of that dollar still continuing. The subsidiary silver coins were redeemable in the standard money, either gold or silver. Sometimes the act of 1834 has been referred to as establishing the gold standard, but this is erroneous. It merely changed the ratio and that, too, by reducing the weight of the dearer dollar, not by increasing the cheaper dollar. Equally erroneous is the assertion that the act of 1853 established the gold standard. That did not in the least change the law relating to the standard money, either gold or silver.

On July 12, 1873, the demonetization of silver was effected by an act entitled "An act revising and amending the laws relative to the mints, assay offices, and coinage of the United States." (A similar law having the same purpose had just before been enacted in England, and a copy of it delivered to the director of our mint.)

When this law was passed the business of the country was being transacted with paper money, both gold and silver being at a premium—silver at a greater premium than gold. No attention was being paid to the subject of metallic money and the purpose of the law of 1873 was not generally understood. In making provision for silver coinage it omitted the coinage of the standard silver dollar, and substituted for it a trade dollar of 420 grains which was intended for use in the Orient, it being thought that the trade dollar would compete with the Mexican dollar in China and other eastern countries. In 1874 (January 20) the federal statutes were revised, and in this revision a clause was inserted limiting the legal tender of silver coins to $5. Neither the act of 1873 nor the act of 1874 was generally discussed, and it is only the recognition of a well settled fact of history to say that this discrimination against silver and in favor of gold was not known among the people and not thoroughly discussed even in congress. When the matter became known an active agitation for the restoration of silver at once began, and nearly all of those who voted for the mesure denied that they knew that the act of 1873 was intended to demonetize silver.

The suspension of silver coinage by the United States alone would not have caused a fall in the price of silver as measured with gold, but other nations joining in the demonetization of silver it soon became apparent that the mints still open could not utilize all the silver available for coinage, and the gold price of silver began to decline. The effort to reopen the mints to silver resulted in the passage of what was known as the Bland-Allison act. The bill, as it passed the house, under the leadership of Richard P. Bland, of Missouri, restored the free and unlimited coinage of gold and silver at the ratio of 16 to 1. The opposition in the senate was sufficient, however, to defeat the bill in its original form, and to compel the acceptance of a substittute framed by Senator Allison, whose name was thus connected with the law. This compromise measure provided that there should be "coined at the several mints of the United States silver dollars of the weight of 412 1-2 grains troy of standard silver as provided by the act of January, 1837," and also provided that such silver dollars "together with all silver dollars heretofore coined by the United States of like weight and fineness" should be "a legal tender at their nominal value for all debts and dues, public and private, except where otherwise expressly stipulated in the contract."

It will be seen that this law restored the coinage of silver dollars under the law of 1837, but did not contain the former provision in regard to the unlimited coinage of silver on private account as gold was then and is now coined. In order to secure the bullion out of which to coin the dollars mentioned in the act of 1878, the law provided "that the secretary of the treasury is authorized and directed to purchase, from time to time, silver bullion, at the market price thereof, not less than $2,000,000 worth per month, nor more than $4,000,000 worth and cause the same to be coined monthly, as fast as so purchased, into such dollars."

In carrying out the provisions of the law, the treasury department purchased the minimum required rather than the maximum permitted.

It will be seen, also, that while the silver dollar was restored to general legal tender, a provision was inserted that permitted the exclusion of the dollar by private contract—that is, private individuals were permitted to discriminate against silver, although they were not permitted to discriminate against gold. The purchase of silver for coinage under this act retarded the fall in the price of silver, but as it did not consume the entire surplus it was not sufficient to restore the price of bullion to the coinage price of $1.29 an ounce.

The Bland-Allison act remained on the statute books until 1890, when it was repealed by what was known as the Sherman purchase act, which provided for the purchase of 4,500,-000 ounces of silver per month, or so much thereof as might be offered at a price not exceeding the coinage value, the bullion to be paid for by the issue of treasury notes, redeemable in coin and after the first of July, 1891, only so much of the silver was to be coined as was necessary to redeem the treasury notes presented.

This act immediately increased the demand for silver and raised the price of silver bullion, not only in the United States, but all over the world, to about $1.21 an ounce. But when it was found that even this demand was not sufficient to utilize all the surplus silver, the price again began to fall.

Secretary Rusk, in the agricultural report of 1890, called attention to the fact that the Sherman purchase law raised the price of silver and declared that that rise in price "unquestionably had much to do with the recent advance in the price of cereals," and added, "The same cause has advanced the price of wheat in Russia and India, and in the same degree reduced their power of competition, English gold was formerly exchanged for cheap silver, and wheat purchased with the cheap silver metal was sold in Great Britain for gold. Much of this advantage is lost by the appreciation of silver in those countries."

The Sherman act was also a compromise, urged by the opponents of silver to prevent the passage of a free coinage law. Mr. Sherman, in his "Recollections," published in 1895, thus speaks of the strength of the free silver movement, and of the purpose of the compromise:

"A large majority of the senate favored free silver, and it was feared that the small majority against it in the other house might yield and agree to it. The silence of the president on the matter gave rise to an apprehension that if a free coinage bill should pass both houses he would not feel at liberty to veto it. Some action had to be taken to prevent a return of free silver coinage, and the measure evolved was the best obtainable. I voted for it, but the day it became a law I was ready to repeal it, if repeal could be had without substituting in its place absolute free coinage."

The treasury notes issued in the purchase of silver were made a legal tender for the payment of all debts, public and private, except where excluded by contract, and were redeemable by the secretary of the treasury in gold or silver coin at his discretion. It will be seen that the option as to the coin of payment was reserved to the government, but another clause in the measure which declared it to be "the established policy of the United States to maintain the two metals on a parity with each other upon the present legal ratio or such ratio as may be provided by the law," was afterward construed by the treasury department to deprive the secretary of the option. At any rate the department adopted the policy of paying in gold when gold was demanded, and although Secretary Carlisle afterward declared before one of the house committees that it would have been better for the government to have reserved the option, he, when he came into office, followed the precedent set by his predecessor.

This ruling of the treasury department was followed by the presentation of treasury notes and a demand for gold, and the drain upon gold which followed was used as an argument in favor of the repeal of the purchase clause of the law. The treasury note was declared to be an endless chain, although it only became an endless chain when the department surrendered the option which the law expressly conferred upon it. It may be added that the same endless chain argument has been made against the greenback, and can be made against the silver dollar if it is ever made specifically redeemable in gold.

What has sometimes been called "the silver movement" began with the discovery of the effect of the law of 1873, and has continued with varying force ever since. It was called the silver movement, not because of partiality to silver, but because silver was the metal discriminated against. It might better be designed as the bimetallic movement, because it was an effort to restore bimetallism, and the supporters of the movement asked for silver nothing more than was already granted to gold. The movement did not originate in the mining states, but extended over the entire country and throughout other countries, the interest being centered in silver as a money rather than in silver as a metal.

During the period that has elapsed since 1873 three international conferences have been held with a view to the restoration of silver (at Paris in 1878 and in 1881, and at Brussels in 1892), but they have been unsuccessful largely because other European countries have hesitated to act without England, and England, being largely a creditor nation, has been unwilling to surrender the advantage which a rising dollar has given her in the increased purchasing power of her credits.

In the summer of 1893, the president, giving as his reason the suspension of the coinage of silver in India, called congress together in extraordinary session and recommended the unconditional repeal of the purchase clause of the Sherman law. Congressman Wilson, chairman of the committee on ways and means, and leader of the administration forces in the house, introduced a bill identical in purpose and almost identical in language with one introduced by Senator Sherman a year before. The object of this bill was to repeal the purchase clause of the Sherman law without substituting any provision for the further coinage of silver. It was supported by all who were opposed to bimetallism, and by some who declared themselves in favor of bimetallism, but criticised the purchase of silver on the ground that it was contrary to the theory of bimetallism. These insisted that as soon as the Sherman law was repealed the remainder of the democratic platform would be carried out and bimetallic coinage re-established. A few were induced to support the measure under the belief that the suspension of silver coinage here would force European nations to an agreement for the restoration of bimetallism throughout the world. After a prolonged contest this bill became a law November 1, 1893. Following this an attempt was made to secure the coinage of the seigniorage which had accumulated in the treasury. This bill passed both houses, receiving the support of many who voted for the repeal of the purchase clause of the Sherman law, but the measure was vetoed by the president. The administration then attempted to secure the passage of a law authorizing the issue of gold bonds, but this was defeated in the house of representatives.

As the act of 1893 virtually opened the campaign of 1896, in which the silver question figured so prominently, it may be well to consider the platforms adopted just before and just after that date.

During the period extending from 1873 to 1896 the platforms of the two leading parties, while more or less ambiguous on the money question, recognized the advantages of the double standard. In 1884 the republican platform declared in favor of an international conference to fix the relative value of gold and silver coin, while the democratic platform declared in favor of "honest money, the gold and silver coinage of the constitution, and a circulation medium convertible into such money without loss." In 1888 the democratic party reaffirmed the platform of 1884, while the republican party inserted the following plank in its platform: "The republican party is in favor of the use of both gold and silver as money, and condemns the policy of the democratic administration in its efforts to demonetize silver."

In 1892 the republican platform said: "The American people from tradition and interest favor bimetalism, and the republican party demands the use of both gold and silver as standard money," and then followed a clause demanding "that the purchasing and debt-paying power of the dollar, whether of silver or gold or paper, shall be equal at all times."

The democratic party that year denounced the Sherman law (the act of 1890) as a cowardly makeshift, and demanded its speedy repeal, and then declared the party's position as follows:

"We hold to the use of both gold and silver as the standard money of the country, and to the coinage of both gold and silver without discrimination against either metal or charge for mintage, but the dollar unit of coinage of both metals must be of equal intrinsic and exchangeable value or be adjusted through international agreement, or by such safeguards of legislation as shall insure the maintenance of the parity of the two metals, and the equal power of every dollar at all times in the markets, and in the payments of debts; and we demand that all paper currency shall be kept at par with, and redeemable in, such coin. We insist upon this policy as especially necessary for the protection of the farmers and laboring classes, the first and most defenseless victims of unstable money and a fluctuating currency."

The populist party, which polled about 1,000,000 votes that year, demanded "the free and unlimited coinage of silver and gold at the present legal ratio of 16 to 1." This was the first national platform which specifically named the ratio, but a majority of the democrats in congress and many republicans had for years been voting for bills providing for free and unlimited coinage at this ratio.

In the campaign of 1896, the money question was the paramount issue. The democratic platform, adopted at Chicago, demanded "the free and unlimited coinage of both silver and gold at the legal ratio of 16 to 1, without waiting for the aid or consent of any other nation." The people's party which met two weeks later, adopted a plank substantially like it, as did also the silver republican party.

The gold democrats, who withdrew from the Chicago convention, met at Indianapolis and declared in favor of the gold standard.

The republican party said: "We are unalterably opposed to every measure calculated to debase our currency or impair the credit of our country. We are therefore opposed to the free coinage of silver except by international agreement with the leading commercial nations of the world, which we pledge ourselves to promote, and until such agreement can be obtained, the existing gold standard must be preserved."

In March, 1896, a resolution was adopted in the English parliament pledging the government to assist in restoring the par of exchange between gold and silver, and this pledge encouraged many in this country to hope for an international agreement.

The campaign of 1896 resulted in the election of the republican ticket by a large majority, but as that party had committed itself to international bimetallism, the verdict at the polls was a victory for the double standard rather than for the single gold standard.

In pursuance of the promise contained in the republican platform, President McKinley, immediately upon taking his seat, sent a commission to Europe to solicit co-operation in the restoration of silver to its former place by the side of gold, but this commission failed to secure any concessions from England and no formal conference was arranged.

In 1900, the democratic party, the people's party, and the silver republican party adhered to the position taken on the money question in 1896, while the republican platform said: "We renew our allegiance to the principle of the gold standard and declare our confidence in the wisdom of the legislation of the 56th congress, by which the parity of our money and the standard of our currency on the gold basis has been secured."

The election of 1900 resulted in an increased electoral and popular majority for the republican ticket, but other questions over-shadowed the money question in this campaign, and the result was again undecisive as to the standards.

The large and unexpected increase in the output of gold in Alaska, the United States, South Africa, and Australia has very considerably increased the supply of money, and to some extent relieved the strain which began with the demonetization of silver in 1873, but with the white metal still furnishing nearly one-half of the world's basic money there is no reason to believe from past or present indications that silver can be dispensed with as a standard money. The gold standard cannot be accepted as a finality in any country until it is accepted as a finality throughout the world, for each nation's supply of metallic money is influenced by the demand created by each other nation. It is probable, therefore, that what is called the money question, will, insofar as it relates to metallic money, increase or decrease in importance in inverse ratio to the supply of money, occupying more attention when a decrease in the volume of money reduces prices and being less considered whenever an increase in the volume of money increases prices.

THE DEMOCRATIC PARTY

Mr. Bryan has written for the Encyclopedia Americana, now being published by the Americana company of New York, an article on the democratic party. This article gives in condensed form the history of the democratic party together with a discussion of some of the more important issues advocated by that organization, and will be reproduced in THE COMMONER by courtesy of the publishers. Papers quoting from this article will please give credit to the Encyclopedia Americana.

THE DEMOCRATIC PARTY.

To Thomas Jefferson belongs the honor of being the founder, and for a third of a century the undisputed leader, of the democratic party. Scarcely had the present constitution been adopted before there appeared a line more or less distinct dividing those who, like Jefferson (q. v.), believed the people fully capable of self-government and trusted them, and those who, like Hamilton (q. v.), thought that the masses needed to be under the control of a strong and centralized government. This fundamental difference of opinion manifested itself in the treatment of every important question, and party organizations were soon perfected.

As Jefferson himself has described the birth of parties in the United States, his opinion can be accepted as authoritative. In a letter written in June, 1823, near the close of his life, to William Johnson, he said:

"At the formation of our government, many had formed their political opinions on European writings and practices, believing the experience of old countries, and especially of England, abusive as it was, to be a safer guide than mere theory. The doctrines of Europe were that men in numerous associations cannot be restrained within the limits of order and justice, but by forces physical and moral, wielded over them by authorities independent of their will. Hence their organization of kings, hereditary nobles, and priests. Still further to constrain the brute force of the people, they deem it necessary to keep them down by hard labor, poverty and ignorance, and to take from them as from bees, so much of their earnings, as that unremitting labor shall be necessary to obtain a sufficient surplus barely to sustain a scanty and miserable life. And these earnings they apply to maintain their privileged orders in splendor and idleness, to fascinate the eyes of the people, and excite in them an humble adoration and submission, as to an order of superior beings. Although few among us had gone all these lengths of opinion, yet many had advanced, some more, some less, on the way. And in the convention which formed our government, they endeavored to draw the cords of power as tight as they could obtain them, to lessen the dependence of the general functionaries on their constituents, to subject to them those of the states, and to weaken their means of maintaining the steady equilibrium which the majority of the convention had deemed salutary for both branches, general and local. To recover, therefore, in practice the powers which the nation had refused and to warp to their own wishes those actually given, was the steady object of the federal party. Ours, on the contrary, was to maintain the will of the majority of the convention and of the people themselves. We believed, with them, that man was a rational animal endowed by nature with rights and with an innate sense of justice; and that he could be restrained from wrong and protected in right, by moderate powers confided to persons of his own choice, and held to their duties by dependence on his own will. We believe that the complicated organiaztion of kings, nobles, and priests, was not the wisest nor best to effect the happiness of associated man; that wisdom and virtue were not hereditary; that the trappings of such a machinery, consumed by their expense, those earnings of industry they were meant to protect, and, by the inequalities they produced, exposed liberty to sufferance. We believe that men, enjoying in ease and security the full fruits of their own industry, enlisted by all their interests on the side of law and order, habituated to think of themselves and to follow their reason as their guide, would be more easily and safely governed, than with minds nourished in error and vitiated and debased, as in Europe, by ignorance, indigence, and oppression. The cherishment of the people then was our principle, the fear and distrust of them, that of the other party. Composed, as we were, of the landed and laboring interests of the country, we could not be less anxious for a government of law and order than were the inhabitants of the cities, the strongholds of federalism. And whether our efforts to save the principles and form of our constitution have not been salutary, let the present republican freedom, order, and prosperity of our country determine."

Jefferson not only gave a history of the formation of parties, but fortunately for later generations, he enumerated the elements which each party contained. In a letter to C. E. Ebeling in 1795 he said:

"Two parties exist within the United States. They embrace respectively the following descriptions of persons. The anti-republicans consist of: (1) the old refugees and tories; (2) British merchants residing among us, and composing the main body of our merchants; (3) American merchants trading on British capital, another great portion; (4) speculators and holders in the banks and public funds; (5) officers of the federal government with some exceptions; (6) office hunters willing to give up principles for places—a numerous and noisy tribe; (7) nervous persons, whose languid fibres have more analogy with a passive than active state of things. The republican party of our Union comprehends: (1) the entire body of landholders throughout the United States; (2) the body of laborers not being landholders whether in husbanding or the arts. The latter is to the aggregate of the former party probably as 500 to 1; but their wealth is not as disproportionate, though it is also greatly superior and is in truth the foundation of that of their antagonists. Trifling as are the numbers of the anti-republican party, there are circumstances which give them an appearance of strength and numbers. They all live in cities together and can act in a body and readily at all times; they give chief employment to the newspapers, and, therefore, have most of them under their command. The agricultural interest is dispersed over a great extent of country, have little means of intercommunication with each other, and feeling their own strength and will, are conscious that a single exertion of these will at any time crush the machinations against their government."

Jefferson's philosophical mind sought not only the facts, but the reason for the facts, and in 1824, in a letter to H. Lee, he thus classified men according to their party tendencies:

"Men by their constitutions are naturally divided into two parties: (1) those who fear and distrust the people and wish to draw all powers from them into the hands of the higher classes; (2) those who identify themselves with the people, have confidence in them, cherish and consider them as the most wide depository of the public interests. In every country these two parties exist, and in every one where they are free to think, speak, and write, they will declare themselves. Call them, therefore, liberals and serviles. Jacobins and ultras, whigs and tories, republicans and federalists, aristocrats, and democrats, or by whatever name you please, they are the same parties still, and pursue the same object. The last appellation of aristocrats and democrats is the true one expressing the essence of all."

Jefferson's purpose was to found a party that would be really democratic in personnel, in purpose and in method. The party, however, was at first called the republican party, and afterward the democratic-republican party. It was not until in Jackson's time that it became universally known by its present name. As there were no natinoal conventions and no national platforms in the early days of the republic the position of the party on public questions must be gathered from the words and speeches of the leaders and from the votes of the members of the party in congress. Jefferson's first inaugural address contained the essence of the party creed as generally accepted during the first quarter of the 19th century. In fact, it is still the creed of the party, and no group of men desiring to maintain an influence in the party can even now admit any essential departure from it. It will be found below:

"About to enter, fellow-citizens, on the exercise of duties which comprehend everything dear and valuable to you, it is proper you should understand what I deem the essential principles of our government, and consequently those which ought to shape its administration. I will compress them within the narrowest compass they will bear, stating the general principle, but not all its limitations. Equal and exact justice to all men, of whatever state or persuasion, religious or political; peace, commerce, and honest friendship with all nations, entangling alliance with none; the support of the state governments in all their rights, as the most competent administrations for our domestic concerns and the surest bulwarks against anti-republican tendencies; the preservation of the general government in its whole constitutional vigor, as the sheet anchor of our peace at home and safety abroad; a jealous care of the right of election by the people—a mild and safe corrective of abuses which are lopped by the sword of revolution where peaceable remedies are unprovided; absolute acquiescence in the decisions of the majority and vital principle of republics, from which is no appeal but to force, the vital principle and immediate parent of despotism; a well-disciplined militia, our best reliance in peace and for the first moments of war, till regulars may relieve them; the supremacy of the civil over the military authority; economy in the public expense that labor may be lightly burdened; the honest payment of our debts and sacred preservation of the public faith; encouragement of agriculture, and of commerce as its handmaid; the diffusion of information and arraignment of all abuses at the bar of the public reason; freedom of religion, freedom of the press, and freedom of person under the protection of the habeas corpus, and trial by juries impartially selected. These principles form the bright constellation which has gone before us and guided our steps through an age of revolution and reformation. The wisdom of our sages and blood of our heroes have been devoted to their attainment. They should be the creed of our political faith, the text of civic instruction, the touchstone by which to try the services of those we trust; and should we wander from them in moments of error or of alarm, let us hasten to retrace our steps and to regain the road which alone leads to peace, liberty, and safety."

The first and most fundamental difference between the democratic party (when it was known as the republican party, afterward as the democratic-republican party, and today as the democratic party), and the party which has opposed it (first known as the federal party, then as the whig party and more recently as the republican party), was upon the construction of the constitution. The former party has insisted upon a strict construction, while the latter has leaned toward a liberal construction of the federal constitution. This difference is a natural one for the democratic party, believing in the right of the people to, and in the capacity of the people for, self-government, has insisted upon giving them as large a part as possible in the control of their own affairs.

It follows, therefore, that the democratic party favors local self-government and opposes the centralization of power in remote centers. It believes that the nearer the people are to their government the more effective will be their control over it. The various parties that have opposed the democratic party have given more or less emphasis to the Hamiltonian view and have increased the power of the representative at the expense of the constituents.

While the distinction has not at all times been clearly marked, and while these views have not been held by all the individual members, the general tendency has existed.

In the very beginning this tendency was illustrated in the alien and sedition laws, enacted by the federalists and in the Kentucky and Virginia resolutions supported by the democrats. Both parties in this instance went to the extreme, the federalists attempting to confer dangerous power upon the federal government, the democrats asserting views which were afterward so misconstrued as to weaken the federal union. The preservation of the balance between the federal government and the state governments has always been a delicate matter, and as the line cannot be drawn with mathematical accuracy there has always been room for dispute; the public sentiment having gone to the one side or the other as it was necessary to maintain the equilibrium. It is likely that this discussion will continue, but the efforts to carry the government to an extreme in either direction will be thwarted by the conservative middle class, which rallies to the support of the side that is attacked.

Beginning with Jefferson's administration in 1801, and continuing to the end of Monroe's administration in 1825, the democratic party held undisputed sway in the nation. Jefferson, like Washington, refused to consider a third term, and his secretary of state, James Madison (q. v.), succeeded him. Madison, following the example set by his predecessor, retired at the end of his second term, and James Monroe (q. v.), who had been his secretary of state, succeeded him.

The war of 1812 was conducted by the Madison administration, and it was during this period that the Hartford resolutions were adopted by a convention of federalists which met at Hartford, Conn., in December, 1814. These resolutions went further in the direction of states rights than either the Kentucky resolutions or the Virginia resolutions. They began by recommending "to the legislatures of the several states represented in this convention, to adopt all such measures as may be necessary effectually to protect the citizens of said state from the operation and effects of all acts which have been or may be passed by the congress of the United States, which shall contain provisions subjecting the militia or other citizens to forcible drafts, conscriptions, or impressments not authorized by the constitution of the United States."

While the Hartford resolutions announced a political policy, they had their origin in the commercial interests which were affected by the war of 1812, and by the embargo act which was enacted as a war measure.

The federalist party which supported Clinton's candidacy in 1812 laid great stress upon the commercial interests. The platform adopted by the New York federalists urged the election of Clinton as the surest method of guaranteeing the protection of those commercial interests which were flagging "under the weakness and imbecility of the administration." The federalists attacked what they called the Virginia regency, and the Hartford resolutions recommended a constitutional amendment making the president ineligible for renomination, and another prohibiting the selection of two presidents in succession from the same state.

It was during the administration of James Monroe that the doctrine, afterward known by his name, and followed ever since, was promulgated. The doctrine was set forth in a message sent to congress by James Monroe on December 2, 1823. The following is the text covering this subject:

"In the wars of European powers, in matters relating to themselves, we have never taken any part, nor does it comport with our policy so to do. It is only when our rights are invaded or seriously menaced that we resent injuries or make preparations for our defense. With the movements on this hemisphere we are, of necessity, more immediately connected, and by causes which must be obvious to all enlightened and impartial observers. The political system of the allied powers (the holy alliance) is essentially different in this respect from that of America. This difference proceeds from that which exists in their respective governments. And to the defense of our own, which has been achieved by the loss of so much blood and treasure, and matured by the wisdom of their most enlightened citizens, and under which we have enjoyed unexampled felicity, this whole nation is devoted. We owe it, therefore, to candor and to the amicable relations existing between the United States and those powers to declare that we should consider any attempt on their part to extend their system to any portion of this hemisphere as dangerous to our peace and safety. With the existing colonies or dependencies of any European power we have not interfered, and shall not interfere. But with the governments who have declared their independence and maintained it we have on great consideration and on just principles, acknowledged we could not view any interposition for the purpose of oppressing them, or controlling in any other manner their destiny, by any European power, in any other light than as the manifestation of an unfriendly disposition toward the United States. Our policy in regard to Europe, which was adopted at an early stage of the wars which have so long agitated that quarter of the globe, nevertheless remains the same, which is not to interfere in the internal concerns of any of its powers; to consider the government de facto as the legitimate government for us; to cultivate friendly relations with it, and to preserve those relations by a frank, firm, and manly policy; meeting in all instances the just claims of every power, submitting to injuries from none. But in regard to these continents, circumstances are eminently and conspicuously different. It is impossible that the allied powers should extend their political system to any portion of either continent without endangering our peace and happiness; nor can any one believe that our southern brethren, if left to themselves, would adopt it of their own accord. It is equally impossible, therefore, that we should behold such interposition, in any form, with indifference."

This message was written after consultation with Jefferson, who was then living in retirement at Monticello. The following extract from a letter written by Jefferson to Monroe in October, 1823, not only shows Jefferson's part in the formulation of the doctrine, but also proves his foresight and his comprehension of American interests, and his devotion to the welfare of his country.

"The question presented by the letters you have sent me, is the most momentous which has been offered to my contemplation since that of independence. That made us a nation, this sets our compass and points the course which we are to steer through the ocean of time opening on us. And never could we embark on it under circumstances more auspicious. Our first and fundamental maxim should be, never to entangle ourselves in the broils of Europe. Our second, never to suffer Europe to intermeddle with cis-Atlantic affairs. America, North and South, has a set of interests distinct from those of Europe and peculiarly her own. She should, therefore, have a system of her own, separate and apart from that of Europe. While the last is laboring to become the domicile of depotism, our endeavor should surely be to make our hemisphere that of freedom. One nation most of all, could disturb us in this pursuit; she now offers to lead, aid, and accompany us in it. By acceding to her proposition, we detach her from the bands, bring her mighty weight into the scale of free government, and emancipate a continent at one stroke, which might otherwise linger long in doubt and difficulty. Great Britain is the nation which can do us the most harm of any one, or all on earth; and with her on our side we need not fear the whole world. With her, then, we should most sedulously cherish a cordial friendship; and nothing would tend more to knit our affections than to be fighting once more side by side in the same cause. Not that I would purchase even her amity at the price of taking part in her wars. But the war in which the present proposition might engage us, should that be its consequence, is not her war, but ours. Its object is to introduce and establish the American system, of keeping out of our land all foreign powers, of never permitting those of Europe to intermeddle with the affairs of our nations. It is to maintain our own principle not to depart with it. And if to facilitate this, we can effect a division in the body of the European powers, and draw over to our side its most powerful member, surely we should do it. But I am clearly of Mr. Canning's opinion, that it will prevent instead of provoke war. With Great Britain withdrawn from their scale and shifted into that of our two continents, all Europe combined would not undertake such a war. For how would they propose to get at either enemy without superior fleets? Nor is the occasion to be slighted which this proposition offers, of declaring our protest against the atrocious violations of the rights of nations by the interference of any one in the internal affairs of another, so flagitiously begun by Bonaparte, and now continued by the equally lawless alliance calling itself holy. But we have first to ask ourselves a question. Do we wish to acquire to our own confederacy any one or more of the Spanish provinces? I candidly confess that I have ever looked on Cuba as the most interesting addition which could ever be made to our system of states. The control which, with Florida Point, this island would give us over the Gulf of Mexico, and the countries and isthmus bordering on it as well as all those whose waters flow into it, would fill up the measure of our political well-being. Yet, as I am sensible, that this can never be obtained, even with her own consent, but by war; and its independence, which is our second interest (and especially its independence of England), can be secured without it. I have no hesitation in abandoning my first wish to future chances and accepting its independence, with peace and the friendship of England, rather than its association, at the expense of war and her enmity. I could honestly, therefore, join in the declaration proposed, that we aim not at the acquisition of any of those possessions, that we will not stand in the way of any amicable arrangement between them and the mother country; but that we will oppose, with all our means, the forcible interposition of any other power, as auxiliary, stipendiary, or under any other form or pretext, and most especially, their transfer to any power by conquest, cession, or acquisition in any other way."

Jefferson died on July 4, 1824, just fifty years after the signing of the Declaration of Independence. The year that marked his demise marked the entrance of the second great democratic leader into the arena of politics.

Andrew Jackson (q. v.) of Tennessee, the hero of the war of 1812, had grown in fame and popularity from the day of his victory over the English at New Orleans. In 1824 he became the nominee of his party, and in the election following received 155,872 votes, as against 105,321 cast for John Quincy Adams; 44,282 cast for Crawford; and 46,587 cast for Henry Clay. In the electoral college, Jackson received 99 votes, Adams 84, Crawford 41, and Clay 37. As no one of the candidates had a majority of the electoral college the election of the president devolved upon the house of representatives; and by a coalition between the friends of Adams and the friends of Clay, the former received the votes of 13 states, while Jackson received but 7 and Crawford 4.

The defeat of Jackson after he had secured a large plurality of the popular vote, and a considerable plurality in the electoral college, aroused great partisan feeling, and from that time until 1828, Jackson was the candidate of the party, his campaign growing in strength as the years proceeded until when election day arrived he had a popular majority of nearly 140,000, and a majority of nearly 100 in the electoral college. Calhoun was chosen vice president at the same time.

The chief features of Jackson's administration were his treatment of the nullification act of the South Carolina legislature, and his veto of the act for the rechartering of the United States bank. He took vigorous steps to enforce the federal authority and, in an elaborate message presented the arguments against the right of secession with a force and clearness never since surpassed. His action in this matter resulted in the alienation of John C. Calhoun, who up to that time had been a staunch political friend.

The fight over the bank charter not only occupied a large part of the time of his administration, but resulted in a controversy that permeated other issues. The senate passed a resolution censuring him for removing the deposits from the bank, and this became an issue. Under the leadership of Thomas H. Benton, of Missouri, the democrats began a fight for the reversal of the action of the senate, and finally secured a majority of that body and expunged the resolution.

While Jackson's military achievements were the foundation for his early popularity, his great political fame was due to championing the cause of the masses, as against the concentrated power of wealth. In his message vetoing the bank charter he presented with emphasis and accuracy the democratic view of the sphere of government. He said:

"Distinctions in society will always exist under every just government. Equality of talents, of education, or of wealth, cannot be produced by human institutions. In the full enjoyment of the gifts of heaven and the fruits of superior industry, economy, and virtue every man is equally entitled to protection by law. But when the laws undertake to add to those natural and just advantages artificial distinctions—to grant titles, gratuities, and exclusive privileges—to make the rich richer and the potent more powerful—the humble members of society—the farmers, mechanics, and the laborers—who have neither the time nor the means of securing like favors for themselves, have a right to complain of the injustice of their government."

Jackson's position on the bank charter represented the views of his party adherents. His veto was sent to congress on July 10, 1831, and it was the main issue of the campaign of 1832, when with Henry Clay as his opponent he secured a popular plurality of 157,000. In the electoral college he had 219 votes as against 49 cast for Clay. His secretary of state, Martin Van Buren, succeeded him as the democratic candidate, and was elected, having both a popular majority and a majority in the electoral college. Van Buren defeated William Henry Harrison in that year, and was defeated by him in the following campaign. In the earlier campaigns the nominations were made by a congressional caucus, or by the various states, but Jackson's renomination in 1832 was made by a national convention held at Baltimore and Van Buren was nominated by a convention held at the same place four years later.

In 1840 the democratic convention was again held at Baltimore, Van Buren was renominated and a lengthy platform was adopted. As this platform was the basis of all platforms adopted from that time to the breaking out of the civil war it is worthy of reproduction. It was as follows:

"1. Resolved, That the federal government is one of limited powers, derived solely from the constitution, and the grants of powers shown therein ought to be strictly construed by all the departments and agents of the government, and that it is inexpedient and dangerous to exercise doubtful constitutional powers.

"2. Resolved, That the constitution does not confer upon the general government the power to commence and carry on a general system of internal improvements.

"3. Resolved, That the constitution does not confer authority upon the federal government directly or indirectly, to assume the debts of the several states, contracted for local internal improvements or other state purposes; nor would such assumption be just or expedient.

"4. Resolved, That justice and sound policy forbid the federal government to foster one branch of industry to the detriment of another, or to cherish the interests of one portion to the injury of another portion of our common country —that every citizen and every section of the country has a right to demand and insist upon an equality of rights and privileges, and to complete and ample protection of persons and property from domestic violence or foreign aggression.

"5. Resolved, That it is the duty of every branch of the government to enforce and practice the most rigid economy in conducting our public affairs, and that no more revenue ought to be raised than is required to defray the necessary expenses of the government.

"6. Resolved, That congress has no power to charter a United States bank; that we believe such an institution one of deadly hostility to the best interests of the country, dangerous to our republican institutions, and the liberties of the people, and calculated to place the business of the country within the control of a concentrated money power and above the laws and the will of the people.

"7. Resolved, That the congress has no power under the constitution to interfere with or control the domestic institutions of the several states; and that such states are the sole and proper judges of everything pertaining to their own affairs, not prohibited by the constitution; that all efforts by abolitionists or others, made to induce congress to interfere with questions of slavery or to take incipient steps in relation thereto, are calculated to lead to the most alarming and dangerous consequences, and that all such efforts have an inevitable tendency to diminish the happiness of the people, and endanger the stability and permanence of the Union, and ought not to be countenanced by any friend to our political institutions."

As the names of several different persons had been presented for vice president the convention of 1840 made no nominations for that office, but advocated resolutions leaving the decision to members of the party in the various states, and trusting that "before the election took place the opinion would be so concentrated as to enable the electoral college to secure the choice of a vice president."

Upon the death of Harrison, John Tyler became president, and during his term vetoed two bills, which had for their object the re-establishing of the United States bank. Tyler favored the annexation of Texas, which had separated from Mexico and had existed under an independent government since 1836. Jas. K. Polk, the democratic candidate, also favored annexation, while Henry Clay, for a third time a candidate for the presidency, opposed annexation.

In the platform of 1844 the first nine resolutions of the platform of 1840 were reaffirmed, and new resolutions added demanding, first, that the proceeds of public lands be sacredly applied to the national object specified in the constitution, rather than distributed among the states; second, sustaining and defending the veto of the president which had "thrice saved the Americans from the corrupt and tyrannical domination of the banks of the United States," and, third, declaring for the annexation of Texas. The campaign resulted in the election of Polk and Dallas, although the majority of the electoral college was proportionately larger than the popular majority.

The campaign of 1848 was waged with Lewis Cass of Michigan and William O. Butler of Kentucky as the democratic candidates for president and vice president. The platform of 1848 reaffirmed that of 1840 and 1844, and added new planks covering new questions. Resolution No. 19 of the platform of 1848 is given below because it reiterates the democratic contention in regard to the value of self-government. It reads:

"Resolved, That in view of the recent development of this grand political truth, of the sovereignty of the people and their capacity and power for self-government, which is prostrating thrones and erecting republics on the ruins of despotism in the old World, we feel that a high and sacred duty is devolved, with increased responsibility, upon the democratic party of this country, as the party of constitutional liberty equality, and fraternity, by continuing to resist all monopolies and exclusive legislation for the benefit of the few at the expense of the many, and by a vigilant and constant adherence to those principles and compromises of the constitution, which are broad enough and strong enough to embrace and uphold the Union as it was, the Union as it is, and the Union as it shall be, in the full expansion of the energies and capacity of this great and progressive people."

The whig candidates, however, Zachary Taylor and Millard Fillmore, were successful that year, having both a popular majority and a majority in the electoral college. In the campaign of 1852, Franklin Pierce of New Hampshire, and William R. King of Alabama were the democratic nominees, and the platform reiterated the leading planks of 1840, 1844 and 1848.

The platform of 1852 also reiterated the principles laid down in the Kentucky and Virginia resolutions, and defended the Mexican war "as just and necessary." The campaign of 1852 resulted in an overwhelming democratic victory, the popular plurality being more than 200,000.

The slavery question was constantly growing in prominence, and at last exerted an influence upon every issue that arose. The position taken by the various parties in regard to the Mexican war was largely determined by the slavery views held by the members of the parties.

The fugitive slave laws of the various states also came up for consideration, and each election showed an increase in the anti-slavery sentiment. In 1856 the democratic platform again reaffirmed the principles set forth in 1840, and reiterated in subsequent campaigns. It quoted resolution 7 of the platform of 1840, and said:

"That the foregoing proposition covers, and was intended to embrace, the whole subject of slavery agitation in congress; and therefore the democratic party of the Union, standing on this national platform, will abide by, and adhere to, a faithful execution of the acts known as the compromise measures settled by the congress of 1850; That 'the act for reclaiming fugitives from service labor' included; which act, being designed to carry an express provision of the constitution, cannot with fidelity thereto, be repealed, or so changed as to destroy or impair its efficiency; that the democratic party will resist all attempts at renewing in congress, or out of it, the agitation of the slavery question, under whatever shape or color the attempt may be made."

The republican party took the name by which the democratic party was originally known, and it held its first national convention in 1856, John C. Fremont and William L. Dayton being the nominees. James Buchanan and John C. Breckinridge were the democratic nominees. They received a majority of 60 in the electoral college and a popular plurality of over 500,000. The American party led by Millard Fillmore and Andrew J. Donelson, secured only 8 electors, but polled 874,000 votes. During the Buchanan administration the Dred Scott decision was rendered, and this, while it was a legal victory for the friends of slavery, resulted in an anti-slavery agitation that inured to the advantage of the republican party.

In 1860 the conflict between the northern and southern democrats became irreconcilable, and the Charlestown convention, which met April 23, having failed to harmonize the differences, adjourned without a nomination. The northern democrats met at Baltimore June 18, and nominated Stephen A. Douglas of Illinois for president and Herschel V. Johnson of Georgia for vice president, while the southern wing of the party met at the same place ten days later, and nominated John C. Breckinridge of Kentucky for president and Joseph Lane of Oregon for vice president. As the platforms adopted at that time represented the positions taken by the **two wings of the party they will be found below:**

"1. Resolved, That we, the democracy of the Union, in convention assembled, hereby declare our affirmance of the resolutions unanimously adopted and declared as a platform of principles by the democratic convention at Cincinnati, in the year 1856, believing that democratic principles are unchangeable in their nature when applied to the same subject matters; and we recommend, as the only further resolutions, the following:

"Inasmuch as differences of opinion exist in the democratic party as to the nature and extent of the powers of a territorial legislature, and as to the powers and duties of congress, under the constitution of the United States, over the institution of slavery within the territories.

"2. Resolved, that the democratic party will abide by the decisions of the supreme court of the United States on the question of constitutional law.

"3. Resolved, That it is the duty of the United States to afford ample and complete protection to all its citizens, whether at home or abroad, and whether native or foreign.

"4. Resolved, That one of the necessities of the age, in a military, commercial, and postal point of view, is speedy communication between the Atlantic and Pacific states; and the democratic party pledge such constitutional government aid as will insure the construction of a railroad to the Pacific coast at the earliest practicable period.

"5. Resolved, That the democratic party are in favor of the acquisition of the island of Cuba, on such terms as shall be honorable to ourselves and just to Spain.

"6. Resolved, That the enactments of state legislatures to defeat the faithful execution of the fugitive slave law are hostile in character, subversive of the constitution, and revolutionary in their effect.

"7. Resolved, That it is in accordance with the true interpretation of the Cincinnati platform that, during the existence of the territorial governments, the measure of restriction, whatever it may be, imposed by the federal constitution, on the power of the territorial legislature over the subject of domestic relations, as the same has been or shall hereafter be finally determined by the supreme court of the United States shall be respected by all good citizens, and enforced with promptness and fidelity by every branch of the general government."

The "Breckinridge platform" was as follows:

"Resolved, That the platform adopted by the democratic party at Cincinnati be affirmed, with the following explanatory resolutions:

"1. That the government of a territory, organized by an act of congress is provisional, and temporary; and, during its existence all citizens of the United States have an equal right to settle, with their property in the territory, without their rights, either of person or property, being destroyed or impaired by congressional or territorial legislation.

"2. That it is the duty of the federal government, in all its departments, to protect when necessary, the rights of persons and property in the territories, and wherever else its constitutional authority extends.

"3. That when the settlers in a territory having an adequate population, form a state constitution in pursuance of law, the right of sovereignty commences, and, being consummated by admission into the Union, they stand on an equal footing with the people of other states and the state thus organized ought to be admitted into the federal Union, whether its constitution prohibits or recognizes the institution of slavery.

"4. That the democratic party are in favor of the acquisition of the island of Cuba, on such terms as shall be honorable to ourselves, and just to Spain, at the earliest practicable moment.

"5. That the enactments of state legislatures to defeat the faithful execution of the fugitive slave law are hostile in character, subversive of the constitution and revolutionary in their effect.

"6. That the democracy of the United States recognize it as the imperative duty of this government to protect the naturalized citizens in all their rights, whether at home or in foreign lands, to the same extent as its native-born citizens.

"Whereas, One of the greatest necessities of the age, in a political, commercial, postal, and military point of view, is a speedy communication between the Pacific and Atlantic coasts; therefore, be it

"Resolved, That the democratic party do hereby pledge themselves to use every means in their power to secure the passage of some bill to the extent of the constitutional authority of congress, for the construction of a Pacific railroad, from the Mississippi river to the Pacific ocean at the earliest practicable moment."

It will be seen that both conventions reaffirmed the Cincinnati platorm of 1856. It will also be noticed that the only difference between the platforms grew out of the slavery question, the Douglas platform leaving the question to the supreme court, promising to abide by its decision; the Breckinridge platform declaring that the people of a territory had the right to decide the slavery question for themselves and also declaring that the citizens of the various states had the right to settle in a territory and carry their property with them (meaning slaves) without being interferred with by congressional action.

The election of 1860 resulted in a victory for the republican party, whose candidates, Abraham Lincoln and Hannibal Hamlin, ran upon a platform denouncing "threats of disunion," and saying that 'the new dogma, that the constitution, of its own force, carries slavery into any or all of the territories, of the United States," was a "dangerous political heresy." The platform did not call for the abolition of slavery in the states where it existed, but asserted "that the normal condition of all the territory of the United States is that of freedom; that as our republican fathers, when they had abolished slavery in all our national territory, ordained that 'no person shall be deprived of life, liberty or property, without due process of law.' it becomes our duty by legislation, whenever such legislation is necessary, to maintain this provision of the constitution against all attempts to violate it; and we deny the authority of congress, of a territorial legislature, or any individuals, to give legal existence to slavery in any territory of the United States."

Lincoln received a popular plurality of over 500,000, and a plurality of 108 in the electoral college. Douglas came second in the popular vote, but fell behind both the Breckinridge ticket and Bell and Everett ticket in the electoral college. This was due to the fact that the Douglas vote was largely in the states which Lincoln carried.

In the war between the states the supporters of Douglas enlisted side by side with the supporters of Lincoln, Douglas himself having urged the support of Lincoln in the war for the maintenance of the Union. During the war, however, many thing were done which aroused criticism from the democratic leaders and by the democrats generally. Among the things complained of were arrests and court-martial in states not in insurrection, and where the civil authority was undisturbed.

The democratic platform of 1864 announced "unswerving fidelity to the Union under the constitution, as the only solid foundation of our strength, security and happiness as a people, and as a framework of government equally conducive to the welfare and prosperity of all the states, both northern and southern"; and then declared:

"As the sense of the American people, that after four years of failure to restore the Union by the experiment of war, during which, under the pretense of a military necessity of a war power higher than the constitution, the constitution itself has been disregarded in every part and public liberty and private right alike trodden down, and the material prosperity of the country essentially impaired, justice, humanity, liberty, and the public welfare demand that immediate efforts be made for a cessation of hostilities, with a view to an ultimate convention of all the states or other peaceable means, to the end that, at the earliest practicable moment, peace may be restored on the basis of the federal union of all the states."

Gen. George B. McClellan of New Jersey was nominated by the democratic party for president and George H. Pendleton of Ohio for vice president. The election resulted in a popular majority of 408,000 for the republican ticket, and in an electoral majority of 191—Kentucky, New Jersey and Delaware being the only three of the 24 states giving their electoral vote to the democratic ticket. It will be seen that the republican plurality was less than it was in 1860.

The assassination of Abraham Lincoln and the inauguration of Vice President Andrew Johnson (q. v.) as president precipitated a struggle in which most of the republican senators and members of congress were arrayed against the president. The democrats took the side of the president, and with the aid of a few republicans prevented the adoption of the articles of impeachment presented by the house.

During the reconstruction period that followed, the democrats insisted that the states which were held in the Union should be given the rights and privileges of other states.

The campaign of 1868 was fought under the leadership of Horatio Seymour of New York and Francis P. Blair of Missouri, and the platform demanded:

"1. Immediate restoration of all the states to their rights in the Union under the constitution, and of civil government to the American people.

"2. Amnesty for all past political offenses, and the regulation of the elective franchise in the states by their citizens.

"3. Payment of all the public debt of the United States as rapidly as practicable—all money drawn from the people by taxation, except so much as is requisite for the necessities of the government, economically administered, being honestly applied to such payment; and when the obligations of the government do not expressly state upon their face, or the law under which they were issued does not provide that they shall be paid in coin, they ought, in right and justice, to be paid in the lawful money of the United States.

"4. Equal taxation of every species of property according to its real value, including government bonds and other public securities.

"5. One currency for the government and the people, the laborer and the office-holder, the pensioner, and the soldier, the producer and the bondholder.

"6. Economy in the administration of the government; the reduction of the standing army and navy; the abolition of the freedman's bureau and all political instrumentalities designed to secure negro supremacy; simplification of the system and discontinuance of inquisitorial modes of assessing and collecting internal revenue; that the burden of taxation may be equalized and lessened, and the credit of the government and the currency made good; the repeal of all enactments for enrolling the state militia into national forces in times of peace; and a tariff for revenue upon foreign imports, and such equal taxation under the internal-revenue laws as will afford incidental protection to domestic manufacturers, and as will, without impairing the revenue, impose the least burden upon and best promote and encourage the great industrial interests of the country.

"7. Reform of abuses in the administration; the expulsion of corrupt men from office; the abrogation of useless offices; and the restoration of rightful authority to, and the independence of, the executive and judicial departments of the government; the subordination of the military to the civil power, to the end that usurpations of congress and the despotism of the sword may cease.

"8. Equal rights and protection for naturalized and native-born citizens, at home and abroad; the assertion of American nationality which shall command the respect of foreign powers, and furnish an example and encouragement to people struggling for national integrity, constitutional liberty, and individual rights; and the maintenance of the rights of naturalized citizens against the absolute doctrine of immutable allegiance and the claims of foreign powers to punish them for alleged crimes committed beyond their jurisdiction."

Besides this statement of the position of the parties, the platform arraigned the republican party for its reconstruction policy, charging that instead of restoring the Union it had so far as was in its power dissolved it and subjected ten states in time of profound peace to military despotism and negro supremacy, and that it had "nullified the right of trial by jury, abolished the right of habeas corpus and overthrown the freedom of speech and press." The republicans nominated General Grant and Schuyler Colfax, and secured a popular plurality of about 300,000 (less than the plurality of 1864), and an electoral majority of 134.

In May 1872, a convention known as the liberal republican convention was held at Cincinnati, O., and nominated Horace Greeley of New York for president and Benjamin Gratz Brown of Missouri for vice president. The platform demanded the recognition of the doctrines of equality of all men before the law, and pledged the party's support of articles 13, 14 and 15 of our amended national constitution. It favored the sacred maintenance of the public credit, opposed repudiation and insisted upon the return to specie payments.

The democrats met on July 9 at Baltimore and nominated the same ticket and adopted a platform substantially like the one adopted by the liberal republicans.

Those members of the democratic party describing themselves as "straight-out" democrats met September 3, following and nominated Charles O'Connor of New York president and John Quincy Adams of Massachusetts for vice president; although both declined, nearly 30,000 votes were cast for the head of the ticket. The platform declared that the Baltimore convention had betrayed the party into a false creed and false leadership, and proclaimed that the members of the "straight-out" democratic party preferred principle to power, and would not surrender those principles in exchange for offices which presidents confer. The election resulted in an overwhelming victory for the republican ticket, Grant and Wilson receiving 286 electoral votes out of 317, and a popular plurality of more than 750,000.

The nomination of Horace Greeley brought to his party a large number of influential republicans and alienatd many democrats, yet the party's vote was only about 125,000 more than the democratic vote of 1868; while the republican vote of 1872 was nearly 600,000 greater than the vote of four years before.

The democrats entered the campaign of 1876 with courage and confidence. The discovery of corruption in several of the departments, and the conviction of officials high in authority, together with the panic of 1873, had broken the prestige of the republican party and caused a wide-spread demand for reform. The democratic party took advantage of the situation, and nominated as its candidates Samuel J. Tilden of New York, who had become conspicuous in reform in his state, and Thomas A. Hendricks of Indiana, who represented all that was highest, purest and best in democratic principle and purpose. The platform described the abuses of power and demanded reform in every department. Among other things, it demanded reform in the tariff, and condemned the resumption clause of 1875.

The campaign resulted in a popular plurality of 250,000 for Tilden and Hendricks. The result, however, was disputed, and charges of fraud were made in the election of several states. The situation grew so serious that congress created an electoral commission to which the whole matter was referred. This commission was composed of five senators selected by that body, five members of congress selected by that body, and the five senior members of the supreme court.

The senate being republican selected 3 republicans and 2 democrats; the house being democratic selected 3 democrats and 2 republicans, and of the judges 3 were republicans and 2 democrats. The electoral commission thus contained 8 republicans and 7 democrats, and on every contested question the vote stood 8 to 7, each member so casting his vote that it would aid his party.

The democrats of 1880 indorsed the principles embodied in the platform of 1876, protested against centralization as dangerous to the government, and denounced the "great fraud of 1876 and 1877 by which upon a false count of the electoral votes of two states the candidate defeated at the polls was declared to be president, and for the first time in

American history the will of the people was set aside under a threat of military violence." The righting of the wrong of 1876 was declared to be the paramount issue. Gen. Winfield Scott Hancock, the democratic nominee, weakened his campaign by putting the tariff question aside as "a local issue." He was defeated, however, by a popular vote of less than 10,000, and only by 59 votes in the electoral college.

In 1884 the democrats met at Chicago and nominated Grover Cleveland of New York for president and Thomas A. Hendricks of Indiana for vice president. A platform of great length was adopted; the tariff question being the one discussed at most length. The platform contained the following plank on the money question: "We believe in honest money, the gold and silver coinage of the constitution, and a circulating medium convertible into such money without loss." This platform also contained a plank reaffirming that portion of the democratic platform of 1856, which indorsed the liberal principles of Jefferson.

The republican ticket, headed by James G. Blaine and John A. Logan, received a plurality of a little more than 20,000 in the popular vote, but Mr. Cleveland had 37 majority in the electoral college.

The democratic platform of 1888 reaffirmed the platform adopted in 1884, and indorsed the president's view on the tariff question as expressed in the tariff message which he sent to congress in December, 1887. The tariff question was made the paramount issue, and the campaign waged on this question, and resulted in the election of the republican ticket, and its candidates, Benjamin Harrison and Levi P. Morton, that ticket having a majority of 65 in the electoral college, although the democratic ticket had a popular plurality of about 100,000.

During the Cleveland administration an attempt was made to reduce the tariff and the Mills bill received the support of the democratic members of the senate and house. The republicans, however, took advantage of the republican victory of 1888 to propose and enact a high tariff law, known as the McKinley act, taking its name from the chairman of the ways and means committee of the house. The passage of this law was followed by an increase in prices of commodities, and it became the paramount issue in the following campaign of 1892. The democratic party that year nominated Grover Cleveland for a third time, and named Adlai E. Stevenson of Illinois as his running mate.

There was a fight in the convention over the tariff plank, and as finally adopted it declared that the federal government had no constitutional power to impose and collect tariff duties except for revenue only. The trusts were denounced, and the party pledged to the enactment of laws made to prevent and control them.

The money plank of the platform was as follows:

"We denounce the republican legislation known as the Sherman act of 1890 as a cowardly makeshift, fraught with possibilities of danger in the future which should make all of its supporters, as well as its author, anxious for its speedy repeal. We hold to the use of both gold and silver as the standard money of the country, and to the coinage of both gold and silver without discrimination against either metal or charge for mintage, but the dollar unit of coinage of both metals must be of equal intrinsic and exchangeable value or be adjusted through international agreement, or by such safeguards of legislation as shall ensure the maintenance of the parity of the two metals, and the equal power of every dollar at all times in the markets and in the payment of debts; and we demand that all paper currency shall be kept at par with and redeemable in such coin. We insist upon this policy as especially necessary for the protection of the farmers and laboring classes, the first, and most defenseless victims of unstable money and a fluctuating currency."

President Harrison was renominated by the republicans and Whitelaw Reid was placed upon the ticket with him. In the election the democratic ticket polled a plurality of 132 in the electoral college and a popular plurality of about 380,000. The people's party nominated James B. Weaver of Iowa for president and James G. Field of Virginia for vice president, and polled a little more than 1,000,000 votes.

During President Cleveland's second term, two questions occupied public attention, the money question and the tariff question. Congress was called together in extraordinary session in August, 1893, and the president recommended the unconditional repeal of the Sherman law. By reference to the democratic platform of 1892 it will be seen that the money plank contained a statement of the party's faith in the double standard, as well as its desire for the repeal of the Sherman act, and an effort to repeal the makeshift without restoring the double standard caused a division in the ranks of the party, but the president succeeded in securing the legislation which he desired; doing this, however, he had the support of a larger percentage of the republican senators and members than he had of the democrats.

Congressman Wilson, chairman of the ways and means committee, reported a measure which bears his name, and the bill as it passed the house was satisfactory to the friends of tariff reform, but it was emasculated by the senate, where a coterie of democratic senators refused to support it until the rates of several schedules were raised. The president refused to sign the bill, but allowed it to become a law without his signature. This bill contained an income tax, but this clause was declared unconstitutional by the supreme court, the vote standing 5 to 4. The decision was rendered at the second hearing; at the first hearing the vote stood 4 to 4, and as the ninth judge who was not present until the second hearing favored the tax, it required a change of opinion on the part of one of the judges to render the income tax inoperative.

After the passage of the tariff law the currency question again occupied the attention of congress and became the paramount issue in the campaign of 1896. The money issue was fought out in the party and the delegates to the Chicago convention were instructed to carry out the financial policy indorsed by the members of the state convention selecting them, who in turn had been instructed by county conventions. As a result of this inter-party contest, the advocates of bimetallism won a decisive victory having more than two-thirds of the national delegates.

The following platform was adopted:

"We, the democrats of the United States in national convention assembled, do reaffirm our allegiance to those great essential principles of justice and liberty, upon which our institutions are founded, and which the democratic party has advocated from Jefferson's time to our own—freedom of speech, freedom of press, freedom of conscience, the preservation of personal rights, the equality of all citizens before the law, and the faithful observance of constitutional limitations.

"During all these years the democratic party has resisted the tendency of selfish interests to the centralization of governmental power, and steadfastly maintained the integrity of the dual scheme of government established by the founders of this republic of republics. Under its guidings and teachings the great principle of local self-government has found its best expression in the maintenance of the rights of the states and in its assertion of the necessity of confining the general government to the exercise of the powers granted by the constitution of the United States.

"The constitution of the United States guarantees to every citizen the rights of civil and religious liberty. The democratic party has always been the exponent of political liberty and religious freedom, and it renews its obligations and reaffirms its devotions to these fundamental principles of the constitution.

"Recognizing that the money question is paramount to all others at this time, we invite attention to the fact that the federal constitution named silver and gold together as the money metals of the United States, and that the first coinage law passed by congress under the constitution made the silver dollar the monetary unit and admitted gold to free coinage at a ratio based upon the silver-dollar unit.

"We declare that the act of 1873 demonetizing silver without the knowledge or approval of the American people has resulted in the appreciation of gold and a corresponding fall in the prices of commodities produced by the people; a heavy increase in the burden of taxation and of all debts, public and private; the enrichment of the money-lending class at home and abroad; the prostration of industry and impoverishment of the people.

"We are unalterably opposed to monometallism, which has locked fast the prosperity of an industrial people in the paralysis of hard times. Gold monometallism is a British policy, and its adoption has brought other nations into financial servitude to London. It is not only un-American, but anti-American, and it can be fastened on the United States only by the stifling of that spirit and love of liberty which proclaimed our political independence in 1776 and won it in the war of the revolution.

"We demand the free and unlimited coinage of both silver and gold at the present legal ratio of 16 to 1, without waiting for the aid or consent of any other nation. We demand that the standard silver dollar shall be a full legal tender, equally with gold, for all debts, public and private, and we favor such legislation as will prevent for the future the demonetization of any kind of legal tender money by private contract.

"We are opposed to the policy and practice of surrendering to the holders of the obligations of the United States the option reserved by law to the government of redeeming such obligations in either silver coin or gold coin.

"We are opposed to the issuing of interest-bearing bonds of the United States in time of peace and condemn the trafficking with banking syndicates, which, in exchange for bonds and at an enormous profit to themselves, supply the federal treasury with gold to maintain the policy of gold monometallism.

"Congress alone has the power to coin and issue money, and President Jackson declared that this power could not be delegated to corporations or individuals. We, therefore, denounce the issuance of notes intended to circulate as money by national banks as in derogation of the constitution, and we demand that all paper which is made a legal tender for public and private debts, or which is receivable for dues to the United States, shall be issued by the government of the United States and shall be redeemable in coin.

We hold that tariff duties shall be levied for purposes of revenue, such duties to be so adjusted as to operate equally throughout the country, and not discriminate between class or section, and that taxation should be limited by the needs of the government, honestly and economically administered. We denounce as disturbing to business the republican threat to restore the McKinley law, which has twice been condemned by the people in national elections, and which enacted under the false plea of protection to home industry, proved a prolific breeder of trusts and monopolies, enriched the few at the expense of the many, restricted American staples of access to their natural markets.

"Until the money question is settled we are opposed to any agitation for further changes in our tariff laws, except such as is necessary to meet the deficit in revenue caused by the adverse decision of the supreme court on the income tax. But for this decision by the supreme court there would be no deficit in the revenue under the law passed by a democratic congress in strict pursuance of the uniform decisions of that court for nearly 100 years, that court having in that decision sustained constitutional objections to its enactment which had previously been overruled by the ablest judges who have ever sat on that bench. We declare that it is the duty of congress to use all the constitutional power which remains after that decision, or which may come from its reversal by the court as it may hereafter be constituted, so that the burdens of taxation may be equally and impartially laid, to the end that wealth may bear its due proportion of the expense of the government.

"We hold that the most efficient way of protecting American labor is to prevent the importation of foreign pauper labor to compete with it in the home market, and that the value of the home market, to our American farmers and artisans is greatly reduced by a vicious monetary system which depresses the price of their products below the cost of production, and thus deprives them of the means of purchasing the products of our home manufactories; and as labor creates the wealth of the country, we demand the passage of such laws as may be necessary to protect it in all its rights.

"We are in favor of the arbitration of differences between employers engaged in interstate commerce and their employes, and recommend such legislation as is necessary to carry out this principle.

"The absorption of wealth by the few, the consolidation of our leading railroad systems, and the formation of trusts and pools require a stricter control by the federal government of those arteries of commerce. We demand the enlargement of the power of the interstate commerce commission and such restriction and guarantees in the control of railroads as will protect the people from robbery and oppression.

"We denounce the profligate waste of the money wrung from the people by oppressive taxation and the lavish appropriations of recent republican congresses, which have kept taxes high, while the labor that pays them is unemployed and the products of the people's toil are depressed in price till they no longer repay the cost of production. We demand a return to that simplicity and economy which befits a democratic government and a reduction in the number of useless offices the salaries of which drain the substance of the people.

"We denounce arbitrary interference by federal authorities in local affairs as a violation of the constitution of the United States and a crime against free institutions, and we especially object to government by injunction as a new and highly dangerous form of oppression by which the federal judges, in contempt of the laws of the states and rights of citizens, become at once legislators, judges, executioners; and we approve the bill passed at the last session of the United States senate, and now pending in the house of representatives, relative to contempts in federal courts and providing for trials by jury in certain cases of contempt.

"No discrimination should be indulged in by the government of the United States in favor of any of its debtors. We approve of the refusal of the Fifty-third congress to pass the

Pacific Railroad funding bill and denounce the effort of the present republican congress to enact a similar measure.

"Recognizing the just claims of deserving Union soldiers, we heartily indorse the rule of the present commissioner of pensions, that no names shall be arbitrarily dropped from the pension roll; and the fact of enlistment and service should be before enlistment.

"We favor the admission of the territories of New Mexico, Arizona, and Oklahoma into the Union as states, and we favor the early admission of all the territories having the necessary population and resources to entitle them to statehood, and, while they remain territories, we hold that the officials appointed to administer the government of any territory, together with the District of Columbia and Alaska, should be bona fide residents of the territory or district in which their duties are to be performed. The democratic party believes in home rule and that all public lands of the United States should be appropriated to the establishment of free homes for American citizens.

"We recommend that the territory of Alaska be granted a delegate in congress and that the general land and timber laws of the United States be extended to said territory.

"The Monroe doctrine, as originally declared, and as interpreted by succeeding presidents, is a permanent part of the foreign policy of the United States and must at all times be maintained.

"We extend our sympathy to the people of Cuba in their heroic struggle for liberty and independence.

"We are opposed to life tenure in the public service except as provided in the constitution. We favor appointments based on merit, fixed terms of office, and such an administration of the civil service laws as will afford equal opportunities to all citizens of ascertained fitness.

"We declare it to be the unwritten law of this republic, established by custom and usage of one hundred years and sanctioned by the examples of the greatest and wisest of those who founded and have maintained our government, that no man should be eligible for a third term of the presidential office.

'The federal government should care for and improve the Mississippi river and other great waterways of the republic, so as to secure for the interior states easy and cheap transportation to tide water. When any waterway of the republic is of sufficient importance to demand aid of the government, such aid should be extended upon a definite plan of continuous work until permanent improvement is secured.

"Confiding in the justice of our cause and the necessity of its success at the polls we submit the foregoing declaration of principles and purposes to the considerate judgment of the American people. We invite the support of all citizens who approve them and who desire to have them made effective through legislation, for the relief of the people and the restoration of the country's prosperity."

The minority, led by Senator Hill of New York, submitted the following, which was refused by the convention:

"To the Democratic National Convention: 16 delegates, constituting the minority of the committee on resolutions, find many declarations in the report of the majority to which they cannot give their assent. Some of these are wholly unnecessary. Some are ill considered and ambiguously phrased, while others are extreme and revolutionary of the well-recognized principles of the party. The minority content themselves with this general expression of their dissent, without going into a specific statement of the objectionable features of the report of the majority; but upon the financial question which engages at this time the chief share of public attention, the views of the majority differ so fundamentally from what the minority regard as vital democratic doctrine as to demand a distinct statement of what they hold as the only just and true expression of democratic faith upon the paramount issue, as follows, which is offered as a substitute for the financial plank in the majority report:

" 'We declare our belief that the experiment on the part of the United States alone of free silver coinage and a change of the existing standard of value independently of the action of other great nations, would not only imperil our finances, but would retard or entirely prevent the establishment of international bimetallism, to which the efforts of the government should be steadily directed. It would place this country at once upon a silver basis, impair contracts, disturb business, diminish the purchasing power of the wages of labor, and inflict irreparable evils upon our nation's commerce and industry.

" 'Until international co-operation among leading nations for the coinage of silver can be secured we favor the rigid maintenance of the existing gold standard as essential to the preservation of our national credit, the redemption of our public pledges, and the keeping inviolate of our country's honor. We insist that all our paper and silver currency shall be kept absolutely at a parity with gold. The democratic party is the party of hard money and is opposed to legal tender paper money as a part of our permanent financial system, and we therefore favor the gradual retirement and cancellation of all United States notes and treasury notes, under such legislative provisions as will prevent undue contraction. We demand that the national credit shall be resolutely maintained at all times and under all circumstances.

"The minority also feel that the report of the majority is defective in failing to make any recognition of the honesty, economy, courage and fidelity of the present democratic adminstration. And they therefore offer the following declaration as an amendment to the majority report: 'We recommend the honesty, economy, courage and fidelity of the present democratic national administration.' "

The main resolutions submitted by the minority were rejected by more than a two-thirds vote, and the platform as reported by the committee was adopted by the same vote. The resolution indorsing the president was defeated by a little less than two-thirds.

The convention named as its candidates William Jennings Bryan of Nebraska, and Arthur Sewall of Maine. The "national" democrats met at Indianapolis in September following, issued a platform indorsing the gold standard and named John M. Palmer and Simon B. Buckner as their national ticket. William McKinley of Ohio, and Garrett A. Hobart of New Jersey were the nominees of the republican convention. The platform contained a plank favoring a protective tariff, and a plank opposing free coinage until foreign co-operation could be secured, but pledging the party to promote international bimetallism.

The people's party, generally known as the populist party, met at St. Louis and adopted a platform containing the same silver plank as the democratic platform and indorsed and nominated the democratic candidate for president. Instead of indorsing Mr. Sewell for the vice presidency, the convention named Thomas E. Watson of Georgia for that office. The silver republicans met at the same time, indorsing the democratic ticket and adopted a silver plank identical with the democratic plank.

The campaign aroused deep feeling on both sides, and was warmly contested in the central states. It became apparent early in the campaign that the democratic ticket would carry the western and southern states, and that the republican ticket would sweep the eastern states. A very large vote was polled, the total that year being nearly 2,000,000 in excess of the total vote of four years before. The republican party secured a popular plurality of 603,514. The electoral vote stood, McKinley and Hobart 271; Bryan and Sewall, 176.

Between 1896 and 1900 there was an improvement in industrial conditions; an increase in the volume of money, and a series of wars throughout the world. In 1898 the United States interferred in behalf of the Cubans and became involved in a war with Spain, which war resulted in Cuban independence, but during the war a naval victory in the Philippines put this nation in temporary control of those islands and resulted in our possession of them as an indemnity for the expenses incurred in behalf of the Cubans. The cession of the Philippine islands to the United States raised a question which has not yet been settled. The sentiment is at present divided, the democrats favoring the immediate promise that indpendence will be given as soon as a stable government is established, this independence to be accompanied by protection from outside interference. Some of the republicans desire that the Philippine islands be held under a colonial system, and others desire that the islands be given a territorial form of government with a view to ultimate statehood.

The democratic convention which met at Kansas City July 4, 1900, indorsed the Declaration of Independence, and adopted the following platform:

"We, the representatives of the democratic party of the United States, assembled in national convention on the anniversary of the adoption of the Declaration of Independence, do reaffirm our faith in that immortal proclamation of the inalienable rights of man and our allegiance to the constitution framed in harmony therewith by the fathers of the republic. We hold with the United States supreme court that the Declaration of Independence is the spirit of our government, of which the constitution is the form and letter.

"We declare again that all governments instituted among men derive their just powers from the consent of the governed; that any government not based upon the consent of the governed is tyranny; and that to impose upon any people a government of force is to substitute the methods of imperialism for those of a republic. We hold that the constitution follows the flag, and denounce the doctrine that an executive or congress, deriving their existence and their powers from the constitution, can exercise lawful authority beyond it or in violation of it.

"We assert that no nation can long endure half republic and half empire, and we warn the American people that imperialism abroad will lead quickly and inevitably to despotism at home.

"Believing in these fundamental principles, we denounce the Porto Rican law, enacted by a republican congress against the protest and opposition of the democratic minority, as a bold and open violation of the nation's organic law and a flagrant breach of the national good faith. It imposes upon the people of Porto Rico a government without their consent and taxation without representation. It dishoners the American people by repudiating a solemn pledge made in their behalf by the commanding general of our army, which the Porto Ricans welcomed to a peaceful and unresisted occupation of their land. It doomed to poverty and distress a people whose helplessness appeals with peculiar force to our justice and magnanimity.

"In this, the first act of its imperialistic program, the republican party seeks to commit the United States to a colonial policy inconsistent with republican institutions and condemned by the supreme court in numerous decisions.

"We condemn and denounce the Philippine policy of the present administration. It has involved the public in unnecessary war, sacrificed the lives of many of our noblest sons and placed the United States, previously known and applauded throughout the world as the champion of freedom, in the false and un-American position of crushing with military force the efforts of our former allies to achieve liberty and self-government. The Filipinos cannot be citizens without endangering our civilization; they cannot be subjects without imperiling our form of government, and as we are not willing to surrender our civilization or to convert the republic into an empire, we favor an immediate declaration of the nation's purpose to give the Filipinos, first, a stable form of government; second, independence; and, third, protection from outside interference, such as has been given for nearly a century to the republics of Central and South America.

"We are not opposed to territorial expansion when it takes in desirable territory which can be erected into states in the Union and whose people are willing and fit to become American citizens. We favor expansion by every peaceful and legitimate means. But we are unalterably opposed to seizing or purchasing distant islands to be governed outside the constitution and whose people can never become citizens.

"We are in favor of extending the republic's influence among the nations, but believe that influence should be extended, not by force and violence, but through the persuasive power of a high and honorable example. The importance of other questions now pending before the American people is in no wise diminished, and the democratic party takes no backward step from its position on them, but the burning issue of imperialism growing out of the Spanish war involves the very existence of the republic and the destruction of our free institutions. We regard it as the paramount issue of the campaign.

"The declaration in the republican platform adopted at the Philadelphia convention, held in June, 1900, that the republican party 'steadfastly adheres to the policy announced in the Monroe doctrine,' is manifestly deceptive. This profession is contradicted by the avowed policy of that party, in opposition to the spirit of the Monroe doctrine, to acquire and hold sovereignty over large areas of territory and large numbers of people in the eastern hemisphere. We insist on the strict maintenance of the Monroe doctrine in all its integrity, both in letter and in spirit, as necessary to prevent the extension of European authority on this continent and as essential to our supremacy in American affairs. At the same time we declare that no American people shall ever be held by force in unwilling subjection to European authority.

"We oppose militarism. It means conquest abroad and intimidation and oppression at home. It means the strong arm which has ever been fatal to free institutions. It is what millions of our citizens have fled from in Europe. It will impose upon our peace-loving people a large standing army and unnecessary burden of taxation, and will be a constant menace to their liberties. A small standing army and a well disciplined state militia are amply sufficient in time of peace. The republic has no place for a vast military service and conscription.

"In time of danger the volunteer soldier is his country's best defender. The national guard of the United States should ever be cherished in the patriotic hearts of a free people. Such organizations are ever an element of strength and safety. For the first time in our history and coevil with the Philippine conquest has there been a wholesale departure from our time-honored and approved system of volunteer organization. We denounce it as un-American, undemocratic and unrepublican and as a subversion of the ancient and fixed principles of a free people.

"Private monopolies are indefensible and intolerable. They destroy competiton, control the price of all material and of the finished product, thus robbing both producer and consumer. They lessen the employment of labor, and arbitrarily fix the terms and conditions thereof, and deprive individual energy and small capital of their opportunity for betterment. They are the most efficient means yet devised for appropriating the fruits of industry to the benefit of the few at the expense of the many, and unless their insatiate greed is checked all wealth will be aggregated in a few hands and the republic destroyed.

"The dishonest paltering with the trust evil by the republican party in state and national platforms is conclusive proof of the truth of the charge that trusts are the legitimate product of republican policies, that they are fostered by republican laws, and that they are protected by the republican administration for campaign subscriptions and political support.

"We pledge the democratic party to an unceasing warfare in nation, state and city against private monopoly in every form. Existing laws against trusts must be enforced, and more stringent ones must be enacted providing for publicity as to the affairs of corporations engaged in interstate commerce, requiring all corporations to show, before doing business outside the state of their origin, that they have no water in their stock, and that they have not attempted, and are not attempting to monopolize any branch of business or the production of any articles of merchandise, and the whole constitutional power of congress over interstate commerce, the mails and all modes of interstate communication shall be exercised by the enactment of comprehensive laws upon the subject of trusts.

"Tariff laws should be amended by putting the products of trusts upon the free list, to prevent monopoly under the plea of protection.

"The failure of the present republican administration, with an absolute control over all the branches of the national government, to enact any legislation designed to prevent or even curtail the absorbing power of trusts and illegal combinations, or to enforce the anti-trust laws already on the statute books, proves the insincerity of the high-sounding phrases of the republican platform.

"Corporations should be protected in all their rights, and their legitimate interests should be respected, but any attempt by corporations to interfere with public affairs of the people or to control the sovereignty which creates them should be forbidden under such penalties as will make such attempts impossible.

"We condemn the Dingley tariff law as a trust-breeding measure, skilfully devised to give the few favors which they do not deserve and to place upon the many burdens which they should not bear.

"We favor such an enlargement of the scope of the interstate commerce law as will enable the commission to protect individuals and communities from discriminations and the public from unjust and unfair transportation rates."

It will be seen that the question of imperialism was made the paramount issue, the trust question coming next in the amount of attention given to it. The convention, however, reaffirmed the principles embodied in the Chicago platform, and reiterated the position taken four years before on the money question and on several other questions.

Mr. Bryan was renominated and Adlai E. Stevenson of Illinois was placed upon the ticket as the candidate for vice president. This ticket was indorsed later by the people's party convention, and by the silver republican convention, both of which parties adopted platforms in line with the democratic platform upon the leading issues. The democratic ticket was also indorsed by the anti-imperialists.

While the democrats tried to focus public attention upon the menace of imperialism, the republicans said: "Let well enough alone," and credited the improved conditions of the people in part to the gold standard and in part to the high tariff law enacted in 1898. They protested against any change in the financial laws or the tariff law, and denied that they intended any departure from the principles of free government.

The republican ticket, headed by President McKinley and Theodore Roosevelt of New York, was again successful, the popular plurality being 849,455. The electoral vote stood, McKinley and Roosevelt, 292; Bryan and Stevenson, 155. The campaign of 1900 did not excite as much interest as the preceding campaign, the total vote being practically the same in 1900 as it was in 1896.

In the foregoing narrative an attempt has been made to present a history of the democratic party from its organization to the present time, and the party's position on public issues has been shown by quotations from the platforms adopted by its national conventions. While the platforms are not so specific as laws, and not so elaborate as speeches, they are probably a better index to the general thought and purpose of parties than either laws or speeches—for the reason that laws are often compromises, and speeches may represent the individual opinions of the speakers rather than the conclusion of the party, while platforms are written by delegates chosen for that purpose.

It will be seen that the party has met with successes and reverses, but it is also noticeable that it has adhered to its principles regardless of the immediate effect of those principles upon it. For instance, it was defeated in 1840, and yet the platform of 1840 was constantly reaffirmed and reiterated for 20 years afterward. The platform of 1892 reaffirmed and even made stronger the platform of 1888, upon which the party had suffered defeat. As the purpose of this article is merely to present as clearly as possible the attitude of the democratic party on public questions, it would be out of place to enter upon the defense of the party's principles.

It may be said, however, in conclusion, that there is today and will continue to be an imperative need for a party thoroughly committed to the defense of the inalienable rights of the individual and to local self-government, and jealous of the encroachments of federal power. Even when such a party is not in power, it exercises a potent influence in molding public opinion and in restraining excesses, because it is very quick to champion the cause of an individual whose rights have been trespassed upon, or the cause of a community whose rights have been ignored. In proportion as the organization is true to the principles promulgated by Jefferson and defended by Jackson, it may hope to appeal to the confidence of those who seek neither favoritism nor privileges, but are content to enjoy the blessings of a government in which each individual is protected in the enjoyment of life and liberty and in the pursuit of happiness.

FARMING AS AN OCCUPATION.

(Written for the *Cosmopolitan*, and reproduced by courtesy of that magazine. Copyright by the *Cosmopolitan*.)

It is with exceeding pleasure that the following suggestions are presented in regard to the desirability of farming as a life occupation.

First—It is an independent way of living, compared with work in the city. The farmer can supply his table with meat, vegetables, bread, milk, butter and eggs, and he is less affected than the residents of the city by fluctuations in the price of these commodities. The clothing account, too, is less for those who live upon the farm than for those who live in town, so that it is much easier and much less embarrassing to practice economy. Not only in dress, but in living, the farmer and his family avoid the rivalry that leads to extravagance, false pretense and the enervating vices.

Second—It requires less capital to begin work upon a farm than to enter any other sort of independent business, and one can usually obtain farm land on the shares, whereas for any mercantile pursuit it is necessary to pay rent, often in advance. If one has not the means to buy horses, plows and agricultural implements, he can usually find a small piece of ground near a town or city where he can raise vegetables, and thus make a start that will enable him to equip himself for larger farming.

Third—All of the members of the family can assist in farming, and that, too, without hardship. The wife can, without sacrifice of dignity or a great amount of drugery, look after the milk, make the butter, and take care of the chickens. The girls as they grow up can assist the mother, and the boys, before and after school and during vacations, can help with the chores and with the farming. Their work is not only of pecuniary value to the household, but it can be rendered in such a way as not to interfere with their schooling, and is of much more value to them in the way of exercise than any sort of sport in which they can indulge.

Fourth—Life upon the farm is healthful. One has outdoor

air and exercise, both of which are strengthening to the body. The vigorous constitution developed upon the farm enables the farmers' boy to outstrip the city-grown boys in the test of endurance that comes later in life.

Fifth—The habits of industry and application acquired upon the farm are valuable capital, no matter to what occupation or profession the mind is turned. The patience, perseverance and energy which are developed in rural life are the foundation upon which one must build in every honorable avocation.

Sixth—Farm life cultivates hospitality and generosity, and without entirely removing temptations gives parental influence a chance to strengthen the child before the seeds of disobedience are implanted by evil associations. People who live miles apart in the country are better acquainted with each other and more attached to each other than the neighbors who are huddled together in the same flat or tenement house, and yet the children who grow up upon the farm can be more careful in their company and are less apt to contract bad habits than boys in town.

In the city there is little manual labor for the boy to do, and to keep him from associating with the boys who are by chance thrown in his way requires a constant exercise of parental authority. In the country darkness shuts out the world and makes the fireside a welcome retreat for all. The farm is also conducive to good morals. Those who till the soil are brought near to nature, and their contact with the earth and its marvelous activities breeds reverence and respect for the Creator of all things. The farmer lives amid miracles and feels each year his dependence upon the Unseen Hand that directs the seasons and sends the refreshing showers. Reverence teaches responsibility and a sense of responsibility is a wholesome restraint upon conduct.

Seventh—The farmer learns early in life the true basis of rewards. By having to give a dollar's worth of labor for a dollar's worth of product he is taught that service, to be fair, must be reciprocal. He never falls into the demoralizing habit of expecting something for nothing. He teaches by example that labor is honorable, and has that sense of proprietorship in his handiwork which only those have who feel that they have honestly earned all that they receive. His ideals of life are, therefore, apt to be high and he imparts to others the stimulus which his occupation and environment excite in him.

Eighth—The husbandman is also the most reliable political factor in the nation. He is the best informed and most independent of all who take part in political life. While he is conservative and not subject to frequent change; while he has convictions and is usually a strong partisan, yet his opinions are his own and as a rule, he can neither be bought nor driven to cast his vote contrary to his judgment.

While it is true that in close states the corruption of voters has sometimes extended to the farm, still it is a well-known fact that repeating and bribe-taking are largely city vices.

The summer days are long and the fatigue of the harvest leaves little energy for study, but the winter evenings bring compensation and the Sabbath day is in the country usually a day for thought and reflection. While the labor organization has done much to turn the attention of its members to the study of economic questions, yet with the growth of great corporations the laboring man has become more and more dependent upon his employer, and the wage-earner is not so free to make his ballot express exactly what he wants as is the man who works for himself, and sells his products in the open market.

Henry Clay, fifty years ago in defending the right of the people of South America to self-government, said:

"Were I to speculate in hypotheses unfavorable to human liberty, my speculations should be founded rather upon the vices, refinements, or density of population. Crowded together in compact masses, even if they were philosophers, the contagion of the passions is communicated and caught, and the effect, too often, I admit, is the overthrow of liberty. Dispersed over such an immense space as that on which the people of Spanish America are spread, their physical, and I believe also their mental condition, both favor their liberty.

In enumerating the advantages of farm life, it is not necessary to say that the farmer enjoys all the benefits that are now within his reach. There is probably no field in which there is greater room for improvement. But if the farm as it is has been the nursery of merchants and ministers, orators and statesmen, the farm as it may be and should be is still more inviting. The introduction of acetylene and other kinds of gas, and the perfection of electrical apparatus, will enable multitudes of farmers to substitute a modern light for the dim candle and the smoking lamp. The windmill and the supply tank are not only saving the muscle of the man, but are contributing to the convenience of the housewife. With water running through the house and supplying both the kitchen and the bath room, the lot of the farmer's wife will be very much improved.

Another invention is likely to have a marked influence upon farm life, namely, the telephone. No one who has not lived remote from a physician can appreciate the anxiety which a mother feels in case of accident or sicknesss in the family. The telephone reduces by one-half the anxious time between injury and relief, and in addition to this makes it possible for the farmer to communicate with his neighbors, receive and send telegrams, and be in constant touch with the outside world. The writer's attention has been recently called to the telephone as a time-saver among farmers, and one now wonders how people could have done without it so long.

The electric car line has already commenced to link city with city and to supply the farmers along the line with cheap and rapid transportation for themselves and their products. It will be surprising if the electric lines and the telephones do not result in the next few years in a large increase in the value of suburban property.

In this connection the Good Roads movement cannot be overlooked. The value of a permanent and at all times passable road is beginning to be appreciated, and the farmer is likely to demand that this consideration be shown to his material, intellectual and moral welfare. The mud embargo is an expensive one to the farmer's purse and not less objectionable in other ways. With good roads it is possible to have larger and better schools, and then will follow the joint intermediate school with its library and its public assembly room. The rural delivery is another boon which the farmer appreciates.

The state universities are giving increasing attention to studies that will fit young men for the intelligent pursuit of agriculture, and what could be more gratifying. If a father is able to start his son in business with $10,000, what business is so safe as farming? Given a young man with a thorough education, good habits, willingness to work and a desire to make himself useful, where can he fare better than upon a farm? He can apply his brains to the enriching of the soil, to the diversification of his crops and to the improvement of his stock, and at the same time give reasonable indulgence to his taste for reading and study. He will have all that contributes to health of body, vigor of mind and to the cultivation of the heart—what occupation or profession can offer him richer rewards?

True, the soil will not yield him the fabulous wealth that he might secure by cornering the production or supply of some necessity of life, but it will respond to his industry and give him that of which dishonest gains would rob him—"a conscience void of offense toward God and man." If he must forego the sudden gains that sometimes come to the stock jobber, he is also relieved of fear of the sudden losses that are still more frequent to those whose fortunes rise and fall with the markets, and the terrors of flood and drouth and wind and hail are, all combined, less to be dreaded than the conscienceless greed of the monopolists who wreck the business of competitors and swindle confiding stockholders.

To the briefless barrister who is not ashamed to work, to the pale-faced clerk who is not afraid of dirt, to all who can labor and be content with moderate returns, the farm offers a welcome. Even the dumb animals are more wholesome companions than the bulls and bears of Wall street, and the harvests will give back smile for smile.   W. J. BRYAN.

THE CRIMINAL CLAUSE.

A Magdalena, New Mexico, reader of THE COMMONER directs attention to an article in which THE COMMONER urged the enforcement of the criminal clause of the Sherman anti-trust law. This writer says that "the criminal clause of the Sherman anti-trust law was repealed by the Elkins law. I mention this because THE COMMONER asks for the enforcement of the crimnal clause when it is no longer in existence. Doubtless this Elkins law game has escaped your notice."

Many people seem to entertain the same idea advanced by our New Mexico reader. The Elkins law passed by the last congress bears no relation whatever to the Sherman anti-trust law. The Elkins bill sought to amend the existing law relating to the publication of tariff rates by railroads and prohibiting railroad managers from discriminating in rates. The original law provided fine or imprisonment for those who violated the provisions of that law. One of the amendments made by the Elkins bill was that which abolishes altogether the penalty of imprisonment and provides for the imposition of a fine from $1,000 to $20,000.

The Elkins bill became a law and as a result, in that portion of the federal statutes prohibiting discrimination in railroad rates, there is no imprisonment penalty; but the Elkins bill did not in any way refer to the Sherman anti-trust law, and does not in any way affect it. The Sherman anti-trust law is intact, and its chief feature—the very first section of that law—provides for criminal prosecution of those who conspire in restraint of trade.

It is easy to see how one may have been misled on this point because it is very easy to confound the law dealt with by the Elkins bill with what is known as the Sherman law. It might be well for newspapers generally to inform their readers on this point because many people have been misled.

son to believe, therefore, that when Judge Grosscup shall make this injunction permanent, it will have any more effective results? The charges made by the attorneys for the government, upon which charges these injunctions were issued, are sufficient as a basis for a criminal indictment. If the representatives of the government really desire to win a great victory, why not proceed against the beef trust under the criminal clause of the Sherman law?

CONSUMERS ARE NERVOUS.

In his New York speech Senator Dolliver said: "Within twenty years every trust magnate will be dead or in a sanitarium for nervous diseases, and the world will be looking for trained men to do the world's work." The Sioux City *Tribune* commenting upon this statement says that the trust magnate should not be permitted to pursue such a cruel fate. But the *Tribune* directs attention to the fact that there is another phase in this quotation from the senator from Iowa. This relates to the position of the public. The *Tribune* intimates that a large number of the consumers will be in the grave or in a madhouse long before this twenty-year period has expired. That paper says: "The situation is something of a mental and physical strain for others than trust magnates. It is no snap to watch the cold, clammy hand reaching out for the currency remnants—and getting them. It is a nerve and body breaking game all around, and if the early grave and the asylum yawn for any of the participants they must yawn for them all, more or less. The need for salvation is large and inviting, and who will say it is not more desirable to save than to allow the drift toward the awful abyss pictured by Senator Dolliver"

VERY POOR ADVICE.

A New York paper recently printed this statement: "The other day the dean of one of the largest of our colleges for women made an impassioned appeal to young mothers not to waste their time in the personal care of their babies, but to give them over to trained nurses or kindergarteners, while they devoted themselves to study and such outside work as would fit them to be companions for their children when they were grown." This is just about as poor advice as could be given. The child in its early days should be kept in close touch with the mother. It is the office of the mother to train the child and the woman who surrenders that duty to others, in the vain notion that she is fitting herself to be a companion for her children when they are grown, may discover when it is too late to provide a remedy that the substitute for the mother has not succeeded in so training the children that they will be a comfort to the mother in her old age. The old-fashioned methods of the mothers cannot be improved upon. It would be better for the children of the future if the mothers would adhere more closely to those old-time methods. A mother can do justice to herself without neglecting her children.

THE VALUE OF AN EDUCATION.

It should not be necessary to quote eminent authorities as to the importance of an early education and yet there are all too many young people who fail to grasp their opportunities in this respect. To be sure, all of life is education and while the college course does not properly terminate endeavor in this line, it is of the highest importance that the young man and the young woman avail themselves of the opportunity of profiting by a college education.

The wisest men of our times have sought to impress upon the youth of their generation the importance of securing an education, and with the present as with preceding generations, it is important that this wholesome counsel be impressed upon the young. Addison wrote: "What sculpture is to a block of marble, education is to the human soul. The philosopher, the saint, the hero, the wise, and the good or the great very often lie hid and concealed in a plebeian which a proper education might have disinterred and brought to life." Benjamin Franklin wrote that "An investment in knowledge always pays the best interest." Washington wrote: "Promote as an object of primary importance institutions for the general diffusion of knowledge. In proprtion as the structure of government gives force to public opinion, it is essential that public opinion should be enlightened." Judson wrote: "Planting colleges and filling them with studious young men and women is planting seed for the world." Varle wrote. "Education is the companion which no misfortune can depress—no crime destroy—no enemy alienate—no despotism enslave. At home a friend; abroad an introduction; in solitude a solace; and in society an ornament. Without it what is man? A splendid slave, a reasoning savage."

To be sure, just as John Randolph said. "All the professors and teachers in the world would not make you a wise or a good man without your own co-operation;" but as E. H. Chapin said: "Do not ask if a man has been through college; as if a college has been through him—if he is a walking university."

The young man or young woman who under disadvantageous circumstances struggles for a college education will certainly appreciate it. Under such circumstances, such a person will not merely seek to go through college. The result will be that the college has gone through the man.

Perhaps it is not possible for everyone to obtain the advantages of a college education. Some are able to surmount the obstacles of life without such an education, but we think it safe to say that the most successful of these will cheerfully testify that their struggle would have been easier had they had the advantages of a college education.

PHILANTHROPHY.

Thomas W. Lawson, a Boston financier, recently issued a satiric letter in which he criticised Andrew Carnegie for the part he played in the formation of the United States steel trust. Referring to the Lawson epistle, the New York *World* says: "The attack was considered in Wall street all the more remarkable, in view of the fact that Mr. Lawson is an ally of Henry H. Rogers, James Stillman, of the National City bank, and others of the so-called 'Standard Oil' crowd who floated the Amalgamated Copper company, the collapse of which securities brought great distress two years ago to small investors throughout the country."

Mr. Lawson begins his letter with the following "ultimatum" which purports to have come from Mr. Carnegie himself:

"When in the course of human events it becomes necessary for a hard working iron monger to supply reading matter to the two greatest countries on earth, it is the duty of all investors, speculators and get-rich-quick warriors to give to the said ironmonger the requisite wherewithal. Therefore I, the philanthropist of Homestead, do now and forthwith demand of said investors, speculators and get-rich-quick hustlers, a sum which shall amount in the aggregate to $300,000,000. Yankee dollars, and may the Lord have mercy upon the souls and pocketbooks of the American people if too much time is consumed by the messenger boy who is to return with their answer to, yours truly philanthropically,

"CARNEGIE."

The Boston financier concludes his epistle in this interesting way:

"The howl that has been resounding through Wall street, the past few days, for the Homestead philanthropist to come forth with $10,000,000 to stay the decline in steel stocks, and thereby balm the lacerated hearts and minds of the thousands upon thousands of widows and orphans who have been cooed into investing their all in his creation, is not only idiotic, but insulting to Mr. Carnegie's 9 1-8 intelligence—$10,000,000 to be paid out for the froth upon the foam resting upon the lake of water which covers his ledge of underlying mortgage, when this $10,000,000 would buy—oh, so many, so many works of imagination, observation and lunification as would compel miles upon miles of press notices— absurd!

"And Wall street can rest easy that this big-hearted Yankee Scot will do no such foolish thing. Wall street could much better employ its time in pointing out to the widows and the orphans who are being passed through the purification and liquefaction state so necessary to Wall street's welfare, the rock-ribbed soundness of the bonds held by the Homestead philanthropist, that they may be getting into line for their purchase when, after the present holocaust is over, Mr. Carnegie, kindly and big-heartedly, places them upon the bargain counter.

"Anyway, Wall street owes it to itself to do all in its power to disabuse the minds of steel stockholders that there is any chance of their sliding any part of their indiscretions on to the broad and generous shoulders of the philanthropist of Homestead; and Wall street certainly owes it to the free-library public to do all that lies within its power to allay any feeling of mistrust that may have come into being because of Wall street's trifling with Mr. Carnegie's steel lake—mistrust that he will even for a moment halt in his noble effort to hammer into the skulls of the people of America and Scotland:

Better far than rising price,
  Better, too, than dividend.
Are the libraries you're a-getting
  With your lucre which I spend."

When any democrat or populist intimates that these trust magnates are not always controlled by high and holy motives, they are charged with an assault upon the property of the country. If any democrat or populist had written as Mr. Lawson has written, he would have been written down as an anarchist.

Can it be possible that the Lawson epistle indicates that in their greed for gold, the "captains of industry" have fallen out among themselves and are disposed to tell the truth concerning one another?

In newspaper circles Mr. Lawson's remarkable letter seems to have created considerable astonishment, and from the opinions expressed, there seems not to be any substantial reason for believing that the example of candor set by the Boston financier will be generally imitated by other men who seek to make a bit of so-called philanthropy cover a multitude of sins.

A SOMERSAULT.

Speaking of the tariff question, Mr. Roosevelt said: "It is exceedingly undesirable that this (the protective) system should be destroyed or that there should be violent and radical changes therein. Our past experience shows that great prosperity in this country has always come under a protective tariff."

Those who have read these remarks of Mr. Roosevelt may be interested in reading something Mr. Roosevelt wrote in his "Life of Thomas H. Benton." On pages 66 and 67 of that book, it will be found that Mr. Roosevelt wrote the following: "The vote on the protective tariff law of 1828 furnished another illustration of the solidarity of the west. New England had abandoned her free trade position since 1824, and the northwest strongly for the new tariff; the southern seacoast states, except Louisiana, opposed it bitterly; and the bill was carried by the support of the western states, both the free and the slave. This tariff bill was the first of the immediate irritating causes which induced South Carolina to go into the nullification movement. Benton's attitude on the measure was that of a good many other men who, in their public capacities, are obliged to appear as protectionists, but who lack his frankness in stating their reasons. He utterly disbelieved in and was opposed to the principle of the bill, but as it had bid for and secured the interest of Missouri by a heavy duty on lead, he felt himself forced to support it; and he so announced his position. He simply went with his state, precisely as did Webster, the latter, in following Massachusetts' change of front and supporting the tariff of 1828, turning a full and complete somesault. Neither the one nor the other was to blame. For free traders are apt to look at the tariff from a sentimental standpoint; but it is in reality purely a business matter, and should be decided solely on grounds of expediency. Political economists have pretty geneerally agreed that protection is vicious in theory and harmful in practice; but if the majority of people in interest wish it, and it affects only themselves, there is no earthly reason why they should not be allowed to try the experiment to their hearts' content. The trouble is that it rarely does affect only themselves and in 1828 the evil was peculiarly aggravated on account of the unequal way in which the proposed law would affect different sections. It purported to benefit the rest of the country, but it undoubtedly worked real injury to the planter states, and there is small ground to wonder that the irritation over it in the region so affected should have been intense."

Mr. Rosevelt seems to have "turned a full and complete somersault." As the author of the "Life of Thomas H. Benton" he declared that "political economists have pretty generally agreed that protection is vicious in theory and harmful in practice," but as president of the United States, he insists that it is exceedingly undesirable that the protective system be destroyed.

As the author of the "Life of Thomas H. Benton," Mr. Roosevelt said that while in 1828 the tariff "purported to benefit the rest of the country, it undoubtedly worked real injury to the planter states and there is small ground for wonder that the irritation over it in the region so affected should have been intense," but as president Mr. Roosevelt declares that "our past experience shows that great prosperity in this country has come under protective tariff."

MARPLOTS.

The Philadelphia Public *Ledger*, a paper that may be depended upon to support republican candidates, refers to democrats who gave faithful support to the national platform as "bourbons and marplots." The same paper insists that "if the democratic party is to have the slightest chance of success in the next national campaign, or if it is even to make a respectable showing at the polls," it must follow the men who in the opinion of the Public *Ledger* "were wise and honest and courageous enough to refuse to support the mischievous heresies of Bryanism as they were promulgated as the party's creed at Chicago and Kansas City." The Public *Ledger* refers to the men who bolted the democratic ticket in 1896 and in 1900 as "the shrewdest and best democrats in the country."

The Public *Ledger* has never been known to manifest genuine concern for the welfare of the democratic party and democrats generally will not accept as a fact, upon the mere statement of a republican paper, that those who supported the democratic ticket and were faithful to democratic principles are "bourbons and marplots," while those who gave aid and encouragement to the enemy, who repudiated the platform when it merely explicitly stated the things for which the democratic party has always claimed to stand, were "the shrewdest and best democrats in the country."

It is not, in the least, surprising that republican papers like the Public *Ledger* should conclude that "the shrewdest and best democrats in the country" are those who support the republican ticket and embrace the policies of the Hannas, while the "bourbons and marplots" are those who support the democratic ticket and defend the principles of Jefferson.

ALTGELD'S PLAIN TALK.

In 1895 the Iroquois club of Chicago gave a banquet. It was said that the banquet was for the purpose of commemorating the birthday of Thomas Jefferson, and yet it was understood that the real purpose was to extend a vote of confidence in the policies of Cleveland's administration, which policies at that time were being seriously criticised by democrats. The late John P. Altgeld was invited to attend this banquet and the invitation was sent to Mr. Altgeld by Mr. Ela of Chicago. Mr. Altgeld's reply may be particularly interesting at this time. It was as follows:

Chicago, March 27, 1895.

Dear Ela: I am in receipt of a letter purporting to be signed by you as chairman of a committee of the Iroquois club stating that the annual banquet of this club, to commemorate the birth of Thomas Jefferson, will be given April 22, and requesting me to be present and deliver an address of welcome. I also learn that a program has been prepared which will make the entire exercises simply a laudation of the financial policy and of the general course of the present federal administration.

In other words, that the program has been so arranged as to convert the whole proceedings into a kind of Cleveland love-feast. As this is simply a repetition of what has been done several times, I take it that you did not prepare this program, but that it was prepared by a few gentlemen who for a number of years have talked reform and then pursued office with the appetite of a wolf. In making this program they remembered the hand that had given the spoils and at the same time they cast a hopeful anchor toward the future.

Last summer one of the great newspapers gave an account of the greatest timber stealing and homestead robbing operations ever carried on in the northwest, involving even the proposition of high office. Recently the country was alarmed at seeing in Washington the most powerful and the most corrupt lobby ever known engaged in trying to force the railroad pooling bill through congress. I notice that two of the men whose names were prominent in connection with one or the other of these scandals have been selected to point out the beauties of Clevelandism, and I will admit that they are the right men for the purpose. Coupled with these is at least one other whose fame in the east is co-extensive only with his ability to injure his party. These three are to discuss the great questions now before the country. All three stand for Clevelandism, but not for democracy of the country. They stand in practice for the theory that government is a convenience for the strong, and were it Hamilton's birthday you wished to celebrate this would all be in accordance with the eternal fitness of things. But not even a resolution of congress, supported by a speech from a senator and an opinion of the attorney general and backed by the federal army, can keep Thomas Jefferson's bones still while you attempt to dump this program into his cradle. These men represent a class which in his day called Jefferson a demagogue, derided his statesmanship and sneered at his patriotism.

Jeffersonism was the first born of the new age of liberty and human progress, while Clevelandism is the slimy offspring of that unhallowed marriage betwen Standard Oil and Wall Street. Jeffersonism brought liberty, prosperity and greatness to our country because it gave its benediction to the great toiling and producing masses, while Clevelandism has put its heel upon the neck of our people, has increased the burdens and the sorrows of the men who toil, and has fattened a horde of vultures that are eating the vitals of the nation.

To make a dollar out of paper by a fiat of government may not be wisdom, but to double the purchasing power of a gold dollar by the fiat of a number of governments in striking down the competitor of gold is ruin. To paralyze the energies of a nation by doubling the burden of the debtor is statesmanship under Clevelandism, but a crime under Jeffersonism. The republican papers praise Clevelandism, but they honor Jefferson by abusing him.

Jefferson's eye took in the continent from the Atlantic to the Pacific. Cleveland is today ignorant of the fact that there is a country west of the Alleghenies. Jefferson belonged to the American people; Cleveland to the men who devour widows' houses. Jeffersonism is an illumination in the American firmament; Clevelandism merely a swamp-light floating around in the Standard Oil marsh. To laud Clevelandism on Jefferson's birthday is to sing a Te Deum in honor of Judas Iscariot on a Christmas morning.

You will excuse me, Ela, if I decline to have anything to do with it, and you will also allow me to say that, as I am not conscious of having done you a wrong, I do not understand why you should have asked me to come and bid a welcome after the program had been practically "packed," as to important issues, so as to stand for hostility to all that is Jeffersonian or democratic, and to favor those measures and acts which tend toward the choking of liberty, the impoverishment of our people and the ultimate destruction of our institutions.

Respectfully,
JOHN P. ALTGELD.

PLATFORM BUILDING.

An Iowa paper claiming to be democratic, says:

"The great trouble with Mr. Bryan is that, not being a democrat himself, he fails to appreciate the true principles, the true object, the true aim, the true scope of democracy. He fails to realize that the democratic party is a party of the people, a party which holds that the right to govern, in party councils or in matters of legislative enactment, emanates from the consent of the governed; he overlooks the fact that democratic doctrines and democratic principles have their inception in the minds of the common people of the country and of the party, and are not taken at second hand from self-constituted leaders and aspirants for honors at the hands of the mass of democratic voters."

It is not necessary to discuss the question raised by the statement of this paper that Mr. Bryan is "not a democrat." It is, however, worthy of note that this organ has outlined a rule which it pretends is followed by the reorganizers when in fact that rule is ignored by the reorganizers and is adhered to by Kansas City platform democrats.

A Kansas City platform democrat does appreciate the true principles, the true object, the true aim, the true scope of democracy. He does realize that the democratic party is the party of the people. He insists that in that party the right of government, in party councils, emanates from the consent of the governed. He insists that democratic platforms shall adhere to democratic doctrines and democratic principles and that the rank and file of the party, rather than "self-constituted leaders and aspirants for honors at the hands of the mass of democratic voters," shall say what the platform shall be.

For this reason THE COMMONER is appealing to democrats who believe in the Kansas City platform to organize and to co-operate in order that their opinions may be reflected in the national platform of their party.

On the other hand, the reorganizers whom this Iowa paper seems to represent, insist that democratic doctrines and democratic principles must be "taken at second hand from self-constituted leaders and aspirants for honors at the hands of the mass of democratic voters."

The Brooklyn Eagle, for instance, recognized as one of the great organs of these reorganizers, tells us, not that the platform should be framed to suit the rank and file of democracy, but that the platform should be framed so that it would be acceptable to Grover Cleveland and men who believe with him.

The platform adopted in 1896 at Chicago, the platform adopted in 1900 at Kansas City, were framed by the rank and file of the democratic party. Men who believe in the principles set forth in those platforms and who insist that the democratic party shall take no backward steps are demanding that the national platform of 1904, shall be framed, not by "the self-constituted leaders and aspirants for honors at the hands of the mass of democratic voters," but shall be framed in accordance with the sentiments of the rank and file of the party.

These reorganizers would not be willing to submit their platform and their candidates to the rank and file of the party in order that the democrats of every precinct in the United States could pass upon that platform and that candidate. Upon the pretense of a desire for harmony they seek to obtain control of the national convention; and if the rank and file of the party should go to sleep, and these reorganizers could thereby obtain control of the party, a platform would be framed without regard to the interests of the mass of democratic voters; but it would be framed to suit Grover Cleveland, who, having been repeatedly honored by the democratic party, brought disaster upon it through his second administration and who deserted the party during the two presidential campaigns when the party's candidates were required to bear the sins of the Cleveland administration.

GORMAN'S LEADERSHIP.

As an exponent of democratic principles as set forth in the platforms adopted at Chicago and Kansas City, THE COMMONER chronicles with regret what may fairly be considered the most important victory thus far scored by the reactionary element in the democratic party, namely, the selection of Mr. Gorman as democratic leader in the senate.

The senator from Maryland is a man of great force and extended legislative experience. Probably no other man in Washington is so well acquainted with public men and parliamentary procedure. Besides this, he is a man of exemplary personal habits, of indefatigable industry and perfect self-control. In other words, he has most of the qualifications considered necessary for leadership and if his sympathies were only with the people he would be an admirable man to speak for the democrats in the senate, but he fails at the crucial point. His record shows that he is too close to the corporations and organized wealth to be commander in chief of the democratic forces in the most influential branch of the national legislature.

There is not a single reform for which Mr. Gorman stands, nor is there a single remedial measure which can be said to have his earnest and hearty support. When the Wilson tariff bill was before the senate he was one of the senators who, by holding the balance of power, forced the emasculation of the bill in the interest of the manufacturers. In the fight for the repeal of the Sherman law he acted with the republicans and is with them still on all phases of the money question. He has never said or done anything to indicate that he desires positive and effective anti-trust legislation. On the contrary, his environment is such as to make it certain that his great influence will be used to strifle rather than promote legislation aimed at the trusts.

The Chicago *Chronicle* of last Friday contained a dispatch from Washington stating that J. Pierpoint Morgan visited the capital the day before and "saw a number of senators, including Messrs. Aldrich, Hanna and Gorman." It does the party infinite harm to have as its leader in the senate a man on intimate terms with the most influential trust magnate and money changer in the United States, for it gives the lie to the party's promises of reform and places our organization on the same level with the republican party. How can we fight the grand larceny schemes concocted by Morgan and his associates if he and our caucus chairman consult together at the capital? No wonder the corporation papers hail with delight Mr. Gorman's return to power and influence. *Public Opinion*, in its last issue, cordially commends the selection of Mr. Gorman and says: "Republicans have been the first to admit that the efficiency of the senate will be increased by Mr. Gorman's reappearance as the leader of the opposition."

The republicans would not be likely to admit that the senate would be rendered more efficient by an honest, earnest fight against their policies. The fact that Mr. Gorman supported the ticket in the campaigns of 1896 and 1900 is used to answer objections from Kansas City platform democrats, and the argument may be satisfactory to those who regard regularity as the only test, but there is an important distinction which must be drawn. A man who, without accepting the platform, supports the ticket can urge his loyalty as a recommendation if he aspires to a position where his views will not misrepresent a majority of the party, but it is absurd to say that because a member of the minority acquiesces in the will of the majority the majority should be willing to put him in a position where he can thwart the will of the majority. Since 1896 Mr. Gorman has never lost an opportunity to reward the men who deserted and helped the enemy. He may as well be recognized as the most potent of all the men who are now trying to reduce the democratic party to servile support of the program arranged by organized wealth. On all economic questions except the tariff he is in agreement with Mr. Cleveland and on the tariff he is even worse than Cleveland. The statement that he is going to unite the party in an attack on the tariff and the trusts simply means that he favors a sham battle on these issues without prospect or promise of interfering seriously with the republicans.

There are in the senate a number of strong and vigorous representatives of sound democratic principles and they will find it more and more galling to march under the banner of one who stands for the commercialism that is corrupting politics and making money the measure of all things.

The fight begun in 1896 was not so much a fight between gold and silver as a fight between the beneficiaries of class legislation on the one side and the advocates of equal rights on the other, and that fight still continues. It would be fortunate if that fight only manifested itself in the contest between the democratic and republican parties, but we might as well face the fact that to a lesser degree it manifests itself in our party, and there is the more reason why the friends of the Kansas City platform, should be on the alert. Instead of retreating, the party must go forward and meet the new questions that are pressing for solution. Until the reform element regains control of the democratic organization in the senate that body will not only not help, but will actually hinder the party's progress.

Unless there has been a complete revolution in the views of several of the democratic senators there will be a protest against Mr. Gorman's leadership and the sooner that protest is made the better for the party.

MUNICIPAL OWNERSHIP.

Municipal ownership of public utilities is rapidly growing in favor. A bill has been introduced in the New York legislature providing that at the next general election voters shall have the opportunity to pass upon the question as to public ownership of all municipal transportation lines and public ownership of municipal gas and electric light plants. While it is not generally believed that this bill will pass at the present session, its introduction shows that a considerable sentiment along this line exists in New York and it may be depended upon that soonor or later those who are opposed to the municipal ownership proposition will be required to defend their position before the people.

Carter H. Harrison, mayor of Chicago, has written for the *Record-Herald* a vigorous and instructive article on the subject of municipal ownership. Mr. Harrison contends that municipal ownership of public utilities contains the only real solution of adequate service to the people. He points out that many of the cities of the old world have adopted this plan and it has proved satisfactory. Mr. Harrison says that while a few years ago this proposition was pronounced impracticable, its correctness from the practical, as well as the theoretical, standpoint, cannot now be seriously disputed. He maintains that in this day municipal ownership is opposed only by those who are prejudiced by ownership of stocks, bonds and other securities, and to all others than these municipal ownership presents the only common sense method of handling a vexatious problem.

Referring to the fact that after all other efforts to distract attention from this plan have failed its opponents have resorted to the cry of "anarchy," Mr. Harrison says: "Whenever through some attempt to give fair treatment to the plain citizen, the wallet of the financier is touched, he flaunts the red flag in an endeavor to frighten the innocent-minded."

Mr. Harrison well describes the situation when he says: "The franchise-holder has gone on enjoying the untrammeled use of the property of the public so long that he seems to have begun to look upon his title as the king or emperor looks upon his right to rule. For generations the guileless public has made a small handful of its fellows the beneficiaries of these franchises, either altogether without reciprocal obligation or with obligations quite incommensurate with the advantages they have enjoyed. Public privileges have been used so long for private gain that apparently to the franchise-holder's way of thinking the title sprang originally from some species of divine origin. The magnates of the street railways, gas plants, telephone plants and other public service utilities seem to claim their franchises through a kindred grace of God. In short, these grants have become the patents of nobility of our moneyed aristocracy.

"For many years the whole public has accepted these conditions without a murmur. The explanations can only be, it seems to me, that these franchises are held by the first citizens of the community. Their general reputation for uprightness and fair dealing has served as a cloak behind which the schemer and promoter have worked secretly and in perfect security. The slightest public clamor has been stilled by the cry that to deny the justice of the claims amounted to inciting to riot; to deny it in fact has been referred to as waving the flag of anarchy."

Mr. Harrison says that there is little if any excuse to even consider the claim that the theory under discussion is a species of anarchy, but he points out that the experience of Glasgow shows the absurdity of such contention. In Glasgow public ownership has advanced to the stage where the city owns not only the waterworks, but the street cars, the gas plant, and the telephone system and all these are operated to the entire satisfaction of the user as well as to the profit of the municipality. The rates charged are low, the profits to the public are so great that taxes have reached low water mark.

Replying to the claim that municipal ownership would result in the erection of gigantic political machines formed on the army of city employes, Mr. Harrison says that this argument vanishes before the fact that every advocate of public ownership strongly favors a rigid civil service provision for the conduct of public utilities, and that a well established merit system would come nearer divorcing any public utility from politics than it is separated now.

Mr. Harrison says that those who object to municipal ownership solely on the ground of the fear that it would result in the creation of a political machine, might at least be inclined to look favorably upon ownership without operation, which plan he maintains is both possible and practicable. He uses the street car system as an example and says that a city may reserve to itself the ownership of the right-of-way and lay rails along it and then let to the highest bidder the right to operate cars upon these rails subject to certain conditions. He points out that this system has been successfully tried at Toronto.

Referring to the immense political power wielded to the disadvantage of the people and to the advantage of the corporations under private ownership, Mr. Harrison contends that, properly administered, public ownership would reach further to purification of politics than any advanced step toward the conduct of municipal affairs that has yet been suggested.

Replying to the argument that private companies can operate with greater economy than would be possible under a system of public ownership, Mr. Harrison denies the claim and says that even though there be truth in the claim, the public obtains no benefit as a result of that economy. He maintains that under public ownership it would be possible to devote profits to improvement of service, reduction of rates and increase of wages, while under private ownership, profits go mainly to the increase of dividends.

While Mr. Harrison admits that public ownership would prove a hard blow to the speculative world, he maintains that it would result in permanent benefit to a legitimate business venture. Under public ownership the reason for watering of stocks would disappear and there would be no great bulk of securities saddled upon an unsuspecting public, wages would reach a fair point and the surplus earnings would apply to lowering the general taxes, not to swelling the bank account of the already over-rich stockholders. And among the various benefits to be obtained from public ownership, Mr. Harrison counts as not the least important the promise that it would "tend to free any city from gang politics with its attendant evils of boss rule, boodle legislation and public spoilation."

It is a good sign when vigorous and enterprising men like Carter H. Harrison take the lead in practical reforms. Doubtless the time will come in this country when under the beneficent results of municipal ownership men will wonder how it was ever possible for individuals to control municipal franchises and grow rich on the profits therefrom.

DEMOCRATIC OPPORTUNITY.

Speech delivered by Mr. Bryan at Wilmington Delaware, February 18, 1903.

Friends and Fellow Democrats: It is very gratifying indeed to meet the representatives of the democracy of Delaware about this banquet board. This gathering is not much like the first meeting I had here. I came to Delaware at a time when you did not know me, and I did not know you. I have often thought of the first speech I ever made in Wilmington. It was not a large meeting; there was plenty of room in the hall for any others who had desired to come. And I introduced myself, because there wasn't a man in the community, so far as I knew, who was willing to take the responsibility of introducing me. That was only about six months before I came as a presidential candidate, when they nearly ruined the building trying to get in.

I have been interested in watching the growth of sentiment in this state and throughout the union, and I am not at all pessimistic in regard to the future. I am confident of the triumph of our ideas, never more confident than now.

It gives me great pleasure to meet with you tonight, as last night, on a similar occasion, I met with some of the loyal democrats of Baltimore. I am glad to meet my old friend, Handy. There was a time along in the early hours of the morning at Kansas City, when he came in mighty "handy." They were discussing the platform down there, and he was loyal when we did not have any votes to spare when it came to a vote. I am also very glad to meet again my friend Gray, whom I learned to know years ago, and others with whom I have become acquainted since—the members of this democratic league, the democrats who have convictions and are not afraid to own them.

The campaigns of 1896 and 1900 brought out a great deal of moral courage. I have known some heroes in my day—men who had the spirit of martyrdom; men who were willing to suffer for what they believed to be right—and a man's convictions are better measured by what he is willing to suffer than by what he is willing to enjoy for those convictions.

You who live in these eastern states have had much more to fight against. The power of wealth is greater here than it is out in our country. You have had much more to contend against than we. You know we sometimes speak of those who come up "through great tribulations." That phrase can be applied to the democrats of Delaware, Maryland and other eastern states, for you have certainly come up amid great tribulations.

There is no doubt of the ultimate triumph of the principles for which you and I contend.

I do not come here tonight as a candidate for office; I do not come as a leader even, for, I am glad to say, the democratic party is in a different condition from that of a few years ago. Ten years ago leaders in the democratic party had more influence than they have now. We had leaders then, and we followed them, often followed them blindly. I remember a time—why, it was when my boy was born—when I was such an admirer of Grover Cleveland and John G. Carilsle that if I had named my child after public men, I would have called my boy Cleveland Carlisle Bryan. You can imagine how I would feel now if I had given him that name.

Now, these were our leaders, and, my friends, we have learned a lesson in regard to leadership. We have found that a leader ceases to be a leader when he ceases to have followers. As some one has remarked, the real leader is the man who is going in the same direction that the people are going, but is just a little bit ahead. That is what a leader is, he must be going in the same direction as the people. In fact, a great many people make a mistake when they think that the people, going in the same direction as they, are following them. If the man who thinks he is leading will just turn and go the other way he will be surprised to find how few of the people will turn back when he does. And so when people tell me that a change has taken place in the democratic party in the last few years, when they talk about the "remnant" who believe in the principles of the Kansas City platform—well, I have had too much experience to believe what they say, for I have spent now more than twenty years trying to change the minds of republicans, and I know what a slow process it is. I know also that the republicans have been trying to change the minds of democrats, and that is a slow process. Therefore I know that a man who talks about 6,500,000 people, turning around suddenly and going in the opposite direction does not know what he is talking about. Those who went down to defeat with us went down because they believed in the things that they fought for, and I know that they were willing to suffer defeat and fight for what they believed, rather than surrender their convictions on great questions in order to win any nominal victory, however great, that might be promised as a reward for that surrender.

I know that these have not changed and will not change their opinions on great fundamental principles. When I hear that people have met at some high-priced hotel and decided to nominate a candidate for the presidency who will accept the nomination only on condition that the platform repudiates the platforms of 1896 and 1900, it does not worry me. I say, "Wait until the fellows at the threshing machines; wait until the fellows in the shops; wait until the fellows who do the working and the voting; wait until these get together, and they will not ask such a man to accept a nomination for the presidency."

My friends, I want to predict that no man in your lifetime or in mine will ever be a presidential candidate on the democratic ticket who will be ashamed to admit that he stood for the principles set forth in the platforms of 1896 and 1900.

If victory were the only things we were contending for; if we would put our argument on the low plane of trying to get the offices only, we could not afford to surrender our convictions.

If a young man comes to me and asks me how he can succeed in life, I tell him that first he must be honest; that, second, he must be industrious, and that if he is honest and industrious, his success will be measured by his ability. If he asks me if I can assure him success immediately, I tell him no; that no person can guarantee anything in the future, either for himself or for anybody else. But I tell him that he cannot afford to build for today or tomorrow; he must build for life. And no man has an ideal that is worth following that is not high enough to keep him looking upward until he dies. No man has an ideal that is worth following that is not so far in front of him that he cannot overtake it while he lives. The young man who will build his life upon a firm foundation, who will be honest, upright and faithful to every trust, cannot live in any community twenty-five years without being called upon to act as the representative and spokesman of his fellows.

And so it is with the democratic party. If we attempt to build for tomorrow, we build in vain. If we attempt to catch a little temporary popularity by selling our principles on the auction block, or buying policies at a junkshop, we will not only fail of immediate success, but we will fail of ultimate success.

There never was a time when this country was more in need of a real democratic party than it is today. Never in this country's history did we need a more complete application of democratic principles than now.

We have suffered for ten years because in 1892 we had a victory for the name, without a victory for the principles of the party. In 1896 the democratic party was disorganized. Why? Because we had won a victory in 1892 that betrayed the hopes of the people who gave victory to the party.

Every little while I see by the papers that they are going to have a harmony meeting; that they are going to bring together the men who have fought each other. I do not believe that we ought to risk a harmony meeting unless we compel the people who attend to leave their revolvers at the door. There is no use in having a harmony meeting between people who dislike each other more than they dislike republicans.

I have been invited to one or two meetings where Mr. Cleveland was invited, and I have refused to attend. And I have refused on the ground that he twice helped to elect a republican ticket, and that he has never intimated in the least that he intended to be a democrat again. I would rather meet at a democratic board an open republican enemy than a hypocrite who pretends to be a friend of the party while opposing its principles.

But I have about made up my mind to accept the next invitation that I receive to a harmony banquet where Mr. Cleveland is to be present, but I shall make my acceptance conditional upon being allowed to take as my toast "Grover Cleveland and His Democracy." I think I can handle that subject in such a way that he and I will not be present at any more harmony banquets.

And I have a right to speak of Grover Cleveland's democracy—for I have borne his sins in two national campaigns. He has made the democratic party the scapegoat for his political crimes, and his record still hangs as a millstone about the neck of the democratic party.

Grover Cleveland cannot come back to the party unrepentant without driving out ten votes for every vote that he can bring back.

What I say of him, I say of other men who have been conspicuous for their treachery; for their treachery not so much to the ticket as to the principles of the democratic party.

I believe in welcoming the prodigal son, while I have had some little sympathy for the feeling of the son who did not go astray, and who could not understand why when he had stayed at home all the time he had no fatted calf killed for him, but reserved for the one who had wasted his substance in riotous living—while I have had, as I say, some little sympathy for him, yet I recognized that there is forgiveness in the human heart and that it is natural to welcome back those who come back really sorry for what they have done.

I think an old colored minister described this forgiving spirit very accurately. He said that the father saw the son coming back, that he could see as the son came that he was sorry. The son had his head down, and he walked hesitatingly, almost ashamed to look his father in the face, and the father's heart went out to him, and the father hastened forth to meet him, and the son was glad and the father was glad. But, said the colored preacher, if the son had come back swaggering as if he owned the place, and had said to his father, "Wha's dat calf?" do you suppose the father would have killed the fatted calf for him?" That is the way I feel about it.

I care not what a man may have done against the democratic party, if he will come back sorry for what he has done, come back anxious to help build up the democratic party and make it strong, strong in the confidence of the people and in democratic principles, I will turn butcher and help kill the fatted calf when he returns.

But the men who are reorganizing the democratic party through the newspapers that did not support the ticket, these men are not coming back as prodigal sons. They come back boasting of what they have done. They come back, not to enter the father's house, but to put the father's house on wheels, and move it over onto some new ground that they demand the right to select. They come back saying that they are better democrats than the people who stayed at home. They come back, not with heads bowed down, willing to be servants in the building up of the party, but they come back and seize the fatted calf, and attempt to kick out the faithful democrats who remained in the house. That is the way they are coming back.

But, my friends, those who talk about reorganizing the party mistake the sentiments of the democrats who have sacrificed and suffered for their principles if they think that they will ever be allowed to take possession of the democratic party again.

I believe that the time is at hand when the democratic party can do great things, but, my friends, it is not by aping the republican ways. We have not room for two republican parties in the United States. One is enough. If the republican policies are right, it is presumptuous on our part to rush in and say, "We have just found it out; now let us administer the offices." If they discovered before we did that those principles and policies were good, we ought not to infringe on their patent.

I believe that the democratic party's greatest opportunity, whether you predicate it upon high principles or upon the low ground of expediency, is to stand erect and show what democracy really means. I believe that there is an opportunity in this country to present to the people higher ideals than the republicans are presenting.

I was delighted tonight to see the large number of young men at our public meeting. I want us to go out and appeal to these young men. I want us to show them that the democratic party is their friend; that it is championing their interests; that we are trying to keep the door of opportunity from being closed against these young men; that we are trying to make it possible for them to reach the highest rewards in the political and industrial world.

And I believe you have here in Delaware as good an opportunity as they have anywhere in the United States to show what real democracy means. I have been talking with some of your people, and they tell me that the condition here has not been exaggerated in the public press; that nowhere in the United States have as many people been actually purchased in proportion to the total vote as in Delaware. But, my friends, I am afraid that the democrats have not always been entirely free from blame. I do not mean to say that the democrats have approached the republicans in the number purchased, but I am afraid that the democrats have not always appealed, as they should have done, to the consceince, while the republicans were appealing to the pocketbook.

I believe that the conscience is the only thing that can be placed against money. If you can awaken a conscience, no money can buy it. It was a conscience that made men stand by the stake and smile as the flames consumed them. Awaken that conscience and all the money of all the world cannot corrupt Delaware!

And instead of trying to "reward" people who are democrats for remaining democrats, or trying to purchase republicans who can be bought, let your motto be that you do not want a vote that has not behind it the heart and the head of the voter; that you are going to fight this battle on democratic ground, and that you are going to purify politics in Delaware by setting the example, and showing how a campaign ought to be run.

You cannot surpass the republicans in the purchase of votes. You cannot imitate their methods, and win. You simply estop yourselves from criticising them. Never until you sell the principles of the party, can you get as much money for campaign purposes as they can. They can always offer five or ten or even a hundred dollars for every vote where you can offer one dollar, and if you go into the market and bid against them, they can outbid you every time.

But if you say to them that you have no money for that purpose, that you do not want any person to vote your ticket because he is paid for it, you will make it an honor to be a democrat in Delaware. You may be few in numbers when you start, but if you will go out and preach this gospel you will increase, and when you do get a vote it will be a vote that will stay, and you will accumulate votes and make yourself an irresistible force in this community.

You cannot adopt any other course without despairing of this republic. Tell me that you are going on from corruption to greater corruption? Tell me that there is no relief except in furnishing more money than the republicans can furnish? I tell you that that theory looks inevitably to the destruction of this republic. You cannot have a republic long under those conditions, and instead of imitating republicans and giving them no reason to leave their party, set before them a higher ideal, and go and appeal to the consciences of those republicans, old men, middle-aged men and young men.

Organize your clubs, and when a man joins, let him do as the old Carthagenian general's child did when his father brought him to the altar and made him swear eternal enmity to Rome. So when a man joins a democratic club in this state, make him walk up to the altar and lay his hand on it and swear eternal enmity to corruption in politics. Let the world know that the democratic party in Delaware, however small it may be, is a party of principles and convictions.

And I believe, my friends, that you will be surprised to find how many republicans, alarmed at what is going on in their party, will be glad to find some place to go, where they can act with ease of conscience, and where they will not be under condemnation for their own conduct. And it may be, if you will do that, that this will be the turning point in our political history, that out of your controversy here, out of your disgraceful conditon here, will come the hope of a better day, and that this corruption having gone to the very limit, will arouse the people to resistance, and little Delaware will lead the way to return to purity in politics.

You are small—and some of the republicans now do not like small states; they do not like to bring in new territories because they are small—but, my friends, virtue is not measured by the size of the man or by the size of the community that exhibits it.

Little Switzerland is not large, but she has given lessons

unto the world. Little Switzerland is not powerful in numbers or in physical strength, but she is leading the way in many reforms to the highest citizenship and to the best government.

And so little Delaware, small in numbers and in territory, may lead the way to purer politics.

I am glad to have been with you. You owe me nothing; I owe you everything. I never can pay the American people for what they have done for me, for while I do not assume that those who have voted for me have voted for me as a personal compliment or that they have placed me under personal obligations for what they have done, yet I do mean to say that the great struggling masses of this country have given to me all I have, or am, or hope to be, and all my life, whether much or little remains, will be all too short to show them how I appreciate what they have done.

All that I ask is for an opportunity to be in the fight until death takes me from the scene. All that I ask is that where the fight is hottest and the danger greatest I may be permitted to go, for no one has more reason than I to make sacrifice or risk danger for the welfare of the people of this country.

As I have seen men who have been republicans all their lives breaking the bands that have tied them to their party, sacrificing all the associations that have grown up in a lifetime; in order to follow their convictions; and as these men have supported me in my campaigns, they have convinced me that it is impossible to conceive of a situation so bad as to be beyond the hope of relief.

If our party will remain true to its principles, if, without yielding to temptation, it will prove to the republicans that there is a party that can be trusted, there will be multitudes of republicans who will turn to this party. They will turn to it and place the government in its hands.

Then this party, superior to the temptations that come from organized wealth, will so revise the laws as to place the burdens of taxation equitably upon the backs of the people; so reform our finances as to give the country a financial system made by the people for themselves; it will drive every private monopoly out of the United States, and open the door of opportunity again to our young men. And it will give to this nation a foreign policy that will make people everywhere lisp with gratitude the name of Democracy, because it will mean justice to people abroad as well as justice to people here.

It was said in olden times that to be a Roman was greater than to be a king. And so I want us to make the word "democrat" so priceless, that to be a democrat will stamp a man anywhere and everywhere as one who has principles that cannot be purchased with money, and purposes that are above the measures of dollars and cents.

ROOSEVELT AND THE COAL TRUST.

An interesting letter was recently written by W. R. Hearst to President Roosevelt. More than three months ago Mr. Hearst addressed a letter to the president notifying Mr. Roosevelt that he, Mr. Hearst, had asked Attorney General Knox for permission to furnish him with conclusive proofs of the existence of a coal trust. Mr. Hearst says that he submitted the proofs to the United States District Attorney of the southern district of New York and that these proofs demonstrated "under the hands and seals of the corporations constituting the trust that a combination of the coal-carrying railroads absolutely controls the country's supply of anthracite and fixes its price to the consumer.

Mr. Hearst reminds the president that the law officer of his administration has been and is remiss in his duty in not proceeding against trusts. He appeals to the president to command his attorney general to proceed against the coal trust both civilly and criminally or explain to the people of the United States his reasons for not doing so if reasons suitable for public avowal he has. The president is further reminded that the people have a right to expect action against the trusts in general and the coal trust in particular.

Mr. Hearst reminds the president that the coal trust continues to exist and continues to plunder because the laws are not enforced and he concludes that the attorney general is responsible to the president and that if the president shall uphold him in his refusal to act against the coal trust, the president will be responsible to the American people.

Mr. Roosevelt will find it difficult to avoid this question much longer. It is significant that when Mr. Knox delivered his famous speech at Pittsburg he did not undertake to explain to the people why he did not enforce the criminal clause of the existing law and although democratic newspapers all over the country called upon republican organs to explain the administration's failure to invoke the criminal indictment no republican editor has undertaken to provide an explanation.

Mr. Hearst's letter is as follows:

To Theodore Roosevelt, President of the United States—Sir: On October 4, more than three months ago, I had the honor of addressing a letter to you, informing you that I had petitioned your attorney general for permission to furnish him with conclusive proofs of the existence of a coal trust.

At the request of your attorney general, I submitted my proofs to General Burnett, United States district attorney for the southern district of New York.

Those proofs demonstrate, over the hands and seals of the corporations constituting the trust, that a combination of coal-carrying railroads absolutely controls the country's supply of anthracite and fixes its price to the consumer.

In the judgment of lawyers whose professional compentency is quite as undisputed as that of your attorney general, those proofs if presented in court would suffice to dissolve the coal trust and subject its members to the civil and criminal penalties provided by law.

Continuously since the submission of those proofs the coal trust has robbed the people, extorting famine prices for coal, a prime necessity of industrial and domestic life, yet no action has been taken against this trust by your attorney general for the enforcement of the laws and the relief of the public.

So remarkable has been the lethargy of your attorney general in the face of a condition of things which reaches the gravity of a widespread public calamity that in both houses of congress a resolution has been introduced calling upon him to disclose the evidence submitted by me through my attorneys in October last.

These proofs aside, sir, neither you nor any other well informed citizen can doubt the existence of the coal trust, nor be ignorant of the organized brigandage which it has practiced and is practicing.

You have but to consult the final report of the industrial commission to learn that the eight lines of railroad comprising the trust own nine-tenths of the anthracite deposits and mine three-quarters of the yearly product. From the same report you can ascertain that in order to crush out competition these railroads have charged extortionate freight rates. Compared with the charge per ton of bituminous coal the rate for carrying anthracite is so high that, in the langauge of industrial Commissioner Phillips, the excess charge "is greater every year than the interest on our national debt," and is "made possible by the railroad monopoly, now euphoniously called 'community of interests.'"

The fact that the coal trust exists is notorious, and its character is universally understood.

A former attorney general of the United States, Richard Olney, on October 11 last, in a public address at Boston, said that the members of the trust are the "most unblushing and persistent of law breakers," and he thus specified:

"For years they have defied the law of Pennsylvania, which forbids common carriers engaging in the business of mining.

"For years they have discriminated between customers in the freight charges on their railroads, in violation of the interstate commerce law.

"For years they have unlawfully monopolized interstate commerce, in violation of the Sherman anti-trust law."

Senator Spooner of Wisconsin, a member of your own party high in your confidence, in last Monday's debate on the Jones resolution directing the attorney general to transmit to the senate the evidence presented to him by me proving that a conspiracy in restraint of interstate trade exists, said:

"I have been of the opinion that probably there is such a conspiracy." And he added that "if there be such a conspiracy it is one that should be prosecuted as one absolutely wicked in its character and far-reaching in its deleterious effects. . . . . If one does exist it is a very merciless one, violating the laws of the United States and most harmful in every way."

You, Mr. President, can have no doubt of the existence of this conspiracy, but if there should chance to remain in your mind any such doubt, I suggest that you remove it by personally examining the evidence which I placed in possession of your attorney general in October.

Sir, these men of the coal trust, enormously rich and politically influential as they may be, are criminals. They swell their great fortunes daily by deliberate law-breaking.

And while your attorney general has remained so strangely quiescent these opulent and political influential criminals have adopted an old trust device for the double purpose of further plundering the public and laying the basis for a fraudulent defense against the evidence now in the hands of the attorney general should he begin proceedings against them. A pretended division between them and the so-called "independent" operators has been arranged, whereby these so-called "independents," who are utterly in the power of the trust, shall seem to compete with the trust, and so prepare the ground for a false contention that the trust is not a monopoly, but a legitimate business organization subject to competition. As the immediate result of this counterfeit rivalry the price of coal has been doubled.

As a citizen regardful of the public welfare, Mr. President, I respectfully represent to you that the law officer of your administration has been, and is, remiss in his duty in not proceeding against the coal trust on the evidence of its unlawful character supplied by me to him last year.

By that failure in duty he has encouraged the coal trust to take advantage of a situation largely of its own creation, not merely to persist in its customary pillage of the people, but to enormously increase the scale of its extortion.

The submission of evidence to your attorney general and my appeal to him to apply the law to the coal trust having up to this time resulted in no action on his part, I turn from him to you.

In your public speeches and messages, Mr. President, you have often declared your conviction that the great combinations of capital commonly known as trusts should be subjected to the fullest publicity and brought within the regulating control of the law, to the end that the public, while profiting by the concentration of capital in business, may be protected against the incidental evil effects of that concentration.

I submit, sir, that there is no other combination of capital in the country more contemputuous of law than the coal trust. And I further submit that the most effective method of subjecting it to publicity is to bring it into court to answer for its illegal offences.

The attorney general of the United States is your servant. He must obey your command or give way to a successor who will do so.

I appeal to you, therefore, Mr. President, to command your attorney general to proceed against the coal trust, both civilly and criminally, on the evidence of its unlawful acts laid before him by me, or explain to the people of the United States his reasons for not doing so, if reasons suitable for public avowal he has.

The people of the United States, President Roosevelt, have a right to expect action from you against the trusts in general and the coal trust in particular. No conspicuous public man of your party has so vehemently as yourself expressed a desire to protect the public from spoliation at the hands of combinations of predatory capital. And you have well said that "words are good when backed up by deeds, and only so."

What better proof of your sincerity could you give, what better deed in support of your words could you do, than by moving at once upon this insolent lawbreaker and wholesale robber of the people, the coal trust?

As a citizen I have done my duty in supplying evidence for the attack to your attorney general. As a citizen I do my duty in turning from him to you when time has shown his invincible reluctance to act.

The coal trust continues to exist and continues to plunder because the laws are not enforced.

For that non-enforcement of the laws, Mr. President, your attorney general is responsible to you, and if you shall uphold him in his refusal to act against the coal trust you will be responsible to the American people. Respectfully,
WILLIAM RANDOLPH HEARST.

One of the greatest mysteries of recent origin relates to the charge that John D. Rockefeller sent telegrams to at least nine senators protesting against any anti-trust legislation. The public generally and many newspapers were loth to believe that Mr. Rockefeller adopted that method of communicating with the senators. It has been well understood that Rockefeller and other trust magnates have used their influence to prevent legislation on former occasions, but it has always been done in a covert way and many people have doubted that Mr. Rockefeller would undertake to improve on his old-time and very eminently successful methods.

But the various opinions entertained by newspapers on this subject may be better understood by reference to certain criticisms.

The Chicago *Record-Herald* appears to take the matter seriously and intimates that the prospects of legislation which Mr. Rockefeller does not like "brightened suddenly after a long period of gloom" and Mr. Rockefeller evidently deemed it necessary to enter quick protest.

The Chicago *Chronicle* quotes Mr. Hanna as saying that "Mr. Rockefeller does not do business that way." The Chronicle thinks that it is possible that some over-zelous member of

Mr. Rockefeller's circle knowing that man's great influence with well-known senators thought he was in the habit of communicating his instructions to them as he would issue orders to the kerosene corporations and that "in this way the telegrams may have been dispatched by one of the Standard Oil attorneys without the direct knowledge or approval of Mr. Rockefeller."

The Louisville *Courier-Journal,* of which Menry Watterson is the editor, says that the alleged Rockefeller telegrams is "a pretense of opposition." The *Courier-Journal* says it is "a pretty trick though not a new one," and that the Rockefeller incident seems to have been planned "to surround with a spectacular eclat of capital's opposition a very innocent piece of legislation."

The Brooklyn *Citizen* refers to it as "the Rockefeller hoax." The *Citizen* says that while there is no doubt as to the interference of the Standard Oil company in national legislation "the American people are not willing to believe that Mr. Rockefeller suddenly lost his senses to the extent that he would send telegrams to senators." The *Citizen* says:

"Such orders as he has to convey are gladly and willingly executed by Senator Aldrich, of Rhode Island, who is the acknowledged legislative agent of the protected interests and who moreover, has close family connections with the Rockefellers. It was a daughter of this Rhode Island senator who recently married the eldest son and heir of John D. Rockefeller."

The *Citizen* adds that "Anyway, there is nothing in the so-called 'trust busting' entered into by republican senators and congressmen to cause the Standard Oil company or any other trust the slightest uneasiness." And the Brooklyn paper adds: "All that President Roosevelt and trust busters of his type are aiming at is to prevent the real trust busters, the democrats, from attaining power. They are simply engaged in fooling the people and pretending to be at war with the trusts."

The Washington correspondent of the San Francisco *Examiner,* referring to this incident, says: "The administration and administration senators appear to have been caught redhanded in the act of pulling the wool over the eyes of the public." This correspondent says that "everybody in Washington is laughing at the boomerang."

The Washington correspondent of the New York *World*, however, insists that he has good authority for saying that Rockefeller did send telegrams to at least nine senators. He says that every one of the men implicated denies that he received such a telegram with the exception of Senator Hale who declines to be questioned on the subject. This correspondent says that these telegrams were signed by John D. Rockefeller, J. D. Rockefeller, jr., W. H. Rogers, Walter Jennings, William Rockefeller and C. R. Archibald. The purport of these telegrams is said to be a general protest against all anti-trust legislation, and a protest against the Nelson amendment. It is bluntly stated by the *World*, correspondent, as well as by other correspondents, that the story relating to the Rockefeller telegrams emanated from the White house; and the attitude of hostility suddenly assumed toward Mr. Roosevelt by republican leaders would indicate that this statement is generally believed in Washington. The *World* correspondent says that "almost every item of distinctive information connected with these telegrams has been traced through various channels back to some confidential conversation with the president." It is pointed out by the *World* correspondent that in these telegrams it was announced that an attorney for the Standard Oil company would follow with a substitute for the Nelson amendments. It is shown that an attorney did come and that the fact remains that a substitute for the Nelson amendment was tendered to Senator Nelson by an unnamed senator, which substitute was refused.

As a matter of fact, few people are surprised to learn that Mr. Rockefeller has communicated with senators on the subject of anti-trust legislation. The only surprise relates to the manner which Mr. Rockefeller is alleged to have adopted. The New York *World* says that this charge affects not only the integrity of the individual senators to whom the telegrams were said to have been sent, but the integrity of the senate as a body, and it calls upon the senate for an immediate and thorough investigation of the truth of the charge. The

World says that the people would like to know who sent the telegrams, who received them and exactly what those telegrams said about pending anti-trust bills.

It is pointed out by a number of correspondents that while the senate could not be expected to investigate every charge made the fact that it has been generally and repeatedly stated that this charge emanated from the White house makes it necessary that the senate call for an investigation as to the truth of the story.

There are, however, a great many people who will be inclined to think that considerable noise has been made over the fact that the Standard Oil magnate sent telegrams to several senators when it is remembered that it has been generally understood that for several years republican leaders in both branches of congress have been doing the bidding of Rockefeller and other trust magnates with respect to every bit of proposed legislation wherein the people could find the least promise of relief. Repeatedly it has been charged that Senator Aldrich is the spokesman of the trust magnates on the floor of the senate and that all proposed legislation by the republican leaders with respect to the trusts was framed in accordance with the wishes of the trust magnates. These charges, so long and so generally made and so thoroughly believed by the American people, have never been investigated and no one has ever seriously proposed an investigation.

"WALL STREET KNOWS."

It may be instructive for those who imagine that the members of the republican congress really intended to provide any effective measures against trusts to read, in the light of the loud boasts now made on anti-trust lines by republican organs, an article written by a republican correspondent for a republican newspaper.

In a dispatch to the Chicago *Record-Herald,* under date of Washington, January 15, Walter Wellman said: "There is no more uneasiness in Wall street as to what congress is to do in the trust-busting line. Wall street knows."

According to this republican correspondent, the representatives of the trust recently held a secret meeting in Washington and in conferences with republican leaders reached an agreement calling for these provisions:

1. Publicity of the operations of inter-state trusts through reports to a government department.

2. More drastic law against discriminations and the payment of rebates by common carriers; shippers who receive rebates to be punishable, the same as transportation company officials who pay them.

3. The administration of the trust law to be turned over to a new department of commerce, to be created by congress and that department to have a bureau of insurance and corporations to deal directly with trust reports and publications.

Mr. Wellman said that it did not matter what the judiciary committee or the sub-committee of the house might do. That sub-committee was just then very active; but Mr. Wellman said "the president, the attorney general, the house judiciary committee and the house itself have not power enough to put through anything which the trusts object to. In trust legislation as in almost everything else the senate is the court of last resort."

Mr. Wellman cannot relieve the president of the entire responsibility nor persuade his readers that Mr. Roosevelt is at all "strenuous" in his famous anti-trust campaign until he can explain how it happens that Mr. Roosevelt's plan for curbing the trusts is not a bit more radical than the plan herein referred to, which plan, according to Mr. Wellman, the representatives of the trusts cordially indorsed.

The opening paragraph in Mr. Wellman's dispatch deserves a place in the scrap-book of every republican who imagines that the people have any reason to hope for relief from trust impositions at the hands of the republican party. In the beginning Mr. Wellman said:

"Anti-trust legislation so-called, but legislation which the trusts are wholly willing to have, is likely to be passed by the present congress. In fact, what amounts to an agreement or understanding has been reached between the leaders of the republican party in Washington, as the party of the first part, and the representatives of some of the most powerful trusts in the country as the party of the second part. The agreement is to pass a nominal anti-trust bill, but to take good care that nothing shall appear in it which the trusts have any objections to."

Referring to the visit of the representatives of the trusts, Mr. Wellman said:

"They declared that they had no objection to the publicity suggestion made by President Roosevelt. In fact, some of the biggest trusts, notably the United States steel corporation, have voluntarily adopted the policy of taking the public fully into confidence as to their operations. The progressive men who are at the head of a number of the greatest corporations are anxious to have as much publicity as possible as to the affairs of companies. Publicity is protection for investors as well as desirable on other grounds of public policy."

This correspondent gave the information that as a part of this program the bill to create a department of commerce would be passed and that Mr. Cortelyou would be at the head.

It is not strange, in the light of such disclosures as these, that sincere and conscientious republicans who realize that the trust system is disadvantageous to their interests continue to nurse the hope that the republican party will do something to protect the people from trust impositions?

THE TREATMENT OF CRIMINALS.

A recent issue of the Philadelphia *Enquirer* contained an editorial giving intelligent consideration to the treatment of criminals after they have satisfied the requirements of the law. It speaks of the difficulty which the ex-convict has in finding employment, and says:

"What is the future of this man? This problem is constantly coming up and it is sad to see that there is little progress made towards solving it. No business man wants to employ an ex-convict; if he is a professional man no one cares for his services. There seems almost no avenue of employment for him. What can he do?"

This sums up the situation, and it deserves serious consideration. How would it do to try a system of probation, say a year or two, during which the ex-convict would have a chance to prove his worthiness? That is, after his term has expired let him have the privilege of working voluntarily under the direction of the state at the same occupation which he followed in the penitentiary, he to come and go at his pleasure as long as he deports himself properly.

Society feels an interest in restoring the ex-convict to his place in the industrial community, but no one is willing to risk employing him until his reformation is proven. If, after his release, he shows by his conduct that he desires to work and establish himself in the esteem of his fellows he will have no difficulty in finding employment. The parole is being used with increasing frequency where someone is willing to become responsible for the good conduct of the convict, and the probationary period would provide for those without friends to stand sponsor for them. The reclamation of those who have fallen before temptation and yet desire to be reinstated in the confidence of the public is certainly to be desired.

NORTHERN SECURITIES CASE.

The opinion delivered by the United States court of appeals in the Northern Securities case is a vigorous rebuke to men who would conspire against public interests by engaging in what Mr. Roosevelt calls "the inevitable process of economic evolution," otherwise and more properly known as trust organization.

If sustained by the supreme court, to which court the case will, of course, be taken, the decision of the court of appeals will result in the complete destruction of the Northern Securities company, which is the name for the trust accomplished by the merger of the Northern Pacific Railroad company and the Great Northern Railroad company.

In its opinion the court of appeals goes directly to the point when it says that the claim that the rate fixed by a combination or a trust is reasonable is of no importance. According to the court, the vice of such a combination is that it confers the power to establish unreasonable rates and directly restrains commerce by placing obstacles in the way of free and unrestricted competition.

According to the court, the New Jersey charter which this combination holds, does not give it authority to violate the federal anti-trust law. The purpose of this merger, in the opinion of the court of appeals, was to destroy every motive for competition between two roads engaged in interstate traffic and the merger is declared to be a trust. The court also says that while the anti-trust law applies to interstate carriers of freight and passengers, it applies to all other persons, natural or artificial; and it is further pointed out that the anti-trust law may not be violated by any device such as entrusting the stock of rival roads to one person with instructions how to vote it, the court declaring that "the result would have been a combination in direct restraint of interstate commerce because it gave power to suppress competition."

The court bluntly declares that the contention that if the proposed merger is held to be in violation of the anti-trust law, then that law unduly restricts the rights of individuals to make contracts and is therefore invalid, is entitled to small consideration. On this point the court says that the constitutional provision with respect to contracts does not exclude congress from legislating with respect to contracts that seek to destroy competition and to antagonize public interests. On the contrary, the court declares:

"The provision regarding the liberty of the citizen is to some extent limited by the commerce clause of the constitution, and that the power of congress to regulate interstate commerce comprises the right to enact a law prohibiting the citizen from entering into those private contracts which directly and substantially, and do not merely, indirectly, remotely, incidentally and collaterately, regulate to a greater or less degree the commerce among the states."

J. Pierpont Morgan has already announced that the case will be appealed to the supreme court. He expresses confidence that it will be reversed by that tribunal. At the same time, he says: "When railroad men know exactly how the law is to be interpreted, they will probably find good ways to see that properties are operated economically and profitably." A fair interpretation of this is that whatever the decision of the supreme court, the trust magnates will find a method of violating the law without laying themselves liable.

The decision of the court of appeals will be accepted as an eminently just one by all who are really opposed to the trust system; and Mr. Morgan and his associates may yet learn that although the lawyers employed by the trust magnates may be ingenious in "finding good ways to see that properties are operated economically and profitably," the people, in whose interests laws are presumed to be enacted, may find "good ways" to see that those laws are vigorously enforced, in spite of the ingenuity of high-priced lawyers and the powerful influences of trust magnates.

ELECTION OF SENATORS BY THE PEOPLE.

The proposition that United States senators be elected by direct vote of the people has the cordial support of the rank and file of all political parties. To be sure, there are many republican politicians who do not take kindly to the suggestion and the republican United States senate has shown its determination to prevent the accomplishment of this important reform. But so strong is the sentiment among the people that even republican legislatures have recognized the sentiment and have given indorsement to the plan.

The Nebraska legislature is republican and although legislation was very generally controlled by the corporations, public sentiment was so strongly in favor of the election of senators by the people that the Nebraska assembly, recently adjourned, adopted the following:

"Resolved, That it is deemed necessary to amend the constitution of the United States so as to make provision therein for the election of United States senators by direct vote of the people.

"Sec. 2. That pursuant to the provisions of article five (5) of the constitution of the United States, application is hereby made to the congress of the United States to call a convention to propose an amendment to the constitution of the United States providing for the election of United States senators by direct vote of the people.

"Sec. 3. That a copy of this joint resolution be sent to each senator and representative from the state of Nebraska in the congress of the United States and to each presiding officer of the senate and house composing the congress."

In 1901 the Michigan legislature adopted a resolution asking congress to call a convention for the purpose of proposing an amendment to the constitution providing for the election of senators by popular vote. A similar resolution has been adopted by legislatures as follows: Montana in 1903, Texas in 1903, Missouri in 1903, Pennsylvania in 1901, Kansas in 1903, Utah in 1903, Nevada in 1903, Tennessee in 1901, California in 1903, Oregon in 1903, Florida in 1901, Washington in 1903, North Carolina in 1901, Minnesota in 1901, Idaho in 1903, South Dakota in 1903.

In 1901 a similar resolution was introduced in the lower house of the North Dakota legislature. That resolution passed the house and on being sent to the senate was referred to the judiciary committee, but it was never reported and hence failed of passage.

The resolution was introduced in the lower house of the Massachusetts legislature and was referred to the committee on federal relations.

The resolution was introduced in the Wisconsin legislature and is pending there.

The resolution was introduced in the New York legislature, but no action was taken by either house.

In the Indiana legislature the resolution was introduced in the house and was defeated.

The resolution was not introduced in the Georgia legislature. The same is true of the legislatures of New Hampshire, Alabama, Wyoming, Rhode Island, New Jersey, Maine and Connecticut.

The resolution passed the lower house of the Delaware legislature, but was defeated in the senate.

"PHILANTHROPY."

One of J. Pierpont Morgan's friends recently announced that Mr. Morgan was planning to build a great art museum and present the same to the American people. Speaking to a reporter for the New York World, this friend said:

"This much can be said definitely, and that is that Mr. Morgan is by nature one of the most philanthropic men in the world. He has not made his vast collections with a view to keeping them secluded for the personal enjoyment of himself and his friends, but he cherishes the ambition of making his collection the most beautiful and valuable in the world. Morgan is today the greatest art collector in the world. He has spent more money for art objects probably than the dozen other most lavish collectors in the world combined. He is a man of rare taste and expert judgment. As an art critic he has few equals, and he has gathered together hundreds of marvellously beautiful things. It is the desire of the owner of these objects that they shall be made available for the American people."

If Mr. Morgan is "by nature one of the most philanthropic men in the world," why does he confine his demonstrations along this line to the field of art? If he thinks it the part of philanthropy not to make his vast art collections with a view to keeping them secluded for the personal enjoyment of himself and friends, and if he things that it is important that these objects be made available for the American people, why does he not show a bit of the same spirit with respect to the people's necessities?

Mr. Morgan is very anxious to have his art collection admitted free of duty and he has been very bitter in his denunciation of the high tariff that would be assessed against these treasures; and yet there is nothing in his brand of philanthropy to prompt him to protest against the high tariffs levied upon the necessities of life.

No one will seriously object if Mr. Morgan's friends can imagine that they find anything of the philanthropic in the greatest trust organizer the world has ever produced; but they ought not to flatter themselves into the notion that they can bring any considerable number of the American people to their way of thinking in the light of the fact that Mr. Morgan is the head and front of the most oppressive commercial system that has ever arrayed itself against the real business interests of a country.

A GOOD SUGGESTION.

The St. Louis grand jury which has been examining into the boodling cases, makes a suggestion which is worthy of consideration. After declaring that there should be a statute making it unlawful for lobbyists to ply their profession in the manner in which they now work, the jury adds:

We believe that laws should be enacted providing for the forfeiture of franchises procured by corrupt methods. The rule of law as to stolen property should be made to apply to franchises obtained by bribery. There can be no vested rights in stolen goods, and there should be no vested rights in public franchises secured by venal methods.

Why should title pass from the public any more than from an individual where fraud is clearly shown? Why not make it the duty of the holder of stock in a franchise-owning company to examine the method by which the franchise was secured? As the grand jury says, title does not pass with stolen goods when the thing stolen is a horse or other piece of personal property. Why should the rights of the public be less carefully dealt with? The jury also advises the passage of a law extending the statute of limitations in case of crimes against the public. It explains that it would have brought in more indictments but for the fact that many of the crimes found had been outlawed.

The investigations that Mr. Folk has been conducting at St. Louis ought to result in great good elsewhere as well as in that state. Those who interest themselves in public affairs —and this ought to include all citizens—may well profit by the facts brought out in Missouri.

JUDGE LOCHREN'S DECISION.

The decision rendered by Judge Lochren in the United States circuit court at St. Paul with respect to the complaint that the Northern Securities company had violated the Minnesota state law, does not directly affect the case already decided by the United States court of appeals, which case is now pending, on appeal, in the United States supreme court.

The case considered by the federal court of appeals involved a violation of the federal anti-trust law.

The case in which Judge Lochren rendered a decision involved a violation of the Minnesota anti-trust law.

But, in principle, Judge Lochren's decision is essentially at variance with the decision rendered by the court of appeals. For this reason and for the further reason that the Lochren decision practically raised the question as to whether a state law aimed at the destruction of competition may be effective, Judge Lochren's decision is of the highest importance.

Minnesota, like many other states, has a statute forbidding the consolidation of parallel railroads. In Minnesota this particular law was enacted in 1874. In 1881 a law was passed permitting one railroad company to consolidate its stock and franchise with the stock of any other roads which might be connected and operate together to constitute a continuous main line with or without branches. At the same time the act of 1881 reiterated the prohibition against consolidating parallel and competing lines. In 1899 the Minnesota legislature enacted an anti-trust law forbidding combinations in restraint of trade and commerce between the state of Minnesota and other states.

In his opinion, Judge Lochren directed attention to all of these Minnesota laws. Yet while admitting that the Northern Securities company is "an investor in and owner of a majority of the stock of each of these two railroad companies," Judge Lochren said: "It has done no act and made no contract in restraint of trade or commerce." Judge Lochren held that the action of Mr. Hill in promoting the formation of this trust 'under the circumstances and for the purposes for which the evidence discloses, and investing in its stock by the sale to it of his stock in the two railroad companies, involved no act or contract in restraint of trade or commerce or affecting transportation or rates more than any ordinary transfer of railroad stock from one person to another."

Judge Lochren admitted that his conclusion is "apparently contrary to that reached by the eminent judges who recently decided the case of the United States versus the Northern Securities company and who will doubtless in another court review this cause upon appeal." But he said that his own sense of duty and the rights of the litigants alike required that his own deliberate judgment guided by his understanding of the authoritative exposition of the law be given in all causes tried before him.

Judge Lochren said that he was compelled to reject the doctrine that "any person can be held to have committed or to be purposing or about to commit a high penal offense merely because it can be shown that his pecuniary interests will be thereby advanced and he has the power either directly by himself or indirectly by persuasion or coercion of his agents to compass the commission of the offense."

It is not at all surprising to learn through the newspaper dispatches that "Judge Lochren's decision was immediately communicated to President Hill of the Great Northern and to President Mellen of the Northern Pacific. The news of his victory greatly pleased President Hill."

The Minnesota laws cited by Judge Lochren show that the merger is distinctly in violation of the state law. If it were necessary that some act, agreement or contract immediately in restraint of trade or commerce be made by companies controlling consolidated parallel railroads, then the law forbidding such consolidation would be a dead letter. Such a law would be wholly useless because, according to Judge Lochren's decision, parallel railroads may consolidate even though the state law explicitly forbids such consolidation, providing no act or contract in restraint of trade or commerce shall be made.

The real evil of such consolidations was well defined by Judge Thayer in the opinions delivered in the United States court of appeals when he said:

"It matters not whether by acting under such a contract the

rate fixed is reasonable or unreasonable, the vice of such a contract or combination being that it confers the power to establish unreasonable rates and directly restrains commerce by placing obstacles in the way of unrestricted competition between carriers who are natural rivals for patronage; and finally that congress has the power under the grant of authority contained in the federal constitution to regulate commerce, to say that no contract or combination shall be legal which is in restraint of interstate trade or commerce by shutting off the operation of the general law of competition."

Judge Thayer further held that if the stock had been entrusted to one person with instructions how to vote it "the result would be a combination in direct restraint of interstate commerce because it gave power to suppress competition;" and it was further held that the organization of the securities company "accomplishes the object which congress has denounced as illegal."

Should the principle of Judge Lochren's decision prevail, then all anti-trust legislation might fall to the ground. Under that principle trusts could be organized, mergers could be effected, combinations could be accomplished and the only thing essential to the avoidance of illegality would be that the managements should not immediately do anything in the way of forcing up prices or directly placing new burdens upon the public.

Commenting upon the doctrine which Judge Lochren says he is compelled to reject, the Des Moines *Register and Leader*, a republican paper, says:

"The whole theory of the law in restraint of crime is based upon the assumption that when a man puts himself in position to commit an offense and his evident interest lies in having the offense committed, it is his purpose to commit it. On what other theory are men every day bound over to keep the peace? On what other theory did a New York judge the other day issue a permanent injunction restraining strikers from even addressing employes who had taken their places on the street?"

This republican paper adds that there is no question in Judge Lochren's mind or anybody else's that the purpose for which the Northern Securities company was organized; that the merger promoters have never been at any pains to conceal it; that they have not only admitted that their pecuniary interests lay in a consolidation, but they have also admitted that the stock of both companies was brought together for the purpose of consolidating them; and the *Register and Leader* adds:

"To pretend now to assume that there is no sufficient reason to believe that the management of the two lines will be brought together in reality, if not in outward form, is to make justice blinder than a bat, too blind to know whether she is even holding scales at all, to say nothing of knowing whether they balance or not.

"It is such rulings as this that make the application of the writ of injunction so often the object of adverse criticism. In New York the judge holds that when a striker speaks to a non-striker it is fair to assume that he intends to violate the law. In Minnesota although a consolidation of two competing railways has been actually effected in broad daylight, Judge Lochren holds it would be unjust to assume that they contemplate any violation of the statute that prohibits such consolidation."

It is gratifying to learn from Governor Van Sant that he purposes to carry on the fight "until the Minnesota laws are vindicated and upheld" and that he says that until it is conclusively shown that "by intrigue results can be accomplisehd which our laws were intended to prevent; that the creation of another state can be used to accomplish in Minnesota that which is against the declared policies of that state; that competition shall be open, active, and potential; that dummies shall not be directors, officers, and agents who so operate the railroads of Minnesota that its law shall be nullified and rendered ineffective." Governor Van Sant says that he has faith to believe that the final decision will be in favor of the state and that the Northern Securities company will be dissolved.

It is to be hoped that Governor Van Sant's faith is well grounded. The power of the state government, as well as the power of the federal government, to deal with the trust evil must be faithfully preserved; and once it be admitted, as the federal court of appeals has said, that congress may by enactment prevent mergers and combinations and impose penalty, in advance of any otherwise overt act, then it is absurd to say that a state cannot legislate in a similar way against the destruction of competition and for the protection of public interests.

MALIGNANT PARTISANSHIP.

President Roosevelt is rapidly acquiring an unenviable reputation as a malignant partisan. In his speech at the opening of the St. Louis exposition he studiously avoided giving any credit to Jefferson for the purchase of the Louisiana territory. The only reference he made to the great American who wrote the Declaration of Independence, added a vast domain to the United States, founded the democratic party and for twenty-five years was the principal factor in the political life of America—the only reference to this illustrious character was an inciental one. There could be no reason for this slight except the president's desire to avoid even a complimentary reference to a democrat.

In his speech at the battlefield of Antietam, however, the president went even farther in his attempt to ignore a democratic character. On that occasion he paid a tribute to the valor of the New Jersey soldiers, mentioned General Lee, President Lincoln, General Slocum, General Grant, and General Greene—going so far as to mention by name General Greene's son, who now holds a position by republican appointment—but in all the speech he never mentioned the name of General McClellan, who commanded the Union forces on that occasion and showed a military skill that gave him a fixed place in the military annals of the nation. General McClellan was the democratic candidate for the presidency in 1864 and his son is a democratic member of congress. These facts may explain why President Roosevelt so studiously avoided a mention of his name. It would be a reflection upon the intelligence of the hero of San Juan hill to say that he did not know who commanded the Union forces at that time. As General McClellan's name was naturally and necessarily connected with the battlefield, the president can only excuse his failure to mention him by saying that a democrat, no matter how great or conspicuous, is not worthy to be complimented or even mentioned by the republican president of the United States.

There is at least one consolation to be drawn from the president's conduct at Antietam, namely, that he has reached the limit of malignant partisanship and that the public can rest easy in the belief that there is no depth beyond to which he can fall. He is at the bottom.

"ASSET CURRENCY."

A constant reader wants to know the "plain meaning of an asset currency, and how it compares with our present system of currency." The term "aset currency" is used to describe the currency which the bankers are now proposing, namely, a currency which does not rest upon government bonds as the present currency does, but merely upon the assets of the bank. The currency is printed by the government and issued to the bank with no security fund back of it except a general lien upon the assets of the bank. As the proposition has not been embodied in a law yet it is impossible to speak of it in detail, but this much is evident: if the government does not guarantee the currency it may become worthless if the officials of the bank abscond with the assets. If, on the other hand, the government guarantees the currency, the bank gets the benefit and the people represented by the government run all the risks.

SERVING GOD AT THE BALLOT BOX.

In a sermon recently delivered, Rev. L. A. Crandall, a Chicago clergyman, said: "Duty is not transferrable. We can not worship God by telephone or fight the battles of righteousness by substitutes. Religion reaches into every detail of life, and includes our duty as citizens. We may serve God at the ballot box as certainly as in the church. The man who evades his duty by leaving the conduct of affairs in the hands of the professionals is guilty before God. Suffrage is not only a privilege, but an obligation; and the man who holds himself too good to vote is too bad for the kingdom of heaven."

It must be admitted that the reverend gentleman stated the case in very vigorous fashion; and yet who will contend that he did not speak with authority?

With evils existing and growing all about us, who will say that we cannot serve God at the ballot box as certainly as in the church?

The man who, on the Sabbath day, sings "Lead, Kindly Light," and then, on election day, casts his ballot in support of policies advanced in the interests of those who oppress the weak and the helpless, is by no means discharging his duty.

Doubtless there are many conscientious Christian men who vote with the trust magnates through ignorance; and yet as much as it is the duty of the Christian to search the scriptures in order that he may not be misled, so it is his duty to observe carefully the events of the day and study thoughtfully the policies advanced by political organizations that call for his vote.

As much as it is the duty of the Christian to refrain from doing evil in the ordinary affairs of life, to withhold his indorsement from questionable transactions, to hurt nobody and to give every one his just due, it is also his duty to withhold his indorsement from political parties or political candidates who would so arrange the policies of the government that the few may live in luxury while the many must struggle for bare existence. It is not only his duty to vote, but it is his duty to vote right; and voting right means that he must make an intelligent and patriotic study of the principles and policies advocated by the respective political parties and, without regard to the prejudices of the past, cast his vote with those who seem most willing and most likely to bring about the best government and to establish policies that will result in the greatest good to the greatest number.

We may, indeed, serve God at the ballot box as certainly as in the church; and when the majority of the American people come to appreciate this clear-cut statement, whenever God is as faithfully served at the ballot box as He is in the church, it may be depended upon that the era of trusts, of imperialism, of spoliation and of corruption will be at an end, and the probability of evils in our public life will be reduced to the minimum.

A MOMENTOUS PROBLEM.

Governor La Follette of Wisconsin delivered an address July 18 at Chautauqua, N. Y. His subject was "Representative Government."

That address should be read by every American citizen. It shows that the evils of the day are recognized by a republican governor who has the courage to speak plainly. It is true that no well informed person denies the correctness of the charges made by the republican governor of Wisconsin; and yet it is significant that other republican leaders keep silent and that those who speak candidly upon these subjects, as the Wisconsin governor has done, are not regarded by party leaders as "thoroughly sound republicans."

In his speech at Chautauqua, Governor La Follette pointed out that the basic principle of this government is the will of the people; that its founders devised a system which seemed to assure the means of ascertaining that will, of enacting it into legislation and enforcing it through administration of the law. This will was to be accomplished by electing men to make and men to execute the law which represent in the laws so made and executed the will of the people. Governor La Follette said that this was the establishment of a representative government where every man had equal voice, equal rights and equal responsibility. And then this republican governor asked his auditors:

"Have we such a government today, or are we rapidly coming to be dominated by force, in making and enacting our laws, which thwart the will of the people and menace the very life of representative government? No man questioned it for a hundred years. Whoever asserts it now is denounced as a 'menace to industrial progress.'"

Governor La Follette quoted from Washington, Jefferson, Lincoln and others to show that the fathers of the country regarded the people as the source of power and he said that it was reserved for Abraham Lincoln, on the field of Gettysburg, to express at once the profoundest and most philosophical, the simplest and most popular definition of American democracy ever uttered, when he declared:

"'We here highly resolve that these dead shall not have

died in vain; that this nation, under God, shall have a new birth of freedom, and that the government of the people, by the people and for the people shall not perish from the earth.'"

Governor La Follette disclaimed any disposition to excite the prejudices of his auditors or to invoke an unfair judgment, but he declared that deep conviction impelled him to appeal to their patriotism to meet an impending crisis. He said: "We owe it to the living as well as to the dead to make honest answer to this question, 'Is our government of city, state, and nation thoroughly representative of the will of the people?'"

Governor La Follette further said:

"One of the causes of revolution proclaimed in the Declaration of Independence was: 'Imposing taxes on us without our consent.' Today, great aggregations of corporate wealth buy immunity from taxation in our legislatures, and throw the burden which they should bear onto the individual taxpayer of every municipality and state. Betrayed by his representative, the individual taxpayer is overtaxed for the benefit of the corporation. Taxation without representation is as much a crime against just and equal government in 1903 as it was in 1776. Government by corporations is as destructive of the liberties of the people of this country as the excerise of the same power by a foreign monarch. The arbitrary control of the price of coal and iron, and corn, and wheat, and beef— whether by an extortionate transportation rate, or by a monster combination, is a more absolute tyranny of the American people than quartering the army of King George upon the American colonists without their consent. There can be no such thing as commercial slavery and individual freedom. We may have the privilege of the ballot, we may have the semblance of democracy, but industrial servitude means political servitude. Monopoly in transportation and coal and iron and the food products, makes a pretense and a mockery of political freedom.

"Let us see if the time be not ripe for a new declaration of American independence. We are building up colossal fortunes, granting unlimited power to corporate organization, and consolidating and massing together business interests as never before in the commercial history of the world, but the people are losing control of their own government. Its foundations are being sapped and its integrity destroyed. 'What shall it profit a man if he gain the whole world and lose his own soul?' What shall it profit a nation if it gain untold wealth, and its people lose their liberty?"

Governor La Follette pointed out that the New York legislative investigation of the Erie railway reported that more than $1,000,000 was spent in one year for "extra legal services," and that money paid to political bosses was charged to the "India rubber account." He also showed that more recently the treasurer of the New York Central Railway company testified that his company had paid for legislation in one year $60,000 and in another year $205,000. He also quoted from the correspondence which passed between the late C. P. Huntington and General Colton in regard to the payment of money for the passage of legislative measures and for the control of congressmen. In one of the letters from Mr. Huntington, that great railroad magnate used this language:

"It is very important that his friends in Washington should be with us, and if that should be brought about by paying Carr, say $10,000 to $20,000 a year, I think we could afford to do it, but of course not until he had controlled his friends."

Having made this showing, Governor La Follette said:

"If there were no further evidences of the power of the railroads in legislation than that which is afforded by the statements from the record of the interstate commerce commission, it ought to arouse the entire country to such action as will bring congress to a sense of its responsibility to the people for some measure of justice and fair play."

And the governor added:

"The gravest danger menacing republican institutions today is the overbalancing control of city, state and national legislatures, by the wealth and power of public service corporations."

In another portion of his speech Governor La Follette read a letter bearing upon the action of the last congress. This letter was written to him by a United States senator under date of February 9, 1903. In this letter this senator wrote:

"'It is expecting too much from human nature that senators, whose every association is with the great railroad corporations, and whose political lives largely depend upon them, should, in good faith, make the railroads a servant of the people and to be subject to the decision of the commission when a question of rates is raised. The senate committee is by a decided majority men who bear those relations to the railroads.'"

Coming to the question of combinations and referring to the coal monopoly, Governor La Follette said:

"This coal trust bears harder even upon the unfortunate, helpless labor that mines the product at a wage level of a generation ago than upon the consumers who are just beginning to feel the burden of its increasing oppression. Its utter indifference and contempt for the constitutional and statutory law, for public opinion, and wide-spread want and suffering should awaken in the people of this free country the spirit which framed the Declaration of Independence and founded a government in which the will of the people should be supreme."

The governor paid his respects to the "elevator combine," and related the history of the meat trust, showing that it was also promoted by the railroads. And then he said:

"The plan developed and consummated in building up the Standard Oil monopoly, the anthracite coal trust, the elevator combination and the beef trust, are indicative of the power of the railroads in combination. There is not an important trust in the United States which does not have the assistance of the railroads in destroying its competitors in business. The limitation and control of these public service corporations in their legitimate field as common carriers is of primary importance in the practical solution of the trust problem which confronts the people of this country. It is manifest that any trust legislation to be effective must go hand in hand with a control over railway rates by the federal government on interstate commerce through an enlargement of the powers of the interstate commerce commission, and a like control of railroad rates on state commerce by each of the states through a state railway commission. Added to this, the railroad companies must be prohibited from using the extraordinary powers conferred upon them by the state for any other purpose than in conducting the transportation business for which they were organized."

Governor La Follette declared that the existence of a wicked alliance between the machine and corporations and the lust for money and power out of which it was born was never more brazenly confessed to the world than in a recent interview by Charles R. Brayton, machine boss of Rhode Island and principal lobbyist for the leading public service corporations of that state. In that interview Mr. Brayton said:

"'I am an attorney for certain clients, and I look out for their interests before the legislature. I am retained annually by the New York, New Haven & Hartford Railway company, as everyone knows. I act for the Rhode Island company (street car interests), and I have been retained in certain cases by the Providence Telphone company. In addition to this, I have had connections, not permanent, with various companies desiring franchises, charters, and things of that sort, from the legislature. I never solicit any business. It comes to me unsought. You see, in managing the campaign year after year, I am in a position to be of service to men all over the state. I help them to get elected, and, naturally, many warm friendships result; then when they are in a position to repay me, they are glad to do it.'"

Then the republican governor of Wisconsin concluded his remarkable speech in these words:

"The problem presented is a momentous one. It calls for no appeal to passion or prejudice or fear. It calls for courage and patriotism and self-sacrifice. It calls for solution. Shall the American people become servants instead of masters of their boasted material progress and prosperity—victims of the colossal wealth this free land has fostered and protected? Surely our great cities, our great states, our great nation, will not helplessly surrender to this most insidious enemy which is everywhere undermining official integrity and American institutions. Surely, we shall not permit this government to abandon its traditions, its memories, its hopes, and become the instrument of injustice and oppression. Surely, the American people will do their plain duty now as they did in the greatest epoch of this country's history. Surely, we shall meet the issues presented with rectitude and unfaltering devotion, strong in the faith of ultimate triumph."

REFERENCE INDEX

Adams, John Quincy, 371.
Adams, Judge, 63, 82, 83.
Alabama, 141, 142, 143, 250, 375, 443.
Alaska, 268, 361, 390.
Aldrich, Senator, 5, 6, 417, 435, 437.
Aldrich Bill, 78, 79, 192, 290, 291, 292, 293, 295, 296.
Alien and Sedition Laws, 367.
Allen, Ex-Sen. W. V., 108.
Allison, Senator, 354.
Altgeld, Gov. John P., 412, 414.
American, New York, 179.
American, Nashville, 120, 121, 249.
Arbitration, 389.
Arizona, 10, 20, 58, 390.
Arkansas, 141, 142, 143.
Asset Currency, 43, 150, 151, 193, 270, 272, 273, 275, 288, 289, 312, 451.
Australia, 361.
Baer, Pres., 179, 180, 181, 182.
Bailey, Senator, 78, 79.
Baker, Congressman, 259, 260, 303.
Bancroft, George, 158, 204, 205.
Belgium, 41.
Bennett, Philo Sherman, 254, 255, 314, 315, 316, 317, 318, 319, 320, 326, 327, 328, 329, 330, 331, 332, 333.
Benton, Thomas H., 191, 372, 410, 411.
Bimetallism, 35, 134, 136, 312, 324, 342, 344, 345, 346, 347, 348, 349, 350, 352, 357, 358.
Black, Gov. Chauncey F., 199.
Black, Judge Jere, 199.
Blackburn, Senator, 58, 78, 80.
Blaine, James G., 5, 384.
Blair, Francis P., 380.
Bland-Allison Act, 96, 224, 354, 355.
Bliss, Ex-Sec., 310.
Boyd, James E., 233.
Bradford, Capt. R. B., 314.
Breckenridge, John C., 376, 377, 379.
Brown, B. Gratz, 382.
Bride, William W., 222.
Bryan, W. J., 11, 40, 43, 44, 51, 74, 76, 77, 98, 107, 108, 109, 110, 111, 112, 113, 122, 133, 149, 155, 160, 196, 199, 201, 226, 227, 230, 231, 232, 233, 234, 235, 236, 237, 254, 264, 265, 266, 286, 312, 314, 315, 316, 317, 318, 319, 320, 326, 328, 329, 330, 331, 332, 341, 342, 362, 392, 393, 397, 403, 414, 422.

Burrows, Sen., 310.
Budd, Ex-Gov., 44.
Buchanan, James, 376.
Buckner, Simon P., 392.
Butler, William O., 374.
California, 141, 142, 143, 443.
Calhoun, John C., 371, 372.
Cannon, Joseph, 240.
Capital, Des Moines, 137, 138.
Carlysle, John G., 151, 357, 423.
Carlyle, Thomas, 104, 115.
Carmack, Senator, 5, 6.
Carnegie, Andrew, 408, 409.
Cass, Lewis, 374.
Central America, 33, 287.
Chicago Platform, 66, 67, 112, 134, 135, 153, 188, 234, 235, 360, 411, 415, 416.
Chronicle, Chicago, 59, 132, 135.
Chronicle, San Francisco, 52.
Citizen, Brooklyn, 435.
Clay, Henry, 371, 372, 374, 401.
Clayton, Congressman, 164.
Cleveland, Grover, 26, 32, 33, 48, 62, 75, 90, 108, 113, 141, 142, 143, 144, 145, 146, 152, 190, 191, 195, 199, 233, 234, 279, 280, 323, 384, 385, 413, 414, 415, 418, 425.
Cleveland, Judge L. W., 334.
Coal Trust, 430, 431, 432, 433, 456.
Colfax, Schuyler, 382.
417, 434.
Colombia, 325, 326.
Colorado, 142, 144.
Commoner, The, 10, 12, 18, 20, 21, 26, 30, 32, 33, 34, 35, 39, 40, 59, 60, 66, 67, 68, 74, 78, 80, 84, 89, 92, 93, 115, 120, 121, 122, 140, 147, 149, 153, 160, 161, 171, 175, 187, 190, 191, 199, 224, 239, 242, 249, 259, 264, 266, 267, 269, 276, 278, 279, 280, 286, 288, 294, 301, 303, 313, 315, 319, 320, 335, 343, 362, 404, 415, 416.
Congressional Record, 79.
Connecticut, 141, 142, 143, 144, 307, 329, 443.
Corbin, General, 314.
Corresca, Rocco, 39, 40.
Cosmopolitan Magazine, 399.
Courier-Journal, Louisville, 90, 435.
Criminals, Treatment of 439.
Crist, J. W., 222.
Crowell, Thomas Y. & Co., 225.
Cuba, 147, 300.
Cuban Treaty, 58.

REFERENCE INDEX

Cunneen, Atty. Gen., 27.
Cushing, Marshall, 196.
DeArmond, Congressman, 37.
Dayton, W. L., 376.
Declaration of Independence, 26, 44, 45, 54, 113, 119, 157, 222, 285, 393, 450, 454.
Delaware, 141, 142, 144, 250, 380, 422, 423, 427, 428, 429, 443.
Demonetization of Silver, 353, 387.
Depew, Senator C. M. 228, 229, 310.
Dewell, Ex-Gov. James D., 329, 332.
Dewey, Admiral George, 98.
Dexter, Henry, 304,, 305.
Diaz, President, 11.
Dingley Law, 397.
District of Columbia, 265, 267, 268.
Dolliver, Senator J. P. 5, 6, 7, 405
Donelson, Andrew J., 376.
Douglas, Stephen A., 376, 379.
Dred Scott Decision, 376.
Durbin, Governor, 249, 250.
Eagle, Brooklyn, 415.
Ebling, C. E., 364.
Education, Value of, 406.
Elkins Bill, 58.
Elkins, John P., ,106.
Elkins Law, 259, 404.
Elkins, Senator, 58.
Embargo Act, 368.
Encyclopedia Americana, 342, 343, 362.
England, 33, 54.
Enquirer, Philadelphia, 439.
Examiner, San Francisco, 435.
Express, Buffalo, 230.
Fairview, 4, 219, 222.
Farmer, Ohio, 178.
Fifty-Seventh Congress, 57, 58.
Filipinos, 87, 119, 185, 242, 243, 252, 265, 266, 267, 287, 300, 301, 394.
Fillmore, Millard, 375, 376.
Fisher, Judge E. L., 340.
Florida, 141, 142, 143, 445.
Folk, Joseph W., 445.
Foreman, Ford & Co., 92.
Foraker, Senator J. B., 11.
Fowler, Congressman, 28, 29.
Fowler Bill, 27, 28, 302.
Frame, Andrew J., 264.
France, 41.
Francis, David R., 195.
Franklin, Benjamin, 406.
Frick, H. C., 38.
Fremont, John C., 376.
Fugitive Slave Laws, 375, 378.
Funk & Wagnalls, 225.
Gage, Lyman P., 310.
Garibaldi, 39.
Garvin, Gov, L. F. G., 20, 21.
Georgia, 141, 142, 143, 250, 376, 392, 443.
Germany, 41.

Gilbert, Judge, 52, 53.
Gladstone, W. E., 154.
Globe-Democrat, 11, 37.
Goebel, Gov. William, 31.
Gold Standard, 151, 191, 338, 361,
Gorman, Senator A. P., 416, 417, 418.
Grant, Ulysses S., 382, 450.
Greeley, Horace, 382.
Gresham Law, 345.
Griggs, Ex-Atty. Gen., 227.
Grosscup, Judge, 405.
391, 397.
Gunton, Sec., 310.
Hamilton, Alexander, 21, 22, 23, 24, 25, 301, 351, 362, 366, 413.
Hamlin, Hannibal, 379.
Hancock, Gen. Winfield Scott, 384.
Hanna, M. A., 44, 152, 310, 311, 312, 336, 337, 417.
"Harmony", 76, 77, 84.
Harrison, Carter, 186, 187, 419, 420, 421.
Harrison, Pres. Benjamin, 170, 384, 385.
Harrison, Pres. William Henry, 372, 374.
Hartford Resolutions, 368.
Harrity, Mr. 233.
Hawaii, 52, 53, 54.
Hay, Sec. John, 238, 325.
Haynes, Rev. Artemus J., 254.
Hearst, William R., 44, 180, 430, 431.
Herbst, E. M., 105.
Hillis, Rev. Newton Dwight, 228.
Hill, David B., 145, 391.
Hill, James J., 262, 446, 447.
Hendricks, Thomas A., 383, 384.
Herald, Boston, 107, 108, 109, 112.
Hoar, Senator Geo. F., 98, 99, 201.
Hobart, Garrett A., 392, 393.
Holt, Hamilton, 198.
Huntington, Rev. Harry, 222.
Idaho, 142, 144, 443.
Illinois, 12, 141, 142, 145, 181, 250, 376, 392.
Imperialism, 25, 26, 184, 263, 300, 337.
Income Tax, 52, 53, 279, 386.
Independent, New York, 39, 199.
Indiana, 141, 142, 144, 145, 181, 250, 383, 384, 443.
Indian Territory, 7, 8, 9, 10.
Inter-Ocean, Chicago, 264, 266, 267, 268.
Institute, Social Economies, 310, 311.
Investor, United States, 289.
Iowa, 5, 6, 142, 144.
Italy, 39, 41.
Jackson, Andrew, 44, 45, 154, 189, 191, 371, 372, 373, 388, 398.
Jefferson, Thomas, 18, 25, 44, 45,

55, 59, 98, 99, 100, 101, 102, 103, 104, 105, 116, 118, 154, 184, 195, 199, 219, 222, 258, 274, 352, 362, 364, 365, 367, 369, 371, 386, 398, 412, 413, 414, 453.
Jefferson-Jackson-Lincoln League, 44.
Jefferson Memorial, 98.
Johnson, Andrew, 380.
Johnson, Herschel V., 376.
Johnson, Tom L., 44, 45, 223, 311.
Johnson, William, 362.
Jones, Dr. Hiram K., 202, 203, 204.
Journal, New York, 50.
Journal, Wall Street, 185, 186, 187, 241, 248, 249.
Judicious Advertising (Newspaper), 341.
Kansas 141, 142, 191, 250, 443.
Kansas City Platform, 14, 16, 20, 21, 32, 46, 47, 62, 67, 73, 112, 113, 135, 149, 150, 151, 153, 188, 195, 234, 235, 237, 286, 335, 393, 411, 415, 416, 417, 418, 423.
Kellar, Helen, 174.
Kellogg, Daniel F., 94.
Kentucky, 30, 141, 142, 250, 374.
Kentucky Resolutions, 367, 375, 376, 380.
King, Grace, 161.
King, W. R., 375.
Kitteridge, Rev. Dr. 65.
Knox, Philander C., 38, 39, 58, 86, 200, 201, 227, 430, 431.
Labor Compendium, St. Louis, 195.
La Follette, Gov., 260, 453, 454, 455, 456.
Lane, Joseph, 376.
Lawson, Thomas W., 408, 409.
Leader, Cleveland, 133, 135.
Leavitt, William Homer, 222.
Lee, H., 364.
Leo, Pope, 237.
Levi, Leon N., 238.
Lincoln, Abraham, 25, 44, 45, 54, 379, 380, 450, 453.
Littlefield, Congressman, 37, 38, 39, 201.
Littlefield Anti-Trust Bill, 37.
Lochren, Judge 246, 446, 447, 448, 449.
Lodge, Senator H. C., 24, 310.
Logan, John A., 384.
Long, Ex-Sec., 310, 321, 322.
Lord & Thomas, 341.
Louisiana, 141, 142, 143.
Louisiana Purchase, 102, 116, 117, 118, 119, 184, 185.
Lucking, Congressman Alfred, 303.
Madison, James, 22, 23, 367.
Maine, 108, 142, 144, 392, 443.
Manning, Daniel, 43.
Maryland, 141, 142, 416, 423.
Mason, Caroline A., 161.

Massachusetts, 35, 142, 144, 145, 443.
McClellan, Gen. Geo. B., 380, 450.
McClure, Phillips & Co., 161.
McDowell, Wm. O., 156.
McKinley, William, 5, 152, 184, 199, 252, 322, 361, 392, 393, 397.
McKinley Act, 384, 388.
Mexican Republic, 11, 324.
Michigan, 141, 142, 144, 145, 374, 443.
Miles, Gen. Nelson A., 98, 148, 247, 314.
Miller, Atty. Gen. 227.
Minnesota, 142, 144, 246, 443, 446, 447, 449.
Mississippi, 141, 142, 143, 250.
Missouri, 37, 72, 141, 142, 145, 195, 380, 443, 445.
Mitchell, John, 181.
Monroe, President, 367, 368, 369.
Monroe Doctrine, 33, 34, 92, 390, 395.
Montana, 142, 443.
Moray, Rev. A. B., 202.
Morgan, J. Pierpont, 201, 240, 279, 417, 441, 442, 444.
Morton, Levi P., 310, 384.
Municipal Ownership, 419, 420, 421.
National City Bank, 197.
National Manufacturers' Assosiation, 196.
Nebraska, 98, 143, 144, 193, 309, 330, 331, 392, 442.
New Hampshire, 142, 144, 375, 443.
New Jersey, 141, 142, 144, 145, 380, 392, 441, 443.
New Mexico, 10, 20, 58, 390.
New York, 27, 141, 142, 145, 307, 380, 382, 383, 384, 397, 443.
Nevada, 143, 144, 443.
North Carolina, 141, 142, 443.
North Dakota, 141, 142, 144, 443.
Northern Securities, 440, 446, 448, 449.
O'Connor, Charles, 382.
O'Farrell, Gov. 232.
Ohio, 10, 31, 143, 145, 181, 310, 311, 382, 392.
Oklahoma, 7, 8, 9, 10, 20, 58, 268, 390.
Oregon, 143, 144, 376, 443.
Oregonian, Portland, 324.
Outlook, The, 321.
Palmer, John M., 392.
Panama, 325, 326, 337, 338.
Panama Treaty, 58.
Parry, David M., 196.
Partisanship, Malignant, 450.
Payne, Postmaster General, 226.
Pendleton, George H., 380.
Pennsylvania, 143, 145, 443.
Pennypacker, Judge, 106.

REFERENCE INDEX

Philippines, 25, 116, 118, 119, 148, 184, 185, 242, 265, 266, 267, 268, 286, 287, 300, 303, 321, 324, 339, 393, 394, 395.
Picayune, New Orleans, 188, 189, 190.
Pierce, Franklin, 375.
Polk, James K., 374.
Pond, George E., 262.
Powers, Caleb, 30, 31.
Post, Louis F., 222, 223.
Post, New York Evening, 281.
Proctor, Sen. Redfield, 320, 321.
Protection, 7.
Public Ledger, Philadelphia, 411, 412.
Public Opinion, 417.
Quay, Senator M. S., 86, 106.
Race Problem, 264.
Reciprocity, 5, 7.
Record-Herald, Chicago, 39, 63, 65, 114, 115, 221, 261, 294, 419, 434, 437.
Reed, Thomas B., 281.
Reid, Whitelaw, 385.
Register and Leader, Des Moines, 63, 288, 290, 448, 449.
Reorganizers, 77, 199, 415, 426.
Republican, Springfield, 149, 150, 151, 152, 153, 154.
Rhode Island, 5, 6, 20, 21, 143, 144, 443, 456.
Robb, C. H., 227.
Rockefeller, John D., 155, 166, 168, 169, 434, 435.
Rockefeller, John D., Jr., 187, 188, 436.
Rogers, Henry H., 408.
Roosevelt, Theodore, 7, 38, 56, 57, 84, 85, 116, 181, 195, 200, 201, 202, 221, 239, 249, 258, 259, 261, 262, 269, 311, 312, 314, 321, 322, 325, 326, 337, 338, 397, 410, 411, 430, 433, 435, 436, 450.
Rusk, Sec. Jerry, 136, 356.
Russia, 18, 238, 239.
Schofield, Gen., 247.
Senators, Popular Election of, 12, 442.
Sentinel, Milwaukee, 235, 236, 237.
Sewall, Arthur, 392, 393.
Seymour, Horatio, 380.
Shallenbarger Bill, 15, 16, 17.
Shallenbarger, Congressman, A. C., 14.
Shaw, Leslie M., 42, 43, 47, 197.
Shearn, Clarence J., 180, 181.
Shepherd, Edward M., 83.
Sherman, John, 75, 141, 356, 270, 290, 295, 296, 311, 312.
Sherman Act., 224, 234, 356, 358, 385.
Sherman Law, 10, 73, 96, 121, 404, 405, 417, 432.

Ship Subsidy, 311.
Short, Dr. W. F., 202.
Silver, Coinage of, 355, 360, 387.
Silver Coinage, Suspension of, 354.
Silver, Demonetization of, 353.
Smith, Charles E., 184, 310.
South Africa, 361.
South America, 33, 287.
South Carolina, 141, 143, 371, 410.
South Dakota, 143, 144, 443.
Spooner, Senator, 432.
Stand Pat, 11.
Star, Lincoln, 277.
Star, St. Louis, 229.
Stevenson, Adlai E., 385, 397.
Stillman, James, 408.
Standard Oil Co., 11, 87, 167, 168, 182, 408, 413, 435, 436, 437.
Sun, New York, 94, 95, 98.
Tariff Reform, 138, 410.
Taylor, Dr. Howard S., 219, 222, 223, 288.
Taylor, Zachary, 375.
Tennessee, 141, 143, 443.
Texas, 141, 143, 250, 374, 443.
Thayer, Judge, 246, 447, 448.
Tilden, S. J., 62, 383.
Times, New York, 155, 156.
Times, Detroit, 303.
Towne, Charles A., 240.
Tracey, Ex-Secretary, 41.
Transcript, Boston, 197.
Tribune, Chicago, 279, 304, 309.
Tribune, Sioux City, 278, 279, 405.
Tryne, Ralph Waldo, 225.
Tuley, Judge, 63, 64.
Tyler, John, 374.
United States Bank, 374.
United States Steel Co., 182.
Utah, 143, 443.
Van Buren, Martin, 372.
Vanderlip, Frank A., 197.
Van Sant, Governor, 449.
Van Vorhis, Flavius J., 25, 26.
Venezuela, 33, 34.
Virginia, 141, 143, 385.
Virginia Resolutions, 367, 375.
Vermont, 143, 144.
Wagner, Charles, 160, 161.
Washington, 143, 144, 443.
Washington, Booker T., 252.
Washington, George, 352, 453.
Watson, Thomas E., 392.
Watterson, Henry, 90, 260, 435.
Weaver, James B., 232, 233, 234, 385.
Webster, Daniel, 19, 20, 410.
Weekly, Harper's, 191, 192.
Wellman, Walter, 39, 261, 262, 294, 437, 438, 439.
West Virginia, 141, 143, 144.
Weinstock, Harris, 225.
Whitney, W. W., 233.
Wilson Bill, 75, 141, 279, 280.

Wilson, Congressman, 75, 358, 386.
Wisconsin, 141, 143, 144, 145, 443, 457.
Wolfe, Jacob V., 222.

World, New York, 89, 142, 240, 241, 311, 408, 436, 437, 444.
Wyoming, 143, 144, 443.

The Commoner

ISSUED WEEKLY

W. J. BRYAN, EDITOR AND PROPRIETOR

SUBSCRIPTION PRICE $1.00 PER YEAR

The Commoner is a weekly journal, which, while devoted in its editorial department to the discussion of political, economic, and sociological questions, furnishes its readers each week a supply of general literature of the highest order. It is hoped that the discussion of political events as they arise from time to time will interest those who study public questions, regardless of their party affiliations. Subscriptions can be sent direct to The Commoner. They can also be sent through newspapers which have advertised a clubbing rate, or through local agents. Advertising rates furnished upon application. Send for free sample copy and clubbing offer. Address all communications to

The Commoner
LINCOLN, NEBRASKA